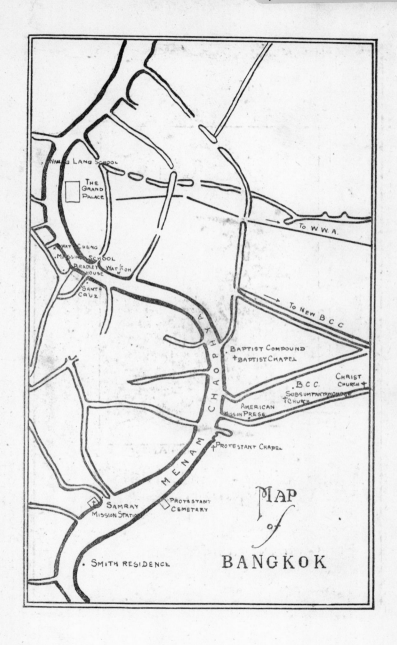

MAP of BANGKOK

H.M. KING PRAJADHIPOK.

HISTORICAL SKETCH

OF

PROTESTANT MISSIONS IN SIAM

1828-1928

❧

EDITED BY

GEORGE BRADLEY MCFARLAND, M. D.

Emeritus Professor, Royal Medical College,
Chulalongkorn University

❧

Printed by The Bangkok Times Press, Ltd., October 1928.

To those, who following in the foot-steps of their Lord and Master, counted not their lives precious but gave their all that others might have life and that they might have it more abundantly,—to their sacred memory this volume is most reverently dedicated.

CONTENTS

CONTENTS

PAGE

APPENDICES.

LIST OF ILLUSTRATIONS

PREFACE

The year 1928 marks the close of a century of Protestant Mission work in Siam, and this seems a fitting time for gathering together and preserving the stories of those who have embarked upon this venture of faith and for summing up the results of this enterprise.

In many of its details the story of this century of Foreign Mission work in Siam is unique in the annals of the Church and were it to be fully told would make a thrilling story—true, but stranger than fiction. It is a story of faith; it is a story of courage and determination of the rarest type; it is the story of great triumph over discouragements of, at times, an almost overwhelming nature; it is the story of prayer—the sort that "removes mountains"; it is the story of the "sower who went forth to sow".

Siam has produced nothing spectacular; there has been no Mass Movement; there has been no "Nation born in a Day"; there has been no large number of baptisms. Were these the only criteria of success, the verdict must be—failure. The seed was planted in faith in prayer, with yearning love and oft with tears. Sometimes the seed-time and the harvest-time seemed unduly separated. Sometimes, "having eyes we see not", because we look for only one manner of fruitage, and fail to recognize the harvest spread before our very eyes. But as one traces the story down through the years, the impression deepens that God has been "working His purposes out" and that the seed sowed in faith and prayer and with repeated call for the prayer of the home churches did bear fruit, a hundred fold. A marvellous story it is—and one inexplicable unless one realize that—" in the beginning, God".

The bond of Christian fellowship binding together the groups of the first Christian workers was real. Not always did they see eye to eye; not always was perfect comity easy; not always did the line of least resistance draw them into close fellowship and harmony. Men and women they were with human weaknesses, but as one Siamese account of the early missionary days put it , "They came as three groups but after they reached here they became one group." Could there be a stronger testimony to the Christian fellowship ?—an answer to the divine petition—" that they may be one".

They were men and women of strong convictions. They came to a land of a different race, a different tongue, different customs and a different religion. Without compromising their personal con- victions , these missionaries of the Cross brought with them that which enabled them to live daily the simple, humble life of their Lord and by the depth of their sympathy and by the genuineness of their affection for the people of the land of their adoption, they were able to establish contact with the needy and also with those in highest places of power. So completely did they win their way by their own breadth of interest and sincerity of purpose, by their lives of unswerving devotion and genuine affection, that an oriental land, hitherto little touched by the lands of the West, not only opened its doors to the missionary but reciprocated their affection and with the truest hospitality accepted him as one of themselves in the brotherhood of the race. Siam, proud in its independence, strong in its position as Defender of the Buddhist Faith, yet reached out and welcomed into its very heart the earnest disciples of another Faith. Religious bigotry found no place in the hearts of either Easterner or Westerner. Each granted to the other the right to decide for himself what is truth and to order his life in accordance with his findings. A miracle this,—in an age when world-unity was scarcely even a dream of the most visionary.

Again, in no other mission field has there been such marked governmental favor. Together the missionary and the government have been working for the advancement of the people of Siam. The personal friendship and the mutual helpfulness of the Kings, princes, nobles and missionaries have often been noted. Beginning with the friendship of H. M. King Mongkut (during the days of his priesthood) for his teacher the Rev. Jesse Caswell and the other missionaries, this chain of friendship, mutual esteem and affection has reached down through the succeeding reigns to the present day. "East is East and West is West and ne'er shall these twain meet" has a truly striking rebuttal in Siam and in the relation between the Siamese and the American missionaries. No race problem exists; no color line can be detected. That all this has happened merely by chance, can one believe? We find here a flower of exceptional beauty, the result of natural causes,—but "in the beginning, God".

Siam has changed greatly in the hundred years just past. From an almost hermit nation without modern civilization it has developed into a land definitely trying to work out its own course of development. From an Absolute Monarchy and a Despotism, Siam has developed into a unique unit in the family of nations—an Absolute Monarchy with limited powers, the *limitation being set by the reigning monarch* and not by the people whom he rules. "Give us the best" is the watchword of the nation. Many aside from the missionary have shared in the development of Siam, but those of us who believe in a God who yearns over the lives of men and who has set "one divine event toward which the whole creation moves" can but feel that the earnest prayers poured out to the Father of all throughout these years, have already found abundant answer—and the full fruitage is not yet. Siam wants the best—truly wants the best, and when she comes to see in Christ the supreme answer of God for human need,—then Siam will find her Saviour; then the prayers of the Church of Christ will be fully answered.

———————

As plans for the centenary celebration of Protestant Missions in Siam were being made, an idea that had already been germinating in many minds, began to grow. The fact that the early history of this hundred years of missionary effort was in very fragmentary form and that the greater part of the source materials were either in manuscript or in books long out-of-print and very inaccessible to most people, made it seem wise to gather this information into permanent and easily accessible form. The task was a large one and the time before the desired record should appear in book form less than a year. That an exhaustive study was impossible in that time is a self-evident fact—especially when the editor and those who have generously given of their time and help must fit this added task into lives already full. No one realizes this more than those who have helped in this task, but whatever short-comings this volume may have, it is hoped that it will serve to preserve some of these interesting facts of mission history and perhaps some one else may then take up the task of revising and adding much that may yet come to hand.

The editor would express his very deep gratitude to those who have contributed chapters to the history and especially to H. R. H. Prince Damrong for the Introduction which he has so kindly and graciously written. His Royal Highness' memory extends over a greater part of the period in which there has been such happy co-operation between the Crown and the missionaries—a period extending over the reigns of four kings of this dynasty. His Royal Highness has himself found many ways to help the missionaries and it was eminently fitting that His Royal Highness should add this another favor to the kindnesses he has shown in days gone by.

The editor would also express his especial gratitude to Miss Irene Bradley whose memory goes back into mission history farther than that of any other foreigner in Siam today, and who has kindly offered endless suggestions and thrown much light on the interweaving of details and seemingly isolated facts, which have made dead facts live.

To include in this book everything of interest would obviously be impossible. For that reason it seemed best to lay special emphasis upon the early period. The illustrations for the most part are those not of modern buildings nor of the missionaries now on the field. Exception has been made in the case of those societies which have opened work within the past thirty or forty years; the present is their day of beginnings. The rule has also been set aside in regard to three institutions of the Presbyterian mission which have originated within the last twenty years. There are many buildings in each mission station and missionary faces which should become familiar through picture if not more intimately, but that must be the task of another time. This is a history of the past,—with the emphasis on the PAST. Those still in the missionary ranks who have been honorably retired or who have fully or nearly completed forty years of missionary service are rightly considered as belonging to the past though they still have a part in the present. Therefore whenever possible to secure them, their pictures have been included.

The past is past, but in a wonderful measure the *past* reveals the *future*. So we who have shared in this effort of bringing together the story of the past century, hope that the reading of the story may bring to the hearts of you readers as it has to us, new courage to carry on the work left us by the Head of the Church, a new appreciation of the worth of the missionary enterprise and a new joy at the realization that we are entered into the labors of those who have gone on before. One sows and another reaps—but God alone gives the increase.

THE EDITOR.

H.R.H. PRINCE DAMRONG.

INTRODUCTORY CHAPTER

By H. R. H. Prince Damrong.

The American Missions in Siam, which are about to celebrate the 100th. anniversary of the establishment of their work in this country, propose to publish, in connection with the celebration, a Historical Sketch of a century of their labour, prepared, with one exception, by their past and present members. The exception is myself, whom the Missions have asked to contribute a chapter to the book. I appreciate the request as one arising from friendship based on mutual respect and confidence. My missionary friends know me for a staunch Buddhist, and their request may surely be regarded as a proof of their confidence that my strong Buddhist feelings do not involve injustice to other faiths than my own. Of the religion of Christ, a reasonable view of a non-Christian must be that its acceptance by countless millions of people of various races of different stages of culture, through many centuries and in many lands, notwithstanding the changes in science and philosophy, entitles it to profound respect even by those who have not accepted Christian enlightenment. Good religions have many essential points in common, and it is impossible to venerate one's own without respecting another faith which teaches similar doctrines. It is a great pleasure to me, therefore, to contribute a small share to the celebration of this important anniversary of the American Missions in Siam.

A history of the American Missions in this country has been prepared by several writers, among whom is Dr. D. B. Bradley, who published his account in the " Bangkok Calendar " for the year 1866. Dr. Bradley's paper is most interesting, and I have had it translated into Siamese as a contribution to the study of modern history. The translation was published by the National Library in 1925. Many other records by other members of the American Missions have been written and published, which will no doubt be utilised by the writers entrusted with the preparation of the other chapters of this present book.   It only remains for me, therefore, to write of the Missions from the Siamese viewpoint, which, necessarily, cannot embrace all phases of missionary work.

The American Missionaries came to Siam thirty-three years before my birth.   I came into contact with them for the first time when, by Command of my August Father, H. M. King Mongkut, I was vaccinated by a medical missionary.   I have the marks of that contact on me still.   When I began to learn to read and write Siamese, the first school books were in manuscript, but later on printed first lessons in Siamese were published by Bradley's Press, and were used in our school.   We boys liked them better, for they contained pictures.

I was about ten years of age when I came face to face with an American missionary for the first time—apart, of course, from the medical man who vaccinated me as a baby. H. M. King Chulalonkorn had then established an English School within the precincts of the Grand Palace, and, outside the school building, there was a lawn on which we played during the interval between school hours.   Outside the school, and close to the playground, was occasionally to be seen a tall spare man with a beard similar to the traditional Uncle Sam himself.   He wore a grey helmet with a chimney-looking means of ventilation, a long black alpaca coat reaching almost to his knees, a pair of duck trousers, with an umbrella in one hand and a number of books in the other.   It was an American missionary, and he was distributing books and pamphlets to bystanders and passers-by.

For the benefit of those who do not know Siam, it may be stated that the Grand Palace in this country is different from the private residences of Royalty in the West.   For, enclosed within its battlemented walls are many of the Government Offices, where the transaction of public business takes place.   The outer precincts of the Palace are, therefore, accessible to the public, and the presence of a missionary seeking to propagate the doctrines of his faith was really nothing out of the way.

It was thus that I first saw the first missionary. He was strange to us schoolboys, and we approached him timidly to listen to his conversation with a small crowd which he had gathered. He spoke fluent Siamese.

I do not remember the actual words which were spoken, but the conversation was to the following effect:

Said the missionary, "Do you not know that your religion is wrong, and can only lead you to hell?"

Some members of the crowd, probably disgusted at such a question moved away. Others laughed, and asked, "What have we to do to avoid hell?"

The missionary, "You must venerate Jehovah, and follow the teaching of Jesus Christ."

"And what is the teaching of Jesus Christ?"

That was the desired question, and out came the books and pamphlets which the missionary handed to his interrogator. "These will tell you," he said, "if you follow the teaching, you will go to heaven."

He proceeded to distribute the books, which were declined by some, but accepted by others. Many of us boys, I among others, accepted them. Personally, the mere possession of new books gave me pleasure, although it was impossible for me, at my age, to understand those which I received from the missionary. Others whom I asked either did not understand or did not read the books, but no doubt there were those who did so. The missionaries at that time knew Siamese sufficiently well for fluent conversation, but their knowledge did not extend to the writing of the vernacular. They had in their employ Siamese writers to whom they communicated verbally the substance of a book to be prepared, and the writers did the best they could.

That particular missionary appeared in the neigborhood of my school frequently. We boys stood listening at a distance from him at first, but soon we became bolder and approached nearer, till at last we spoke to him, and he to us. I well remember my discomfiture when the missionary replied to the first question I asked him.

On that day, before speaking to the missionary, I had heard it remarked that he always used the same clothes, the same hat, and the same umbrella. I approached him without intending to say anything; but he smiled, and I gave voice to the first question that occured to me: why did he always wear the same clothes?

He replied politely, "I have used this hat more than ten years. This coat also has been in use for nearly ten years, and this umbrella is older than the two."

There was nothing more to be said. His argument was overwhelming. People had pointed out his stinginess in the matter of dress; he spoke of it as economy, and therefore a virtue. I was also impressed by the manner and the words with which he argued his points on religious matters, and the absence of anger when his arguments were sharply questioned. It was thus that at ten years of age, I first made friends with a missionary.

In later years, when I had learned to speak English, and when my English tutor desired me to practise conversation, he took me to English-speaking households to give me as much opportunity as possible. Roads were few at the time, and communication was mainly by boat. Of the missionaries whose houses were within easy reach were Dr. and Mrs. Chandler at Ta Tien, and Dr. and Mrs. D. B. Bradley on the Bangkok Yai Canal. We paid frequent visits to their houses. I remember meeting Dr. Bradley once or twice in the later years of his life, but after his death we continued to visit his family, of which Mrs. Bradley was then the head. The lady lived long after the death of her husband, and once she said to me, "I am old, and it matters little when I die. Only one thing weighs on my mind and it is that the King of Siam is not a Christian yet. When he is converted, I shall die happy." I must confess that, being young, I felt amused at the time, but subsequent reflection convinced me of the most earnest good-will on her part.

Apart from the Bradleys, the McFarlands were a family with whom I was on terms of friendship from my youth. After leaving school, I became an officer of the King's Body-guard, and accompanied His Majesty on most of his trips into the country. At Bejraburi I met the McFarlands for the first time. Dr. S. G. McFarland was in charge of the Mission in that town, and, with him I visited the Mission schools for boys and girls, little thinking that we would, in time to come, become colleagues in the same Government Department. Some years after, when I was in charge of the Department of Education, Dr. McFarland served as headmaster in a Government School under the direction of my Department. The doctor impressed me, as he impressed all who came into contact with him, by his excellent pronunciation of our language. To hear him speak without seeing him, we would not recognise the voice of a foreigner. Of the Europeans or Americans who have come to Siam, many study the language of the country and know it very well, but I have not met one with a pronunciation superior to that of Dr. S. G. McFarland.

Other missionaries I met in that day were, among others, Dr. House, Dr. N. A. McDonald, Dr. Dean and Dr. D. McGilvary. With the last named I came into contact again later, when, having become Minister of the Interior, I visited Chiengmai during the course of my inspection of the provinces, and there renewed the friendship which had started many years before.

My acquaintance with the missionaries began, as above stated, in my boyhood. As I came to know more of them, I began to learn the value of their work. Many of the American missionaries, notably Dr. MacDonald, Dr. Chandler and a son of Dr. Bradley, acted as English interpreters to the Government. As A.D.C. to King Chulalonkorn, it was my duty to attend on His Majesty at private audiences granted to foreigners, and it was such occasions which increased my friendship with the missionaries who came to interpret. The King understood English, but did not care to speak it. The interpreters knew this, and usually remained silent when a foreign visitor spoke to the King, only translating H. M.'s words each time he spoke. There was, however, an interpreter who did his work conscientiously, and tried to translate everything said in English into Siamese, and vice versa. The careful interpreter was Dr. Chandler, who always spoke Siamese with the utmost deliberation, and in spite of his thorough knowledge of our language, took more time to utter a sentence than any other one I have met. It was amusing when Dr. Chandler, having got half-way with his translation from English into Siamese, the King started to reply, and the interpreter had to stop his translation to the King, and begin translating His Majesty's words to his guest.

When I was appointed to take charge of the Education of the country, it was necessary for me to pay greater attention to the work of the American missionaries. In Siam the work of imparting knowledge in the vernacular has always been entrusted to the Buddhist monks, who have from time immemorial instructed the youths of the country. But the teaching of a European language and other forms of education based on such language, had been introduced by the American missionaries (the Catholics had not yet started the Assumption College). For the immediate future, education in Siam, as I saw it, depended not alone on continuing to utilize the services of the monks, but also in enlisting the aid of the missionaries. Would it be possible, considering the divergence of their religious points of view, to induce the two classes of people to co-operate so far as the temporal education of the youths of the country was concerned. It behoved me, as organzier of a new system of education, to study the work of the missionaries.

The primary object of the establishment of the American missions in this country is, of course the propagation of the Christian faith. But while the aim is common to all missions, methods appear to differ. Apart from spreading the knowledge of Christ and of religious instruction, the American missionaries have adopted, from the beginning, the humane work of providing medical service to the communities among whom they work, and also of assisting in the introduction, or the expansion, of education along western lines. The medical and educational services are a means to an end, of course, but the means has been widely appreciated apart from the end itself. The first American missionaries came here on their way to China, and came with some knowledge of the Chinese language, acquired in Europe and Singapore. It was therefore among the Chinese residents of this country that the missions originally confined their teaching in Siam. But, in spite of their ignorance of the Siamese language, the missionaries were able to render medical service to the people, who consequently regarded all missionary men as doctors. That is why even today a missionary man is usually addressed as "Doctor" in the interior of Siam.

.The establishment of the first American missions in Siam coincided with the time when changes began to take place in this country on the question of her foreign policy. Siam's old antagonist, Burma, had fallen to the British, who thus became a close neighbor to us. The British had established a trading centre at Penang, and had begun to carry on commerce with Siam. On the East we went to war with Annam, and it brought us more into touch with foreign powers. Many Siamese of high-standing, notably the younger members of Royalty, realized the necessity, in order to keep up with the times, of acquiring a knowledge of foreign tongues as a step to further learning, and King Mongkut (then in the monkhood) and some of his brothers, began to take lessons in English. They were followed by many of the younger members of the nobility. Needless to say, it was the American missionaries who taught them. After acquiring a fair knowledge of the English language, the Siamese went on to the study of subjects such as history, politics, military science, medicine, engineering, ship-building, and so on. By the middle of the 19th century (Christian era) their anticipation proved correct, for our relations with Europe and America increased to a degree not realized by men of the older generation, and treaties of friendship and commerce came to be made between Siam and most of the countries of Europe, and the United States of America. The American missionaries, who rendered invaluable service to the Siamese in the initial stage of their occidental education, and of their contact with the western world, continued to serve the Government as interpreters up to the time of my youth, when I personally had occasion to observe them at work as translators at interviews.

But in assisting the Siamese Goverment as above described, the missionaries neglected no part of their own work, which, however, did not run as smoothly as might have been the case. As an instance of the attitude of the highly-placed Siamese at an early period, I may quote a passage from a book by Chow Phya Dibakarawongse, translated by the late Henry Alabaster, F. R. A. S., into English, and published in a book entitled " The Wheel of the Law ". I hope to make clear presently my object in giving the quotation.

Chow Phya Dibakarawongse was the first Minister for Foreign Affairs under King Mongkut, who ascended the Throne in 1851. His position naturally brought him into contact with foreigners, among whom, of course, were the American missionaries. According to an English contemporary, the aforesaid Henry Alabaster, the nobleman was much esteemed by those who knew him. He was always open to argument, and never let anything disturb the urbanity of his manner. It was his wont, after an official interview, to open a private discussion on some theoretical and transcendental subject. Thus by verbal inquiry and the reading of such books as were accessible to him in the vernacular, he managed to acquire some knowledge of European sciences, and of foreign religions. Needless to say, he realized the value of foreign education to the full.

But the old nobleman was a Buddhist of Buddhists. Broad-minded in all other things, in matters of religion he was less so. In 1861 he published in book-form such knowledge as he had gained from his foreign friends. Subjects like education, geography and astronomy were treated, and where he considered that the existing Siamese beliefs or methods were wrong, he had the courage to say so. On the subject of religion, he gave his own staunch views, and cited his conversations with American missionaries, of which I propose to quote passages here:

"Dr Caswell remarked to me that if the religion of Buddha prevailed throughout the world, there would be an end of mankind, as all men would become monks, and there would be no children. This, he urged, showed it was unsuited to be the universal religion, and therefore could not be the true religion. I replied that the Lord Buddha never professed that his religion would be universal. He was but as a transient gleam of light, indicating the path of truth. His religion was but as a stone thrown into a pool covered with floating weeds; it cleared an opening through which the pure water was seen, but the effect soon died away, and the weeds closed up as before. The Lord Buddha saw the bright, the exact, the abstruse, the difficult course, and but for the persuasion of angels would not have attempted to teach that which he considered too difficult for men to follow. The remark of the doctor really does not bear on the question (i. e., on the truth of the religion)."

"Dr. Gutzlaff declared that "Samana Khodom only taught people to reverence himself and his disciples, saying that by such means merit and heaven could be attained, teaching them to respect the temples, and Bo-trees*, and everything in the temple grounds, lest by injuring them they should go to hell, a teaching designed only for the protection of himself and his disciples, and of no advantage to any others." I replied, "In Christianity there is a

---

* This Bo, or Bodhi tree, is the tree under the shade of which Buddha attained to omniscience. It is to be found in most, if not all, Siamese monasteries.

command to worship God alone, and no other; Mahomet also taught the worship of one only, and promised that he would take into heaven every one who joined his religion, even the murderer of his parents, while those who would not join his religion, however virtuous their lives, should surely go to hell; also he taught that all other religions were the enemies of his religion, and that heaven could be attained by injuring the temples, idols, and anything held sacred by another religion. Is such teaching as that fit for belief? Buddha did not teach that he alone should be venerated, nor did he, the just one, ever teach that it was right to persecute other religions. As for adoration, so far as I know, men of every religion adore the holy one of their religion. It is incorrect of the doctor to say that Buddha taught men to adore him alone. He neither taught that such was necessary, nor offered the alternative of hell as all other religions do."

"The doctor told me that "Jehovah, our Creator, although jealously desirous that men should not hold false religions, permits them to hold any religion they please, because in His divine compassion, doing that which is best for them, He will not force man's conversion by the exercise of His power, but will leave it to their own free will." I answered, "Why did the Creator of all things create the holy chiefs (teachers) of the religions of the Siamese, Brahmins, Mahometans, and others? Why did He permit the teaching of false religions which would lead men to neglect His religion, and to suffer the punishment of hell? Would it not have been better to have made all men follow the one religion which would lead them to heaven? Mahometans hold that Allah sent prophet after prophet to teach the truth, but that evil spirits corrupted their teaching, and made it necessary for him to send an emanation from himself in human form (Mahomet) to teach the truth as they now have it. Brahmins hold that God the Father, ordering the descent of Siva in various avatars, as Krishna, and others, has so given rise to various sects; but that, whichever of these sects a man belongs to, he will, on death, pass to heaven, if only he has done righteously according to his belief. The missionaries hold that God Jehovah made all men to worship in one way, but that the devil has caused false teachers to arise and teach doctrines opposed to God. Such are the various stories told by Mahometans, Brahmins, and missionaries. My readers must form their own opinion about them."

"In the Bible we find that God created Adam and Eve, and desired that they should have no sickness nor sorrow, nor know death; but because they, the progenitors of mankind, ate of a forbidden fruit, God became angry, and ordained that thenceforth they should endure toil and weariness and trouble and sickness, and, from that time, fatigue and sorrow and sickness and death fell upon mankind. It was said that by baptism men should be free from the curse of Adam, but I do not see that any one who is baptized now-a-days is free from the curse of Adam, or escapes toil and grief and sickness and death, any more than those who are not baptized." The missionary answered, "Baptism for the remission of sin is only effectual in gaining heaven after death, for those who die unbaptized will certainly go to hell." But the missionary did not explain the declaration that by baptism men should be free from pains and troubles in their present state. He further said, "It does at times please God to accede to the requests of those that pray to Him, a remarkable instance of which is, that Europeans and Americans have more excellent arts than any other people. Have they not steamboats and railways, and telegraphs and manufactures, and guns and weapons of war superior to any others in the world? Are not the nations which do not worship Christ comparatively ignorant?" I asked the doctor about sorrow and sickness, things which prevail throughout the world, things in which Christians have no advantage over other men, but he would not reply on that point, and spoke only of matters of knowledge. Where is the witness who can say that this knowledge was the gift of God? There are many in Europe who do not believe in God, but are indifferent, yet have subtle and expanded intellects, and are great philosophers and politicians. How is it that God grants to these men, who do not believe in Him, the same intelligence He grants to those who do? Again, how is it that the Siamese, Burmese, Cochin Chinese, and other Roman Catholic converts, whom we see more attentive to their religion than the Europeans who reside among us, do not receive some reward for their merit, and have superior advantages and intelligence to those who are not converted? So far as I can see, the reverse is the case: the unconverted flourish, but the converted are continually in debt and bondage. There are many converts in Siam, but I see none of them rise to wealth, so as to become talked about. They continually pray to God, but, it seems, nothing happens according to their prayer". The missionary replied. "They hold an untrue religion, therefore God is not pleased with them". I said to the missionary, "You say that God sometimes grants the prayers of those who pray to Him; now, the Chinese, who pray to spirits and devils, sometimes obtain what they have prayed for; do you not, therefore, allow that these spirits can benefit man?" The missionary answered, "The devil receives bribes".

The above extracts are, as before stated, taken in translation from the work of an old Siamese nobleman, which was published nearly 70 years ago, when the higher class of our men had just begun to acquire Western knowledge. To us of the present day, the extracts indicate, in the first place, that on religious matters, the attitude of mind of men in Siam, be they Buddhists or Christians, was less liberal than it has since become: for, in upholding their religion, men were apt to indulge in fault-finding and other forms of malice against all faiths which were not their own. The good points of other religions were studiously overlooked. In the second place, it is evident from existing records that, in spite of aggressive speech and lively opposition to their respective views, neither Siamese nor American abandoned the good fellow-feeling which one entertained for the other. Thus the missionaries were ever ready to render service to the Foreign Minister, which the old nobleman reciprocated with warm friendship and willing assistance whenever desired. It is a source of pride to us to be able to state that neither King nor people, official and non-official alike, have ever taken exception to the religious views of the missionaries, who have thus been able to establish themselves without let or hindrance from the time of their first arrival in Siam.

Of the benefits introduced into the country by the American missions, their educational and medical services stand out in especial prominence. In Education, the teaching of English at a time when there was no other means of acquiring knowledge of that language must be emphasized as an important piece of work. In spite, however, of the fact that knowledge of a Eupropean tongue was recognized to be useful, it was not easy for the missionaries to find pupils. The Americans came here to teach Christianity, and it was supposed, erroneously or otherwise, that the teaching of their language was a preliminary to the systematic instruction of the Christian doctrine. If the truth be told, the early missionaries were not well-advised in picking out and criticizing severely what they thought were the faults of Buddhism. They took pains to show contempt for the religion of the land, and thus created the natural impression that their schools were opened for the ultimate purpose of teaching the youths of the country to despise the faith of their fathers. It was in consequence of such attitude on their part that the early missionary schools did not thrive to the extent that they do to-day.

As regards the medical service, the introduction of vaccination and Western surgery, by Dr. D. B. Bradley, conferred inestimable benefit on the country. Later on missionary hospitals were established, and of these I shall have more to say.

I will now resume the narration of my contact with the American missionaries, into which my duties brought me. As Minister of

Education, my friendship with them enabled me to enlist the aid of missionaries interested in Education. Thus Rev. Colombet of the Catholic Mission, Dr. S. G. McFarland, Dr. J. A. Eakin, Dr. E. P. Dunlap, Miss E. S. Cole of the American Presbyterian Mission, assisted in many ways in my work. I imagine that the missions began about that time to pay greater attention to education, and to make it one of the most important branches of their work.

Of their medical service, much was seen by me later when, as Minister of the Interior, my inspection tours took me to all parts of Siam. Among their hospitals in the interior of the country, those at Bejraburi, Nagara Sridharmaraj, Bishnulok and Chiengmai have rendered excellent service to the people of those respective localities. To see such munificent work is to recognize the sterling quality of the men and women who, thousands of miles from the land of their birth, willingly serve humanity without the least expectation of material gain, their sole object being the conversion of alien communities to the faith which, to them, is the only enlightened one. Whether or not they succeed in their initial aim, or whatever the extent of success, their humane and altruistic work must be regarded with admiration. To them are due the grateful thanks of the communities among whom they work, even if the major part of such communities do not accept the path which is pointed out to them.

Speaking from my own observation, the present work of the American missions in this country has prospered beyond comparision with the work of their pioneers. The reason appears to me to be this : that the missionaries, having lived long enough in Siam, have come to appreciate the character of her inhabitants, and have changed their methods to suit such character. Thus, instead of abusing Buddhism as a first step to the extolling of Christianity, they set about to exhibit Christian virtue, and thus inspire faith in a religion which possesses such good points. Aggressive works have been abandoned in favour of a gentler method, and the results must surely be more satisfactory from the missionary view-point. Whereas in the opinion of a contemporary foreign observer, the missionaries could not produce one good Siamese convert for every £ 10,000 they spent sixty years ago, I imagine the present volume will show that such is very far from being the case today.

The attitude of this country from time immemorial has been that of complete toleration of the freedom of religious thought. The State religion has always been Buddhism, but the state does not interfere with its people in the matter of faith. More than that, the Kings of Siam have always assisted other religions in the country, the most recent instance of such help being King Chulalonkorn's gift of the land on which the British Christ Church stands in Bangkok. It is also the desire of the Sovereigns that foreign religions shall not be persecuted, and this has been emphasized in an announcement recently made by command of his present Majesty, wherein the King offers a prize each year for the best essay on Buddhism. In that announcement it is plainly stated that an essay submitted in competition for the prize shall not refer to other religions in contemptuous terms. It is recognised that religions confer happiness on the people, and the King's support of all faiths is, in effect, the support of all his people. Consequently, although we are essentially a nation of Buddhists, the King's Government puts no obstacle in the way of any of His Majesty's subjects belonging to another religion, be it Christianity, Hinduism, Islam or any other Faith. This fact is well-known to all who know Siam.

As regards the American missionaries, their sterling qualities and the good work they have done in educational and medical matters have always been fully recognised, and their friendship with the people of the country extends to all classes.

In conclusion I would express the hope that American Presbyterian missions would continue to receive support from the United States of America as well as in Siam, and be thus enabled to keep up the good work they have done.

PIONEERS

CHAPTER I

THE BEGINNINGS OF PROTESTANT MISSIONS IN SIAM

THE PATHFINDERS

THE very first Protestant missionary effort on record for the land of Siam was made by a woman who never saw Siam. Mrs. Ann Hazeltine Judson, the young wife of the Rev. Adoniram Judson, D. D., Burma, became so deeply interested in the numerous Siamese colony of captives she found in Rangoon that in April 1818, she wrote a friend, " I have attended to the Siamese language for about a year and a half, and with the assistance of my teacher, have translated the Burman catechism, a tract containing an abstract of Christianity, and the Gospel of Matthew, into that language." Her Siamese version of her husband's Burman catechism was published in 1819 by the Baptist Press at Serampore, India, but the Gospel of Matthew apparently was never published.

To the Rev. W. H. Medhurst, it is believed, belongs the honor of first planning a Protestant Mission to Siam. In 1826 he proposed to visit Siam for the purpose of distributing books among the Chinese, but for some reason he did not accomplish his purpose. Then in 1828 he actually set out from Batavia intending to join the Rev. Jacob Tomlin and the Rev. Carl Gutzlaff who were on their way to Bangkok, but arrived in Singapore just two days after they had left. He worked his way up as far as Singora, hoping still to get to Bangkok but there being no boats available he had to return to Singapore and apparently never reached Bangkok.

The first to actually arrive in Bangkok were a German, the Rev. Carl Augustus Friedrich Gutzlaff, M. D., who had severed his brief connection with the Netherlands Missionary Society, and who visited Bangkok at his own expense, and an Englishman, the Rev. Jacob Tomlin of the London Missionary Society. These two men embarked from Singapore on the 3rd of August, 1828 on an " old crazy Chinese vessel and after an exceedingly toilsome and dangerous passage " arrived at the capital of Siam on 23rd August. The Portuguese Consul, Segnior Carlos de Silveira, himself a Roman Catholic, received them with great kindness and took them into a house on his own premises about three rods above the landing of the Portuguese Consulate. This Consul was ever most gracious and it was no doubt due in large measure to his kindness that they were so well received and that the subsequent opposition of the Roman Catholics was in vain and ceased. At their first interview with the authorities, the new missionaries received permission to reside in Bangkok and to labor among the Chinese. The Gospel was quite new to the people, though the Roman Catholics had been in Siam many years and had at the time four churches in Bangkok and one each in Ayuthia and Chantaboon. Their Siamese converts were not numerous nor influential for they were still feeling the results of the persecution they had sustained in the 18th century. Foreigners were very few in Siam at this time. The result of all this was that their lodgings were constantly crowded with people seeking books and medicines. People even from remote regions heard of these missionaries, and came to see them, some coming three or four days journey for the purpose. In two months the whole stock of Bibles they had brought with them was exhausted and scattered among the Chinese population.

So great was the interest aroused in these new-comers that a persecution arose, probably instigated by the Roman Catholics. The Phra Klang or Foreign Minister, requested Mr. Hunter, an English merchant, to take them out of the country. But they at once appealed to the Phra Klang asking what their offence was and for papers that they might carry to the representative of the British Government with whom Siam had recently made a treaty, which

Rev. Carl Friedrick Augustus Gutzlaff

would satisfy the British Government that they were rightfully expelled from Siam. These treaties to which they referred—of which there had been two, one in 1822 and a second in 1826—were with the East India Company and not with the British Government as such. The remonstrance, however, had the desired effect and permission was given for them to remain but they were admonished to be more sparing in the distribution of their books, one of which had actually been translated for the King as he feared there might be something seditious in it. A Royal edict forbade the receiving of Christian books by the Siamese. This storm quickly blew over and the confidence of the people returned and the opposition of the Roman Catholics ceased. Throughout this time of difficulty and stress, the Portuguese Consul de Silveira had been their staunch friend and had saved them discomfort and serious trouble.

They realized that Siamese books were needed and set themselves to learn the Siamese language. They must have made wonderful progress with this study for they started in at once on a translation of the Chinese Bible into Siamese. They worked through a Chinaman named King (who had Siamese but imperfectly) and Hon, a Burmese (who also knew Siamese) the latter writing down in Siamese from the mouth of the former who read from the Chinese version. During the first six months after their arrival these two men, Messrs. Gutzlaff and Tomlin, with the help of their assistants, had completed the translation of the four Gospels and the Epistle to the Romans in Siamese and had proceeded with an English and Siamese dictionary as far as the letter " R ".

Mr. Tomlin left on 14 May 1829 for Singapore to recuperate his health and to get a fresh supply of books and medicines. Mr. Gutzlaff himself remained until the close of the year. At length, having prepared a tract containing a brief " View of the Christian Religion ", together with the translation of parts of the New Testament, Mr. Gutzlaff followed Mr. Tomlin to Singapore to get these printed. The first Siamese type of the Baptist Mission Press in Serampore, India, had been brought to Singapore and was in the possession of the Rev. Robert Burn, Chaplain of Singapore, and Mr. Thomson, a missionary to Malaya under the London Missionary Society. While on this visit to Singapore, Mr. Gutzlaff married at Malacca Miss Maria Newell, a zealous missionary under the London Missionary Society. Together they returned to Siam 11th February 1830. These two devoted themselves to studying Siamese and translating, hardly allowing themselves time to eat or sleep, and daily employing a number of copyists. Thus they succeeded in evolving a very imperfect translation of the whole Bible in Siamese, a considerable portion of it into the Lao and Cambodian languages, and preparing a dictionary and grammar of the Siamese and Cambodian. These translations were later delivered by Mr. Gutzlaff to Mr. Robinson of the American Board of Commissioners for Foreign Missions and the dictionary was taken over by Mr. Jones of the Baptist Board and became the foundation of the dictionary later prepared by Mrs. Eliza Grew Jones.

Both Mr. and Mrs. Gutzlaff found the new climate trying and their arduous labors still further undermined their strength. Mrs. Gutzlaff gave birth to twin daughters on 16 February 1831, dying a few hours later. One child died at birth and the other lived about four months. Burial was made by special permit at the upper side of the Portuguese Consulate gate. This plot of ground continued to be the burial ground of the missionaries and others until H. M. King Mongkut made a grant for this purpose in 1853, and in 1893 this earliest cemetery which had eventually been bought by the Baptist Mission, was sold and the graves moved to the new Protestant Cemetery. Thoroughly discouraged by the death of his devoted wife, and conscious that he himself was rapidly failing in health and strength and feeling that death was near, Mr. Gutzlaff reluctantly decided to leave for China. Almost too weak to walk, he was escorted to his junk bound for Tientsin, 3 June 1831, by Mr. Robert Hunter, Captain Dawson and Mr. Mac Dalnac. These men, and especially Mr. Hunter, had been his constant benefactors and were most reluctant to see him leave thus alone. Mr. Gutzlaff still prayed to be spared to work in China, the country of his first love. Before leaving Europe he had studied the Chinese language and long before leaving Bangkok he had become a naturalized subject of the Celestial Empire by adoption into the clan of Kwo, from the Tung-an district of Fukien. He took the name of Shik-lee and occasionally wore Chinese dress. He lived for twenty years after leaving Bangkok, exploring the coast of China and after a notable career died in 1851. The Churches of Christendom are under lasting obligation to this devoted missionary for the attempts he made to penetrate China and to facilitate the more direct communication of the Gospel to the Chinese. A life of great danger he lived; his purpose was noble and the results great.

Passing down the Menam Chaophya, he nearly died before reaching the Bar. All deserted him; he felt death near. But the attack passed and he began to improve. While at the Bar, he received word of the death of the infant daughter he had left with her native nurse until such a time as she could be put into the care of Mrs. Thomson in Singapore. This news was a great grief to him and severed the last tie that bound him to Siam. But in his brief stay, Gutzlaff had rendered Siam a lasting service though but one convert—a Chinaman named Boon-tee—had been baptized at his hand.

The American trading-vessel commanded by Captain Coffin, which in 1829 took to America the famous "Siamese-twins" also carried an earnest appeal for aid in the evangelizing of that almost unknown land of their birth. This appeal came from the Rev. Carl Gutzlaff and his associate the Rev. Jacob Tomlin. Their own missionary societies not favoring the taking up of work in Siam, these men appealed to the American churches to do so. It was in response to this appeal that the Rev. David Abeel, M. D., the first American missionary to Siam, was sent out by the American Board of Commissioners for Foreign Missions, then supported by the Congregational and Presbyterian Churches jointly.

Under instructions from his Board to open work in Siam if he deemed the opening favorable, Mr. Abeel reached Singapore just as Mr. Tomlin was starting on his second trip to Bangkok. Knowing of Dr. Gutzlaff's ill-health and his plan to go to China, Mr. Tomlin was eager to reach Bangkok before he should leave, hoping to be able to persuade him to remain at least six months or a year longer in Siam. These two men arrived from Singapore on 30 June 1831, just twelve days after Gutzlaff had left, and took up their residence in the house so recently vacated by him,—owned by the Portuguese Consulate. This house had been moved from its original site to land adjoining the Consulate. Mr. Abeel at once rented this house of the Consulate. They found the people as eager as formerly for books and soon their small supply of Siamese tracts was exhausted. They were much encouraged and found several persons whom they felt were really interested. They made special mention of one priest who copied considerable portions of the New Testament. Soon after arriving they established public worship in their own house and this was conducted in Chinese every Sunday.

Under date 25 August 1831, Mr. Abeel reported to his Board, " One thing I feel anxious to urge, and that is, *immediate assistance.* A host of missionaries with the spirit that can hazard their lives for their Lord and Master would have little difficulty in finding stations and employment. As Bangkok is a new station, and one which should by all means be retained, it appears highly important that at least *two or three* should be sent to this place as soon as possible". He adds in the same communication, "The claims of Siam are perhaps of more immediate urgency than any other place in these regions. Besides, my fellow laborer (Mr. Tomlin) is not likely to continue long in Siam. He has left Singapore now without a Chinese missionary, and his family are still there."

Mr. Abeel appeared to feel that Siam was his own proper field

Phya Bibadh Kosha

(Son of Seignior Carlos De Silveira)

มหาอำมาตย์โท พระยาพิพัฒ์โกษา

of labor and nothing but continued ill-health would have induced him to leave. A remarkable overflowing of the river which covered the whole country for two months, and the subsequent lack of exercise brought on Mr. Abeel a low lingering fever which induced him to go with Mr. Tomlin to Singapore in an effort to regain his health. So after a stay in Bangkok of a little over six months, Messrs. Tomlin and Abeel left for Singapore on 7 January 1832, arriving on the morning of the 13th. After visiting Singapore and Malacca and being partially restored in health, Mr. Abeel embarked alone on a Chinese junk for Bangkok on 18th April, anxious to reach Bangkok before the junks there should embark for China, hoping to distribute tracts and books on them. After a tedious voyage of one month, he arrived in Bangkok on 19th May and was welcomed by his friend Segnior de Silveira. A second Royal Edict had been issued prohibiting the distribution of books. This ban was lifted however to the extent that he was allowed to distribute literature on the junks leaving for China. There were some fifty of these still lying at anchor in the river. The people flocked about him for medicines and he had abundant opportunities of teaching the people of Christ. The Sunday services for worship had kept up all during his absence and regularly there were from twelve to twenty Chinese present.

Mr. Abeel baptized none himself but the one Chinaman whom Mr. Gutzlaff had baptized—Boon-tee—returned from a visit to China on 6th July and became a very helpful assistant in the Sunday services and otherwise. Mr. Abeel wrote of him as one who "appears to know the truth in the love of it ".

Continued ill-health made it imperative that Mr. Abeel should again leave Siam. His last interview with his little flock was most interesting and touching. He wrote under date 14 October 1832, " Since the commencement of our Sabbath service, I have never seen such fixed and thoughtful attention as was apparent toward the close of this morning's exhortation. The spirit of the living Saviour was doubtless in our midst, and the hearts of many, I sincerely believe, felt his sacred presence. Again the sadness of separation came over my spirit, and again I commended this little band to the Shepherd and Bishop of souls." This little band of worshippers was much on his heart and while in Singapore, before he continued on his way to U. S. A., he met the Rev. John Taylor Jones then en route for Siam, and requested him to encourage them to meet as they had done till other missionaries should arrive.

Mr. Abeel did not leave Singapore at once on his homeward journey but tried to recuperate there. During his stay in Singapore the Chaplain, the Rev. Robert Burn, died. Mr. Abeel ministered to him in his last illness and at request of the community remained temporarily to carry on this man's work after his death, hoping that the trip to the U. S. A. might prove unnecessary. An interesting fact regarding the association between Mr. Abeel and this Mr. Burn lies in the fact that Mr. Burn had ever taken a keen interest in missions and had himself studied several eastern languages, among which was Siamese. He had assisted in correcting Mr. Gutzlaff's translation. He had also spent a large sum of money in purchasing fonts of type in the native character and together with the Rev. C. H. Thomson, a missionary whose work was chiefly among the Malays, was proprietor of the Printing establishment in Singapore. Apparently after the death of Mr. Burn the Siamese part of this equipment was sold to the A. B. C. F. M. Board. When Dr. Bradley arrived in Singapore in 1835, the press and type were turned over to him and he brought them to Bangkok. The Baptists had already been having printing done on this press.

His health still failing, the Rev. David Abeel embarked on 25 May 1833 for England in an English ship, en route for America. He never returned to Siam, though it is apparent that he only gave up his work in Siam because of failing health. His Board, too, apparently considered him as their first missionary to Siam and not merely as an explorer.

Gutzlaff not only appealed to the churches of America but also to the Baptist missionaries in Burma, urging them to send someone to take up work in this promising field. In response to that appeal, the Rev. John Taylor Jones, D. D. and Mrs. Jones were transferred to Siam where they did much notable work among the Siamese. En route for Siam, Dr. Jones met Mr. Abeel in Singapore and whether from him or through some other hands, received the dictionary begun by Gutzlaff. On his arrival in Bangkok he naturally sought the Portuguese Consul Segnior de Silveira who had been such a friend and benefactor to his predecessors, and doubtless through his help succeeded in renting the land adjoining the Consulate which was apparently later sold to the Baptist Mission.

In 1837 the Presbyterian Board of Foreign Missions was organized. One of its first acts was to establish a Mission for the Chinese in Singapore. In 1838, the Rev. R. W. Orr of that mission spent one month in Siam, touring about with Dr. Dan Beach Bradley and his favorable report led to the appointment of the Rev. and Mrs. William P. Buell who arrived in Siam August 1840—the first of a long line of Presbyterian missionaries in this country.

Thus the needs of the new field were made known and definite beginnings were made toward the entrance of three American Missionary Societies into Siam.

CHAPTER II

THE WORK OF THE AMERICAN BOARD
OF COMMISSIONERS FOR FOREIGN MISSIONS
AND
THE AMERICAN MISSIONARY ASSOCIATION

1831—1893

In response to the earnest appeal sent directly to the American churches by the Rev. Carl Gutzlaff, M.D., and his associate, the Rev. Jacob Tomlin, the American Board of Commissioners for Foreign Missions took steps toward the occupancy of Siam if this should on further investigation seem advisable.

The Rev. David Abeel, M.D., went to Canton under the auspices of the American Seaman's Friend Society as chaplain. He took with him a "conditional appointment" from the American Board of Commissioners for Foreign Missions in case he should consider it his duty to devote himself exclusively to missionary work. After one year in Canton he started on a tour with a double purpose, viz. (1) To ascertain important posts for mission stations, and (2) to make himself useful in whatever "station presented the strongest claim upon his services."

Mr. Abeel reached Singapore just as Mr. Tomlin was on the eve of embarking on a second visit to Bangkok. Mr. Tomlin had long been waiting for this opportunity to return to Bangkok. The very day of Mr. Abeel's arrival in Singapore the boat obtained her port clearance. For Mr. Abeel's accommodation the Captain delayed the sailing three days, enabling Mr. Abeel to join Mr. Tomlin on this trip. They arrived in Siam on 30 June 1831, a few days after Mr.

Gutzlaff, thoroughly disheartened by the death of his devoted wife and by his own desperately weakened condition, had sailed for China on the first of his memorable voyages for missionary exploration up that coast.   He had been in Siam for parts only of three years and had baptised but one convert, Boon-tee (in some accounts given as Bunty).

The new-comers finding the people eager for the books and medicines they had brought, labored faithfully for the good of the many Siamese and Chinese of high and low degree who came to visit them.   In six months, however, Mr. Tomlin was called away and Dr. Abeel also was obliged to leave Siam on a trip to Singapore to recruit his impaired health.   Returning to Siam, Dr. Abeel labored until 5 November 1832, when continued ill-health drove him finally from the field.

The next missionaries sent out by the A. B. C. F. M. to arrive in Siam were the Rev. Chas. Robinson and the Rev. Stephen Johnson, who with their wives had embarked at Boston on 11 June 1833, but, detained in Singapore nine weary months waiting for a vessel to Siam, did not reach Bangkok until 25 July 1834, having been more than a year on their way.   Mr. Johnson entered at once into active labors for the Chinese and Mr. Robinson for the Siamese part of the population.   Since the Baptist mission was devoting itself exclusively to those among the Chinese who spoke the Teh Chiew dialect, the A. B. C. F. M. undertook Chinese work with those who spoke the Hokien dialect.

Shortly after their arrival, Messrs. Robinson and Johnson succeeded in renting a plot of ground of a civil officer of some rank, —one Nai Clin.   This plot of ground was about six rods square, on the left hand of the landing at Wat Koh as one ascends and but two or three rods from it.   The plot was hemmed in on three sides by bamboo houses thatched with attap leaves; in front was low swampy land which could only be traversed by boats through a narrow ditch or by a long foot-path one plank in width.   Being at the foot of the bazaar, the situation was excellent for coming into contact with the people but being a sort of "sink of the off-scouring of creation" it left much to be desired as a place of residence for the missionary families. Two rough barn-like dwellings were erected at once which became the homes of these two families.

Dan Beach Bradley, M.D., and Mrs. Bradley under the A.B.C.F.M., together with the Rev. and Mrs. William Dean under the Baptist Board, sailed during the summer of 1834 from Boston for Singapore. In Singapore they had a long delay. There two babies were born, the infant son of Dr. and Mrs. Bradley living but a few hours. Then ensued a fierce fight for the life of Mrs. Dean. Medical science had not yet made blood transfusion common, but even that extreme measure the young doctor was willing to attempt, using the blood of the young husband in the vain effort to save the life of his dying wife. A baby daughter—Matilda Dean—survived her mother and was adopted by Dr. and Mrs. Bradley. It was not until the 18 July 1835, a year after the little party had sailed so bravely out of Boston harbor, that these courageous young missionaries reached their chosen field. But all three of them were destined to play a very important part in the Christian work of Siam,—and Dr. Dean had the additional joy of rendering many years of invaluable service to China.

On arrival, Dr. and Mrs. Bradley took up their abode with Mr. and Mrs. Johnson until Dr. Bradley could erect a house for himself on the already crowded mission plot of ground. A few days later he opened a medical dispensary in one of the rooms under the Johnson house and entered with faith, zeal and energy, which neither illness nor tropical heat could abate, upon a course of preaching, writing, translating, printing and medical labors for the good of the Siamese. These never ceased until his death in June 1873—thirty-eight years later.

Ten days after his arrival in Siam, Mr. Hunter came to Dr. Bradley with a message from P'ie-see-pee-p'at (the man who

Rev. Dan Beach Bradley, M.D.

subsequently became the Somdetch Ong Noi) requesting him in the name of the king to go immediately to try his skill as physician on a company of slaves and captives who were sick of small-pox and cholera. The dignitary who acted as interpreter on this occasion carefully explained to Dr. Bradley that this call was not because the king had any interest in these captives and slaves but because the king wanted to test out the skill of the new physician before calling him to attend great men. The interpreter himself formed a very poor impression of Dr. Bradley's skill because the latter frankly admitted that he could not tell by merely looking at a man whether or not he would recover. Siamese physicians who always combined their knowledge of medicine with soothsaying, were able to do this; therefore Dr. Bradley was not their equal. Unfortunately Dr. Bradley had little opportunity to display medical skill on this occasion or to relieve the sufferings of the poor captives for the squalor in which they were and the absolute lack of all attempts at nursing made his efforts futile. However, Dr. Bradley was not dependent upon royal favor or approval to popularize his dispensary. About a hundred patients came daily to the dispensary for treatment and, they being mostly Chinese, Mr. Johnson availed himself of the opportunity of preaching to them there.

Dr. Bradley had things well systematized and could care for a large number of people easily. He thus described the routine, " Mrs. Bradley with her female assistant takes the main charge of administrating medicines to the females while my John, assisted by a Chinaman, attends to the males; I am seated so as to oversee all that is done. My Siamese teacher sits on the opposite side of the table, engaged in writing passages of Scriptures on the backs of all cards given to the patients and is ready to answer any questions which I may wish to ask regarding the language."

Meanwile the storm-clouds were gathering. The increasing popularity of the missionaries, and the constant benefactions they

distributed with open hand awakened jealousy.   Nai Clin began to
fear royal displeasure since he had rented this land to the foreigners
without royal sanction, and so he began to urge them to move.
With the assistance of Mr. Hunter, the English merchant who had
gained great power in high circles, the missionaries tried to secure
the consent of the Phra Klang to their continuing residence there.
Just at that time a very unfortunate incident occurred.   Mr. Hunter
and Captain Wellar called on Dr. Bradley one afternoon, carrying a
gun with which they intended to shoot pigeons and crows which
were numerous in that part of the city.   Captain Wellar strayed out
alone with his gun and into a temple compound where he shot
several birds.   The Buddhist monks rushed out in great excitement
for Buddhism teaches the sacredness of all life, and this was
sacrilege.   Capt. Wellar was seriously wounded. Mr. Hunter made
large demands of the government and even threatened British
rule in Siam.   The affair was eventually settled, but the episode
doubtless did little to help the cause of the missionaries who were
personally not involved in the affray.   But after nearly a month of
negotiations the ultimatum was that they must leave the premises
within five days for H. M. the King was about to make a visit to
Wat Koh bazaar and they must be gone before that time.   No place
was even suggested where they might go.   A sad, anxious time it was;
places of residence must be found for three families; the infant
daughter of Mr. and Mrs. Johnson lay at the point of death, and five
days hence the transfer must be completed.   It was finally arranged
that Mr. Robinson should go with his family into a small Portuguese
house near the Baptist mission, Mr. Johnson and family should occupy
a floating-house moored in front of the Roman Catholic Church at
Santa Cruz on the west side of the river, and Dr. and Mrs. Bradley
and their adopted daughter Matilda Dean should occupy a small rented
house in the Santa Cruz Catholic village, near the church.   The
moving was delayed until the very last day granted them for occupying
the old site but, fearing dire consequences were they to overstay their

time limit, they moved on the 5th October and the following day the immortal soul of the little Mary Johnson took its flight. Burial was made by the side of Mrs. Gutzlaff and her two daughters and two children of Dr. and Mrs. Jones. For five days the Johnsons continued to stay with the Bradleys in their tiny house and then moved to their own floating-house which had been bought for the purpose of making it into a floating-dispensary, and which Dr. Bradley described as being one of the smallest of floating-houses. The house occupied by Dr. and Mrs. Bradley at this time, which continued to be their home for nearly three years, was about 12 by 25 feet, with a narrow veranda on one side; it was built of wood and had an attap roof. The addition of two other verandas increased the capacity of the house and provided for the dispensary which Dr. Bradley shortly afterward opened at this new location.

A new site was finally selected on land belonging to the Phra Klang, just across the canal which ran near the house occupied by Dr. Bradley. On this land the Phra Klang promised to erect two houses according to agreed specifications for which the Mission was to pay a rental of Tcs. 65.00 per month. Any further buildings desired were to be erected by the Mission at its own expense. These houses were roughly made of wood, two tall stories high, with plank floors and tile roofs, and with verandas all around. Though crude, they were very comfortable. In 1838 they were completed and the missionaries were able to move into them : this remained the home of the Congregational mission for some fifteen years to come.

A friendship early developed between Dr. Bradley and the son of the Phra Klang named Luang Nai Sit. This young man had built the first brig ever constructed in Siam,—the "Ariel." In 1835, he invited Mr. and Mrs. Johnson to go with him to Chantaboon where his father was making preparations for war with Cambodia. The suggestion was that Mr. and Mrs. Johnson should teach the family of Luang Nai Sit and then have the opportunity to preach and teach all through the region of Chantaboon. They spent six months on this trip.

Dr. Bradley who had begun to have dysentery about the time of their ejection from the old Wat Koh quarters went with the party for a month's trip hoping that his health might be fully restored. He did return greatly benefitted by the change but soon the dysentery returned and it was four years before he finally succeeded in curing himself. He never allowed his ill-health to interfere seriously with his missionary and medical work however.

Though Dr. Bradley had brought with him to Bangkok the printing press that had fallen into the hands of the A. B. C. F. M. in Singapore,—the press upon which all of the Siamese printing thus far had been done,—it was apparently not until the year after his arrival in Siam that time was found to set it up and start printing. The first printing actually done in Siam was a sheet tract in Siamese printed by Mr. Robinson on this old-fashioned press made of wood and stone, with type cast in Bengal and brought with the press to Bangkok. Both press and type were said to have been " very ugly." This tract, containing eight pages, was a brief account of the giving of the law on Mount Sinai, the Ten Commandments, a short summary of the commandments, explanations, a short prayer and three hymns. An edition of 1000 copies was printed with the assistance of Mr. Davenport. Three other tracts were ready for the press—but no printer. That very year 1836, the Baptist mission received a press that carried with it all of the necessary accompaniments of a thorough printing office. The following year (1837) two new printing presses, two standing presses and other materials for the establishment of another complete printing office arrived for the A.B.C.F.M. Thus both missions were well equipped for supplying the printed page—a task which formed a very important part of the mission work for many years to come. It was this press that on 27 April 1839 printed for the Siamese Government a Royal Proclamation contrabanding opium. This was the first government document ever printed in Siam : the edition was 9,000 copies.

The Phra Klang's temple was dedicated on 13 January 1837

and during the celebrations a cannon burst killing many and wounding many more. That night Dr. Bradley successfully amputated the arm of a priest. This is believed to have been the first modern surgical operation ever performed in Siam.

The medical services of the missionaries and their medicines and the Christian books distributed without money and without price, were eagerly sought and there was free access for making known the new religion to the people in their streets, homes, and even in their temples. During these early years none of the Siamese seemed savingly impressed. Such was the dread of the King during those days that no Siamese could even be brought to entertain the thought of forsaking his religion. Those were the days before religious toleration was decreed.

The Chinese settlers in Siam had less to fear, being allowed entire freedom of conscience;—it was only the displeasure of their kinsmen that they had to fear when they changed their religion. So there were converts among the Chinese. In 1837 the first Chinese Baptist church was organized with eleven members. It was not until the following year however that the A. B. C. F. M. baptised its first convert,—a Chinese teacher of Mr. Johnson's baptised by him. The second baptism was in 1844 when Mr. Johnson again had the pleasure of baptising another of his teachers, Sinsaa Ki-eng Qua-Sean (กี่เอ็ง ก๊วยเซียน) a Chinese of very respectable literary attainments.

The year 1838 was a notable one for the Congregational mission not only because in that year the first convert was baptised, but also because Dr. Bradley was then successful for the first time in inoculating for small-pox. This scourge was endemic in Bangkok and annually caused the death of many persons. For several years attempts were made to introduce vaccination but without success. Finally in desperation, the missionaries inoculated their own children successfully from small-pox patients. His Majesty, King Somdetch Phra Nang Klao was much interested and sent his chief physician to the missionary physician to learn the art of thus inoculating. The following year this king distributed premiums amounting to several thousands of ticals to the royal physicians and to Dr. Bradley for the services they had rendered in inoculating for small-pox during a period of three months. Fortunately they had been very successful. It was not until 1840 however that vaccination was really successful in Siam. Vaccine scabs were sent out from Boston by the new missionaries and on 31 January 1840, after four years of effort Dr. Bradley at last succeeded in vaccinating. This was continued week by week until about the first of the following May. Again in 1842 being surrounded by small-pox and without any possibility of vaccination, the missionaries once more resorted to the inoculation of their children and others, but not without the loss of some lives. In 1844 vaccination was again revived after an interval of four years. Again in 1846 we find record of a third revival of vaccination by the Rev. J. Goddard, who used scabs sent from Boston. In 1861 also, vaccination was successful, being produced from a vaccine scab sent out from Brooklyn, N.Y. overland, reaching Siam when it was five and a half months old. This had been encased in a little beeswax. Out of twelve persons vaccinated, seven cases were reported successful. This enumeration of inoculations and vaccinations helps to reveal the extreme difficulty under which the early physicians labored and the really remarkable and persistent efforts to introduce the results of modern medical science into Siam.

Until 1838 the three Congregational families labored without reenforcement. In November of that year, Dr. Bradley was ordained a minister of the gospel by his Congregational associates, a step that was both fitting and important. But the year 1838 marked the beginning of many changes in the Congregational mission. In April, the Rev. Mr. Robbins and the Rev. Stephen Tracy, M. D. joined the mission but left the following year. Early in 1840 the Siamese department of the mission was strongly reenforced by the arrival of the Rev. Jesse Caswell, the Rev. Asa Hemenway, the Rev. N. S. Benham and their wives together with Miss M. E. Pierce,—the pioneer among single women missionaries coming to Siam. One month after his arrival Mr. Benham was drowned in the Menam Chaophya when his boat capsized as he was returning from an evening prayer-meeting. In May of the same year the Rev. H. S. G. French and the Rev. L. B. Peet and their wives arrived for the same mission. But in 1841 the widowed Mrs. Benham returned to the United States and Mrs. Johnson died of brain fever. The following year Mr. French died of tuberculosis and his widow returned to the United States. In September 1844 Miss Pierce who had come out as missionary teacher but who had been unable to gather a school, died of tuberculosis. Then in 1845 the Rev. Charles Robinson and his wife left for America and he died at St. Helena on his passage home; his wife never returned to Siam. This same year, Mrs. Bradley died of tuberculosis in Bangkok, in the triumph of faith after ten years of efficient and loving missionary service for her Saviour,—a most valuable helper in her husband's work. She left three motherless children. Serious losses these deaths were to the work of the Congregational mission and greatly depleted its force just at the time when it seemed about ready to take big strides forward.

During this same year (1845), a very important opportunity came to the Rev. Jesse Caswell of this mission. H. R. H. Prince Chao Fah Mongkut, who later became king, then head-priest in the royal monastery Pavaranives, within the city walls, invited him to become his private tutor. So anxious was this Prince-priest for instruction that he offered an inducement which he knew would weigh heavily with the missionary—the use of a room in a building on the temple grounds, where, after his hour of teaching was over, he could preach and distribute tracts. The arrangement was made and carried out for over a year and a half. So much of the future of Siam in Providence was to hinge on those hours of intimate intercourse between the faithful missionary teacher and his illustrious and most diligent pupil that all of the particulars are of interest. The Prince was then about forty years of age—his teacher a graduate of Lane Theological Seminary, a member of the Presbytery of Cincinnati and in the service of the A. B. C. F. M.

Gradually China was opening up more and more and seemed to offer a wider field and a more promising one for labors among the Chinese-speaking peoples, so in 1846 the A. B. C. F. M. decided to give up the Chinese department of their mission in Siam and instructed the Messrs. Johnson and Peet to proceed to China and establish a new mission at Fuh Chow Fuh. This left the Baptists as the only missionaries in Siam working directly for the Chinese. The Presbyterians had already made several attempts to send missionaries to work among the Chinese in Siam but in every case the missionaries had chosen to go on to China proper.

In February 1847, Dr. Bradley and his three motherless children left on a visit to the U. S. A., his ship passing in the Gulf of Siam, the boat on which were travelling the newly appointed missionaries of the Presbyterian Board,—the Rev. and Mrs. Stephen Mattoon and Samuel House, M.D., who were on their way to re-open Presbyterian work which had been closed since 1844. Upon their arrival in Bangkok these new-comers were welcomed by the members of the Baptist mission and of the A. B. C. F. M. mission and took up their abode temporarily with the Messrs. Caswell and Hemenway who were the only remaining members of the A.B.C.F.M. in Bangkok at this time. Other houses on the Congregational mission premises were soon put in order for the accommodation of the new missionaries. Dr. House was soon forced to re-open Dr. Bradley's dispensary, which had been closed when he left for America,—and the work of caring for the sick continued in the floating-dispensary moored in front of A.B.C.F.M. premises.

The A. B. C. F. M. mission and the Christian work of Bangkok suffered an irreparable loss in the death of the Rev. Jesse Caswell in September 1848. He was a man of most earnest purpose and pos-

H. R. H. Prince Vongsa Dhiraj Snid.

พระเจ้าบรมวงศ์เธอ กรมหลวงวงษาธิราช สนิท

sessed rare fitness for the missionary work. It was largely due to the enlarged and liberal ideas in government and religion which Mr. Caswell had given to the Prince-priest that he opened Siam to commerce and improvement when he succeeded to the throne. H. R. H. Prince Chao Fah Mongkut attended the funeral of his beloved teacher and in observance of Siamese custom, presented a roll of white silk to Mrs. Caswell. After he became king he erected a handsome stone over his teacher's remains and sent to Mrs. Caswell, who had returned with her children to the United States in February 1849, a gift of $1000.00, and subsequently $500.00 more, as token of his regard for his former teacher.

The death of Mr. Caswell and the steadily failing health of Mr. Hemenway put the A. B. C. F. M. mission in a very serious condition. When the Presbyterian mission organized its first church on 29 August 1849, Sinsaa Ki-eng Qua-Sean, the Chinese teacher who had been baptised by Mr. Johnson in 1844, was encouraged to unite with that church by certificate before the last representatives of the Congregational Board should take their departure from Siam. The last week of 1849, the Rev. Asa Hemenway and his family left never to return. This ended the work of the A.B.C.F.M. in Siam. For fifteen years the missionaries of the A.B.C.F.M. had cultivated this interesting and inviting, but as to visible results, most barren field. From none of the native races of the land had they gathered one reliable convert. These missionaries had labored, and labored well, but others were to enter into their labors. The books they had prepared, translated and distributed ; the favor won by their gratuitous healing of the sick ; the introduction first of inoculation and afterward of vaccination against small-pox ; the training given in habits of industry and order and in the knowledge of the Christian scriptures to those employed by them in their printing-offices and in their families—these were not lost nor was the high opinion which the Siamese learned to entertain of their truthfulness, benevolence, and goodness in vain.

While still in the U.S.A., Dr. Bradley severed his connection

with the A.B.C.F.M.—this step had apparently been contemplated
before he left Siam as he and Mr. Caswell planned jointly to take
this step—and persuaded the American Missionary Association, then
working for the negroes in the U.S.A., to undertake a mission to
Siam. Siam became their first field of foreign service and Dr. and
Mrs. Bradley, whom Dr. Bradley married while on this trip to
America, were their first foreign missionaries. Sunday School children contributed a certain sum of money which made Mrs. Bradley a
member of the mission for life. Dr. Bradley spent some time in collecting funds to buy over from the A.B.C.F.M. their properties in Siam.
This was accomplished before Dr. and Mrs. Bradley sailed for
Siam, which they reached on 16 May 1850. The new mission was
formally opened on 1 July of that year. With Dr. and Mrs. Bradley
had come out the Rev. L. B. Lane, M.D. and Prof. Josiah Silsby and
their wives, making six members in the new mission, Mr. Caswell
who was also to have been a member of the new mission having died.

Though to the A.M.A. had been made over the residences, dispensary, printing-presses, chapel and lease of the A.B.C.F.M., yet
when the party arrived in Bangkok it was to find the Presbyterian
mission in full possession. They had been making strenuous efforts
to secure other quarters for themselves but in vain. So the first
few months of the new mission were marked by a serious crowding
on their premises which was only relieved when the new King came
to the throne in 1851 and made a grant of land to the Presbyterian
mission.

Soon after this grant to the Presbyterian mission, the A.M.A.
in 1852 was likewise granted the rental of a beautiful site adjoining
the palace of Krom Luang Wongsa T'iratsanit and the fort at the
mouth of Klong Bang Luang for the location of their mission.
There Dr. Bradley, Dr. Lane and Prof. Silsby erected homes for
themselves.

Early in 1852 the A. M. A. mission organized themselves into a
church but entered into agreement with the Presbyterian church that

Mrs. Dan Beach Bradley

the two organizations were to unite in the observance of the Lord's Supper, the place of meeting to alternate. The records of the Presbyterian church bear a tragic entry on 6 August 1853. "On motion it was voted to withdraw from the mutual arrangement made with the members of the American Missionary Association's mission in April 1852 by which they and we have been alternately guests at each other's table on our sacramental occasions. In a communication made to them by the Pastor Rev. S. Mattoon the ground of that withdrawal was stated to be the fact that as there were two Communion tables in that Mission we felt that we could not become involved in any diversity of views, wishing to avoid this, lest it destroy the peace and harmony so desirable between the members of the different missions on the field."

Prof. Silsby had come out chiefly for educational work but shortly after his arrival in Bangkok was ordained to the Christian ministry by his associates. Expecting to find educational work of college grade awaiting him, he was greatly depressed at finding he must begin by teaching boys the most elementary English. A child born to Prof. and Mrs. Silsby died. Other causes of discouragement and rising grounds of friction finally led to the departure of both families,—Dr. and Mrs. Lane and Prof. and Mrs. Silsby in 1855. Shortly after that event the record of the Presbyterian Church contains the following brief entry,—"We have with us again today— participating in the privileges of the occasion, Dr. and Mrs. Bradley— the only remaining member of the A. M. A." A short entry—but one reads between the lines the record of broken and bleeding hearts, of bitter disappointment but of friendship and sympathy.

No other recruits joined the A. M. A. but in 1866 Dr. Bradley accepted Mr. George Graham, who had recently married in Bangkok, as lay assistant. Whether or not the A. M. A. Board considered Mr. and Mrs. Graham as fully appointed missionaries is an open question. But it is certain that Dr. Bradley so considered them, and as there were no funds required of the Home Board at this time to finance the

Siam Mission of the A. M. A. it is fair to suppose that any appointees
of Dr. Bradley would also be considered appointees of the Board. They
continued with the A. M. A. until after the death of Dr. Bradley in 1873
when they left to enter the employ of the Rev. S. J. Smith, then
carrying on an independent printing-office, having severed his connection with the Baptist mission.

The only other reenforcements of the A. M. A. were the Rev.
and Mrs. Cornelius B. Bradley who came out in 1871. Continued
ill-health made permanent stay in Siam impossible and the year
after his father's death, Prof. Bradley and his wife left Siam permanently. Prof. Bradley later became Professor of English in the
University of California.

The Rev. Dan Bradley, M. D., died in Bangkok 23 June 1873,
having lived a very remarkable pioneer missionary life. He came
to Siam in 1835, and spent thirty-eight years of active missionary
life in his adopted home. Only once in all these years did he
return to the land of his birth, and then after he had been left
with three motherless children. Twice married to remarkable
Christian women who shared with him his labors and inspired him
to deeper devotion, he achieved much for his Master. With amazing
energy and zeal, he healed the sick, preached the Gospel, translated and printed scriptures and other literature, edited for several
years the Bangkok Calendar, which is one of the fullest records
extant of the early years of Protestant Missions in Siam, affiliated
closely with missionaries of other Boards and especially with
those of the Presbyterian church. To Dr. Bradley the Presbyterians
owed much for his help through their period of greatest strain
and stress and discouragements that nearly drove them from Siam.
With amazing faith and courage he launched on a mission career
of self-support, asking no help whatsoever from his Board in
the United States. In his own words we find a statement of his
convictions along this line — "The American Missionary Association
has never thrown me off on a self-supporting plan. It was my own

THE BRADLEY HOME

independent, unconstrained movement which led me to propose the plan of self-support to my Board. Indeed it was a plan I had in view from the time of leaving the United States in 1849, under the auspices of the A. M. A. Board, and I even then determined that whenever I could find a way fairly open for the experiment, I would try it. It was about fifteen years ago (1857) when I first thought the time had come to commence it, and accordingly then proposed the plan to the Board. The Board was at that time young and comparatively feeble. My proposition was to seek my own support, not independent of the Board, but by the use of their property which was then in my hands. That property was of a kind which I thought I could employ without any extraordinary expense of time or trouble, and in the meanwhile continue my usual missionary work. The Mission had then vacant houses on their premises which the foreign merchants were glad to rent. It also had a printing establishment which those merchants felt it was to their own interests to patronize. In view of these facts my Board fully approved of my views in managing to pay my own way with such use of her property, and at the same time holding herself ready to supply all deficiencies that might occur in procuring comfortable support for my family on the field. From that day to this (1871) I have never requested the Board to aid me in that direction, nor have I ever felt the need of such help."

For years the Bradley compound was the rendezvous of all of the missionaries and of most of the foreigners in Bangkok. In those days there were no clubs where they could foregather, so, weekly the young people and their elders would meet for tennis and croquet and social fellowship at either the Bradley home or at that of the McFarland's nearby at Suan Anan. There were young people in both homes and so these homes became the natural centres for all gaiety.

But the Bradley home was a religious centre as well. Weekly prayer-meetings of the three missions were held there for years. Then too the early days of the three missions were days of great beginnings and all were working together for the spread of the Gospel. The rich experience and the deep sympathy of Dr. and Mrs. Bradley made them the counsellors for all. The founding of the Presbyterian station at Petchaburi and the later founding of one at Chiengmai, were both enterprises in which Dr. and Mrs. Bradley deserve "honorable mention". Miss Sophia Royce Bradley had married the Rev. Daniel McGilvary before the opening of the Petchaburi station and Dr. Bradley had been most enthusiastic over the new venture. Then during the days of the persecution in Chiengmai, when no one knew what a day might bring forth, Dr. Bradley did much to save the young station from an unfortunate ending.

After Dr. Bradley's death, Mrs. Bradley continued to live in the old Bradley home with her youngest daughter Irene. Together they ran the press and together they gave out tracts and talked with the people, telling of the Saviour. Mrs. Bradley died in 1893, having spent forty-three years in Siam without once leaving it.

For almost the entire one hundred years of Protestant missionary effort in Siam, the Bradley family has had a part in the work. Dr. Bradley himself arrived when the work had been started but seven years and served thirty-seven years. Mrs. Bradley survived her husband twenty years. One son, Cornelius B. Bradley served for a time under the A. M. A. Two daughters, Mrs. Daniel McGilvary and Mrs. Marion Cheek entered missionary service under the Presbyterian Board. Miss Irene Bradley still lives in the old Bradley home on Klong Bang Luang where she was born. One grandson, Evander McGilvary and two granddaughters, Mrs. William Harris and Mrs. Roderick Gillies followed in the steps of their parents and grandparents. Thus in many ways it is true that the work begun by the A. B. C. F. M. in 1831, is still going on, though the official connection between the A. B. C. F. M. and Siam ended in 1850.

No 104

Wat Pavaranives
29th March, 1850.

To Dr S. R. House

Dear Sir, I have heard some person said Uncertainly that Dotor B Bradley was now arrived Singapore. but he detain at the same for being afraid of the occasioning irregularly of Cholera here in... Is it true & How did you hear of him?

Your friend
T.Y. Chaufah Mongkut

A letter written by King Mongkut.

CHAPTER III

THE WORK OF THE AMERICAN BAPTIST MISSION IN SIAM

1833—1893

SIAM was the second field of foreign service chosen by the American Baptists and one in which they did pioneer service: here some well-beloved missionaries gave years of faithful, loving service for their Lord. One thinks with deep emotion of the little group of Baptist missionaries in Burma. In 1832 they numbered only six men and their wives. But the Rev. Carl Gutzlaff and the Rev. Jacob Tomlin had sent them a thrilling call for help in this new field of Siam. In great faith and deep devotion the little group set aside two of their number—the Rev. John Taylor Jones and Mrs. Jones, for work in the new land. They were no longer new missionaries, having spent about two years in Burma. They brought with them a lad of twelve years, Samuel Jones Smith, whom they had adopted in Burma. Thus in faith and with real sacrifice on the part of the missionaries in Burma, the work of the Baptist Board was started in Siam. This was but the outgrowth of an interest that Mrs. Ann Hazeltine Judson had long felt because of her work among the Siamese captives of war whom she had found in Moulmein and for whom she had been translating the Gospel of Matthew, the catechism and a tract of her husband's. Thus the seed she had planted bore fruit in the opening of Baptist work in Siam by a man who is remembered as the translator of the New Testament, which she had begun herself to translate into Siamese.

The Rev. John Taylor Jones, D. D., and his wife arrived in Siam 25 March 1833. At the time of their arrival in Bangkok, the Hon. E. Roberts, U. S. Envoy, was concluding the first American treaty with Siam, which gave full protection to the missionaries in their new field. But even so, Siam was very far distant; foreign mail arrived only once in a year; and as there was no postal service, the ship captain gave out the mail to the foreigners as they came alongside and claimed it.

This entrance into Siam was felt to be a step toward China and though Dr. Jones was definitely appointed to work for the Siamese and did give the main effort of his life to the work for these people yet he was asked to investigate and report on the possibilities of entering the "walled empire," and the best way of approach, whether from the rear through Siam and Burma, or along the eastern coast. A large proportion of the city's population proved to be Chinese, and worship in the Chinese language was early established in Dr. Jones' own house. His first three converts, baptised on 22 Sept. 1833, were all Chinese. This was the first Christian baptism by immersion in the river Menam Chaophya. One of these three was Boon-tee, who had professed conversion and had been baptised by the Rev. Carl Gutzlaff, himself a pedo-baptist. For a time Boon-tee became the mainstay of the little Chinese Christian group, but in the latter part of 1836 he fell away entirely from his profession. The other two baptised at the same time were Chek Peng and Chek Seang-seah. It was not until the following year, 1834, that a missionary was definitely appointed to serve the Chinese. This was the Rev. William Dean, D.D., who reached Bangkok in July 1835, his wife having died at Singapore en route. He was soon sufficiently master of the Teh Chiew dialect to preach to the little congregation of Chinese that Dr. Jones had gathered together.

Thus two departments of the work were started almost at once. Dr. Jones continued to have charge of the Siamese branch and as soon as possible began the preparation of tracts and scripture portions. As early as the second year following his arrival in Siam, he made a trip to Singapore to print some literature on the press there equipped with Siamese type. A memorial to the earnest efforts of

Early Baptist Mission Residences

(Copied from " Malcom's Travels ")

those early days still remains in the Siamese New Testament translated and revised by him, which he saw through two editions before
his death in 1851. Mrs. Eliza Grew Jones prepared a Siamese
dictionary, using as her guide the dictionary prepared by Dr.
Gutzlaff and later turned over to Dr. Jones. The distribution of
tracts and scripture portions soon became one of the main forms of
missionary activity, for the pamphlets were eagerly desired by people
who would not linger long to listen, and printed matter could go
anywhere, often being carried far inland by waterways or on
Chinese junks. There being no printing press in Siam in that day,
literature was precious and rare. A floating-house early became
the source of literature distribution. The Baptist mission press was
established in 1836, to serve both branches of the mission. This
rapidly developed into a valuable organ of the mission, capable of
casting type, and it handled a great amount of work. Before the
Presbyterians established their press in 1861, they had their printing done on this Baptist press and on the press of the A. B. C. F. M.

Dr. and Mrs. Jones, en route to Bangkok, having met the Rev.
David Abeel in Singapore, very naturally learned from him of the
kindness shown to the early missionaries by the Portuguese Consul,
Seignior Carlos de Silveira. Probably through his assistance, Dr.
Jones was able to rent a small piece of ground at the rear of the
Portuguese Consulate. There he built houses which were of very
crude construction: the framework was of wood but the sides were
enclosed with bamboo wattling: one was enclosed with teak boards
roughly fastened together. This was partly because of the difficulty
of securing proper workmanship no doubt, but also because the early
missionaries felt they should thus show their allegiance to the
Master who "had not where to lay His head." Apparently this
property was later sold to the Baptist mission.

Siam has the distinction of having the first Protestant Church
organized in the East. This church was organized by Dr. Dean in
1837, in Bangkok, with eleven charter members. This church grew,

though slowly, and when a distinct mission to China was recognized by the Baptist Board in 1843 with Hong Kong as its centre, the First Baptist Church of Siam supplied not only the missionary to take charge of the work,—the Rev. W. Dean,—but the first church organized there on 28 May 1843 had as charter members signing its constitution, two men who had been baptised in Bangkok—Tang Tui and Koe Bak. Siam also trained several other missionaries who became pioneers when the Chinese Empire was opened to Christian work; and Siam continued to be a Christian training-school for that country. Beside the Rev. W. Dean who was transferred to Hong Kong in 1842 and did not work again in Siam until 1865, there were, Miss A. M. Fielde, the Rev. Josiah Goddard, Mr. J. L. Shuck, the Rev. W. Ashmore, Sr., and the Rev. and Mrs. S. B. Partridge, who gave the first years of their service to Siam and then were transferred to China.

Work progressed slowly—especially among the Siamese. In 1838, there were from thirty to fifty Siamese attending the Sunday services. The New Testament in Siamese was almost ready; preaching places were being established away from the centre; a small boarding school in each department cared for a few children. Dr. Dean early gathered together a little class of assistants for special study of the Bible and training in the work.

Many discouragements were faced bravely by the little group of workers. Ill-health came to many in the hot climate and there were many untimely deaths among the adults, while the infant mortality was alarmingly high. For a time the school work was given up by the women of the mission who had not the strength to carry it on with their other duties. It was never possible to send as many workers as were needed. Work for the Siamese had to be entirely suspended when Dr. Jones was away, while the transfer of forces to China further depleted the Chinese department.

One of the tragedies of those early years was the great fire of 1851 in which the entire Baptist mission property was destroyed,

Rev. S. J. Smith

including dwellings, chapel, printing-press, type-foundry, book-bindery, libraries, school and personal property. The new second edition of the Baptist New Testament printed in 1850 was completely destroyed. The Presbyterian and American Missionary Association representatives, foreign consuls and Siamese noblemen as well, surrounded the little group with special kindness at this time and greatly helped them. After the crisis was over the sister missions continued to render a much appreciated service in supplying scripture portions and other Christian literature for distribution until the Baptist mission press was once more established. Other encouragements came: there was evidence that tracts were read and appreciated; though the school work had been given up, it was started again; translation work progressed and shortly before his death Dr. Jones began the translation of the Old Testament into Siamese.

The year 1851 brought another serious loss to the Baptist mission and to the Christian work of Siam, when in September, Dr. Jones who had given twenty years of his life to missionary service,— eighteen of them in Siam,—died of dysentery. This was especially serious for the Siamese work, as there was no one upon whom Dr. Jones' mantle could fall. The Chinese work however, continued to be promising: by 1858 it had two houses of worship on important highways; by 1859 the mission as a whole could say that not less than from one hundred fifty to two hundred heard the Gospel at the Sunday services. A missionary society was formed in 1860 sending out one native colporteur, and a sewing society was also doing good work. The press was meeting the increasing demand for Christian literature.

The Government of Siam was graciously permitting free access to all parts of the country and the missionaries were treated with marked respect. At the request of H. M. King Mongkut, the Baptist ladies joined with the ladies of the other two missions in teaching in His Palace. They were permitted even there to tell the story of the Christ to the ladies of the Court. This favor of the Court meant favor with the people. This was lost for a time when a Singapore paper published a criticism of the Government which was mistakenly laid at the door of the Baptist mission. All of the missionaries suffered at this time from the restrictions imposed. But the misunderstanding was cleared up and the old freedom of travel was granted again. The contact with the ladies of the Court was lost but royal favor was shown in money given in support of mission schools.

In 1860, it was decided that the time was ripe for the organization of a separate church for the Siamese that the two branches of the work might be separate. Accordingly the Siamese Baptist Church of Bangkok was organized in April 1861, with fourteen charter members, after which the Siamese church then had a few difficult years.

In 1865, Dr. Dean returned to Siam with his wife and daughter and began a ministry for the Chinese that yielded much fruit. He wrote at the end of his first year's work, "I expect not to be happier in the present world than I have been during the present year." Under his experienced leadership, with his prestige at Court and the veneration in which the people held him, there began a period of great promise. Forty were baptised in 1867. These together with the five baptised the year previous made a total equal to the whole number baptised through the first thirty years of missionary effort. Two chapels were built before long; a pastor was ordained for the first time in the history of the mission; Dr. Dean began a revision of translated portions of the scriptures: church membership grew from 53 in 1867 to about 500 in 1882. There were six churches and seven chapels doing good work.

In 1869 it was decided best to suspend the Siamese mission. The Rev. S. J. Smith who had joined the mission in 1849 after returning from America, (in 1853 marrying the widow of Dr. Jones) left the Baptist mission at this time and opened an indepen-

Residence of the Rev. William Dean, D. D.

dent printing office at Bangkolem, down the river. This property he had bought while still in the mission. There he edited and published in English The Siam Weekly Advertiser, The Siam Repository, The Siam Directory, and in Siamese, Sayahm Samai, an English-Siamese Grammar, a Siamese-English Grammar, an Arithmetic, a Christian Catechism, a Comprehensive Anglo-Siamese Dictionary, a Comprehensive Siamese-English Dictionary (which was ready for the press at the time of his death but never printed) and he printed Siamese prose and poetry in great quantities, making the printed page very common and selling presses and fonts of type to Siamese and Chinese job-printers who opened presses everywhere.

There was a growing question in the minds of the Baptist missionaries as to the wisdom of having a separate Chinese mission in Siam when the work in China proper was so well opened up and established. When Dr. Dean was absent the work suffered but it was found impossible to send relief. Mrs. Dean's death in 1882 and the failing health of Dr. Dean brought a fresh crisis.

In 1893, the Rev. L. A. Eaton, then acting-U.S. Consul and the sole surviver of the Baptist mission in Siam, sold the Baptist Compound, and the old burial grounds of the missions near the Portuguese Consulate and transferred the remains of those buried there to the Protestant Cemetery granted to the Foreign Protestant Community by H. M. King Mongkut in 1853. He then turned over the Baptist work to the care of Dr. H. Adamsen and left for America. His wife, a sister of Dr. M. A. Cheek of the Presbyterian mission, had died in 1891 and he had then taken his children to U. S. A. The work of the Baptist mission in Siam practically ended at this time.

Dr. H. Adamsen was born in Siam, and was sent to U. S. A. by the Rev. S. J. Smith where he studied medicine, and after his return to Siam, established himself in a successful medical practice. Much encouragement for a time came from his generous devotion to evangelistic endeavor. A special feature was the vigorous carrying on of work for the Peguans (Talains). In 1896, twenty-four of the seventy persons baptised were Peguans, forty-three were Chinese and three Siamese. Two new chapels were completed in 1897. Day and night schools were well attended. A new city mission was opened. Other things consumed an increasingly large part of Dr. Adamsen's time and finally absorbed his entire interest. Dr. Adamsen then gave over the charge of the work to a representative of the South China Baptist mission, since no resident missionary was to be found.

For a time the Rev. J. M. Foster, D. D., was able to make annual visits to Bangkok from Swatow. It was hoped that students might go from Siam to study in South China, returning to preach and teach in their adopted country. The Peguan work became a missionary enterprise of the Baptist Talains (Peguans) of Moulmein, Burma. Other missions were doing vigorous work for the Siamese. The Talains of Moulmein continued their contact through translation work.

The Baptist mission property was finally sold and the Baptist mission definitely gave up its work in Siam in 1927. One small piece of land occupied by the chapel where the Chinese Baptist Church worships is still retained, for a place of worship of the Chinese Baptist Church of Bangkok—the one organized in 1837 by Dr. Dean.

For sixty years, the Baptist Church of America sowed the seed in Siam. Many souls were born anew as the direct result of this effort. But owing to the close unity between the Baptist missionaries and those of the other missions, and due to the extent of the preaching, teaching, printing and literary work of the early missionaries who helped to lay the foundations for all of the Christian work in Siam, the story did not end when the Baptist Church finally withdrew its resident missionaries. Others have entered into their labors and now carry the burden they laid down.

ONE OF THE BAPTIST MISSION RESIDENCES,

Residence on the Baptist Compound

CHAPTER IV

THE WORK OF THE PRESBYTERIAN MISSION

1840—1860

"THE PIONEER PERIOD"—THE GREAT BEGINNING

THE Rev. Robert W. Orr, one of the first Presbyterian missionaries to the Chinese, but stationed at Singapore, made a visit to Siam in the autumn of 1838. The following year, the Presbyterian Board of Foreign Missions, upon his hearty recommendation, determined to open a mission in Bangkok for the Chinese and also one for the Siamese. The Rev. William P. Buell and his wife were the first to be set apart for this new mission and, appointed to Siamese work, arrived in Bangkok August 1840.

The Congregational mission had already been founded nine years, and the Baptist mission seven years. Both missions were well manned, there being no less than 24 adult missionaries of the two missions in Bangkok at this time.

Each mission was a separate entity and developed independently but it was also true that a very close union existed between the three groups. After the arrival of the Rev. C. Robinson and the Rev. S. Johnson and their wives (A. B. C. F. M.) in 1834, a weekly religious service in English was held at the houses of the missionaries of both missions turn about, the missionary at whose home the meeting was held conducting the service and reading the published sermon of some other man. In 1837 or 1838 they began preaching their own sermons.

When the Rev. and Mrs. W. Buell arrived they entered into this happy fellowship of the other two missions though naturally the bond connecting them to the Congregational missionaries seemed the closer one. It is probable that Mr. and Mrs. Buell lived with the A. B. C. F. M. missionaries on the west side of the river, just below Klong Bang Luang, in one of the houses built for them by the Phra Klang: no record is available to substantiate this theory.

A physician and his wife were appointed to this field in 1841 and a minister and his wife in 1843,—all for Chinese work—but on reaching Singapore and finding the door to China open, they felt led to proceed to China rather than to come to Siam, which still was considered as merely a means of entrance into China proper. Mr. Buell devoted himself to the study of the Siamese language and acquired a sufficient mastery of it to be able to preach in Siamese and to explain the scriptures and other books and tracts which he distributed among the people. He was encouraged and eager in his work but when his wife was stricken with paralysis they reluctantly decided to return to America.

In 1844, the first steamer ever seen in Siam made its appearance and greatly astonished the Siamese and Chinese of Bangkok. On leaving it took as passengers to Singapore Mr. and Mrs. Buell—still after three and one half years in Bangkok, the only Presbyterian missionaries. With their departure on 24 February 1844, the Presbyterian mission in Siam was apparently ended. It was more than three years before it was re-opened.

The task of establishing permanent Presbyterian work was entrusted to the Rev. and Mrs. Stephen Mattoon and Samuel R. House, M. D. This little party had sailed from New York for China in the ship Grafton in July 1846, after a five months' voyage arriving at Macao on Christmas Day. No opportunity thence direct to Bangkok, they proceeded to Singapore. Finding there a native-built trading ship belonging to the King of Siam but commanded by a European,

หมอมัตตูน

Rev. Stephen Mattoon

they secured passage in it and, after an additional tedious journey of twenty-four days, arrived in Bangkok on 22 March 1847—eight months after leaving New York.

As the work of the Presbyterian mission really began with the arrival of these three missionaries, (at least no record is available of the work of Mr. and Mrs. Buell) it might be well to summarize briefly the situation in 1847 and the foundation upon which the Presbyterian missionaries began to build.   H. M. King Phra Nang Klao had been on the throne twenty-three years.   His reign had been characterized by revolt.   Fearing English encroachments because of their interest in Burma, he sent an expedition to Kanburi in 1824.   The same year the Chinese at Chantaburi rebelled.   This was followed by uprisings among the Chinese at the mouth of each river emptying into the Gulf of Siam, viz.—at Nakawn Chaisee (1842 and 1847), Langsuen (1845), Cherng Sao (1848).   The Laos were led in revolt, first by the Prince of Vieng Chan (1826), then at Luang Prabang (1835) and later at Chiengrung (1846); the Cambodians and Yuans organized a serious revolt (1833) which had far-reaching political effects on both countries ; the Malays of Saiburi rebelled (1830) and Malay pirates (1838) added to the difficulties of the King of Siam. No less than eleven distinct uprisings during a reign of twenty-eight years meant almost constant unrest and far from easy lay the head that wore the Siamese crown.   England had (1824) taken Burma and a prophecy that a foreign king would conquer Siam, increased the king's fear of the foreigner within his gates. Commercial treaties had been made reluctantly with England (1822 and 1826) and with the U. S. A. (1833) more or less to keep peace with the threatening western powers.   Twenty three years of rebellions and intrigues had not softened the king's disposition nor served to allay his suspicions.   The Protestant missionaries had come ; they had done no harm truly, but only good—but why? To perform acts of merit occasionally and to distribute books at stated times—as at Cremation ceremonies—this could be under-

stood. But to spend their whole time in doing meritorious acts
and constantly distributing literature: that was queer and inexplicable, and a thing that looked so suspicious would wisely be
discouraged rather than encouraged.

The Baptist and A. B. C. F. M. presses were well equipped
and were turning out much literature. Dr. Jones, Mr. Robinson
and Dr. Bradley especially had done much translation and writing
in Siamese. A Baptist translation of the New Testament (which
stressed the Baptist baptismal beliefs) and a Congregational translation of parts of the New Testament were in print—also a number
of tracts, a Life of Christ by Dr. Bradley and a series of Old
Testament histories of various periods written circling about outstanding characters like Joseph, Moses etc.

Foreign medical science had been introduced and Dr. Bradley's
medical practice was a firm foundation on which the new physician
could build.

The other two missions were by this time greatly weakened.
The Baptist mission had lost several of its workers to start work
in China: it never recovered from this loss. The Congregational
mission was nearing the close of its career.

The earlier missions had put down their roots and their
growth and development were healthy. Into this united Christian
body the Presbyterian mission was grafted. From them the new
graft drew strength and vigor, and though not weakening them
by its presence and growth, it did gradually become the thriving
branch of the tree and after the first ten years or so, almost the
whole story of the mission enterprise must be told in terms of
the Presbyterian branch. This continued true down to the beginning
of the 20th century when other societies began to come into the
field.

A letter from the Rev. W. Lowrie, the General Secretary
of the Presbyterian Foreign Mission Board, to these new missionaries—Dr. House and Mr. and Mrs. Mattoon—as they were about

แหม่มมัตตูน

Mrs. Stephen Mattoon

to start on their long journey is very touching in its counsel and instructions. In referring to the estimated expense of the mission for the first year he said, "The salary of Mr. Buell when in Siam, was fixed at his own request at six hundred dollars per annum for himself and his wife and fifty dollars for each child. In the usual proportion that of a single missionary would be four hundred fifty per annum. These sums for your salaries may be taken for the present, but if you find on experience that they are too low or too high they can be altered to what is found to be the proper amount." The total budget for the year was:

Salaries	...	$ 1050.00
House Rent	...	200.00
Teacher	...	75.00
Incidentals	...	175.00
		$ 1500.00

Upon their arrival these missionaries were most cordially received by the missionaries of both the A. B. C. F. M. and Baptist missions. The Messrs. Caswell and Hemenway—then the only remaining members of the A. B. C. F. M.—welcomed them into their own homes until the vacant houses on the A. B. C. F. M. mission premises could be made ready for their occupancy. They were visited soon by many of the nobles and the princes and they themselves took early opportunity of paying their respects to the Phra Klang and Prince Chao Fah Mongkut (the Prince-priest) at his residence in Pavaranives Monastery. They were most kindly received by both of these men, especially by the latter whose regard they ever retained.

The tidings spread rapidly that a new foreign doctor had come to Siam and patients of every description and of all classes flocked in for relief until Dr. House was forced to re-open the floating-house dispensary which had so long been maintained by

Dr. Bradley in front of the mission premises. This was really a sore trial to this young doctor, for he had looked forward to having the experience of Dr. Bradley to assist him in his practice, little knowing that before he should reach Siam, Dr. Bradley would be homeward-bound. The tremendous responsibility of caring for the sick was ever an almost unbearable burden on Dr. House and finally led to his giving up medical practice when he could be relieved. During the first eighteen months he prescribed for 3117 patients. It seems that Dr. House's own reluctance in the practice of medicine did not arise from inefficiency—for he was highly esteemed as a physician—but rather from his own humility and keen realization of the great responsibility of life and death which is the physician's peculiar burden. Mr. Mattoon applied himself successfully to the study of the language and soon entered upon the work of tract distribution, visiting for this purpose the various temples of the city. None were more eager to receive these tracts than the monks themselves.

In the ensuing cool season many tours were made with the brethren of the other missions—going to Petchaburi, Ayuthia, Prabat and Patrieu. Everywhere they found a ready reception for the books and tracts they carried with them.

In 1849, the Presbyterian missionaries were made glad by the arrival of their first reenforcements—the Rev. and Mrs. Stephen Bush. In July of that year a frightful epidemic of Asiatic cholera swept away a full thirty or forty thousand of the population of Bangkok. During the height of the epidemic, 2000 deaths occurred in 24 hours in Bangkok alone. Fortunately none of the mission families was attacked, but the time and strength of the missionary doctor was entirely consumed in caring for the stricken in palace and in bamboo hut. Many lives were thus spared and many life-long friendships resulted. Of all those who died of this plague, but one was a Christian. This was an old man who had recently arrived in Bangkok from his home five days distant.

Rev. Samuel House, M.D.

He had learned to trust in the Saviour through reading the Christian scriptures and books though he had never seen a Christian teacher until this visit to Bangkok. He was among the first of the cholera victims and to the last expressed his abiding trust in the Saviour.

The Presbyterian missionaries had arrived at a most opportune time, for the Congregational mission was passing through a serious crisis. Dr. Bradley, who was in the U. S. A., severed his connection with the A. B. C. F. M. and in 1848, the Rev. Jesse Caswell died. In 1849, his widow returned to America and the last week of that year the Rev. and Mrs. Asa Hemenway,—then the only remnant of the Congregational mission,—left for America never to return. This closed the operations of the A. B. C. F. M. in Siam, and the Presbyterian missionaries who were at the time living on the A. B. C. F. M. premises fell heir to a certain extent to the work of the A. B. C. F. M. The Presbyterian Board entered negotiations with the A. B. C. F. M. for the purchase of their buildings and press, but when Dr. Bradley was accepted by the A. M. A. he succeeded in raising enough money to buy over the A. B. C. F. M. property and clearly had the first option on it.

On the 31st August of that year which marked the close of the A. B. C. F. M., the little band of Presbyterian missionaries met and organized the first Presbyterian Church of Bangkok. An act of faith it was, for this first communion was composed solely of missionaries—the Rev. and Mrs. S. Mattoon, Dr. House, and the Rev. and Mrs. S. Bush. Eight days later Sinsaa Ki-eng Qua-Sean the Chinese teacher who had been baptised by Mr. Johnson in 1844, was received by certificate from the A. B. C. F. M. church.

Sinsaa Ki-eng Qua-Sean at once entered the employ of the Presbyterian mission as an assistant and went about talking with his countrymen and distributing tracts among them. Later, in 1852, when a school was started, he became the first teacher of it.

During the larger portion of that year, Mr. Mattoon sustained

the preaching service in the mission chapel. Three days in the
week, with a good degree of regularity, he visited the tract house
in the bazaar for tract distribution. In the afternoons he received
those who called at the station for books; these visitors, except
during the time of cholera, were from fifteen to twenty daily.
From the presses belonging to the American and Baptist Boards,
554,500 pages were purchased, aud widely distributed. In extensive missionary tours, there was found as heretofore, a general
readiness to receive tracts and scriptures. It was found also, that
where the visits of the missionaries had been the most frequent,
there the demand for books was the greatest, showing an increasing
desire for reading where the publications of the press had been
most widely diffused. Six days in the week Dr. House was accustomed to spend two hours daily at the floating-house dispensary,
except when absent on tours in the interior. The majority of
his patients were Siamese,—a marked change from the earliest
experience of the missionaries when they found the Chinese patients
more numerous than the Siamese. The missionaries had also
taken three or four native children into their own homes to give
them a Christian education.

In May 1850 the Rev. Dr. Bradley returned with his children
and Mrs. Sarah Blachly Bradley whom he had married in America.
Together with them were Prof. Josiah Silsby, the Rev. L. B.
Lane, M. D. and their wives. It then became imperative that the
Presbyterian mission should have a home of its own but all
previous attempts to procure one had failed. The knowledge of
the reluctance of the Government to give the foreigner any foot-
hold upon the soil deterred the owners of land from selling to the
missionaries. And when at last one braver than the rest consented
to part with enough land for a suitable mission station in the upper
part of the city, and when permission to purchase this particular
piece of land had been obtained, and when the money had been paid
over and when one of the missionaries had removed in a floating-

Rev. Stephen Bush

house to the spot to commence building, a peremptory order came from a still higher official revoking the permission already given. The money was refunded and the hope of obtaining property seemed vague indeed. The only reason given was that the location was at "the head of the waters," that is above the king's palace. No suitable site could even be rented.

During this year (1850) The United States of America sent the Hon. J. Ballestier, to make a new treaty between the U. S. A. and Siam. His efforts were entirely unsuccessful. Four months later, England made a similar attempt and sent Sir James Brooke as British Envoy on a like mission. He too was entirely unsuccessful. It happened that owing to the rebellions within his own borders, the King of Siam had dispatched from Bangkok all of those upon whom he was accustomed to rely for translation of English documents. He was in no position to negotiate new treaties wisely. Furthermore the Siamese were accustomed to hold the actual document sent by a king in deep reverence, giving to it the honor which would be accorded the person of the king. These envoys did not appreciate this and one cannot but smile at the naive description the Rev. S. J. Smith gave of himself as interpreter for the Hon. J. Ballestier. He said, " It fell the task of Rev. Smith to carry the box containing the documents. Mr. Smith with the box in one hand and his umbrella in the other was ushered into the presence of the Siamese Government Officials. The Siamese criticized the bundling and handling of the documents by Mr. Smith." The result of it all was that neither American nor British Ambassador was even permitted to meet the King of Siam. At this time several teachers and writers in the employ of the missionaries were imprisoned because of their relations to the missionaries. This all had a very depressing effect upon the missionaries and their work. Especially was this true because they were unable to trace the causes of the hostile attitude of the Government and were not able to see the reasons for royal disfavor. Twenty-three years, with no less than eleven actual rebellions to quell and the constant menace of a strong western power which actually had subdued his neighbor Burma had not caused the king to open his doors gladly to the foreigner. The missionaries failed to see the relation they themselves bore to this political situation, for truly they personally had nothing to do with it.

Another fact must be mentioned too.   H. M. King Phra Nang Klao, third king of his dynasty, was a strong and zealous Buddhist. Rumor had it that the man who would win his favor must build a wat. The first king of the dynasty chose warriors as his favorites; the second chose those with learning; but the third chose those who like himself were zealous Buddhists. The star of the foreigner had not yet risen. Therefore the three Presbyterian missionaries were fearfully discouraged. For a time they seriously considered leaving Siam for some other field of labor—the province of Wellesly, Sarawak, Borneo, actually being under consideration. The Board gave its reluctant consent, but strongly urged their remaining if possible and commended its little band of five missionaries in Siam "to the special prayers of God's people".

On 3 April 1851, the death of the king brought the Prince-priest to the throne as King Mongkut. For twenty-six years he had been in the Buddhist priesthood. Apparently he had been eclipsed by the brother who had usurped the throne. In reality those years of semi-seclusion were years of wonderful preparation for the task of laying the foundations of a modern kingdom. During those years of seclusion he had had leisure for study—an opportunity he had eagerly seized. He had studied English, and acquired remarkable proficiency in that foreign tongue. He had been much interested in arts and sciences and in his quest for knowledge he had come into contact with the American missionaries who were most sympathetic and who tried to do all within their power for the royal priest, little realizing how royally he would later make return for every service rendered. He learned to know not only the foreigner but his own people as well. As a mendicant priest he went among his own people and

H.M. KING MONGKUT.

learned their actual condition and needs. No king ever had a better training for the responsibilities placed upon him and the task before him.

This accession of King Mongkut to the throne was the turning point in the affairs of the Presbyterian mission, as well as of the nation he was to rule. For years he had been most friendly to the missionaries, and this elevated position offered him the opportunity he had long wanted to show his gratitude to these men and women who had opened his eyes to the new world of learning and thought. On 21 July 1851, the Presbyterian missionaries were allowed to lease land near Wat Cheng and to build homes for themselves there. Two brick houses were then erected.

On 14 August 1851, H. M. King Mongkut made a request of the three American missions that the three missionary women Mrs. D. B. Bradley, Mrs. S. Mattoon, and Mrs. J. T. Jones teach the women in his palace the English language. It was agreed that these ladies should take turn about each one teaching two days a week. This plan was carried out for about three years, during which time no small amount of knowledge was communicated to His Majesty's large and interesting family. This was the first zenana work attempted anywhere in the world.

It appears that to the three or four native children which they had received into their homes in 1850 had been added others so that in 1853 twenty or more formed the nucleus of the boarding school. In 1848, Mrs. Mattoon had begun to teach some little girls and boys and later she opened a school in a Peguan village near the mission compound. This was later transferred to the mission compound. These children were each paid one fuang a day for attending school. At one time this school had an enrollment of 27 pupils.

Two of the children taken into the missionaries' homes became leaders in the Christian community. These were Kru Naa, given by his dying father to Dr. House in 1853, and Esther given by her father to Dr. and Mrs. Mattoon in the same year. Esther lived with them and when finally Mrs. Mattoon was obliged to return to America because of ill-health, Esther accompanied her and the children. She returned three years later with them and with Dr. Mattoon who had joined his family as soon as reenforcements had made it possible for him to be spared from Bangkok. Esther then continued to live with Mrs. Mattoon teaching a little class of eight or ten children to read Siamese. She united with the church in 1860. Nai Naa married Esther in 1863 or 1864, before he had become a Christian. He was baptized on the 3rd February and on 2 November 1867 was ordained elder—the first native Presbyterian elder to receive ordination. Together this man and his wife translated Pilgrim's Progress into Siamese. Kru Naa became a Christian teacher,—dying a number of years ago. Nang Esther has the distinction of being the first trained midwife and practical nurse among the Siamese people. For years she was called to the palaces and homes of those who knew her—both Siamese and foreigners—where she was much in demand as a nurse and midwife. As a skilled laundress, expert seamstress, and housekeeper she had no equal among her own people. A very wonderful opportunity was hers to bear witness for her Lord—a testimony which always rang clear and true. Nang Esther is still living—at the age of eighty-four, having outlived her four children but honored and cared for by over a hundred grand-children and great-grand-children,—the first woman convert and the oldest living Protestant Christian in Siam.

At the request of the Foreign community, on 29 July 1853 H. M. King Mongkut made a royal grant of land for the Protestant cemetery. Many times had the little community been called upon to lay away its dead in the burial plot north of the Portuguese Consulate where for a time burial was " by permission ". In 1893 a Mortuary chapel was erected in this Protestant cemetery. Especially fatal had the climate and improper food proven to the children born to the missionaries, but even of the adult missionaries, death had claimed no less than ten in the twenty-five years since the work had started.

Nang Esther Naa Pradipasena

But it is a noticeable fact that not once does one find reference to this cause for grief as the thing that depressed the souls of the intrepid missionaries. Their hearts were saddened and their loneliness increased—but the thing that was reiterated in nearly every report and letter was the desire for reenforcements that Siam might be won for Christ, and the pleading for the prayers of God's people that the seed they were planting might grow. Month after month they watched for news of reenforcements. Applicants were considered and then appointments definitely made, only to have the appointees sail for some other field of labor. In 1855 it seemed as though at last the hoped-for recruits were about to arrive. The Rev. and Mrs. M. M. Carleton arrived in Singapore and had passage engaged for Bangkok when information was received that the King of Siam would permit no Europeans or Americans to enter Siam. After remaining eleven weeks in Singapore—the missionaries in Bangkok not even hearing of their arrival in Singapore—they decided that the best thing would be to attempt to join the Presbyterian mission in India, and so sailed for Calcutta. One can picture their intense disappointment when word of this finally reached the little band in Bangkok—now only three again, for Mrs. Bush had died in 1851 and her husband with failing health had left for America, hoping to return but never doing so.

This difficulty about entrance into Siam was caused by some ill-advised criticism of the King of Siam which appeared in a Singapore paper. This was erroneously attributed to some of the Baptist missionaries in Siam and the result was that for a time all missionaries fell under royal displeasure and the missionary ladies who had been teaching in the palace were temporarily debarred. The difficulty was eventually cleared up, the ladies continued their teaching and the free exit and entrance of foreigners was again allowed—but it cost the Presbyterian mission its two recruits.

About this time it was decided best for Dr. House to take a furlough and he left for the U. S. A., the Mattoons remaining in sole charge of the mission. The failure of Mr. and Mrs. Carleton to secure entrance into Siam would have prevented securing recruits for a time. Dr. House's arrival in New York and his assurance that the trouble had blown over was timely, and the next few years were to be marked by strong reenforcements for the Siam mission. Dr. House began the work of securing reenforcements in the old, old way for in 1856, he returned to Siam from furlough bringing with him a bride,—Mrs. Harriette M. House, of blessed memory. For twenty years these faithful missionaries were to labor together for Siam before ill-health finally forced them to leave. With them came the Rev. and Mrs. Andrew B. Morse, but their stay was brief for they left in 1858. Though their stay was so short, they gave the little band new courage and they began to look forward to bigger things. They all thought that the land they had been granted behind Wat Cheng gave little chance for expansion so sold their buildings there and secured a new grant on the same side of the river some five miles down stream—quite in the out-skirts of the city. This new grant of land was subsequently enlarged by purchase and two brick buildings were erected; one building still stands. Here permanent work was begun and developed rapidly. An entry in the journal of Mr. Morse throws an interesting side-light on the beginnings of work on this site, now known as Samray. "Oct. 24,—With Mr. Mattoon and Mr. Vail, Mr. King's agent, went down to stake off the new ground; the Siamese official surveyor also present. Now don't imagine a theodolite, chain, stakes and nice mathematical calculations. The lands in this country are very few of them fenced. The boundary marks of our territory are on one side the canal, and on two sides narrow ditches which a man could leap; front 850 feet on the river. The Siamese surveyor did survey, but only the ditches, underbrush, etc, through which our course led, and then in disgust assigned his part of the work to one of his men and laid himself down to sleep in his boat. The assistant took all of the instruments, i. e., the stakes and went with us to stick them down in the corners

HOME OF THE REV. S. BUSH, WAT CHENG

of the lot and the work was all done, and the official could take oath before the government that he had seen all the land surveyed. Covered with mud and thoroughly heated by our long tramp through ditch, and brake, and briar, but nevertheless much benefitted bodily, we returned home."

But other strides were being made during this particular period. In 1855 Great Britain sent Sir John Bowring to Bangkok to draw up a treaty of friendship and commerce. This time the attempt was opportune, and the treaty-making was successful. This was followed the next year by the arrival of the Hon. Townsend Harris, Envoy from the U. S. A. on a similar errand which was likewise successful. As a result of these treaties a British Consulate was established in June 1856 and an American Consulate a month earlier, with Mr. Mattoon as Consul—a position which he held until 1859 when he turned it over to Mr. Chandler of the Baptist mission. Previously the Portuguese Consulate (established in 1820) had been the only foreign consulate in Siam. This making of new treaties marked the real beginning of diplomatic relations with western countries. In 1857, Siam sent her first Envoy to England and in 1861 she sent one to France.

In 1858, the Rev. Daniel McGilvary and his friend the Rev. Jonathan Wilson, with his bride, arrived; in 1860 the Rev. and Mrs. S. G. McFarland and the Rev. and Mrs. N. A. McDonald joined the Siam mission. The arrival of these missionaries marked the beginning of the transition from the pioneer period into quite a new era in the history of the Presbyterian work, not only because it meant a swelling of the missionary force but also because they were all permanent additions, each giving many years to the work, except Mrs. Wilson alone who died in 1860. They were all able, consecrated men and women of vision and abounding strength and energy which they used freely in the cause so dear to their hearts. In 1860 this group was strengthened by the addition of Miss Sophia Bradley who became Mrs. Daniel McGilvary, thus cementing the already strong ties binding the little Presbyterian group to the veteran missionaries,—Dr. and Mrs. Bradley.

The strengthening of the Presbyterian mission during this period is of great significance because it was a time of greatly diminished strength of the sister missions. In 1860 the only other missionaries in Bangkok, aside from the Presbyterian, were Dr. and Mrs. Bradley of the A. M. A.,—and the Rev. and Mrs. S. J. Smith, the Rev. and Mrs. R. Telford and Mr. and Mrs. J. H. Chandler of the Baptist mission.

In September 1878 the first Presbytery of Siam was organized with four members, viz, the Rev. S. Mattoon, Dr. House, the Rev. D. McGilvary and the Rev. J. Wilson.

This period was also memorable in the Bangkok Presbyterian mission for on 5 August 1859, the first Siamese Christian convert was baptised,—nineteen years after the arrival of the first Presbyterian missionaries. This man was Nai Chune who became the teacher in the Samray school after the death of Sinsaa Ki-eng Qua-Sean on 23 Nov. 1859. For fifteen years Sinsaa Ki-eng Qua-Sean had been a strong leader and his death was sincerely mourned by his American missionary friends who had all learned to trust and love him. This change in teacher also resulted in a change in the language used in the school — from Chinese to Siamese. This was exceedingly significant in the later development of the work.

In 1860 the Presbyterian mission had actually existed twenty years—years of great beginnings, in face of great difficulties and great discouragements. But the foundations had been laid strong and well. The next few decades were to behold notable strides forward.

"Missionary House — Sunray"

One of the two first Missionary Houses erected at Samray in 1848-9

EXPANSION

CHAPTER V

BANGKOK—" The Period of Expansion "

To set any one date as the end of one period of history and the beginning of another is largely arbitrary; transition from one period into another is of necessity gradual. But the date 1860 has been chosen as the close of the " Pioneer Period " and the beginning of the " Period of Expansion" with good reason. Up to that time the history of the Presbyterian mission centers in three persons,—the Rev. S. Mattoon and his wife and Dr. S. R. House. These three had borne the burden and heat of the day ; they had shaped the policy of the Presbyterian mission ; they had much of the time faced all of the problems and discouragements alone. Three other families had been connected with the mission at various times, but in no case did any of them remain long enough to accomplish anything permanent. To Mr. and Mrs. Mattoon and Dr. House belongs the praise for sticking to their post through everything and planting the seed in faith. True pioneers they were—brave and patient and persevering.

With the advent into the Presbyterian mission of Mrs. H. M. House, the Rev. and Mrs. J. Wilson, the Rev. and Mrs. D. McGilvary, the Rev. and Mrs. S. G. McFarland and the Rev. and Mrs. N. A. McDonald the number of the missionaries was greatly increased. The early putting down of stakes and the holding together of work already begun was all that could be thought of before this time ; with the increase in the force, the first impulse was to reach out to larger things.

Petchaburi was a place very much in everyone's thought at this period. During 1860, H. M. King Mongkut made no less than four visits to Petchaburi where he was building a palace and a temple. But the interest of the missionaries in Petchaburi did not begin with the royal interest. For years tours into the interior and to Petchaburi in particular, had led the missionaries to see the desirability of placing a mission station there. In 1858-9 the two friends, Wilson and McGilvary definitely planned to start work there. The rival interest which drew Mr. McGilvary to the Bradley home and the untimely death of Mrs. Wilson ended the possibility of taking this step for a time. But when Miss Bradley had become Mrs. McGilvary and when the Rev. and Mrs. S. G. McFarland had arrived, the way seemed open for the new step of faith. In June 1861 these four young people formally opened the first out-of-Bangkok station at Petchaburi. The work at Petchaburi was robbed of many of the difficulties which had attended work in Bangkok and from the very first the new mission station seemed to flourish. The Governor was a man who had already represented H. S. M.'s Government as Minister at the Court of St. James. He later became Minister of Foreign Affairs for Siam and was given the title Chao Phya Bhanuwongse Maha Kosa Tibodi. This Governor was a staunch friend of the missionaries, helping them to secure land for their mission and helping them in countless other ways. Once when the life of one of the missionary women was in danger and immediate medical assistance was imperative, this Governor-friend provided his own house-boat with double crews of oarsmen that the invalid might be rushed to Bangkok because no medical aid was nearer. This timely kindness doubtless saved her life. A church was organized in 1863 and a Siamese licentiate was ordained by Presbytery in 1867. Thus was the first move toward "Expansion" made.

A second move toward "Expansion" was the establishing of the Presbyterian mission press in 1861. The Congregational and Baptist missions had early established fully equipped presses for printing the scriptures which the missionaries had translated into Siamese, and other religious literature which they prepared for teaching their message of salvation.

Rev. Jonathan Wilson, D.D.

Mrs. Maria Wilson

With the opportunity before them of purchasing printed literature from the other mission presses, and with their own limited force of missionaries and with the still more limited funds at their disposal, the Presbyterian mission delayed establishing a press of its own. But the early missionaries were not indifferent to the need for such a press and persistently wrote to their Board asking for such equipment. As early as 1854 there appears in "The Foreign Missionary" —a publication of the Presbyterian Board of Foreign Missions, — a letter from a little boy invalid in which he says he is sending a small sum of money towards the buying of the press asked for by Mr. Mattoon. But though without a press of their own, the early Presbyterian missionaries persisted in translating and writing, printing what they could on the existing presses, but ever preparing for the bigger work that would be possible when they too should have a press of their own. This press was started by the Rev. N. A. McDonald in 1861, and before the end of that year they had struck off the first form. The report for Bangkok for the year ending 1 Oct. 1862 indicates that already 588,000 12mo pages had been printed. The work of the press consistently and abundantly justified the early expenditure of money. The press was at first housed in a dark basement under a missionary dwelling at Samray. In 1892 it was removed to larger and better rented quarters across the river, and in 1897 was again moved to what became known as the Press Compound, where a building suitable for both press and godown were erected and where the press continued to stay until it was eventually sold in 1919. The press had long been self-supporting, paying its expenses by job work and annually printing thousands of pages of religious literature and scriptures at little or no cost to the mission. Not only had it paid its way as it went along, adding its improved equipment as needed, but when the press was sold it netted Tcs. 60,000.00 for the mission, which became an endowment fund for the printing of mission literature. This fund was diminished by Tcs. 30,000.00 given to the Wattana Wittaya Academy when it was struggling to find funds for erecting its new buildings, and Tcs. 10,000.00 given toward the support of the Chinese Department of the Bangkok Christian College. The reason for the final sale of the press was the fact that it required the full time of one missionary. Since many printing presses had been established in Bangkok and elsewhere which could do the work efficiently, it seemed unwise to set apart one of the missionary force for this secular work. But at the time the press was founded, the hands of the mission were tied for want of proper printing facilities. The Presbyterian press served the mission long and well, its work being still the criterion for all fine printing in Siam. For its achievement all credit is due the Rev J. B. Dunlap, D.D., whose energy, skill and devotion made the press what it was and made it accomplish what it did. From 1891 Dr. Dunlap was Press Manager, until he was relieved by Mr. E. M. Spillman in 1909; then he entered direct evangelistic work.

Not only were the Presbyterian missionaries reaching out to bigger things but the Protestant community of Bangkok also began to feel new life. From the time of the establishment of the A. B. C. F.M. it had been the habit of the missionaries of all denominations to meet together weekly for Divine Worship. At first the meetings were in the homes of the missionaries turn about attended only by missionaries: subsequently other foreigners came to Bangkok and joined in this worship. Later the Presbyterian chapel at Samray was the place of meeting. But the Foreign community of Bangkok had grown greatly since the arrival of the first missionaries and on 3 April 1861 the Protestant community petitioned H. M. King Mongkut for land on which to erect a chapel for its own use. His Majesty was graciously pleased to grant this request on 9 May 1861, giving a piece of land fronting on the river, adjoining on the north what later became the premises of the Borneo Co. Ltd. A subscription list was circulated and the Protestant Chapel erected, Mr. Mattoon and Mr. Wilson giving very largely of their time to the purchasing of ma-

Rev. N. A. McDonald, D. D.

Rev. J. B. Dunlap, D.D.

terials and overseeing the work of construction. The funds not being entirely sufficient, the British Government generously gave the additional needed amount on condition that the church edifice and lot be under the control of H. B. M's Consulate. The first service held in the new chapel was conducted by the Rev. S. Mattoon on 2 May 1864. The text chosen was taken from the 122nd Psalm— " I was glad when they said unto me, Let us go into the house of the Lord ". There was a very general attendance of the Protestant community at this service. It was subsequently arranged that the pulpit should be supplied by the Protestant missionaries resident in Bangkok, in alphabetical rotation as had been the custom of the same religious service for a period of nearly thirty years.

In 1868 the English service began to be used in this Union Protestant Chapel. The following year, at the annual meeting of the Protestant community held at the British Consulate, it was decided to suspend the Anglican service for one year. However a later decision of the Protestant community established the Anglican form of service permanently. The American missionaries continued to conduct the service until it was finally decided that the Protestant community could support a Chaplain of its own. A subscription list was circulated and as a result of this effort, the Canon William Greenstock came to Bangkok in 1894 and continued to serve the Protestant community as Chaplain until 1903 when he resigned to take up work for the Siamese and Eurasian people under the S. P. G. mission. His place as Chaplain was filled by the Rev. Dr. Hillyard who was in turn followed by the Rev. C. R. Simmons of the S. P. G. mission.

A memorial window was placed in the Protestant Chapel 5 March 1877, in memory of Mr. Blythe, late Manager of the Borneo Co. Ltd. When it was finally decided that the Foreign community was ready for a larger and better building, the site which has been given by H. M. King Mongkut was sold with permission of H. M. King Chulalongkorn, and with the fund thus raised, together with other funds secured by subscription, a new building was erected on a new site given by His Majesty. The memorial stained glass window was removed from the old Chapel to the new building—now known as Christ Church, which was dedicated for use in 1904.

Christ Church is entirely supported by voluntary contributions. It is controlled by a Committee of which the British Minister is Chairman ex-officio, by condition of the grant made by the British Government toward the erection of the first building. This Church is often called the English Church, but that is really a misnomer for it is what it has been from the first,—a Union Protestant Church, designed to serve the needs of the entire Christian Protestant English-speaking community.

Before the movement toward providing a permanent place of worship for the Protestant community was started, the Presbyterian missionaries began building a permanent chapel for their mission. Funds were not sufficient and the completing of this chapel was delayed because they were not willing in any way to hinder the progress of the Protestant Chapel by appealing to the Foreign community for contributions. A gift of $100 from a local foreign merchant started the work again and it was opened on the last Sunday in May 1862, by services in both English and Siamese.

Two years later the brick church at Samray was built. In 1910 this building was so greatly in need of repair and enlargement that the old building was pulled down and the Siamese Christians themselves circulated a subscription list and erected a new building on the old site following practically the old lines.

In 1861, Esther, the Siamese girl who had lived with the Mattoons since 1853, and who had gone with Mrs. Mattoon to America when failing health had driven her home ahead of her husband, united with the church. Not until 1867 were there further accessions to the Presbyterian church. Then three others were baptised. This was a happy day for the older missionaries especially, for they had sowed the seed which had seemed so long in bringing forth fruit :

Christ Church, Bangkok

at last the Siamese were beginning to turn to Christ. One of these three was Nai Tien Hee,—the late Phya Saurasin. Nai Tien Hee went to the U.S.A. with Dr. House. He was there surrounded by Christian influences, being educated by a Christian physician, Dr. Elliott. Desirous of studying medicine, Nai Tien Hee was placed in the Medical College of Columbia University where he was graduated in 1871 and returned to Siam to practice medicine. In 1880 he was put in charge of the first Siamese government hospital to be run along foreign lines. Dr. Tien Hee, being the only Siamese physician qualified for such a post was put in charge of this hospital of sixty beds, providing for Siamese soldiers only. Rise in government favor and certain temptations drew Dr. Tien Hee—later called Phra Montri and finally Phya Saurasin—from the close fellowship he had previously enjoyed with the Christian church. But he ever counted himself a Christian and shortly before his death, in 1925, he asked the Rev. W. G. McClure, D. D., to come to his home where he had been a great sufferer for years with both gout and asthma, to administer to him the sacrament of the Lord's Supper. The Supsampantawongse Church building where the Fourth Church of Bangkok worships, was largely built with funds given by this man as a memorial to his firstborn son, whose death was a sore blow to this nobleman.

Another of these converts was Nai Keo, a Lao from Vieng Chan who had been a Buddhist priest of considerable learning at Wat Krua-wan. Kru Keo became a preacher of the Gospel and distributed Bibles with Dr. Carrington and was faithful until his death. One of his daughters— N. S. Kaa —became a teacher in the Harriet M. House School.

The third was Meh Delia, who ended her life tied to a post in a Governor's house, — a victim of gambling. In this same year in which these three were baptised Kru Klai of Petchaburi was licenced by the Siam Presbytery as the first Siamese preacher.

The founding of the Petchaburi station had proved a wise venture. That success increased the longing to reach out to other parts of

Siam.   While Mr. McGilvary was living near Wat Cheng shortly after his marriage, the Prince of Chiengmai, — H. H. Prince Kawilorot — made a visit to Bangkok and moored his boats at Wat Cheng.   Mr. McGilvary had ample opportunity to make the acquaintance of this irascible prince who was then on his good behavior.   The interest awakened by the prince and his people at that time, was deepened as Mr. McGilvary met and talked with some captives of war which had been brought from the north-country, though not from Chiengmai itself.   These Laos were living near Petchaburi and seemed quite responsive to the teaching of Mr. McGilvary who visited them as often as possible.   Work in Petchaburi was progressing favorably and encouragingly and it seemed as if others might take up the work there and the call of the Laos in northern Siam began sounding very loudly in Mr. McGilvary's ears.   He talked with his old friend Jonathan Wilson and together they took a trip to Chiengmai in November 1863 to investigate the possibilities of opening work there.   So encouraging did they feel the opening was that they returned in January 1864 ready to urge upon the Bangkok mission the setting apart of missionaries for this particular task.   Both were eager for this and had the way been open they would have urged that they themselves be released for the task.   But they returned to Bangkok to find that Mrs. Mattoon was forced to leave at once for the U. S. A. and the Mission had already decided that it was best for Mr. Wilson to take his furlough at the same time.   Thus the door to opening work in the North was closed for the time being.   But the return of Mr. Wilson in 1866, with his bride, again made these friends McGilvary and Wilson see visions—visions of a Lao people won for their Master. The Board had previously given its permission to the opening of the new station.   Request for royal sanction was made of H. M. King Mongkut who replied that he himself was very willing but that he would not force such a mission upon his vassal the Prince of Chiengmai: however, if that Prince was willing for the missionaries to

H.M. PHRA PIN KLAO,
SECOND KING DURING THE REIGN OF
H.M. KING MONGKUT

establish a station there, H. S. M's Government would have no objection. Very opportunely, the Prince of Chiengmai came to Bangkok at this time for a visit and it was possible to wait upon him in person. With great longing in their hearts and much prayer, a little band of missionaries and the U. S. Consul waited upon the Prince laying before him their proposition. He seemed quite favorable to the idea and gave ready sanction. Thus apparently was the way opened for starting the long-planned mission to the Laos. But before the two families could make the necessary preparations, it became impossible for Mr. and Mrs. Wilson to go earlier than the following year. This was a sore blow to the eager Mr. McGilvary. He and his intrepid wife decided that they would not wait but would go alone and allow the Wilsons to follow them the following year. And so it was settled and Mr. and Mrs. McGilvary with their two little ones started out on a long, long journey by boat, alone. Marvellous courage and fortitude they showed in that step of faith—and plenty of need for all their courage and fortitude they had before the new mission was firmly established. But with true missionary faith and zeal they ventured forth, nothing doubting. Thus a second out-of-Bangkok centre for Christian teaching was established ; easy to tell ; hard to live—but of momentous importance to the cause of Christ.

The change of personnel of the missions was not all on the side of assets. The continued ill-health of Mrs. Mattoon made the resignation of these noble missionaries imperative. They had borne the burden of the early years; they had spent themselves freely in the cause for which they had dedicated their lives. Others were entered into their labors and though their leaving meant a serious loss to the mission, there were others who at last could carry on. At about the same time the death of Dr. Bradley (1873) and the departure of his son for the U.S.A. the following year ended the active work of the A.M.A.

Though the Baptist mission did have certain reenforcements for a time which strengthened their hands, it too had reverses. Dr. Dean

who had already done notable work among the Chinese in Bangkok
and in China, returned to Siam in 1864.   Beginning with his return
the Baptist work among the Chinese especially began to flourish as
never before.   But in 1869 it was definitely decided to withdraw
from work among the Siamese.   At the same time the Rev. S. J.
Smith withdrew from the Baptist mission and started a printing
press of his own.   The death of Mrs. Dean in 1882 and the breaking
health of Dr. Dean ended that brief period of Baptist activity and
the closing of the mission in 1893 was approaching.

Another notable event of this period was the building of a
school building in 1862 for the boys' school at Samray.   This school
had really had its birth in 1852 when the Mission took action authorizing Sinsaa Ki-eng Qua-Sean, the mission's Chinese assistant, to
commence a school for the sons of Chinese.   On 30 Sept. 1852
this school was started.   The records tell with what loving care the
missionaries fostered this infant school.   Children taken into their
own homes fed the school.   A little school in the Peguan village
begun by Mrs. Mattoon seventeen days before this school was opened,
was four months later transferred to the school under Sinsaa Ki-eng
Qua-Sean and incorporated with it.   In August 1856 is the first mention of Siamese in connection with the school.   In May 1859 a girl
was added to the ranks—the first girl pupil.

The first beginnings were back of Wat Cheng on the mission
premises there.   In 1862, the time had come for the erection of a
real school building at Samray and the report of 1862 tells with
what joy this was accomplished.   This building sufficed until after
the Rev. J. A. Eakin joined the mission in 1888, bringing with him
his sister Miss Elizabeth Eakin, and the Rev. and Mrs. J. B. Dunlap.
These three had been associated with Mr. Eakin in an independent
school which he had started at Kadee Chen.   Upon their request the
four were received into the Presbyterian mission in 1888 and Mr.
Eakin brought with him his school called the Bangkok Christian
High School.   Mr. Eakin was put in charge of the boys' school at

Original Mission Chapel at Samray, Bangkok

Christian High School for Boys, Samray

Samray and it was under his supervision that the Samray Boys' Christian High School building was erected in 1892, with funds he had collected to build his own private school. In 1900, the time seemed ripe for the opening of another boys' school across the river and a plot of ground was acquired there and a new Bangkok Christian High School was commenced, Dr. Eakin being placed in charge of it. The name was changed in 1913 to Bangkok Christian College, but this present school counts its years from the founding of the private school by Dr. Eakin at Kadee Chen, of which he took with him as much as possible to Samray, strengthening that school and giving to it the name Bangkok Christian High School.

Though with such tiny beginnings, that boys' school did notable things. It taught many a boy who later became a leader in government affairs. The English taught there gave entree into many a high place. Some of the boys went abroad for study.

But not all of these boys entered government service. All four of the ordained pastors which Bangkok Presbyterian churches have had, received their training there. Many other Christian men owe their debt to the training of the Samray School or the later Bangkok Christian College. The Christian leaders of the present, in South Siam, are practically all the products of these schools.

In 1876, the Rev. S. G. McFarland, D.D., gathered together the hymns already translated into Siamese, translated others and with his own hands on a wooden and stone press printed the first Siamese Hymnal containing 213 hymns and 68 tunes. This more properly belongs in the narrative of Petchaburi where the work was done but being a task of interest to the whole Christian church it also deserves mention at this place.

The starting of a dispensary on 18 Jan. 1888 where medicines were sold, not given away, was a innovation by Dr. T. H. Hays. Foreign medicine no longer must be given away; the people had learned the value of it and were ready to pay for it. This is but the beginning of the countless dispensaries which to-day are seen on every corner of Bangkok.

At this place it will be well to pause a little to trace some of the other developments of this particular period—the latter days of H. M. King Mongkut who died in 1868. It has already been narrated how the King gave to the Presbyterian community land for their chapel. On 19 August 1861 the Foreign community again addressed a petition to the King requesting that he open a proper road behind the Consulates and merchantile establishments on the east side of the river. His Majesty was pleased with the idea and readily acceded to the request. The road, which has ever since been called New Road, was opened to traffic on 16 March 1864. It was deemed by His Majesty a step of such importance to his capital city that the event was marked by a big celebration.

About this time there was a very severe earthquake—an almost unprecedented thing in Bangkok—which struck terror to the hearts of many, especially of the most conservative. The innovations of their new king had seemed to many almost sacrilegious. His marked favor for the foreigner seemed almost traitorous to some. So when the earthquake occurred they at once attributed it to the fact that the great fish which made its home in the Menam Chaophya flowing through the heart of Bangkok, had been so disturbed by the building of this road that he had turned over in his river-bed, shaking the earth to its foundations. But nothing daunted by such criticisms, H. M. King Mongkut went calmly on with his innovations.

H. M. King Mongkut was very eager that the English language should be studied and widely disseminated among those of higher rank, but in this he was retarded by many things. However, in 1862 he secured the services of an English woman, Mrs. Leonowens as governess for his son and as English instructress in His Palace. He also found her services as private secretary very useful for the brief time she remained in Siam. Though King Mongkut had two sons before he entered the priesthood, when he ascended the throne they were too old to study. With the exception of the eldest son,

Somdet Chao Phya Prom Maha Srisuriyavongs

who became King Chulalongkorn, the children born to the King after he became king were too young to make great progress in the study of English. So that great desire which lay close to the heart of King Mongkut was slow in being satisfied. After his death however the full realization came and his sons became the best educated among their people, proficient in the use of European languages.

In 1862, the Bangkok Police force was started under the superintendence of Captain S. J. B. Ames. During the same year the cowrie shells which had been legal tender in Siam were replaced by flat coins. But the Royal Mint was not realized until 1 June 1876. Nai Mode Amatyakul who then became Director of the Mint, started his education in chemistry and machinery under the influence of H. M. King Mongkut.

Five men studied English and "foreign knowledge" together under the missionaries. These were H. M. King Mongkut (then the Prince-priest), his young full-brother Phra Pin Klao who became Second king under H. M. King Mongkut, the man who became Regent for King Chulalongkorn — the Luang Nai Sit of the early days of the missionaries, who had taken Mr. Johnson and Dr. Bradley on the trip to Chantaboon in 1835. The other two were Prince Krom Luang Vongsa, grandfather of Dr. Yai Snidhavongs who took up the medical profession and began his study under the missionaries and Nai Mode Amatyakul, later Director of the Mint. These five studied with Mr. Caswell and with the other American missionaries and became the first pro-Europeans of the period.

To the close of his reign, H. M. King Mongkut was eagerly reaching out to develop his country: canals were built, printing presses were established, buildings of European architecture were erected, a Custom house was built, foreign trade was encouraged, free intercourse with other countries was encouraged. The eighteen years of his reign were marked by tremendous advances. Though not a part of the missionary story *per se* they had important bearing on missionary work and on the lives of the missionaries themselves.

The missionary story cannot be told without them any more than the history of Siam can be written without mention of the missionaries.

Two other events mark the closing years of King Mongkut's life — events one wishes need not be mentioned but events which both of them affected the missionaries and their work. In 1867 the American Consul Hood, began to issue protection papers to all orientals who would pay for them. This resulted in a period of Christian popularity among the Chinese. These papers were much desired and though the issuing of them did not depend at all upon the religious profession of the applicant, and the missionaries were not involved in this issuing of these papers, yet in the mind of the ignorant Chinaman there was a relation and it did have its influence on the church roll, for a time. The American missionaries found it very hard to endure the sight of these little Chinese boats plying the waters, flying the American flag. They felt each one was a stain on their nation's honor: for *pay*, the highest representative of their country was taking advantage of the friendship of Siam for America and was giving them the privileges Siam had denied them herself. But the perfidy of the Consul was eventually disclosed and he made a hasty exit from Siam; then the period of bought protection ended.

The other tragic event of this period was the beginning of French encroachments. In September 1863 the startling news reached Bangkok that the King of Cambodia, long a vassal of the King of Siam, had signed a treaty with France granting her full and exclusive rights of commerce along the Cambodian river. This was done even though there had been no break between France and Siam, nor had the King of Siam received any intimation of the plans which eventually led to the ceding of a huge tract of Siamese territory in the eastern part of Siam to France in 1893. The bearing of this on the missionary enterprise is apparent when one studies the situation of the station of Nan and the work that naturally falls under that

พระยา กระสาปน์ กิจโกศล
Phya Krasapana-Kit-Kosol (Mode Amatyakul)

station.

When H. M. King Mongkut died on 1 October 1868, it marked the end of a notable career. He had been the first to step from the past into the modern world of thought and action. It is notable too that the very cause of his death was his love of knowledge. A solar eclipse was to be visible from Sam Roi Yot in southern Siam. An expedition was undertaken that the King might see that eclipse. He there contracted a chill and fever which proved fatal. A remarkable man he was, passing on a remarkable heritage to a remarkable son.

Prince Chulalongkorn was but sixteen years old when his august father died. A Regent was appointed to carry the responsibilities of the government until the young prince should be able to assume the burden. This Regent was none other than Luang Nai Sit, the friend of Dr. Bradley. A better man for the post could not have been found. In 1873 the young King entered the Buddhist priesthood to fulfil his religious obligations before he should become of age and fully enter his kingly office. After this was finished, he was again crowned and the Regent retired. A long reign followed in which H. M. King Chulalongkorn followed the lead of his father and laid the foundations for the present government and the pursuit of learning and the best that other countries had to offer his people. But before taking up the further government developments it will be better to trace some of the mission developments of the early period of King Chulalongkorn's reign.

This is not the place to detail the events of the new station in Chiengmai but two incidents must here be chronicled as they show how closely interwoven were the lives of the missionaries of that day though separated by a six weeks to two months river journey. Dr. House was sent to the two families in the North in 1868 as there was no physician there and a doctor would soon be needed. While still several days out of Chiengmai, Dr. House was gored by his elephant and after giving himself first aid treatment he wrote a hasty note and sent it on to the waiting missionaries. His wound had been alarmingly serious and he himself feared it might prove fatal but his life was spared and in due season he did arrive in Chiengmai—but too late to render the service for which he was hastening thither : two new babies were already there to greet him. The pioneer period with its need for intrepid hearts and sturdy faith, was not wholly past even yet.

Later in that same year (12 Sept 1868) two of the four men who had openly confessed their Saviour in Chiengmai were put to death by the Prince of Chiengmai. Then followed a time of intense anxiety for the missionaries who were in the midst of unknown dangers and also for their friends in Bangkok who did not know exactly what had happened or what to expect next. Mr. McDonald and Mr. George both hastily started North to visit their brethren and to give them whatever help they could, leaving Bangkok 5 Nov. 1868. For a time it seemed that the new station must be given up but a respite before the withdrawal was made possible because of a trip to Bangkok by the Prince of Chiengmai. A fatal trip it was for him for when he next approached Chiengmai, it was with the honor given a deceased monarch. His son succeeded him, and no longer was there any need for the missionaries to fear expulsion.

This martyrdom was during the early years of King Chulalong-korn under the regency. In 1870 the Regent issued a decree of religious toleration which secured to everyone in the land of Siam, the right to worship without fear the god of his own choice. The Regent, be it remembered, was the Luang Nai Sit of Dr. Bradley's days. Little did the good Dr. Bradley realize the far-reaching influence of his friendship in those early days in Siam. This decree of religious toleration was confirmed by King Chulalongkorn in 1878 and perhaps no other decree of any King was ever more faithfully obeyed. Siam is today a land of religious toleration.

The young King Chulalongkorn entered upon the task begun by his revered father — the development of a modern Siam. This is not the place to trace in detail the steps of his progress nor even to

H. M. King Chulalongkorn
(Wearing the Kathin Crown)

mention all of the wise reforms he instituted. One of his advance steps must be mentioned however because of its bearing on the mission story. For seventeen years the Rev. S. G. McFarland, D. D. had been developing the mission work in Petchaburi. When H. M. King Chulalongkorn was ready to begin government schools, he asked Dr. McFarland to take charge of the new enterprise. A boys' school for the sons of princes and nobles was to be started at Suan Anan, on Klong Maun on the west side of the river in Bangkok. After much consideration and council with his fellow-missionaries, it was mutually agreed that this was an opportunity for service which should not be ignored. So in 1878, Dr. and Mrs. S. G. McFarland resigned from the mission force, turned over to other hands the Petchaburi station they had helped establish, and which ever remained dear to their hearts, and started on educational work for H. S. M's Government. For ten years, Dr. McFarland continued his work, laying the first stones of the foundation of the present educational system.

The stations at Petchaburi and at Chiengmai had proved far more encouraging in many ways than the parent station at Bangkok. They had their discouragements too, but they also found the people far more ready to listen and to accept the Christ who could save from sin. But little by little the way seemed to open up and the starting of other new stations was felt to be a necessity. In 1885, Lampang was established; in 1893, Prae; in 1894, Nan; in 1897, Chiengrai; in 1899, Pitsanuloke; in 1900, Sritamarat; and in 1910, Trang. Thus the ten stations of Siam under the Presbyterian church were all started before the end of 1910. In 1917 a trek to the still further north was made when the station of Chiengrung was opened among the Lao-speaking peoples of south-western China. The story of each of these is told in turn and need only be referred to here in passing. But those ventures out into the far-regions were all a part of the " Expansion " anticipated by the pioneers in their many tours, and actually started by the Mission in 1861 when the first out-of-Bangkok station was opened at Petchaburi.   But the "Period of Expansion" will not be ended until the whole of Siam shall have heard the glad message.   There are reasons to feel that the real "Period of Expansion" lies yet ahead.

But the "Spirit of Expansion" was manifesting itself in still another way.   As one reads over the early records, one rarely finds mention of the wives of the missionaries.   They usually were not mentioned at all or were designated as "and family".   They bore their full share of the burdens, they taught, they visited the sick, they accompanied their husbands on tours and into all sorts of places. Some of Dr. Bradley's accounts of how he and Mrs. Bradley visited palace and wat arm in arm in stately fashion, make one realize how far we today have travelled from the customs of the long ago.   But before the early sixties one finds no mention of the good ladies having minds of their own.   Dutiful wives they were, one and all. Perhaps just as dutiful were those who followed, but they too began to develop and to seek opportunity for individual expression.   In 1862 occurred the "first of a series of social meetings of a social and improving character, superintended by the ladies of Bangkok," and held at the British Consulate.   In 1866 a Ladies Bazaar Association was organized for charitable purposes.   The proceeds of their first bazaar were given to the infant mission station of Chiengmai, just formed.   In 1869 the same society decided to organize a Library Association and thence-forth to support that institution.   The library they then established has developed into the Neilson Hays Library of the present day—continuously managed and supported by the women of Bangkok through a period of sixty years.

A Womans' Christian Temperance Union was formed and flourished greatly.   It was through their efforts that aerated waters were first introduced into Bangkok and the owner of one of the firms dealing in these waters today, got his start in business from these very W. C. T. U. women.   They carried on a Sailors' Rest for a number of years and did much for the cause they represented.

W. C. T. U. of Bangkok.—*Sitting left to right :*—Miss Mary McDonald, Miss Lizzie Eakin, Miss Jessie Ackerman, Mrs. Loftus, Miss Van Emon. *Standing :*—Mrs. D. J. Collins, Miss Mary Stokes, Mrs. S. G. McFarland, Mrs. T. H. Hays, Mrs. Belbin,

In mission affairs too, women began to make their presence felt. Finally women were given a vote and at last were actually placed on the same basis as the men. But it came as the result of a long struggle to find themselves and to make themselves felt and recognized as as integral part of the mission.

Perhaps one of the most far-reaching and noteworthy events of this "Period of Expansion" was the establishing of a boarding-school for girls. Girls were not eager for education nor did their parents favor it. Long years before Miss E. M. Pierce had come out under the A. B. C. F.M. to start a school — whether for boys or girls is not stated — but four years later (1844) died having been unable to gather her school together. The time was not yet ripe for this phase of the work. Mrs. Mattoon had already been teaching girls. In 1865 Mrs. S. G. McFarland had begun an industrial school in Petchaburi. In March 1871 Mrs. Carrington obtained station sanction to gather about her a little group of girls for industrial instruction which later apparently became the nucleus of the Wang Lang Girls' School. Mrs. Carrington was granted an appropriation of Tcs 12 per month for her school. The mission women were eagerly looking forward to female education. In 1870 a new site was bought about five miles up the river from Samray and the residence there was started by Mr. George. His wife's failing health sent them home, and when Mrs. House was on furlough in the U. S. A. she began raising money for the completion of this building which should house the "female seminary". The building was completed in 1874 and Dr. and Mrs. House and Miss Arabella Anderson, who had come back to Siam with Mrs. House, took up their residence there. The following May the school opened its doors and Siam had a real girls' boarding-school— in name at least. The vicissitudes of the next few years gave the school little chance to grow. That it did not actually die is evidence of the faith of the women and of the faith in them that they had inspired among the men of the mission—and an answer to fervent prayers. The Wang Lang School as it was known all over Siam, and the Harriet M. House School as it was later known at home in memory of Mrs. House whose energy and faith gave it life, came to bear yet another name on the lips of all Siam—"Mem Cole's School". For fifty three years that girls' school has had existence and has perhaps done more than any other one institution to build Siam and to mould a new womanhood here.   What it has achieved through all those years is largely due to the life and influence and devotion of one woman.   Others here helped and to them be all honor; but Siam pays its affectionate and involuntary tribute to Miss Edna S. Cole who guided this school for so many years, when she speaks of "Mem Cole's School".   But Miss Cole was no narrow educationalist. To her, educated womanhood meant trained, broad, efficient Christian womanhood.   She was asked to write the narrative of the Harriet M. House School and in that story is told the story of Siam during those years.   She could not tell the story of The Harriet M. House School otherwise, for the two were inextricably intertwined.   And so the next chapter of the story of the "Period of Expansion", follows on in the narrative of The Harriet M. House School by the pen of Miss Edna S. Cole.

Mrs. S. C. George

Rev. S. C. George

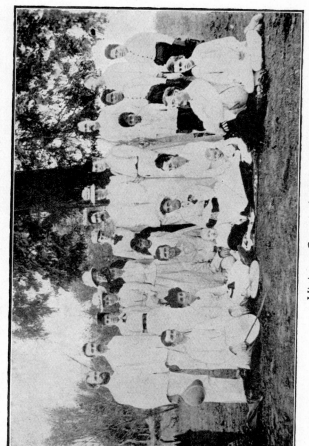

Missionary Group in the early 90's

CHAPTER VI

THE NARRATIVE OF THE HARRIET M. HOUSE SCHOOL AT WANG LANG

Established in 1875

SIAM has long had a system of education for her boys. To place a boy in one of the Buddhist temples to serve as an attendant on one of the priests was considered an act of merit. For such service he was taught to read, transcribe the sacred books and was given some knowledge of numbers and science. Some of the monks were famous educators with flourishing popular schools within the monasteries. As soon as our American missionaries were able to use the language, they opened schools for boys.

It had been for years the custom of the Siamese to seek better opportunities for their daughters by permitting them to live in the homes of those of superior rank or culture. The prejudice of the Siamese against schools for girls was never so great as their failure to realize the value of education to them. It thus follows that as soon as the ladies of the American mission became friendly with the people, one or more of the little girls found entrance into their homes, and thus began to be gathered together the nucleus of a girls' school. Some of these children learned to read, write, speak a little English and became quite famous among their own people.

In the year 1866, the question of opening a sub-station for the mission in the neighborhood of Wang Lang was proposed. But it was not until four years later that a small piece of land was purchased by Mr. George, and a substantial two-storey brick house of six rooms,—quite a palatial building for that time, was com-

menced.   Ill-health caused Mr. and Mrs. George to resign their work
and return to the U. S. A. before the building was completed.   The
Mission then appointed Dr. and Mrs. House to finish the building
and she arranged the upper rooms for a girls' school.   Mrs. House went
to America for a rest and change which she gained as best she
could, while soliciting funds for completing and equipping the new
building.   In time these were secured, and also the appointment of
Miss Arabella Anderson as teacher for the new school.

Thus in 1875, the first boarding school for girls in Siam was
organized with some ten or fifteen little pupils, all of them being the
children which the missionaries had been teaching in their homes.
Thus the little school was launched, and from the beginning labored
under two disadvantages—crowded accommodations and little possibility for expansion.   Mrs. House was so well trusted and beloved by
the Siamese people that as long as she remained in the country the
school was popular and several girls of the highest families were
sent to her to be educated.

In 1876, Miss Anderson was married to the Rev. H. B. Noyes, D. D.
of Canton, China, and Miss S. D. Grimstead came to take her place.
At that time the roll of the school showed an attendance of twenty
pupils.   The health of Mrs. House had become so seriously impaired
that to remain in the country was out of the question, so in 1877,
most reluctantly, she gave over to others her cherished work of women's education in Siam.   With sincerest regret, Dr. House left
the people whom he greatly loved and for whom he had given thirty
years of his life. However, they continued their work for Siam by taking with them two boys to be educated,—one of these was our revered
Kru Boon Itt, and the other Nai Karn, who later became Phya Winit,
and who on his return was appointed to and held with distinction, a
high position in the Government Educational Department.

In 1877, Miss Grimstead returned to her home and Miss Jennie
Korsen arrived to take her place.   At the close of the next year,
she was married to the Rev. James McCauley, D. D., who was one of

The Wang Lang School in 1875

the finest educators our mission has ever had. His poor health forced him to leave Siam. He went to Japan and there spent many years in educational work, one of the great men instrumental in establishing the Mejii Gaka In.

Miss Belle Caldwell arrived in 1878 and became superintendent of the little school which she reported to be in a flourishing condition, having an enrollment of twenty-nine pupils, the expense of the year being $490.00 with an income of $40.00.

Miss Caldwell was soon married to the Rev. J. Culbertson and until 1885 the school was under the care of Miss Mary E. Hartwell and Miss Laura A. Olmstead. Thus in ten years the school had been in charge of eight different superintendents, all coming to it with new ideas and plans of work and with utter ignorance of the Siamese customs and language. This school could never have grown under such conditions but for the faithful and continued service of Nang Tuan, the mother of our beloved Boon Itt. She was an exceptional woman. Mrs. House had appointed her to be both teacher and matron. She was dignified and wise, and it was to her earnest service that the school owes its very existence. It was entirely through her influence that pupils were secured and retained. Nearly all of those early pupils were contracted by their parents to remain from three to five years, and for this favor the missionary promised to provide food, clothing and education. Some things were accomplished with these little folks; they did learn the primary branches of education and to sew, and to knit, with a smattering of English, and quite a good idea of house-keeping, for they did all of the work of the school even going to market. And best of all, many of them gave their hearts to our Lord Jesus and lived more or less according to his ideal all their lives.

During this first decade, the outstanding event in the history of the school was the part it was permitted to take in the Exposition given to commemorate the 100th anniversary of Bangkok's becoming the Capitol with the present dynasty firmly established on the Throne of Siam. This celebration was arranged with much magnificence. Efforts were made to show all the advancement in civilization by comparing its past with the present. It was a most commendable and successful undertaking, the first of its kind. A large, beautiful park was arranged and many artistic buildings were erected, in which were collected the treasures of the Kingdom, and some of the finest specimens of Oriental art. A museum, still in existence, was organized where the flora, fauna and all the products of the country were exhibited. By this Exposition a great impetus was given to international interests and to modern education. Our school was asked to prepare an exhibit of its work in sewing, embroidery and lace making for it. This was graciously permitted space in the Queen's Apartment in the Grand Hall. This very modest exhibit attracted the attention of H. M. King Chulalongkorn, who graciously purchased the whole display, and presented the school with a silver medal.

At the close of 1885, Nang Tuan Boon Itt, very tired and much discouraged, resigned her position and with her all of the older pupils and helpers left. When Miss Olmstead's health demanded an immediate return to the U. S. A., the death of the school seemed imminent. But just at that time, at the close of 1885, there came to the mission a young woman who was permitted to take the puny orphan and nourish it for forty years to vigorous growth.

In order to have a trusted helper with the American teacher, Kru Yuan Tieng-Yok and family were given that position and most happy was the selection. Kru Yuan Tieng-Yok, patient, gentle yet truly forceful, filled well that position for ten years until chosen pastor of the Samray Church and ordained. To his faithful, loyal assistance is due much of the success of the school.

Early in 1886, Miss Mary J. Henderson joined Miss Edna S. Cole and together they began experimenting to find solutions to their many problems. They seemed gigantic to these young women, handicapped on every side by a meager knowledge of the language

HARRIET PETTIT HOUSE

and surrounded by a strange people. The buildings were much out of repair, with practically no equipment for the school. Pinching poverty was theirs and strictest economy must govern every act, for the income of the school was but Tcs. 9 per month. They soon learned that the Siamese were not a poor people, but like the majority of humanity, "cared little for what cost them little." An attractive school would attract pupils and patrons. No more "contract" children were received, each new applicant must pay Tcs. 5 per month.

The first term there were but sixteen little girls; Meh Soy, who had been in school with Miss Olmstead, was the teacher. She remained a valuable assistant for a year or two until she married Nai Boon Yee, the younger son of Nang Tuan. At present she is an outstanding Christian woman in Chiengmai, exerting a wide influence for good together with her husband.

At this time Meh Tim became teacher in the school and gained her first experience showing that fine executive ability that twelve years later made her so celebrated in Goverment schools for girls.

The advanced class of four little girls with an education about equal to second Pratome, were our only prospects for future teachers. With this objective, training of them began at once. Marriage claimed all of these girls, but before that occurred Meh Soowan, Meh Chang and Meh Ploy responded well to our efforts, and it was a glad day for the school as well as for multitudes of Siamese women when these three little girls consented to become teachers. For twenty years Meh Soowan shared the burdens and successes of Wang Lang. Though frail and delicate in body, and gentle in spirit, she was withal of a brilliant mind. For the twenty years that she was head Siamese teacher great was her influence in molding the school. With unusual tact she met the parents of the pupils and won their friendship. By her deep interest in the welfare of the children and the gentleness with which she always dealt with them, she won their hearts and bound them to the school. With her wisdom, foresight and willingness to explain to the foreign teachers the disposition and the customs of her people, she enabled them to guide the school past many reefs and shoals.

Meh Tow was another who gave most loyal service to the school as teacher for some ten years or more, and then she became a valued assistant in the Queen's College until prolonged sickness and death took her from us.

Some good church friends in America sent us a box of unusually expensive dolls, really more and far better than our little pupils needed. As equipment for the school was so greatly needed just then, and as no beautiful American dolls were to be bought in the shops, we arranged a bazaar with the sewing and fancy work of our school together with these dolls, and had a very successful sale. Each child at Christmas time received one of the smaller, less attractive dolls,—and was quite satisfied. When later, twenty-four beautiful, automatic desks came from America, few saw the exchange from dolls to desks, and those who did, rejoiced. So by dint of workable exchanges, the ball of poverty rolled down hill never to return.

The marriage of Miss Henderson to the Rev. W. G. McClure, D. D., and her successor, Miss Van Emmon, a year later to the Rev. Christian Berger, kept the school somewhat in confusion. It seemed wise to request the Mission to change its policy and permit the school to occupy and control the whole of the Wang Lang Compound. This permission being granted in 1888, made possible the first steps toward the expansion of the school.

About this time, an event occurred that gave the school the widest publicity and the highest approval it had ever received. H. R. H. Prince Naradhip Prabandhu Bongs was the first of the Royal Princes to patronize the school. His Royal Highness was pleased to place his eldest daughter, Princess Barnbimal with us. This fact proved the changing sentiment in regard to the education of girls and marked the beginning of a new epoch. From this time on, many other children of royalty and nobility began to be number-

Mrs. Laura Olmstead Eakin

ed among the pupils and the school became recognized as a school for higher, as well as for lower classes of people.

The first little Princess was so bright and friendly that she won the admiration and love of the whole house. On the day of her arrival, an accident occurred that I feared would immediately close the period of her school life. The nurse who had come with her took her to bathe in the teachers' bathroom, where on the table was a bottle supposed to be filled with perfume, but alas, it was filled with carbolic acid. The nurse, quite unknowingly sprinkled the child with a generous supply of this. Then followed several hours of terrible suffering while the little one rolled and tossed on my bed, bravely trying to be quiet and endure the agony. In the morning when the pain was gone, the nurse returned to the palace and told her story. I know not where she placed the blame, but a few hours later, the revered Grandmother of the Princess came in a boat filled with ladies from the Palace, to examine every burn on the little body, and to decide what should be done next. We were all relieved when the child decided for herself that she was well and happy and would remain. They returned home and the process of education continued. When in 1900, Her Serene Highness died of cholera, we mourned for her as if she had been our own child.

About the same time, several ladies in the Royal Palace of the King sent some of their little "maids in waiting" to be pupils. In 1890 Miss S. E. Parker and Miss L. J. Cooper arrived from America and joined the school. The next year Miss Parker became the bride of the Rev. A. W. Cooper and always afterward devoted her time to education in our out-station schools.

Miss Cooper, greatly beloved by all her pupils, greatly gifted in acquiring the language, wise in all counsels for the advancement of the school, was associated with us nearly twenty years and then went to Sritamarat to continue educational work in our boys' school there until her death in 1918. At this time, Miss Elsie Bates joined us and gave seven years of helpful, happy service. Her excellent judgment helped to solve many a problem.

The second decade closed with many improvements. The school was filled to capacity and to a large extent was self-supporting. Through the influence and good fellowship of the Rev. E. P. Dunlap, D. D., sufficient money was collected from Siamese friends to purchase an adjoining piece of property, on which were erected additional accommodation for class rooms, dormitories, a dining-room and other necessary buildings. Other improvements—a bund along the river front, a new landing, and the compound surrounded by high walls, soon followed.

A lamentable event transpired in 1880 that caused great national sorrow but one destined to give an impetus to the education of girls. H. M. Queen Sunandha Gumaree Ratna while taking a pleasure trip on the river to the Summer Palace at Bang Pa In was drowned with her two children, some trouble having occurred with the steam launch. Her Majesty, the Queen, had been interested in education and had frequently expressed a desire to establish a school for the peeresses over which she should have full supervision. So in pursuance of this wish, two beautiful memorial buildings were erected on the river bank, and dedicated to education. This school was not actually organized until several years later.

In 1893, the political sky clouded over threateningly. France claimed and took from Siam, a generous slice of her territory bordering on the Cambodian river. Siam was too weak; she could only rewrite her treaties with France, and suffer the humiliation.

The next event of far reaching influence occurred in 1898. His Majesty took His first tour to Europe. His Majesty graciously appointed H. M. Queen Sowabha Pongsi, Regent during His Majesty's absence. So successfully were all the affairs of state conducted, that the honors given to her were, with reflected glory, extended to all the women of the country, arousing them to higher ambition. Education received an added impetus. Several day-schools were then opened by the Government throughout the capitol, and our graduates

Miss Edna S. Cole

were in demand as teachers. Private schools for girls became popular. The following letter received from one of our graduates shows the trend of the times :

"After my marriage, my husband was called to a Government position in this city (150 miles from Bangkok) and I came with him. As soon as the Governor knew that I was a graduate of Wang Lang, he urged me to open a school for the children of officials. This was very difficult for me to do as I had just left my mother's home and the duties of housekeeping were hard for me, but he was so urgent that I consented." Thus in every province and in all our mission schools were the graduates of the Wang Lang School to be found, giving that which they had received.

His Majesty had been sending his sons to the most celebrated schools in England and Europe for education, and the older Princes were already returning and helping to solve the problems of State. For years, competitive examinations had been held for young men in the Departments of State and many of them had been sent to Europe and America to continue their education along technical lines.

The return of H. M. the King, from Europe, brought forth many new plans for the improvement of the country. Schemes for extending the railroads, opening out new and better roads, and the advancement of education were introduced. The King's College, especially for the study of Law, was planned. Schools of Agriculture, of Surveying, of Irrigation, of Civil Engineering, of Medicine and Nurses' training,—in fact, steps looking toward a University for Siam began to be taken, but were not fully matured until years later. New hospitals were opened and those in existence received better equipment and wider approval.

A large tract of land in the northern part of the city was transformed into a beautiful park and in it a noble palace for His Majesty was erected. A broad, well shaded Parisian boulevard was laid out, connecting this park with the Grand Palace,—by far the loveliest highway the Siamese people had ever beheld. Thus the whole atmosphere of Siam was charged with the spirit of progress.

The Queen's Memorial School for girls was then launched and placed under the supervision of several ladies brought from England for the sole purpose of organizing and conducting it.   This institution is now known as Queen's College and is under the management of H. S. H. Princess Bichitr Chirapa.   Many Siamese women have been educated there, two of whom are now continuing their studies in the Chulalongkorn University.   This school has always worked in happy co-operation with the Wang Lang School.

At the death of Mrs. House, her friends in America who had known of her work for and continued interest in the Wang Lang School, requested the Presbyterian Board of Foreign Missions to give her name to the school as a suitable memorial.   Henceforth it was known in America as the Harriet M. House School, but the name of Wang Lang, so designated from the district of the city in which it was located, could not be changed in Siam.

Slowly, the entire character of the school had improved.   Our teachers had raised the standard of teaching until teachers themselves held a higher social position.   Some of them had become Life Members of the Government Educational Association, which helped to keep our school in close connection with Government Educational work.

In 1895, realizing that the pupils must have some real objective, a definite course of study was arranged at the completion of which a certificate should be awarded.   In accordance with this plan, seven of the most advanced pupils, N.S.* Um, Kaa, Pleek, Chamroen, Waa-o, Poon and Agoon, were formed into a class and graduated, receiving home-made diplomas, properly sealed and be-ribboned.   The grade of scholarship was not above Matayome 4th, but the first steps had been taken and future years brought out classes each a little more advanced than the last.

As soon as the Government Educational Department organized yearly examinations for the boys' schools, we obtained permission

---

* Nang Sao (and its abbreviated form, " N. S.") are the equivalent of " Miss."

H. S. H. Princess Barnbimal

for our pupils to enter the lists. The first class to climb this mountain peak was composed of N. S. Tart, Chee, Tong Sook and Cham. They all passed with honors equal to those of the boys, which was indeed a triumph for the school. Since then, our pupils have regularly taken the Government examinations. This proved a most wholesome step in advance. It opened doors of competition, comparison and criticism,—always a source of growth and strength.

The aim of the school had been from the first to give Siamese girls an opportunity for the highest education that would be of service in Siam,— the truest ideal in the world of woman's position as mother and home-keeper. To this end, household arts were included in its curriculum. Each child must do her share of the daily housework—sweeping, dusting, washing dishes, spreading tables, making her own clothing, attending to her own laundry, as well as learning to sew, embroider, knit and weave lace.

The teachers were trained to do and supervise all this work. In a land like Siam, where all have servants and where menial service is considered only for the poorest, the difficulties of upholding such a curriculum were greater than at first imagined. Patrons accepted the theory as fine, entirely agreeing with their own ideas for a girl's practical education; practical demonstration was however less pleasing. Many a parent said, as he brought his little daughter to us, " I do not wish my child to do house work, she will never have to do it at home. " After sympathetic explanation of the plan, willing consent was usually granted, if not, the applicant returned to her home. If the child remained, the regular routine of house and class work was looked upon as of equal pleasure and importance.

To have trained mature women to do the work of the school would have been an easier task, but the development of expert home-keepers for the country could never have advanced so rapidly. A happy solution of our problem was in the organization of Duty Day. On this all-inclusive day, the teacher,—American or Siamese,—

would rise, dress and be ready for duty by the time the rising bell rang at 5.30 a.m.; she then supervised every item of the daily program until the retiring bell rang at 8.00 p.m. when she saw each child safely into bed. It was indeed a strenuous day but as the teachers took turn about, it would be followed by eight or ten days of only class-room duties.

The school family was divided into circles of fifteen or twenty and these were trained to do all of the work. In the dining-room each table was presided over by a teacher,—this to secure good manners, and to assure abundant and well-cooked food. At the close of the meal, a circle of ten girls put away the remaining food and gathered up the dishes; another circle of twenty brought in pans of hot water with mops and clean towels and the dishes were washed and put away; meanwhile, sweeping and dusting circles were busy in the dormitory and class-rooms. The entire work of the morning was finished before the bell rang for Prayers and Bible study at 8.30 a.m. Class work followed until noon. Lunch followed with all the attendant work-circles. The afternoons were given to sewing, drawing, singing and gymnastic drills which rounded into a jolly play hour after the supper at 5.00 o'clock. Our only helpers were a matron of the kitchen to plan the meals and to do the marketing, assisted by two or three cooks, and two coolies to do the heavy work of the compound.

One day each week was free from lessons, that time being given to the laundry-work or other extra demands. A couple of hours every day after lessons were given to play.

A weekly meeting with the teachers to check up the daily programs was a necessary part of an organization that gave the maximum of service, co-operation, companionship and economy. Duty Day was the most important development of our institution and produced many heroines,—the shirks soon finding less exacting places elsewhere. At the present day this plan is followed more or less closely by all our mission schools and the best of the Government schools for girls.

Kru Tow

Kru Soowan

Miss Ednah Bruner joined the school in 1903 and her keen artistic interest gave the school its first glimpse into the joys of picture-making.   A few years later, her marriage to Dr. L. C. Bulkley took her to Trang, where in the mission hospital she still serves the people she loves.   In 1905 Miss Margaret C. McCord joined us and is still giving faithful, consecrated service to educational work.

The opening of a kindergarten was another dream.   Our primary teachers could not understand how instruction and play could be worked together and neither could we drop our regular burdens long enough to teach them.   The going of N. S. Aroon to America to take the two years' course in the Normal Training College of Connecticut led to the consummation of our plans.   An ideal little building was erected under the shade of our beautiful trees at Wang Lang and there began the first model kindergarten with primary children and the training of teachers.   Some of those teachers thus trained, have become the best educators for girls in the country.

Miss Bertha Blount joined our faculty in 1908 and spent many years in most efficient service, holding the position of Principal several times, and carrying the school with her fine judgement through several serious crises.   Even after her marriage to Dr. McFarland in 1925, she held the arduous position of Principal for a considerable time.

With the need of expansion ever before us, we gratefully accepted an undreamed-of opportunity to extend our borders.   A large building in the immediate neighborhood of Wang Lang had been erected by the Government and leased to Chinamen for a public gambling-shop.   This nefarious business was permitted a few years only, for when the Government fully realized that the public gambling with all its accompanying evils was ruining the people, the dens were closed and public gambling was prohibited. This commodious building, vacated by all its inhabitants (except a venerable and vastly enlarged pig) we leased from the Government.   A thorough cleaning of the place both within and without brought about a condition to which the

pig failed to respond: one day of his own free will he died. The
congestion of our school rooms was relieved by removing several of
the classes to this converted place which we named Utitsatarn
(Dedicated to God). This not only provided class-rooms, but a little
dispensary for the neighborhood was opened there. Experiments were made in developing our first domestic-science kitchen
over which Miss McCord presided. Well-cooked rice, delicious curry,
fluffy muffins and far-famed American cakes were provided for
many a happy school event.

The Second Presbyterian Church of Bangkok which had had its
home at the Wang Lang School since 1878, was now moved to the
Utitsatarn and the transformed gambling shop echoed to hymns of
devotion. Many jolly times, Christmas trees, cinematograph shows and
picnics were held there. Not until bubonic plague came into the
neighborhood several years later did we close the doors and withdraw within the more sanitary walls of Wang Lang.

Vacation days brought their own special problems but not one
moment of less work, the question being how to accomplish, along
with the care of our large family, the necessary cleaning, repairing
and much needed recreation of vacation days. Our orphan children
knew no other home and for many of our pupils coming from distant
provinces, vacation time did not allow a return to their homes. Many
delightful plans were tried, but the most successful was leaving the
compound to the head Chinese coolie and his staff of workers to attend
to the cleaning, whitewashing and repairs, while we took the whole
family to some seaside village—wherever we could secure a house
large enough to shelter us. One time we chartered all the deck space
of one of the East Asiatic Co. steamers for a twenty-four hour
trip down to Koh Lak on the sea-coast. That night we witnessed one of the beautiful electric storms that often come in the
tropics during the dry season. The ship seemed a living thing with
balls of fire dancing from every spar and rope as she dipped
rhythmically through a sea of liquid silver, so filled was it with

First Three Graduates of the Harriet M. House School

phosphorescence. What a memorable month we had; with the daily tumble in the sea with the jelly fishes; with long walks along the beach that every tide left strewn with treasures of seaweed, starfishes, rare shells and hermit crabs; with long walks over low mountains, around whose rugged peaks, made fanciful by their resemblance to humble household things, this following romance had been woven:—

"A valley nook sheltered the cabin of Father and Mother Chung, with whose lovely daughter no maiden in all the country could compare. She was engaged to be married to a brave young fisherman. In distant China, a prince dreamed that in the south land by the sea, a most charming maiden was waiting for him. In a magnificent junk sailed the Prince. The winds and waves brought him straight to the home of Father Chung. The maiden was far more beautiful than his dream had pictured and the Prince, deeply enthralled, promised honor and riches to the parents if he might make the maiden his bride and return with her to China. Every person concerned except the young fisherman, willingly gave consent. Somehow, right being truly on the side of the discarded lover, tornadoes, sea and earthquakes were all invoked to bring about the awful revenge that followed. The cabin became a giant promontory jutting out into the sea; the junk broken to pieces formed several rocky islets that cluster to the outer horn of a small crescent-shaped bay; and all the household furniture tossed up into the sky, came down again forming the chain of mountains called the "Three Hundred Peaks". One of these peaks having a circular hole through which the sky can be seen, is sure proof that the mirror is held there. Could any place be more delightful for vacation days and happy girls? Other pretty places were found—but none so educationally satisfactory as this.

One year H. E. Chow Phya Surisakdi Montri took our entire vacation family to his summer home at Sriracha and made us most comfortable in one of his own houses by the sea, and near to a great forest where we might see elephants dragging huge logs to the mills, and monkeys playing "hide and seek" in the trees. Sometimes we took our study books along and tried to follow some classroom schedule, but books were weary things; the great outdoors was a better teacher for vacation days.

Early one morning in September 1910, as our school family was beginning the duties of the day, a little boat rounded up to our landing and whispered the message, "Our King has passed into Nirvana", and hurried on with the message of grief. There was a moment of silence and then a great wail—"Our Royal Father, our most august and revered Lord, Ruler of our heads, Prince of our hearts has gone from us. We are orphans", wailed the children, all duties forgotten as they sat on the ground and wept. This little scene of heart-felt sorrow was being enacted all over the country as the sad tidings spread abroad.

Someone was hastily sent to the bazaar to purchase several hundred yards of black cotton cloth and in a few hours, all were dressed in the prescribed mourning garb. Formerly, the national mourning for a Sovereign had been white clothing and shaven heads for every subject. The universally beloved King Chulalongkorn had reigned forty-two years over Siam. The most progressive of all her monarchs, he had brought about autonomy peacefully, friendly international relations and to the people, progress and contentment.

Would the old unsightly custom of shaving the head be thought necessary? We hoped not but waited for the word of authority. It came—"Owing to our great national sorrow, all people of Our realm are requested to wear black, the garb of mourning, for six months or until the Royal Cremation rites are completed."

His Majesty had been failing in health for several weeks so the announcement was not unexpected. His Majesty had died in the beautiful new palace that had been erected after His first visit to Europe. The Royal body must be removed to the Grand Palace and enshrined in state in the priceless golden, jewelled urn

KRU TIM

in the most exquisite of pavilions to await the funeral rites.

Words can never express the dignity, solemnity, and grandeur of the procession—the army with arms reversed, navy, officials, noblemen, and Princes, all in full uniform—each person holding a lighted taper in clasped hands. In the midst drawn by loving subjects was the gorgeous, teak-wood royal chariot richly carved and incrusted with gold, bearing the magnificent golden urn in which the body of His Majesty had been placed. The bands of music were silent, scarcely a sound was heard save the muffled tread of the multitude, until the funeral chariot reached the gate of the Grand Palace; then with a mighty blare from every band burst forth the National Anthem as the beautiful gate opened to receive for the last time its revered Ruler. Silently, our band of grief-stricken children crossed the river to our school home.

The school, with the standard of Junior High, had developed extensively, intensively, downward into the basement, upward into the attic, even outward as far over the river as we dared to go; there were no more corners to be utilized. The school was filled to capacity with pupils and was sending away applicants by the score every term.

Miss Alice J. Ellinwood joined the school in 1911 arriving just in time to witness the magnificent scenes that marked the coronation ceremonies of H. M. Rama VI. Several European Princes accepted invitations to this event and no expense was spared to give the public parades and royal functions the utmost regal splendor that Siam could produce. To the royal guests was extended every courtesy, even to providing for their pleasure a tiger hunt in the jungles and an elephant drive in the forests. Miss Ellinwood has served the school most faithfully all these years, her special duty being the supervision of class work and daily oversight of the teachers' preparation hour for the next day's lessons. This has been an arduous but fruitful undertaking and has been the lever by which the school has been raised to High School standard.

Each year closed with a garden party for the graduating class to which hundreds of their friends were invited. We staged many original playlets for their entertainment and held many bazaars of our own sewing, embroidery, cakes, candy, preserved fruit, for the school's own profit. As we could purchase no adjoining land at Wang Lang, we realised we must seek a new nest, and every stang we could get would be needed. Several fine expositions were conducted by the Educational Department in some one of the beautiful parks or temple grounds and to our school was always tendered space for display. These were times of real growth and resourcefulness, for each member of the school was asked for ideas, and anything that seemed feasible was tried. We gained pleasing publicity and approval by one time giving an exhibition of all branches of our industrial arts—a class of girls, each girl with her lace; another class sewing; another modeling plaster of Paris figures, an art that had just been taught us by a travelling American. But most attractive of all was a class under the direction of Miss McCord making muffins and cooking them in small electric ovens that had been recently introduced into Bangkok. Many Siamese tasted muffins for the first time and approved.

Some of the fine things were the yearly Conferences of Christian Workers conducted by delegates from all of our churches and schools and the monthly meetings of the King's Daughters Circles; and the daily Bible study by which our girls were enabled to turn their faces heavenward to grasp the things of the spirit and the human-divine ideals of Jesus Christ for His redeemed world.

Many visitors, — some truly famous people,—visited our school, giving the inspiration of earnest achievement. Some travelers came and led us into strange lands of scenes and people. An Indian philosopher came and talked of the charms of Buddhism. An Indian juggler came with his monkey, his basket of cobras, his mango seeds from which grew little trees in five minutes. The Sultan of Keddah spent an hour with us and a Princess of Cambodia charmed us with

Women's Club Organized by Miss Cole and holding its meetings in the Palace of
H. R. H. Princess Chirtchome

an account of the schools she maintained in Penomphen. Agents of the Richard Burton Holmes Travelogues took cinema pictures of the school for our American friends.

When the first International Federation of Christian Students met in Tokio, we were permitted to send two delegates with Miss McCord to bring back to us the inspiration of such a gathering.

During the World War, Siam entered the ranks of the Allies by sending an Expeditionary Force to France. Our school opened a tea-room where, every Thursday afternoon, were dispensed tea, coffee, sandwiches and cakes, gaining thereby some thousands of ticals that were sent to the American Red Cross in France for the starving war-orphans. And thus the flying years were filled.

In 1914, the school purchased twenty-five rai of rice fields, some seven miles across the city east from Wang Lang. It was an isolated place and then could be reached only by boats through a beautiful, shaded canal. This region is now rapidly opening up and the Government is building a road which means much to our school. We divided this tract into orchard, garden and building lot,—the latter needing to be raised some four feet to lift it above flood-water during the rainy season.

Gifts of fruit trees and flowering shrubs were sent by friends to beautify the place. Two hundred well-sprouted cocoanuts, more than one hundred well-rooted mango slips, some fifty mahogany saplings, several hundred banana shoots, oranges, limes, pumalos, custard-apples,—trees of many kinds were given in rich abundance for the new place. Even five tiny quinine trees were sent by a good doctor friend as his donation. Owing to our lack of knowledge of tree culture, some plants died, but many are to-day bearing rich fruitage for the benefit of the school.

Meanwhile, friends and patrons were solicited for funds; more than one hundred of our former pupils gave one hundred ticals each, —a generous gift when we knew that not one of them was earning more than eighty ticals per month. With Tcs. 75,000 collected,

Mr. C. A. Steele of our mission supervised the building of our beautiful Recitation Hall.

The architect's plan which had come from Manila, being the plan for a twenty-room school unit, was made by the U. S. A. for the schools in the P. I. The year 1920 saw the completion of the first dormitory erected with money from churches in America. The many years we had spent in crowded quarters had given us time to plan ample accommodation for two hundred boarding pupils with suitable rooms for teachers,—three commodious dormitories, dining-commons, infirmary, comfortable quarters for the servants and all the other necessary buildings and equipment for them, play grounds, tennis courts and sufficient land to permit each pupil a little plot of ground for a flower garden of her own. Paper plans cost little but the time was long.

Early in 1921, the herculean task of moving the boarding department of the Wang Lang School commenced. Those who took part in the vast undertaking will never forget how, with boats, wagons, coolies, astonishing make-shifts, hair-breadth escapes and many amusing accidents, the work was accomplished. It was "camp life" for many weeks. The school was re-organized and by the last of March, we were ready to graduate the class that was the last at Wang Lang and the first at the Wattana Wittiya Academy,—our new name meaning only "High School", for our curriculum had already reached that standard.

Several hundred friends who had made possible this day, responded to invitations to a garden party for the Graduation of the Class of 1921. We staged a symbolic play—"The Motherhood of Siam", —with her children receiving gifts of wisdom from sages of India, China, Palestine, Persia and Greece, she herself being presented with this new "Temple of Learning" from the Christian Womanhood of America. The glorious afternoon sun dropped unclouded behind the great city in the west; the full moon arose over rice fields bathed in the soft afterglow; friends with hearty congratulations said goodbye; the

-oup of Missionaries Connected with the Harriet M. House School and Wattana Wittaya Academy

Front Row, Left to Right.—Mrs. A. W. Cooper, Miss S. A. Watterson

cond Row.—Mrs. W. G. McClure, Miss A. Galt, Mrs. G. B. McFarland, Mrs. J. B. Dunlap, Miss M. C. McCord

Third Row.—Miss J. Sloan, Miss F. Kilpatrick, Mrs. L. C. Bulkley, Miss M. Jordan, Miss E. Twelker

Fourth Row.—Rev. W. G. McClure, D.D., Rev. J. B. Dunlap, D.D.

school girls in happy excited groups were all around the place;— and only the teachers fully realized how wonderful was the dream come true.

The Wang Lang School, under the care of Miss McCord, was continued as a day school only, two or three years longer, until it was sold to H. R. H. Prince Songkla who purchased it that it might become a home for nurses in training in the nearby Siriraj Hospital.

A copper plate has been placed in the reception hall of Wattana Wittiya Academy in honor of Mrs. Harriet M. House, giving to her the honor due her for founding the first girls' boarding-school in Siam, and thus the present is linked with the past. The old Wang Lang School has turned over to the new Wattana Wittiya Academy the sacred traditions that have grown up during all these years, and the responsibility for the training of Christian Siamese women.

CHAPTER VII

THE NARRATIVE OF PETCHABURI STATION

Established in 1861

PETCHABURI, one of the most delightful places for residence in Siam, was the scene of the first "Expansion" movement of the Presbyterian mission. It is situated about eighty miles west of Bangkok in the midst of a rich, alluvial rice-plain, thickly dotted with tall sugar palms. The horizon is broken by low hills, one of which towers over the city itself. It is on this hill that H. M. King Mongkut built his palace and temple. In another of these hills are to be found the celebrated Petchaburi caves. The city itself takes its name, meaning "City of Diamonds", from the fact that diamonds were found in the Petchaburi river, having been washed down from the hills above. The climate of this region is congenial and the country prosperous.

There were many consultations of the missionaries in Bangkok over the advisability of establishing a station in this place. The Mission went so far as to take action appointing Dr. and Mrs. House to the task. Dr. House visited the field, procured a lot, made ready for the work and then falling from a horse was so severely injured that he was unable to fulfil the appointment. Later Mr. McGilvary and Mr. Wilson definitely planned to take up this work—only to have the plan fail of fulfilment.

Finally the time seemed fully ripe for the starting of the new station. There were two reasons which especially led to this forward step at this time, viz.—the acting-Governor, พระเพ็ชรพิไสยศรีสวัสดิ์ later bearing the title เจ้าพระยาภานุวษ์ มหาโกษาธิบดี เสนาบดี จตุสดมภ์ กรมท่า was very eager to have the missionaries come

Chao Phya Bhanuvongs Maha Kosa Tribodi

so that his son might be taught English and as an inducement he offered them a place for a school; and the mission had received strong reenforcements in the persons of the Rev. S. G. McFarland, the Rev. N. A. McDonald and their wives and Mrs. Daniel McGilvary. Evidently the time was ripe for "Expansion". A third fact might also be mentioned — that the opening of this out-of-Bangkok station appealed strongly to the Rev. Daniel McGilvary and the Rev. S. G. McFarland and their wives, who were all four eager to be assigned to the new station. It was a heavy responsibility that was being laid upon these four young people but they put their whole hearts into the task before them.

The Remarkable Story of Nai Kawn.

Within a month after the station was opened, the missionaries reported the story of a Siamese man who had come to believe on God and Christ without ever having seen a missionary and without ever having met a Christian. The name of this man was Nai Kawn,— the first gem found in the "Diamond City". He was of middle age, was converted solely through the reading of the Gospel according to John, the Acts of the Apostles and the Epistle to the Romans, all of which he had committed almost entirely to memory. He had taught his little son the Lord's Prayer and the Ten Commandments and he could repeat whole chapters from memory without missing a word. He seemed delighted to meet the missionaries, and wished to come and live with them that he might learn more perfectly about the Gospel and assist them in teaching and distributing books. He desired no compensation, as he had a few hundred ticals and needed no more. He was very firm in his faith in the new religion and assured his new-found friends that under no conditions would he give up his trust in Christ.

Nai Kawn was never formally enrolled in the Church. The honor of being the first Siamese member of the Church at Petchaburi was gained two years later by Nai Kao.

The Period of the Civil War.

The terrible time of the American Civil War was keenly felt by that little band of missionaries, located half-a-world away from the scenes of conflict. Mr. McGilvary was from North Carolina and sympathized ardently with the South; Mr. and Mrs. McFarland were from western Pennsylvania and their feelings were just as strongly enlisted on the side of the North. Mail came to them once a month; then they shut themselves up in their homes with letters and periodicals, eagerly reading the news of the war. But when they met afterward they never dared speak of those things which so filled their hearts and minds. On one occasion, after a day spent in such reading, Mr. McGilvary went over to call on the McFarlands. They talked about the Church; they talked about the work; but there were long pauses when they were thinking of a very different subject which must not even be mentioned. One such pause was broken by Mr. McGilvary asking, "Mr. McFarland, have you noticed in the papers what an enormous national debt England has?" That was a safe topic. Surely in the annals of foreign mission life and work, there is not a more tremendous example of Christian forbearance and self-repression. Those people lived and labored together in most intimate contact all through the war without one word of friction.

Educational Work.

Under the fostering encouragement of the acting-Governor, the educational work seems to have developed rapidly. The first school house was a small building placed in the front of the compound. It had a teak floor raised about three feet above the ground, one brick wall and three walls of bamboo with an attap roof. It also served as the first chapel. The school was opened under the superintendence of Mrs. McFarland, and the enrollment of the Governor's son set an example which the other officials and the common people were not loath to follow.

The teaching of the women and girls was a slower and more difficult development. Mrs. McFarland felt distressed to see the

Rev. S. G. McFarland, D.D.

Mrs. S. G. McFarland

utter lack of even the most elementary knowledge of books on the part of the female population. Her invitations to come to the mission compound for instruction were disregarded. They all had their work to do in the house, the shop, or the field; learning had no attraction for them. At length she resorted to the plan of paying the women for their time while they were in school, and thus secured a few pupils who assembled for study and to engage in industrial work. They were taught to make neat jackets for themselves. These buttoned closely up the front—a style which rapidly spread into other parts of the country. When sewing machines were first introduced into Siam by the missionaries, Mrs. McFarland introduced them into Petchaburi and it later became known as "sewing machine town". In this modest way the first instruction of women and girls was begun in Petchaburi.

Evangelistic Work.

From the beginning, Mr. McFarland was engaged in the local work of the station, conducting religious services and training candidates for baptism. Very soon we find record of Mr. McGilvary engaged in touring to the outlying country villages. He had been interested, while living in Bangkok, in the Lao prince who came down from the North and anchored his boats in front of the A. M. A. mission compound where Mr. McGilvary was then living. Later this interest was deepened by finding villages near Petchaburi occupied by Lao captives taken in war and held as hostages. These people spoke a different dialect, and their knowledge of the Siamese vernacular was limited but they readily responded to the presentation of the Gospel, and their open-mindedness and their helpless condition appealed powerfully to the generous-hearted missionary. Here we find the seed planted which developed afterward into a great religious movement. Mr. McGilvary began to have visions of a people in the North in dire need of the Gospel. In 1863 he challenged his old classmate, the Rev. Jonathan Wilson, to accompany him on a tour of investigation to that region. That tour occupied seventy-nine days and was full of encouragement.

Meanwhile the local religious work went on apace, and in that year the Petchaburi church was organized with three Siamese members and the missionaries; from the beginning its growth was rapid.

Mr. McGilvary was impatiently waiting for a favorable opportunity to follow up work in the North. This opportunity came in 1867 and the result was that Mr. and Mrs. McGilvary and their two little ones left for Chiengmai. This left Mr. and Mrs. McFarland alone at Petchaburi temporarily.

During this time much of Mr. McFarland's time and strength were spent in erecting a brick dwelling for his family. It was substantially built and continued a pleasant residence until it was demolished only a few years ago.

At the meeting of the Presbytery of Siam in 1867, Nai Klai of Petchaburi was licensed as the first Siamese preacher of the Gospel, having been trained by Mr. McFarland. Thus the hopes and prayers of these devoted missionaries were speedily answered. The next important business to occupy the mind of Mr. McFarland was the building of a house of worship. It must be constructed of brick and they must make and burn the brick by the painfully slow process which then obtained in Siam. The form of the building and the details of construction, had to be revealed item by item to the workmen; it required great patience, unwearied attention to details and constant oversight to prevent disastrous mistakes. These qualities were not lacking in the young missionary; and after three years of unremitting labor, the work was completed and the new church was dedicated in 1872.

It was a glad day for the little company of believers in Petchburi when they saw their new church building, erected mainly by the labor of their own hands, formally opened for the worship of God. The dedicatory sermon was preached by the Rev. Cornelius B. Bradley, the eldest son of Dr. Bradley of Bangkok. The missionaries at this time included the Rev. and Mrs. J. W. Van Dyke and Miss E. S. Dickey.

เฮ็บโรน   L. M.

HEBRON. L. M.

Selected by Kru Poon, Petchaburi, SIAM.

บท ๑๙   L. M.

๑ มีที่ หนึ่ง นั้น ชื่อ เมือง สวรรค์
อยู่ ชั้น บน ฟ้า เปน ที่ ผาศุก
สนุก หนัก หนา คน ถือ สัชา
แม้น ว่า ตาย ไป อยู่ ใน ที่ นั้น.

๒ มีที่ หนึ่ง ไซ้ร์ ล้วน แต่ เปลว ไฟ
ติด ไหม้ ทุก วัน เรียก ว่า นรก
คน ตก อะนันต์ สำหรับ โทษ ทัณฑ์
คน อัน ทำ ผิด เปน นิจ ไม่ เว้น.

๓ ผู้ ใด มี โทษ พระองค์ พิโรธ
ลง โทษ เข้า เอย็น อยู่ นรก ใหญ่

ไฟ ไหม้ ไม่ เว้น ฝูง ยีศาจ เปน
เพื่อน ใน ไฟ นี้ เปน นิรันดร.

๔ เรา ท่าน ได้ รู้ ว่า มี บาป อยู่
มาก นัก แน่ นอน แต่ ข้า อยาก ให้
บาป ได้ หลุด ถอน ก่อน วัน ม้วย มร
ขอ ไป สวรรค์ บาป นั้น หาย ไป.

๕ ข้า ยัง ไม่ ม้วย ขอ พระเจ้า ช่วย
คน จิตร คน ใจ ให้ ข้า พ้น ชั่ว
ก่อน ตัว บันไลย ให้ กลับ ดี ได้
พ้น ไภย พ้น ทุกข์ เปน ศุข นิรันดร์.

16

After this the good work went on steadily. When Kru Klai, the faithful licentiate was prepared to conduct the Sunday morning service, Mr. McFarland felt free to follow the Master's guidance and engaged in itinerating. For this work, on the river and canals, he used a house-boat, equipped as a sleeping room at night and as a tract-dispensary in the daytime. For the work on land, he had invented and constructed a wheelbarrow, with a load nicely balanced over the one wheel, and geared with a dial showing the distance travelled; many a journey was taken by the missionary on his little pony, accompanied by his Siamese helpers, with provisions, books and bedding carefully arranged upon this barrow. As a result of this work, all of the villages round about Petchaburi were early visited and the Gospel was preached. Thus the seed was sown over a large part of the province, bringing forth fruit in later years.

Meanwhile, the local work of the station was carried on vigorously by the ladies and Mr. Van Dyke, who superintended the work of the school on the compound, the Sunday services and the midweek prayer-meeting. In those days, it was the policy of the mission to have as many as possible of the Christian families live on the premises; but the bamboo fence surrounding the compound was not strong enough to keep out the devil and his agents, and frequent inroads were made which brought sorrow to the heart of the workers, and provided problems for the Church Session to solve.

After more than twelve years of service, Mr. and Mrs. McFarland, with their four children, left Siam for a well-earned furlough in the homeland, leaving the work of the station to the care of Mr. Van Dyke. In the following year (1874) Miss Mary L. Cort, Miss S. M. Coffman and Miss S. D. Grimstead arrived and were located at Petchaburi; but Miss Grimstead remained only a short time. Miss Coffman took charge of the Industrial School which had been closed on the departure of Mrs. McFarland, and Miss Cort turned her attention mainly to outside day-schools. Toward the end of 1875, Mr. and Mrs. Van Dyke were transferred to

Bangkok to provide for the Wang Lang Girls' School.

When the McFarlands returned early the following year, they brought with them music plates for a Siamese hymn book. This was printed on a wooden press made by Mr. McFarland. A number of Sunday Schools and missionary societies had been interested in in the plan to print this hymnal, and contributed five dollars each to purchase music plates for printing the notes, each one selecting a favorite hymn to be translated. Kru Poon, the language teacher, was the only one available to translate these hymns into Siamese, but he knew nothing of foreign tunes. It was necessary first of all, to teach him the tune, and then he had to make the translation of the hymn fit the tune. By such a tedious process was this first attempt carried to a successful conclusion. The name of the contributing school or society was printed in the book in connection with the hymn.

As the buildings were not sufficient to provide for the growing work of the Industrial School, the next step was the erection of a large brick building, which occupied two years in the building, and cost $4,000.00. Of this sum, $2,000.00 was appropriated by the Board with the promise that the remainder would be appropriated later. With this assurance, Mr. McFarland started the work. Lumber was ordered from Bangkok and brought over by boat. All lumber must be prepared and trimmed by hand locally. A work-shop was rigged up under the McFarland house and there the simple machinery which he brought from America and other home-made machines turned out the prepared lumber. Owing to unexpected difficulties, the Board was unable to fulfil its pledge and Dr. McFarland was informed that he could not count on any additional appropriation that year. Still lacking $2,000.00 of the amount required to complete the building, the situation looked serious. A Siamese friend of the work suggested that this amount might be secured by subscription in Siam, since the Siamese Government Officials were in such hearty sympathy with the cause. A petition was prepared

House-boat of Petchaburi. Siam.

and submitted to H. M. King Chulalongkorn who subscribed $1,000.00 of the amount needed: the rest was given by Siamese princes and nobles. Thus a two storey school building was built and has been used continuously down to the present time.

The McFarlands were accompanied on their return from furlough by the Rev. and Mrs. E. P. Dunlap, who afterward helped make history in Siam for many years. Their first assignment was to Petchaburi but they later had a part in the work of all of the other stations of south Siam, except Pitsanuloke alone.

A Momentous Change.

About this time, Dr. McFarland accepted the position offered him by H. M. King Chulalongkorn and removed with his family to Bangkok, founding the Royal School for the Nobility at Suan Anan in 1878. Before leaving Petchaburi, he had the joy of organizing the first country church in south Siam,—the church at Bangkaboon with nine charter members. This church was the outgrowth of Mr. McFarland's many days and nights spent at the mouth of the Petchaburi river at Bangkaboon, where he had to go frequently to receive lumber sent over from Bangkok which was there loaded from the large boats into tiny boats that could ascend the river.

The next few years were a time of much vicissitude and lightning changes in the personnel of the Petchaburi station. A year later the Rev. and Mrs. E. P. Dunlap were obliged to return to the homeland because of the failure of his health. The Rev. and Mrs. J. M. McCauley were stationed at Petchaburi; but within a year his health failed, and they withdrew to Japan. The Rev. and Mrs. Charles C. McClelland arrived and were located there and remained only two years when the failure of his health compelled his withdrawal from the field. The Rev. J. M. Culbertson was transferred from Bangkok but remained only a short time. Dr. E. A. Sturge arrived in 1880 and built in Petchaburi the first mission hospital in all Siam. He married and for a

time was the only man in the station.   The Rev. and Mrs. E. P.
Dunlap returned in 1883 and labored until 1889 when another
breakdown of his health made it necessary to leave Petchaburi, to
which he never returned.   Broken in health, Miss Coffman had left
in 1882.   Miss Jennie Neilson arrived in 1884 and worked in Petchaburi until she married Dr. T. Heyward Hays of Bangkok in 1887.
During Miss Cort's furlough in 1884-5 Mrs. McLaren came to Petchaburi and took charge of the schools.   Miss Cort left permanently
in 1890. Dr. and Mrs. Sturge withdrew from Siam for health reasons in 1885; their place in the medical work was left vacant until
the arrival of Dr. Paddock in 1888.

A Retrospect.

Notwithstanding these sudden and often unexpected changes in
the personnel of the station, the main features of the work were
continued almost without interruption : the station schools, the Sun-
day-school, the Sunday morning preaching-service and the mid-week
prayer-meeting were never allowed to lapse.   As much as possible
evangelistic touring was carried on. During this period country churches were organized at Pak Talay on 5 January 1884 with sixteen
charter members : at Tah Rua Ban Pai on 26 July 1885 with eleven
members and at Ban Laam on 27 February 1887 with twelve charter
members.   These country churches thrived for a time and all received accessions but eventually they all were disbanded and ceased
to exist as church organizations though preaching services are still
held at some of these places from time to time.   At sometime during
this period two other men were licensed as preachers–Kru Kaan and
Kru Rit.   Kru Kaan lived an earnest Christian life and finally was
buried in the church cemetery.   His son Kru Klan followed in the
footsteps of his father and is now an old man pensioned by the
Petchaburi church.   Kru Rit and Kru Klai both finally fell away
from their profession and were lost to the Church but before
that time, each spent many years in earnest work for the Christian
church.   In reviewing the history of this decade, it seems fitting to

Residence at Petchaburi
Built by Rev. S. G. McFarland, D. D

to give a brief characterization of the principal workers.

The Rev. E. P. Dunlap was an untiring evangelist, with a real passion for souls; earnest, spiritual, sympathetic, warmhearted and open-handed: an effective speaker in Siamese, he preached the Gospel wherever he went, and trained Siamese preachers who took upon themselves his likeness. He felt especially interested in the people of fishing villages along the sea-shore where he organized two churches. When he was obliged to leave suddenly on account of complete health failure, the bottom fell out of Petchaburi.

Dr. E. A. Sturge was a very quiet, modest, unassuming gentleman, fully equipped as physician and surgeon, overcoming great difficulties in building the hospital, developing a large medical practice, and by his personal magnetism making friends everywhere. Lacking the gift of foresight, or perhaps failing to find the proper man, he trained no Siamese assistant and when he had to take his invalid wife to the homeland, the hospital was left with no one to care for it. His subsequent success among the Japanese in California shows what he might have done in Siam had he been spared to the work.

The Rev. J. M. McCauley was a man of great ability as a scholar and teacher but was not an aggressive evangelist. Mrs. McCauley was most energetic and whole-hearted in the work that was theirs. On one occasion when he had baptised and received into the church several new members, his wife said to him on the way home, "Mac, aren't you glad?" He quietly replied, "Yes, Jennie, I'm very glad; but I had nothing to do with it."

Miss S. M. Coffman was a woman of intense spirituality, diligent as well as fervent, and deeply sympathetic with all the woes of others; the situation tried her beyond what she was able to bear; she was obliged to leave Siam, and soon afterward passed to her heavenly reward.

Miss Mary L. Cort was a bright-faced, genial, practical Christian with great good sense, whose kindness of heart would not allow her to inflict corporal punishment upon one of her pupils without weeping over the delinquent; she used to speak of going to heaven with a jolly little laugh as though that was the most delightful thing she could think of.   She opened day-schools here and there in the city and surrounding villages and carried them successfully; but it was hard for those who came afterward to follow in her steps and maintain the work.   Her book on Siam was for many years the standard authority on the mission enterprise in this country.

The faithful old Siamese language-teacher Kru Poon deserves a paragraph all to himself.   One time when Mr. McFarland was starting for Bangkok, he gave this teacher a piece of white cloth and a copy of the Ten Commandments in Siamese, instructing him to paint the Commandments in large letters on the cloth to be hung up in the church.   When he returned home the task was not nearly completed.   He criticised the teacher for spending too much time on the job, saying that it was not necessary to take so much pains with this work.   The teacher replied, " Hereafter, when anyone looks at this work, he will not ask how many days it took to complete it; he will only ask who did it ? " Kru Poon never professed to have faith in the Christian religion.   Knowing that there were no old-age pensions for employees of the mission, he gave all of his savings to the monks of the principal monastery on the condition that he should be taken care of there until his death.   When he retired to that refuge, it was common talk that two religions were taught in that monastery;—the Christian as well as the Buddhist.   On the night of his death, an old monk declared that he had been awakened by the trampling of the horses which had brought a chariot to carry the soul of the " teacher " to heaven.

The New Régime.

At Mission meeting in 1888, it was decided that the Dunlaps be allowed to retire on sick-leave and that the Rev. and Mrs. W. G. McClure be transferred to Petchaburi to fill the vacancy.   Shortly after this the Mission adopted rules forbidding the missionaries

Subscription For The Girls' School Building, Petchaburi

to lend money to the national Christians or to help them in their law-suits. The reasons for this measure need not be considered at this place but the application of these rules at Petchaburi filled the pathway of the McClures with briars and thorns. Naturally disaffection quickly arose among the church-members for their difficulties with their non-Christian neighbors were often serious. Siam was just in the beginning of its effort at establishing modern courts and equal justice for all. Feeling suddenly deprived of the strong hand that had helped them, naturally many were alienated and for years the work seemed on the down-grade. Great praise is due the faithful missionaries who struggled through this hard period and patiently grappled with the difficulties before them. The patient, systematic, practical and persistent labors of these young missionaries in time produced their legitimate effect, and a period of growth followed.

When Mr. and Mrs. McClure arrived at their station they were welcomed by Miss Cort, Dr. Paddock and Miss Small, a recent arrival in Siam but who about a year afterward made the supreme sacrifice, a victim of the dreaded Asiatic cholera. In her last lucid moments, she said, " We have everything at Petchaburi except a missionary's grave; and the Lord knew that was needed. "

Thus there was no evangelistic missionary left to pass on the good will of the old regime to Mr. McClure; yet for a little more than a year Miss Cort remained with them to unfold and explain the traditions of the past. The new couple had a clear field but no favor. Gradually reenforcements came to their support: the Rev. C. E. Eckels joined them in 1889; Dr. Paddock left to enter Government service, but Dr. and Mrs. Lee arrived the same year to supply the vacancy in the medical work. Mrs. Lee was a trained nurse, a genial soul and an efficient worker: her husband was a well-qualified medical man but unfortunately not optimistic. In 1891 he resigned from the mission and entered the Government service, and has no more place in this story. The vacancy was filled in 1892 by the arrival of Dr. and Mrs. W. B. Toy who extended the hospital and did considerable medical itinerating.   Mr. Eckels accompanied the Rev. J. A. Eakin on the first tour to Sritamarat in 1892, and Dr. Toy substituted for him in subsequent tours to the same region up to the year 1896; then the Toys were transferred to Rajburi and their place at Petchaburi was supplied by Dr. J. B. Thompson who had returned from furlough without his family.

Meanwhile, in 1893, Miss Ricketts had arrived, remained a few months, and was sent home on sick-leave, never returning.   The station received a very desirable addition to its working force in 1891 in the arrival of Miss Margaret Galt and her cousin, Miss Annabel Galt.   Not long afterward, Miss Margaret Galt and Mr. Eckels were married and continued to labor in Petchaburi until they were asked to assist in the starting of the new station at Sritamarat.

Finding the work of the station provided for by the ladies and Mr. Eckels, Mr. McClure turned his attention more and more to itinerating.   Where Dr. McFarland had toured with a saddle pony and a wheelbarrow, and Dr. E. P. Dunlap with a light spring-wagon and a team of stallion ponies, Mr. McClure used an ox-cart for his baggage and other impedimenta and trudged along the trail on foot.   It was slow work but it was seed-sowing.   He covered more ground than either of his predecessors and came very close to the hearts of the people as he followed the criss-cross trails all over that province to a distance of thirty miles north, one hundred miles south, east to the sea and west to the mountains; yet it was not until years afterward that any fruit was gathered from that extensive work.   To those who faithfully preached the Gospel, praying earnestly for the people with whose lives they became so closely identified, who had not the joy and encouragement of seeing the seed spring up into abundant harvest—to such be all praise.   Those years of weary treading the rough trails were not only years of preaching; they were years of soul-training for the preacher.   To those who came under the influence of this godly

Miss Mary Cort

Miss S. Coffman

man in after years, there came a rich blessing: he had come close to the heart of man in his long and weary and lonely journeys; but he had also come very close to the heart of his Master and all who knew him knew that he "had been with Jesus".

At such times as touring was impracticable, Mr. McClure spent his time largely in training the two Siamese preachers, Kru Boon and Kru Song. The former had been a Buddhist monk, converted under the preaching of Dr. Dunlap, and employed as a colporteur. He could neither read nor pray aloud; but he had a prayer written for him which he committed to memory and used exclusively for several years. Under the painstaking training of his preceptor he developed into a useful preacher of the Gospel.

Kru Song was a Mohammedan by birth and early training; likewise converted under Dr. Dunlap's preaching but out of harmony with the new regime, he held himself aloof from the missionaries at first though still in the employ of the Mission. During this period, he spent much time in the study of Buddhism, thus forming a substantial groundwork for the Christian training which he received later on. Now after thirty-five years of active service, his "bow still abides in strength"; he preaches occasionally though now retired from regular duties on account of his age.

In 1894, Mr. and Mrs. McClure and their four children went on furlough, leaving the work of the station well provided for under the care of Mr. and Mrs. Eckels, Dr. and Mrs. Toy, Miss Annabel Galt and Miss Hitchcock who had recently been transferred to that station from Chiengmai. She did faithful service in charge of the day-schools until she returned to the North as the bride of the Rev. J. H. Freeman.

Dr. J. B. Thompson, who took the place of Dr. Toy when the latter was transferred to Rajburi, was notably successful on different lines of work: he trained a Siamese medical assistant who, after serving the Mission for many years, still continues in successful private practice. He was also at that time the only elder of the church.   But Dr. Thompson's chief labors were put forth in medical itinerating in which he combined the service of physician and evangelist.   His life was brought to an untimely close by an attack of cholera in 1898, leaving his wife and four children in the homeland to mourn their bereavement.

Soon after the return of the McClures from furlough, Mr. and Mrs. Eckels went on furlough.   When they returned, Dr. and Mrs. W. J. Swart arrived to take up the medical work.   In 1899, the Eckels family was transferred to Sritamarat to open the new station there and so pass out of this story : though still continuing in the work of the mission.

Dr. and Mrs. Swart were transferred to Sritamarat in 1903 and and Dr. and Mrs. McDaniel arrived to take their places at Petchaburi.   Miss Annabel Galt was transferred to Bangkok and her place was taken by Miss Bruner, who came over from Wang Lang and took charge of the school which at that time included both boys and girls.   The day-schools had been closed for want of anyone to superintend them.   The Rev. and Mrs. R. C. Jones were transferred from Bangkok (1901) and he took charge of the local evangelistic work, while Mr. McClure continued his touring and training of Siamese preachers.

It was somewhere about this time that the little band of workers at Petchaburi decided to venture on an enterprise hitherto unused in connection with the work in Siam.   They called a Conference for Christian Workers, asking some of the strong Christians from elsewhere to assist in the program which was to last three days and nights—from Friday morning to Sunday night, closing with a Consecration service.

The purpose of this Conference was two-fold ; to develop a feeling of solidarity among the Christian workers assembled from different stations, and to quicken the members of the local church into a new spiritual life.   In both of these purposes it was successful.   The annual Conferences for Christian Workers were

Petchaburi Girls' School Building

continued and furnish spiritual uplift and refreshment for the Christian people, and many believers from the country groups made long journeys to attend these meetings, carrying back with them new ideas of worship and of service which set them on a higher plane of Christian living.

From this time on, the work continued very much as has been described. There was little or no change in the personnel of the station until the time came for the furlough of Dr. and Mrs. J. A. Eakin in 1903—then at the Bangkok Christian High School in Bangkok—when the McClures were transferred to Bangkok for a time to take charge of the school in their absence. On the return of the Eakins from furlough, the McClures returned to their former work. But it soon became evident that the Lord had other plans for these faithful servants. When it transpired that Dr. Eakin must take his wife to Hong Kong for a surgical operation, the McClures were brought back to the Christian High School and the appointment was made permanent.

When Dr. and Mrs. Eakin returned from China, they were located at Petchaburi and assigned to the work laid down by the McClures. The itinerating was not altogether new to Dr. Eakin as he had made various trips to Sritamarat and elsewhere. But the time was not auspicious for touring for it was in the midst of the rainy season. There seemed a very definite need for work in the local church community. To that he turned his first attention. During this period too, the Siamese preachers were being trained for extensive touring on their own after the rains should be over.

Just at the close of the rainy season Dr. Eakin sustained a very severe injury to his spine as a result of a fall, with the result that desk-work became torture and he never again felt so comfortable as when trudging on foot along the ox-cart trails. Owing to this injury, the course of evangelistic work continued to be turned strongly toward itinerating work. Dr. Eakin had the diary kept by Dr. McClure on former tours and followed the same routes. At first,

the mode of operation was simple : the ox-cart was loaded with provisions, clothing, bedding, a small tent, a fair supply of books, a
stereoptican and an outfit for vaccinating.   At the first sitting, forty-
seven persons were vaccinated.   In his ignorance, the missionary
supposed that it was necessary to draw blood in order to make sure
that it would "take".   His chair was surrounded by a crowd of
Siamese mothers with their babies.   The infants took fright at the
sight of the bloody arms, and in a few minutes twenty or more were
crying at once.   The mothers seemed panic-stricken and a general
bolt was imminent.   Just then a young woman offered her arm for
vaccinating and he saw his opportunity.   As he scratched her arm,
he said in the same soothing tones he had been using to the babies,
"Don't cry now; don't cry."   Those standing by took up the
admonition; everyone laughed, the babies smiled and the crisis was
safely past.

Evangelistic work was done mostly at night where they
camped in the rest-house or under a green tree; the simple-minded
villagers gathering around stared in amazement at the beautiful
pictures, while they listened to the old, old story of the Gospel.

Gradually, as the ties of friendship were formed and tested, it
was found that the homes of villagers were open to receive the missionary; it was no longer necessary to come and go as a stranger and
camp out in the jungle.   The custom of family worship was established, and in time, there were at each stopping-place homes where
Christian families made "the teacher" welcome, and he had the joy
of seeing the people develop in the graces of the Christian life.

After a time, as the Government doctors increased in numbers
and penetrated farther into the country, the custom of administer-
ing medicines and vaccinating was abandoned; and the missionary
came to depend solely on the printed Word and the living testimony
of believers to awaken an interest on the part of outsiders in his
message.

When Miss Bruner first took charge of the school, owing to

EARLY HOUSE AT PETCHABURI
(COPIED FROM "SIAM & LAOS")

EARLY HOUSE AT PETCHABURI
(COPIED FROM "SIAM & LAOS")

Kachang Church, Petchaburi

the lack of workers and the frequent changes, the school for boys and the school for girls had been combined in one, and it was rather a small one. On the arrival of Mrs. Eakin at the station it seemed possible and wise that the two schools should be developed separately and that the building which originally had been erected for the girls' school should be kept for that purpose alone. To do this, required time and patient effort; finally a new compound was secured for the boys' school, a building was erected as a memorial to Mr. William Rankin, to house the boys' school. The girls' school building has been restored to that school and its original name restored—The Howard Memorial. After Miss Bruner married Dr. Bulkley and removed to Trang, Miss Bertha M. Mercer took charge of this school.

Two temporary reenforcements were received during this period in the persons of the Rev. Paul A. Eakin (1913) and Miss Ruth O. Eakin (1914) who were provided for in cramped accommodations with their parents in the Howard Memorial School building. Miss Eakin only stayed six months to study the language; then she passed on to her appointed work at Trang. Mr. P. A. Eakin remained in Petchaburi three years, where in addition to studying the language, he greatly assisted his father in his touring work. It was he who contributed largely to the development of the boys' school; he erected the new building, and stayed by the work until it was firmly established, with a fine playground and separate dormitories, no longer a mewling infant requiring a missionary's constant attention, but a vigorous youth with a new name—the Rankin Memorial.

As the time drew near for the home furlough of Dr. and Mrs. Eakin in 1911, the station planned to invite the Rev. and Mrs. R. W. Post of Sritamarat to supply the vacancy. The transfer was effected and in this way the touring work was provided for without considerable loss. After the furlough, it was decided to appoint Mr. and Mrs. Post to the work of the North Petchaburi field and Dr. and Mrs. Eakin to the work of the South Petchaburi field, which includes the town of Petchaburi. The North field includes Rajburi where no missionary is now located but where regular preaching service and two schools are maintained, Kanburi and several other points on the river Me Klong. These points on the river are occupied with work among the Chinese, which constitutes the greater part of Mr. Post's work. At one of them, Look Kaa, a Chinese church has been organized, and regular preaching services are held at the two points. The church at Look Kaa had its own pastor and Session. This Northland was by far the more populous part of the territory belonging to the Petchaburi station.

The South field, outside of the town itself, consisted of more than forty small groups of believers, where religious worship was maintained only in the homes of the people, and in which the widely-separated groups could be visited only once or twice a year. When Dr. McDaniel went on furlough in 1915 it was necessary to discontinue the medical work of the station until Dr. and Mrs. Bulkley were transferred from Trang. When Mr. and Mrs. Post went on furlough, Dr. Eakin extended his efforts to cover the work of Mr. Post and when Dr. and Mrs. Eakin went on their next furlough the Rev. and Mrs. Paul A. Eakin took charge of their work. When Miss Mercer went on furlough, Miss Beatrice Moeller was borrowed from Sritamarat and the school was still maintained.

In 1924, the Board had adopted a new rule, whereby Dr. and Mrs. Eakin were automatically retired from active service ; but they were unwilling to leave their work until it had been provided for by the appointment of a successor and as there was no possible candidate for the position in sight, the Mission asked the Board to continue Dr. Eakin for another year. At the end of that time, the Rev. S. E. Kelsey was transferred from Sritamarat to provide for the work.

About that time a young Siamese licentiate whom Dr. Eakin and others had been training for the ministry was accepted for ordi-

Rev. W. G. McClure, D.D.; Mrs. M. J. Henderson McClure

nation by Presbytery and being called to the Petchaburi church, was ordained and installed as pastor of that church. Thus the burden laid upon Mr. Kelsey was somewhat lightened. Assistance was provided from another source also.

Mr. Charles Hock who had been educated in Moody's Bible School, Chicago, was engaged in chapel-preaching in Bangkok. He was invited to come to Petchaburi for a month to assist in a whirl-wind campaign which was to cover all of the territory of the South Petchaburi field, in order to introduce Mr. Kelsey and make him acquainted with all of our people in that region. It was quite an undertaking to cover the greater part of four provinces in one short month—February—but it was the most favorable time of the year; the weather was perfect; the people were at home threshing their rice and their cordial welcome was a great joy to the visitors. This visit of Mr. Hock to Petchaburi led to his later appointment to work there.

Shortly previous to this campaign, Miss Wan Piroshaw, R. N., a Siamese graduate from the School for Nurses connected with Columbia University, who had been in Government service in charge of the first Public-Health Centre in Bangkok, found her health break-ing and came to Petchaburi to recruit. By this time Dr. and Mrs. Bulkley had gone on furlough and Dr. and Mrs. Neils Nedergaard were in charge of the medical work of the station. Miss Piroshaw became interested in that work and offered to assist without remu-neration. This was a very happy arrangement and when she mar-ried Mr. Hock a few months later all rejoiced and felt the working force of Petchaburi had been greatly strengthened.

As the months passed it became evident that Mr. Kelsey would not be able to continue his work, because of failing health. Mr. and Mrs. Post were due to go on furlough. To add to the stress of circumstances, Dr. and Mrs. Nedergaard were on furlough. The Rev. and Mrs. J. L. Eakin were appointed to Petchaburi and on them fell the responsibility for the work in both the North and South Petchaburi fields and the hospital as well. The assistance of Mr. and Mrs. Hock was invaluable: the two trained nurses Mrs. Chas. Hock and Mrs. J. L. Eakin threw themselves into the breach and undertook to do all they could to maintain the medical work. The hand of Providence was very plain in this provision for the work of the station; but it left a heavy burden of responsibility upon the young and untried shoulders.

However, even then there was not a complete break-off in the personnel of the station. Miss Mercer, after sixteen years of service still upholds the traditions of the past and faces the future with high hopes for the Howard Memorial School. A large and most desirable site for a new school compound has been purchased with funds secured locally, and funds amounting to almost the estimated cost of the new building are now in hand. In 1915, when a fierce fire swept over Petchaburi and attap roofs, dry as tinder were leaping into flame, the course of the fire lay directly in line with the church. A dead frond of a sugar palm hung down over the attap roof of the Sunday School room in the rear of the church. That caught fire—and the building seemed doomed. But instantly the wind changed and blew strongly from the west—and instantly the threatened buildings were out of danger. The market chapel had an even more miraculous escape as buildings on both sides of the road leading to the market chapel were razed to the ground, yet that stood with its attap roof. The strongest opponents of Christianity recognized this as from the hand of God.

For sixty-seven years Petchaburi station has existed and many are those who have labored there, sharing its joys and sorrows. Dangers untold have repeatedly threatened—but through it all, a Providence has shaped things. Over and over the hand of the Lord has been revealed and repeatedly prayers have been answered. Many jewels have been found and polished: many more are still awaiting the touch of skilful hands.

Rev. J. A. Eakin, D.D.   Mrs. J. A. Eakin

CHAPTER VIII

THE NARRATIVE OF CHIENGMAI STATION

Established in 1867

CHIENGMAI at one time had the unique distinction of being the most remote station under the care of the Presbyterian Board of Foreign Missions. It owes its beginning to a philosophy of venture rather than a philosophy of safeguards. It is located in a delectable valley of the River Ping and includes Chiengmai and Lampoon provinces, with a population of half a million. There are twenty-three organized churches with a membership of over thirty-six hundred, (about two fifths of all the Christians in the Kingdom). Its institutions are the McGilvary Theological Seminary, Prince Royal's College, Dara Academy, McCormick Hospital, Nurses Training School and the Chiengmai Leper Asylum.

Any history of mission work in Chiengmai must of necessity be more of less the story of Dr. McGilvary's life. His dream was to see the whole Tai family brought within reach of the Gospel message.

He came to Siam in 1858 and his interest in the Lao of the North, as they were then called, was aroused soon after his arrival while still living in Bangkok, through his acquaintance with the Prince of Chiengmai whose stopping place on his visits to Bangkok was near to Dr. McGilvary's home. This interest was kept alive after he was stationed at Petchaburi through visits to a colony of Lao war captives living near that city.

The plan for opening mission work so far away, while as yet Bangkok and the surrounding country were so inadequately manned, did not make a strong appeal to the Mission; but the two old classmates, Dr. McGilvary and Dr. Wilson kept the subject alive and in

113

1863 they made a tour of exploration to the North. They remained ten days in Chiengmai but, as Dr. McGilvary says in his autobiography, "one day would have been sufficient to convince us and I left it with the joyful hope of its becoming the field of my life work."

But it was not till the fall of 1866 that opposition in the Mission was overcome and the final arrangements were made to open mission work in Chiengmai.

The story of those early days can best be told in Dr. McGilvary's own words :—

"When Mr. Wilson arrived in Bangkok from furlough in the fall of 1866, a letter was awaiting him, asking him to visit us in Petchaburi to talk over the question. On his arrival we spent one Sunday in anxious consultation. He was still eager to go to Chiengmai, but could not go that year. His preference would be that we should wait another year, but that might be to lose the opportunity. So next morning, leaving Mr. and Mrs. Wilson to visit with my family, I hurried over to Bangkok. There was no time to be lost. The Prince of Chiengmai had been called down on special business, and was soon to return. The whole plan might depend on him—as, in fact, it did.

"Dr. Bradley accompanied me to our Mission and taking Mr. McDonald and Mr. George with us, we proceeded next to the United States Consulate, where Mr. Hood readily agreed to give his official and personal aid. The two greatest obstacles remained yet : the Siam Government and, as it turned out in the end, the Lao Prince also. The Consul wrote immediately to the King, through our former Petchaburi friend, who had recently been made Foreign Minister, a formal request for permission to open a station in Chiengmai. It was Friday evening when the reply came that the decision did not rest with the King. He could not force a mission upon the Lao people. But the Lao Prince was then in Bangkok. If he gave his consent, the Siamese Government would give theirs. He suggested that we have an audience with the Prince, at which His Majesty

Daniel McGilvary

Daniel McGilvary

MRS. DANIEL McGILVARY

would have an officer in attendance to report directly to him.

"So on Saturday morning at ten o'clock we all appeared at the landing where the Lao boats were moored asking for an audience with the Prince. We were invited to await him in the sala at the river landing. In a few moments His Highness came up in his customary informal attire, a phanung about his loins, no jacket, a scarf thrown loosely over his shoulders, and a little cane in his hand. Having shaken hands with us, he seated himself in his favorite attitude, dangling his right leg over his left knee. He asked our errand. At Mr. Hood's request Dr. Bradley explained our desire to establish a mission station in Chiengmai and our hope to secure his approval. The Prince seemed relieved to find that our errand involved nothing more serious than that. The mission station was no new question suddenly sprung upon him. We had more than once spoken with him about it, and always apparently with his approbation. To all our requests he now gave ready assent. Yes, we might establish ourselves in Chiengmai. Land was cheap; we need not even buy it. Timber was cheap. There would be, of course the cost of cutting and hauling it; but not much more. We could build our houses of brick or of wood, as we pleased. It was explained, as he already knew, that our object was to teach religion, to establish schools, and to care for the sick. The King's secretary took down the replies of the Prince to our questions. The Consul expressed his gratitude, and committed my family to his gracious care. We were to follow the Prince to Chiengmai as soon as possible.

"Such was the outward scene and circumstances of the official birth of the Lao Mission. In itself it was ludicrous enough; the audience chamber, a sala-landing under the shadow of a Buddhist monastery; the Consul in his official uniform; the Prince en déshabillé; our little group awaiting the answer on which depended the royal signature of Somdet Phra Paramendr Maha Mongkut authorizing the establishment of a Christian mission. The answer was, Yes, I was myself amazed at the success of the week's work. On the part both of the Siamese Government and of the Lao Prince, it was an act of grace hardly to be expected, though quite in keeping with the liberality of the truly great king who opened his country to civilization and to Christianity. And the Lao Prince, with all his faults, had some noble and generous traits of character.

"Friends in Bangkok gave us their hearty assistance. The Ladies' Sewing Society made a liberal contribution to the new mission. Dr. James Campbell supplied us with medicines and a book of instruction on how to use them. The German Consul gave us a Prussian rifle for our personal protection. All our missionary friends added their good wishes and their prayers.

"We had great difficulty in securing suitable boats and crews for the journey. On January 3rd. 1867, we embarked, leaving Mr. and Mrs. Wilson to follow us the next year."

It was indeed launching out on an adventure in faith; no friends or home awaited them at their journey's end and in that jungle city there would be no mail or telegraph service connecting them with the outside world; houses for rent or hotels did not exist; their box of medicines with Moore's book, " Family Medicine for India", their only material help in illness; their reception friendly or otherwise depended entirely on the whim of a tempermental ruler (who, according to a Siamese official of high rank, " was a hard nut to crack.")

Before them lay the long tiresome river journey with its more than forty rapids. It was not until 3rd April three months after leaving Bangkok that their boats finally crawled into Chiengmai, their desired haven. They found a public rest house twelve by twenty feet in size, partially enclosed, with a tile roof, and a teak floor. In this and other temporary buildings they lived for more than eight years and received the throngs that pressed about them. Privacy was a thing that did not exist, the people crowding about them as they ate, handling knife or fork and even bread in their attempt to satisfy their curiosity. Such briefly told was the

Mrs. J. Wilson and children

beginning of Chiengmai station and the Lao mission.

Of the first year Dr. McGilvary writes :—

" No year ever passed more rapidly or more pleasantly than that first year of the mission. We were too busy to be either lonesome or homesick, although, to complete our isolation, we had no mails of any sort for many months. Our two children, the one of three and the other of six years, were a great comfort to us."

The year 1868 was marked by three outstanding events. In February Dr. and Mrs. Wilson arrived to share the joys and responsibilities of this pioneer work; the first church amongst the Lao or Tai of North Siam was organized, an organization wholly of faith for as yet there were only interested listeners, and the first convert Nan Inta was baptised.

These first two years might be designated as years of popularity. Many friendships were formed of which Dr. McGilvary mentions two, a princess the mother of the last Lao Prince or Chief, Chao Intanon and a Buddhist monk. While neither ever professed faith in Jesus Christ yet both acknowledged the beauty of His life. The monk, even during the dark days of martyrdom, when all others feared to show any friendliness to the missionaries, visited them regularly and continued to do so till his death.

As the people gained confidence and trust in the missionary they came seeking medical treatment. Even with what little knowledge Dr. McGilvary possessed he relieved much suffering and laid the foundation of the medical work in Chiengmai. He demonstrated the efficacy of quinine for malaria and vaccination for the prevention of small-pox, thereby saving many lives and winning many friendly listeners to his Gospel message.

In 1868 a piece of land was secured for permanent residences. In accordance with the old feudal system that all that a man hath belongs to his prince, the Prince magnanimously gave to the Mission a fine plot of land belonging to certain of his subjects. He refused all offers of compensation, and came in person to designate the boundaries.   Later when it was learned that the real owners had received no remuneration, they were paid a price which quite satisfied them.   On this plot were built residences for Dr. McGilvary, Dr. Wilson, and a girls' school building with a residence for the foreign teachers.   These four buildings are still in use by the Mission.

By the middle of 1869 three more outstanding men in their communities had cast in their lot with the new faith and it became an anxious question in the minds of all where-unto this was to grow; especially in the mind of that redoubtable Prince.   There were ominous hints, dark forebodings, furtive looks, innuendoes which the Christian nationals could interpret better than the missionaries and they knew long before the missionaries that trouble was brewing.

The Prince, outwardly friendly to the missionaries, was never-the-less plotting their down-fall.   He was jealous of their popularity and was also abetted by an unscrupulous Portuguese whom he had attached to his court.   His plans were known to the people long before his hostility was apparent to the missionaries.   Even after the order had gone out that all who had embraced Christianity should be killed he still maintained an outward show of friend-liness.

Those were stirring days and gave to the church in the North a heritage of faith that places it with the churches of the apostolic age.   On 14th Sept. the Prince's order was executed and Nan Chai and Noi Sunya were brutally clubbed to death.   It was two weeks before the missionaries knew the truth.   That something dire had occurred, they were sure for their servants on one excuse or another, left them; but few came for medicine and the Christians failed to attend the usual services.   Finally two weeks after the fatal deed, a Shan neighbor of the martyrs with much secrecy and demanding what was virtually an oath that he would not be betrayed, told the tale not by words but by significantly drawing his hand across his neck.

Sixty five Descendants of Noi Soonya, one of the two first martyrs.

The air was full of rumors and fear was in the hearts of all. Not knowing what was in store for them, the missionaries began writing a history of those days on the margin of the books in their library. No Lao could be hired to take letters telling of their condition to Bangkok; finally a Burmese, a British subject offered; so word finally reached Bangkok, and a Royal Commission was appointed and started on its way to the help of those two isolated families.

The party was within one day of Chiengmai when the first news of its existence reached the city. On 27th Nov. the Royal Commissioner with eighteen elephants and fifty-three attendants entered Chiengmai. With the Commissioner were Dr. McDonald and Mr. George of the mission in Bangkok. What an awful cloud of anxiety and uncertainty their arrival must have dispelled !

The next morning after the arrival of the Golden Seal, as the Regent's letter was called, it was carried on a golden tray, under the royal umbrella and delivered to the Prince. He seemed much relieved on hearing it read and said "This letter does not amount to much. It gives the missionaries privilege to remain if they wish, or go if they prefer."

But for the courage of Dr. McGilvary the affair would have ended in ignoring the vital question. Dr. McGilvary boldly accused the Prince of killing the men because they were Christians and the Prince as boldly acknowledged the fact and said a like fate awaited all who should leave the state religion for Christianity. This was certainly definite enough and proved that the missionaries had not made false accusations.

It was decided to abandon the mission at least for a time, but Dr. McGilvary obtained permission to remain until the Prince who had been summoned to Bangkok should return. Time, Dr. McGilvary felt, would reveal God's will in the matter.

Events proved the truth of this, for the Prince did not return alive. He died on the return journey just a few miles below

Chiengmai. The law which forbade the passing of a dead body through any gate into the city prevented him, whose word had been law, from lying in state in his own palace, inside the city walls. This according to the beliefs of the country was a sign of great demerit.

Thus was removed the most active opposition to mission work, although sporadic cases of minor persecution occurred from time to time, the most serious being the imprisonment in 1889 of Elder Noi Siri. He was arrested on the charge of teaching in Chieng Dao region that converts were exempt from taxation. The charge was false but eight months passed before the fetters were taken from his ankles. During the eight months and ten days of his imprisonment 133 persons were received into the church.

The first woman to be received into the church was Pa Kamun the widow of Noi Sunya, the martyr. The widow of Nan Chai, the other martyr refused to accept the religion that had brought such dire sorrow into her life. Shortly after the martyrdom she prepared her gifts and on her way to the temple stopped at the gate of Pa Kamun and called on her to join in cursing the God that had made them widows and come along to the temple to worship according to the custom of former happy days. But Pa Kamun refused. At night behind closed doors she would gather her children about her and pray with them as best she could to the God whom their father loved. Today her descendants in the church are numbered by the score but not one of the family of Nan Chai, the other martyr, has become a Christian.

In Jan. 1872 C. W. Vrooman, M. D., the first physician to the Lao, reached Chiengmai and those who have lived through strenuous times of illness without medical aid can appreciate what his coming meant. He began treating the sick on the day of his arrival and from that time until the present the medical work of the station has been an active and growing part of mission work. The medical plant now includes a general hospital of sixty beds, a separate maternity ward of six beds, a special ward for Buddhist priests, a

Miss Mary Campbell

four room building for European patients, and an operating pavilion with service rooms. In connection with the hospital is a nurses training school which graduates its second class this year.

Relief work during malarial epidemics must be mentioned though briefly if the record of the activities of the station is to be complete. Not only the doctors of the station but non-medical members have gone out into the districts stricken with malignant malaria and literally raised the dead. Two organized churches are the result of such work by the Rev. Howard Campbell, D. D., during the last severe epidemic of 1911 and 1912.

During ten years the station laboratory made its own vaccine and supplied both the Government and the other mission stations of the North. It was an inspiring sight to see those one hundred and fifty vaccinators, all Lao Christian men, starting out on their life-saving service. This work practically stamped out these awful epidemics of small-pox that swept the country and left deserted villages to the unburied dead. It was carried on by the station until the Government was in a position to institute compulsory vaccination throughout the Kingdom.

Not only did these men vaccinate against small-pox but they carried simple remedies which they could use with safety. They went long distances into regions where the main-stay of the people in illness was spirit-charms and offerings or noxious concoctions of outlandish things. They also distributed the Scriptures and preached the Gospel.

Early in the history of the mission Mrs. McGilvary gathered about her little children whom she taught as strength and time permitted, but no regular organized school work was begun until Miss Edna S. Cole and Miss Mary Campbell joined the mission in 1879 when they organized a school for girls. By this time there was a sufficient Christian constituency upon which to draw so that children from Christian homes predominated in the school and this condition is still true in both of the boarding schools of the station.

Contrary to the usual custom in mission fields the school for girls was founded before one for boys. It was not until 1887 that the first organized school for boys was started by the Rev. and Mrs. D. G. Collins. These two boarding schools have developed into The Dara Academy for girls and Prince Royal's College for boys.

An event of far reaching importance to the country at large occurred in 1878. It began in a very trivial way and was of mere local interest, being the first Christian marriage to be celebrated. Besides the Christians, a few princes and special friends were invited, and a marriage feast prepared.

But the head of the clan was not a Christian and insisted that six rupees be given him as a spirit-fee, the payment of which legalized the marriage. The young couple had renounced the worship and feeding of spirits and refused the fee. The patriarch forbade the marriage and the matter came to a deadlock. There was nothing to do but to apologize to the guests, eat the feast and wait. Every appeal to those in authority was met with the statement that they had no jurisdiction in the matter and advised going to those still higher until the matter finally reached H. M. King Chulalongkorn in Bangkok, and had grown from the original request for the privilege of Christian marriage to a request for a proclamation of religious toleration in general. The request met a hearty and immediate response. On 30 Sept. 1878, the King's order that religious toleration should be proclaimed in all the Lao Provinces was read before the princes, nobles and high officials of Chiengmai. Thus ended happily another period of anxiety for the little group of Christian believers.

During the two years of popularity a monk, Nan Ta by name, who was a "Luk Keo", adopted temple son, of the Prince, often came to visit Dr. McGilvary and evinced much interest in Christianity. He soon left the priesthood, married and settled in the country, still keeping up his visits as opportunity offered. When the order for the death of the Christians was given, he was told by a former

Dr. McGilvary's Residence

(The first missionary home built in Chiengmai)

Second Missionary Residence, Chiengmai

(Built by Rev. Jonathan Wilson, D. D.)

monk friend that his house was to be burned. He did not return to his home but fled the country taking nothing with him save a copy of Matthew's Gospel in Siamese. For nine years he wandered, not venturing back to his old home until after the proclamation of religious liberty. He found his wife faithful, his child born after his flight a fine big girl, and he at once identified himself with the Christian community, became a ruling elder and later the first ordained Lao minister. Thousands heard the Gospel from his lips and he was a power in the church till his death.

No account of mission work in Chiengmai would be complete without mentioning the part witchcraft has played in the history of the church. The stories that are a part of the church's heritage sound like chapters from the Acts of the Apostles.

Accusation of witchcraft was one of the most dreaded means of persecution and was a favorite way of getting rid of an envied rival or a disagreeable neighbor. When once a rumor was started that a certain family or one member of the family was using occult powers that family's fate was settled and no rank was safe from such attacks. Anonymous letters would first warn the victims to flee, or dire would be the result. It soon become known that Christianity offered a refuge for such homeless ones and many of the pillars of the early church were from these refugees; and today their descendants are found in the ministry, as teachers in our schools and men and women of worth in the church. This is readily understood for it was not as a rule the ne'er-do-wells of a village who became the victims, but the prosperous, aggressive, possibly dominating characters, such as the man who owned two elephants or Nan Chiwana whose house was teak and whose rice bins were full of rice. Through Dr. McGilvary's efforts Nan Chiwana's home was restored to the family; the wrecked buildings were reassembled, and a Christian center established which banished forever the black magic. The church later organized in Nan Chiwana's house was called Bethel.

Demon possession was common and the victims often found

relief in Christian prayer and medicine. One Christian woman found the vigorous application of her Christian hymnal on the head of her crazed sister exorcised the demon and restored the reason of her possessed relative. The possessed woman declared that the devil was chasing her as she ran screaming up and down the rice field, angry with her because she had decided to become a Christian.

The women of the church, as well as the men, have shown bravery and loyalty to their faith. Christians in a non-Christian land often find themselves in trying positions. Just by way of illustration; Pim Pa, a country woman, found it necessary to appear in court together with her non-Christian neighbors in regard to the adjustment of taxes on their rice fields. She knew she would be asked to take the oath before an idol; but she determined that she would not do this, let the consequences be what they might.

The company were seated on the floor before the judge as he administered the oath and they bowed their heads before an idol as they murmured in unison, "I promise", all except this one lone woman. She sat bolt up-right. The judge motioned her to come forward; she rose but her limbs shook so, she said, that she scarcely could take a step. When asked why she did not bow to the idol as the law required, she replied "I'm a Christian and do not worship idols." The judge said "You are an honest woman and I'll take your testimony without an oath." It ended happily but with a less noble judge might easily have been a case of contempt of court. As a result of this incident the chief judge gave permission to place Bibles in the courts under his jurisdiction for the use of Christian witnesses.

Siam has the rather unique distinction of having two sets of alphabetical characters, the Lao provinces having their own, a relic of the days when they were a free and independent kingdom. The mission labored under the disadvantage of having to use the Bible and tracts in the Siamese character. While the majority of Lao men were literate in their own character, few if any could read

Edict of Toleration by H. M. King Chulalongkorn

ทัพเท้า   พระยาเทพประชุนที่ปฤกษาราชการในกะบาทสมเด็จพระเจ้า
อยู่หัว   ทั้งหลวงใหญ่ฉิงสำเร็จราชการเมืองนครเชียงใหม่   เมืองนครลำปาง   เมืองลำพูน
ประกาศให้เจ้านายผู้ใหญ่ผู้น้อยยกกะบาลาการทำแสนแลกะฎา   ในเมืองนครเชียงใหม่
เมืองนครลำปาง   เมืองลำพูนกภบกว่ากันว่า   จิตภกระทั่งให้ประเทศกลางประเทศกะหม่อม
ชั้นผาสึกทั้งเท้อมูขฯวงความว่า   จิตเกษเกริกวิจักเกลกสุระเผใกัน   จิตหมาย
เายผู้เท้าพนักงานกรมกว่า   หมวมแกยินเวี   หมวจักจิงอุณเมืองเชียงใหม่
จิตหมายไปยังกงสุกระเผใกว่า   คนที่ถึงสาศนากะเยชูแล้วนั้น   จะทำการฉิงก
ฉิผู้จักราง   ให้ทำกามภาษขบ้านเฉิงฉิงเกยฉิงมาแก่ก่วน   เท่านักงนกรมกว่า
ได้นำความชันกรบบังคมทุล   แกกระบาทสมเด็จพระเจ้าอยู่หว่าทรบลัววงบุฉิกะบาท
เจ้า   ชิงฉิพระบรมทรัวงการมวภกะบัณกรสุงฉิงหากากำหนสึเหนึงกล้าเหนึง
กะหม่อมฉิงว่า   การสาศนานั้นไม่เป็นฉิจักรางฉิงใคในกรการแผ่นฉิน   มิ่กเหนึงว่า
สาศนาใกระฎกรัง   ก็ฉิงกามชรบใารงผู้นั้น   ฉกฎกรบยุก่ผู้ที่ฉิงสาศนานั้นเฉ
ในหนฉิสั่งฎฎาแลมรยเนียมในกุเทพฯ   ก็ไม่ได้หายปกมคนกิจะฉิงสาศนา   ถ้าผู้ใก
ในหกรสาศนาในกระเยชูกี   ก็ให้เกฉิงกามชรบใา   เฉิงฉิกราการบ้านเฉิงหวังให้ผู้กี
ฉิงสาศนากะเยชูนี่กิเรก็   สาศนาหาเป็นฉิงจักรางหัมปกมในกรการไฉ่
แกฉิฉิงไฉ่   ถ้าผู้ใกะฉิงไฉ่ฉิงสาศนาใก   ก็ให้ผู้นี่ฉิงกามชรบใา   ระฎให้ทำนาย
พระมาสรกำว่าแสนแลกะฎูฉิงเป็นภูกิฉินวังแลมุกะายชนผู้ที่ฉิงสาศนากะเยชูนี่นั้น

ชักชวนห้ามปกมการสิ่งใด ซึ่งสมควรจะยอมรู้ทำไม่ให้สิ่งไม่ให้ทำ สิ่งให้สิ่เสียงส่
ทำการงานต่าง ๆ ในวันหาทิตย์ ก็เอาให้กกลับคืบคยให้สิ่งให้ทำเป็นวันทก เว้นสิ่ย
แต่เป็นการสิ่งบุคคม เหตุเป็นการกัรกัญญ์าระทรุ่งใช้ผู้นินในวันหาทิตย์ก็รู้ได้
แก่เขาให้เป็นการมกลัง ประการหนึ่ง ถ้าคนสะทำมาหากินเป็นลูกจ้ะ
การะเมริกนู้า.......ก็เอาให้เท้นายพะยาทาวต้าแสนรักงวง
ห้ามปกม........ให้เป็นกัดงปุ่นธอวงทางกะทรป์มักไม่ได้ ถ้าท้านายพะยาทาวต้าแสน
แตการสิ่รู้....ร้หนยสิ่ฉนัน....วนมีวา เห้ถวงประกาศ.ปแต่ชว่หนึ่งทว่ใคได้.เป็นวันทก
ประกาศ..............๒๕............ทกใค้   ศักรา ๑๒๔๐   ยะ

Siamese although the Bible when read to them was perfectly under-standable so nearly alike are the spoken languages. Dr. S. C. Peoples secured the first font of Lao type in 1892 and the Rev. D. G. Collins set the press in operation and remained its manager until his death. The first book to be printed was Mrs. McGilvary's translation of the Gospel by Matthew. Aside from the Bible the most popular book ever printed on the press was a hymnal prepared by Dr. Wilson. A lover of music himself he chose those hymns which have stood the test of time and through these he has sung the Gospel message into the hearts of thousands. The Siamese Government patronized the mission press for many years as they found it necessary to have documents of all kinds for use in the Northern Provinces in the Lao character. The Lao character is not now being taught either in government or in mission schools and soon it will be the dead alpha-bet of a living language. Practically the only demand for printing in the Lao character now is literature to be used in the most distant parts of the Lao Provinces and amongst the literate Tai of China and French Indo-China.

As soon as Chiengmai station's future was finally established Dr. McGilvary began his tours of exploration, visiting Lampang, Prae, Luang Pra Bang and the Camoos in their mountain retreats in French territory, Chiengrai, with the Moosurs near by in their mountain homes, Chieng Tung in British territory and Chiengrung beyond the Chinese border, seeking to find the extent of the Tai speaking people. Everywhere gathering little companies of believers, he marked these places for future occupation. Chiengmai station believing in that age long paradox that " there is that scattereth and yet increaseth " gave of its own forces to open Lampang, Chiengrai and Chiengrung stations.

There are two pictures that come to the minds of those who were fortunate enough to accompany Dr. McGilvary on his tours. One is in the evening in some peasant's home. Gathered around his touring lamp, which to the simple villagers was a curiosity, is a row of eager faces bending over a book, the book invariably being the shorter catechism.   Dr. McGilvary with a sliver of bamboo is patiently pointing to the words, saying them over and over till word and text are familiar.   Variety of books was limited so he chose the shorter catechism because the words were often repeated.   By the time the students could read they were likewise well grounded in the basal beliefs of the Christian religion.

No matter how short his stay in a village was to be, he always started his reading class.   Hundreds learned to read in this way or received that urge to learn which always finds a way.

The other scene is in camp by the road-side.   It is meal time. Dr. McGilvary is seated at his touring table while behind him stands that mountain of flesh his gentle old s'daw elephant, patiently waiting for the titbits that Dr. McGilvary from time to time hands up to him.   He had a boyish delight in the tricks and doings of his travelling animals, elephants or horses, that shortened the trail and eased the monotony of slow jungle travel.   Good roads had not been constructed during Dr. McGilvary's life.   Three weeks before his death at the age of 84 he rode horseback one Sunday morning to the church of the martyrs, a round trip of twenty miles.   Was it a coincidence that the last public worship he attended was with the descendants of Noi Sunya the martyr ?

The completion of the railroad in 1925 brought Chiengmai within twenty-six hours of Bangkok at all times of the year and marked the passing of that interesting though tedious river trip. The chug of that first engine was the death knell of those graceful, picturesque Lao house-boats.   During the fifty years that the entrance and exit to and from   Chiengmai was by way of the river, literally years of missionary time were spent in the restricted cabins of these boats.

Good metalled roads are now being built from the city in all directions.   Out-stations that once required a camp outfit, cook and three or four days travel in order to spend a Sunday with a

Chiengmai Church

Christian community can now be reached in a couple of hours by motor.

Boys and girls who once walked one hundred miles to attend the boarding schools now come by train and there is a taxi waiting to carry them the two miles from the station to the schools.

The church in Chiengmai is now entering a new stage in its development. The missionaries like John the Baptist must decrease and the church, the body of Christ, must increase; not only in numbers but in responsibility, in directing the activities, bearing the burdens, making the sacrifices and carrying the Gospel to the untouched regions. If they fail in this, the missionaries have failed in their task of foundation laying.

In March 1928, Chiengmai Church celebrated for three days the sixtieth anniversary of its founding. It was a far cry from those martyr days of anxiety and danger, not only in years but in changes wrought. Then a hiding and fleeing for one's very life, now a joyous flaunting, as it were, of their faith; a confidence due to a feeling of stability that comes from age and a measure of success; a pride in speaking of "our godly ancestry."

But perhaps we can get a clearer view of those three full days through the eyes of a sympathetic visitor, Mrs. Geo. B. McFarland.

"The celebration was planned and carried through by the Lao people themselves. A large temporary pavilion, accommodating fifteen hundred persons was erected on the lawn in front of the McGilvary Theological Seminary. This was repeatedly packed and children sat on the ground on mats, placed just in front of the platform thus economizing both space and chairs. Sleeping and eating accomodations for visitors from other stations were provided in the Seminary, but with no elbow room to spare.

"For three days and nights, these ardent, enthusiastic Christians fore-gathered, narrating the events of those sixty years. Older men gave reminiscences, telling of lives lived and of hardships bravely borne, telling of the changes wrought during this period, and ever and anon in accents tender and almost reverent, the names of Dr. and Mrs. McGilvary were mentioned. To them was given the rare privilege of planting the first seed, and of continuing their labors for more than half a century. The roll-call of the other missionaries filled a memorable half-hour. Some were unable to stand the strange climate and turned their faces homeward : some have been called to the eternal home to hear the Master's "Well done" : but for the most part these who have given their lives for North Siam are still daily giving of their best that Siam may know the Christ".

"But there was one thing they failed to tell—a thing they could not even know. That was the profound impression made by their happy faces, by their quiet, simple grace, by their ability to put across such a celebration and by the unconsciously expressed testimony of victorious lives in which Christ was revealed. A venture of faith it was when Dr. McGilvary and his young wife bravely faced solitude, privation, hardships and even danger to bear the glad tidings to the uttermost parts of the earth. Yes, a marvellous venture of faith for them and for those who later entered into their labors and "planted their lives in North Siam." But what a harvest ! Thousands have thus heard of the Saviour, and hearing have been born anew : hope has come into hopeless lives : fear of the power of evil has given way before the greater power of the Son of God. North Siam is one irrefutable answer to the oft-recurring question, " Do Foreign Missions pay ? "

The Original *Girls'* School Building, Chiengmai
(Residence in front; school rooms in the rear :
all built more than forty years ago.)

Mrs. Sarah Bradley Cheek

CHAPTER IX

THE NARRATIVE OF LAMPANG STATION

Established in 1885

THE opening of Lampang station reads like a page from the Book of the Acts. The wonderful zeal and faith of Phya Sihanat, the first convert, is quite equal to that of Cornelius the centurion and his conversion fully as striking. Twenty years before this remarkable man was baptised he came into possession of the Word but like the Eunuch had no one to interpret it to him until he Providentially met Dr. McGilvary in Chiengmai. There on 8 May 1878 he was baptised and on returning to his home he taught the Christian faith to his wife and children and to a few others, among them a fellow-officer. Two years later the number of Christians was sufficient to warrant their organization into a church of which the Phya was made the first elder. In 1885 the first resident missionaries were located in Lampang. Many had been the inducements to start the work. H. M. King Chulalongkorn had given orders that a lot should be provided for the station and in addition had sent a gift of two thousand rupees as a contribution towards the new station and a hospital. "Who," writes Dr. McGilvary, "could fail to see the guiding hand of the Lord was in it?"

The Rev. S. Peoples, M. D., and Mrs. Peoples were the first resident missionaries. Dr. Peoples' double profession and other qualifications fitted him especially for the opening of the new station. Later when the Rev. Jonathan Wilson, D. D., returned from his furlough accompanied by his niece Miss Katherine Fleeson, they too came to join in this new work. In 1888 the Rev. and Mrs. Hugh Taylor came. Though resident missionaries arrived in Lampang in 1885 the station

129

was not formally organized until 1889. But on the 21st day of January of that year six missionaries met in the home of Dr. and Mrs. Peoples for the purpose of formally organizing Lampang station. Dr. Wilson, being the senior member in both age and experience, was naturally chosen chairman. A committee was appointed to draw up a constitution and by-laws—thus was the new station launched on its career.

It would appear that in the first years of the station it was neither necessary to meet often nor to keep very elaborate records of the few meetings held. But from these meager records of the first years we find the young station six months after its organization launching a project not only for the advancement of its own work but for the benefit of all other stations. "Moved and carried that we hereby authorize Peoples, to obtain a font of type for printing the Laos language while he is in America and request the Chiengmai Mission to join us in this." This was the origin of the Chiengmai press which proved such a help in all the work of the North for nearly half a century.

No notice ever appears in these old records of the arrival of new recruits. Once they appear in these brief accounts they are already at work; thus on 14 January 1890 William Briggs, M. D., is found looking after his part of the Hospital and Dispensary fund. Evidently there was no time for receptions. The Rev. Robt. Irwin came to the station at the same time that Dr. and Mrs. Briggs did but he and Dr. Peoples were busy in getting the industrial department of the boys' school into action.

One would like to look between the lines of these old records and see how these early missionaries were housed but while they mention, with great dignity, meetings in their "parlors" and studies in this and that "residence" not one glimpse of a building is given. In 1891 however, permanent houses were being thought of and we read of the purchasing of teak logs for a marvellously small sum and arrangements being made for the sawing of the same. The station appears to have been very successful in securing land. In the record of

SEGUR. 8s. 7s. 4s.

ဍ ၃၄၆   Guide me, O Thou great Jehovah.

၁ ြၐယၜဟၜဝၬၾၿၙ္ဇြဇၳရ္ဂၸ
  သျဝသ္ၡ္ၡုၡ္ဓၬၾၿၬၿၸ
  ၼ္ၼၒႅ္ၹၵ ၾၹ္ဖ္ၿၾ္ၾၼၸ္ၾၸ
  ပ္ျၚၸၿ္ၿ္ၚၿၣ္ၷၾ္ၾၾၰ္ၾၸ
  ၾ္ဇႅ ြၹး္ၿ္ၿ ၊
  ၾၿ္ၿၿ္ၿဖ္ၿၿ္ၷ္ၿ္ဝ္ၿၵ္ၿၸ

၂ ၿ္ျၿၾ္ၾ ၾၿၷၵ္ၾၿ္ၡ္ၿၾ္ဇၾဃ
  ၰၿၿ္ဗ္ၾၾၾ္ဟ္ဇၾ္ၾၵ္ဇၸ
  ၵ္ၾၿၼၿၙ္ဇ္ၯ္ၾ္ၿၹ္ၯ္ၾ္ၿၿ္ၾၾၿ္ၾၾၸ
  ၿၡ္ၾၼ္ဇၰ္ၾၸ္ၿၵ္ၾ္ၿ္ၸ
  ၿ္ၺၿ္ၿၿ္ၿ ၊
  ၾ္ၾၾၿၷ္ဃၾၵ္ဇၿၵ္ၾ္ၼ္ဝဝ

၃ ၿ္ၾၵၼ္ၾ္ၿ္ၯၵ္ၾျၸ္ၾ္ၿ္ဇၾၾ
  ၡၼၾၷၿ္ ၾ္ၸၿၵ္ၾၵ္ၿ္ၷ္ၺ
  ၾ္ၾၿ္ၾၼ္ၿ ၾၾ္ၷ္ဂၡၵၿ္ၿ္ၸ
  ၾ ၾ္ၷ္ၡ္ၼၾၾၵ္ၾၾ္ၷၴ
  ၿ္ၡၿ္ၝၵၵၿ္ၿ ၊
  ၾ္ၾၵၼၿၸၶ္ဇၷ္ၿ္ၿၯ္ၾၾ

19 February 1891 we read, "Dr. Peoples reports, 'we are assured of the place we requested (boys' school) and we hereby express our gratitude to God for granting us this success.'" This was the land for the Kenneth McKenzie Memorial School and the beautiful tract of land adjoining it.

As one goes through the records of those early years the three departments of the work—church, school, and medical work—all seemed to progress with about the same amount of success. The medical work was started in a very simple, primitive way by Dr. Peoples but with his skill, tact and sympathy it grew into a work of commendable proportions both as to volume of work and buildings. While the records do not say so, we infer that Dr. Peoples turned over the medical work to Dr. Briggs after his arrival, and took up other lines of station work in which he was also eminently successful.

For years the church life of Lampang station centered around two men, the Rev. Jonathan Wilson, D. D., and the Rev. Hugh Taylor, D. D. These two men carried on in the face of all discouragements with unbounded enthusiasm. The early Christian community which grew up around the first convert Phya Sihanat, is to-day a well-organized church. While this early church stands as an ever-lasting memorial to Dr. Wilson it is not the only result of the labors of this prince among missionaries. His poetic nature, his rare musical ability fitted him for his own peculiar task—a greater one was never performed by any missionary in the North than the preparation of the Lao hymnal. Dr. Wilson translated over five hundred of our best English and American hymns, in a land where the very language of the people is replete with music. Dr. McGilvary in his autobiography pays this tribute to his life-long friend, "His influence in the Lao church may be compared to Watts and Wesley for the English race".

The early church gradually extended its influence to the nearby places and little by little the more distant places were reached by the missionaries or by the devoted national evangelists.

The missionary founders of this church were ever mindful of the Lord's commission of "beginning at Jerusalem". In a brief record in 1891, Dr. and Mrs. Taylor are mentioned as making a tour up the river to the north and the Station noted the great importance of this tour. This was the beginning of an out-village church at Chaa Home. The following year the records note a tour by Mr. Irwin to Muang Nyon where some years later the first out-village church was organized. And so as the records unfold their treasures we see the different centers being opened to the Gospel message.

Later came others who put their unstinted energy into the evangelistic work in the out-villages. Of these we can speak only a word. In 1894 the Rev. and Mrs. L.W. Curtis came to Lampang and added their efforts to the evangelistic work and other departments as the need arose. Mrs. Curtis was the author of "The Laos of North Siam". In December 1896 the minutes of the station were written by the Rev. C. R. Callender—the first intimation that he and Mrs. Callender had arrived in Lampang. Mr. Callender was pre-eminently an evangelist and in this capacity he served with very evident success. However in time of special need he and Mrs Callender took over other lines of work and carried them on with their usual skill and enthusiasm. Returning in 1909 they were a second time located in Lampang, appointed to the pastorate of the city church and extensive evangelistic touring.

After Dr. Taylor was transferred to Nan in 1908 there were three ordained missionaries who served before the coming of the Rev. Loren Hanna, now in charge of evangelistic work—the Rev. Roderick Gillies, D.D., who was co-pastor with Dr. Wilson and who also did extensive evangelistic touring, the Rev. Howell Vincent, D. D., who was later also co-pastor with Dr. Wilson and the Rev. J. L. Hartzell who besides being pastor of the city church also did very extensive evangelistic touring. During these various pastorates covering some fourteen years the growth of the church was healthy and uniform and the nationals were gradually taking over more and

Miss Katherine Fleeson

more responsibility for their own church. In 1926 the Fleeson Memorial Chapel was completed. The nationals themselves have given most generously to the building of this church and it is conceded to be one of the most handsome church buildings in Siam. At last after all these years the city church has a building worthy of the name. In the last decade the city church has made splendid progress toward self-support. In 1923 the church installed its own pastor and in 1928 it assumed the full responsibility for his salary. As one thinks of the first little group of Christians and then turns to the Church as it is today with the pastor's salary and all the church expenses met by the congregation, the contrast is inspiring. The church today is marked by a deepening of spiritual life and a joy in the discharge of its responsibilities.

As we turn once more to trace the medical work, we find Dr. Briggs added much to the buildings and to the general prosperity of the work. On 11 August 1893 he left Lampang to start the new station in Prae. A year later the records are written by a new hand — that of the Rev. J. S. Thomas, M. D. At this time the station force was increased by three new workers, — Dr. and Mrs. Thomas who took over the work of the hospital and Miss Julia Hatch — now Mrs. Hugh Taylor. These three made splendid contributions to the work for several years and then went to the new station in Prae where they were much needed.

At this time the medical work was taken over by Carl C. Hansen, M. D., and Mrs. Hansen. This marked a new era in medical work. For fourteen years the work was carried on under their leadership and the prestige of the hospital was much increased. In 1908 on the resignation of Dr. Hansen, Charles H. Crooks, M. D., and Mrs. Crooks came to Lampang to take over the work. Except for furloughs they have since then had continuous charge of the medical plant known as the Charles T. Van Santwoord Hospital and Lampang Dispensary. This institution has in recent years made some very useful additions in equipment and buildings. Two private wards have been erected. A modern operating room with a laboratory was built in 1920; in the same year brick kitchens were added. In 1922 a water plant was installed, paid for by hospital receipts, thus furnishing an abundant water supply for the hospital and the three residences. In 1923 modern bathrooms with hot and cold baths, a laundry, a latrine and septic tank were installed. In 1928 electric lights were put in. In the last two decades the hospital staff has been greatly increased and these men have been under daily instruction with lectures and clinical work. The staff is now able to carry on with some degree of efficiency during the absence of the doctor-in-charge. This was demonstrated during the recent furlough of Dr. and Mrs. Crooks.

While the church was going forward the two schools were keeping pace but it can be recorded that school work followed rather than preceded evangelistic effort. Mention had already been made of the land obtained for the boys' school through the efforts of Dr. Peoples, who, after the coming of Dr. and Mrs. Briggs to the station, gave his time to the school—especially along industrial lines. The Rev. Robert Irwin was his associate. They continued in this work until 4 November 1891 when we read "On motion Mr. and Mrs. Taylor were requested to take permanent control of the boys' school". This regime continued for seventeen years and they guided the school from a mere handful of boys in a little bamboo school-building until with increased enrollment they occupied the Kenneth MacKenzie Memorial School, a building amply adequate for the school at that time. Too much appreciation can not be expressed for the loving, patient work which they gave to that generation of boys. With the coming of Dr. and Mrs. Vincent to the school, industrial instruction was greatly emphasized; the dignity of labor with one's hands was a very real lesson taught during this period. The school grew and prospered and the industrial plant established by Dr. Vincent has won the universal appreciation of the Siamese. The next principal of that school was Mr. Arthur McMullin. While not an experienced

Mission Meeting at Lampang, 1917

Front row sitting, from left to right:—Miss Cole, Mrs. Peoples, Chao Ying of Lampang, Chao of Lamp ang,
Rev. S. Peoples, M.D., Mrs. Collins, Rev. W. Dodd, D.D., Rev. D. Collins, Rev. H. Taylor, D.D.

Second row standing behind :—Dr. Dodd, Mrs. Dodd, Mrs. Taylor.

educationalist he proved himself earnest and the school continued to prosper and the standard of class room work was gradually raised. Mr. McMullin was a musician and made large contributions along musical lines not only to the school but also in the church work. Between the time that Mr. McMullin left and the coming of the present principal other members of the station served as acting-principals, keeping up the work of the school. Many have contributed in bringing the school to its present prosperous condition. In 1925 Mr. and Mrs. Asher B. Case were placed in charge of this school and together they have brought it to a higher degree of efficiency with the largest enrollment in its history.

As the other departments progressed, so did the girl's school. As the Christian community grew, Miss Fleeson gathered a few girls around her and in due time the school numbered ten. Miss Fleeson also took an active part in the evangelistic work for we read of several long tours which she and Dr. Wilson took at various times. She also kept up the social side of the station life. "Mission met in Miss Fleeson's parlor" is often repeated in these brief records. Between these lines we read of the tea parties following these meetings which must have been like oases in the daily routine of the new station, for Miss Fleeson was blest with rare social graces and had much to contribute to this side of the station life. As the Christians multiplied so the school grew but there do not appear to have been many pupils except from the Christian community. At first the school had no special abiding place; it appears to have been like a moveable feast. However in January 1922 Dr. Wilson, who ever took a keen interest in this school, proposed "That the mission take action towards securing a place between the two compounds (present ministerial and medical residences) for the Girls School". It does not appear to have been a very easy matter to accomplish. In August 1894 the records give this information, " It is suggested that Miss Fleeson call on the old lady now living there (the owner who was determined not to sell), then call on the prince having authority over the owner, then call on the Governor to see what can be done about purchasing the land ". While all this may have helped, yet the land was not secured until a few years later when Dr. Briggs, by methods unrecorded, got the land from the ancient owner ; Dr. Briggs was always able to do quite a canny job of persuading people.

Then Miss Fleeson began to plan for a new building—the present building which unfortunately was completed only a short time before her death. This was erected with materials and funds which Miss Fleeson herself solicited largely in Lampang itself. The school she left is a monument to her faith and efficiency. Her school work was of a high grade and the girls she trained are among the capable mothers of the younger generation of women who cherish memories of her in loving and grateful hearts.

Two principals succeeded Miss Fleeson—Miss Elizabeth Carothers and Miss Hazel E. Brunner (now Mrs. Loren S. Hanna) each having the school for one term of service and Mrs. Hanna again for several years after her marriage. Under the efficient leadership of these two principals the school continued to grow and prosper with increasing prestige. Industrial work — especially sewing and weaving — were prominent features at that time. During Miss Carothers' time the plan of sending the girls to higher schools for training was started and has proven beneficial. Mrs. Hanna continued this plan and our present group of teachers is the result of this effort.

The school was then placed under the principalship of Miss Lucy Starling. Under her able management the school has become one of the largest and most progressive of our out-station schools. The grade and quality of the class room work has been steadily improved. The school both in the boarding and day school departments has long outgrown the present building. Last year a commodious primary department building was erected by Miss Starling from funds collected by herself. These were gifts of friends who

Laos Boat moored in front of Wang Lang ready for the six weeks or two months trip to North Siam

appreciated the great value of the school and gladly helped provide for its needs.

There have been others who, when the emergency arose, have taken charge of the school. Truly many have labored and sacrificed to bring the Lampang girls' school to its present prosperous condition.

In closing this very brief narrative of Lampang station one thinks tenderly of those who worked for a brief time but who nevertheless left their impress here and there on the lives of the people. There are also those who not only gave *some* but who gave their *all* and are now lying sleeping in our midst—a constant reminder of their love and devotion,—Mrs. W. A. Briggs who had scarcely reached her field of labor when she was called to a higher sphere; Mrs. C. A. MacKay who also lived so brief a time but whose loving devotion is still remembered; and Dr. Wilson, beloved by all who knew him who gave fifty-three years of his life in unswerving devotion and service to the land of his adoption, that Christ might be made known.

CHAPTER X

THE NARRATIVE OF RAJBURI STATION

Established in 1889

THE name Rajaburi, meaning Royal City, is often clipped to the shorter form Rajburi. This thriving town is located on the west bank of the Meklong river, and is the capital of a large and populous province which includes Petchaburi and several other large towns.

Christian work there was started chiefly by tours from Petchaburi, which then involved 24 hours or more of travel each way, on two rivers and out into the Gulf of Siam. Later the Rev. E. P. Dunlap secured from the Siamese Government the use of a two-storey brick house, rent free, the mission paying only for needed repairs or improvements. The first resident missionaries were James Thompson, M. D. and wife, (1889-1893)—and they, while still the only workers, started all lines of work,—medical, school, and evangelistic. A few years later the government required that property for other uses, but allowed the mission in exchange and also rent free, a larger building and one more centrally located. This was remodelled into a double house for two families with other buildings for schools. A small dispensary building was added later.

The roll call of the sowers of the seed during those early years might read as follows: the Rev. A. W. Cooper, 1890-92; Mr. and Mrs. Cooper, 1897-1902 and 1908-1913; Dr. and Mrs. E. Wachter, 1894-1908; the Rev. and Mrs. C. E. Eckels, 1892-93 and 1898-1900; the Rev. and Mrs. R. W. Post, 1902-05; the Rev. and Mrs. Hugh Moody, 1905-08; the Rev. and Mrs. H. W. Stewart, 1910-12. For periods averaging less than a year each

138

Rev. E. Wachter, M.D. and Mrs. Wachter

were: Miss Cooper, 1890-01; the Rev. and Mrs. Lyman, 1897; Dr. and Mrs. Guy Hamilton, 1901; Dr. and Mrs. Harry Boyd, 1901-02; Dr. Lucius Bulkley, 1908-09.

Medical work was always maintained, but not on a large scale. During some years there was much evangelistic touring; much of the rest of the time little beyond local work could be attempted. Regular Sabbath-school and preaching services were maintained, but the converts were never organized into a local church. The most effective work was done in the schools; quite a number of boys and girls who received their first start in these day-schools went on to Bangkok for higher education, and developed into notably useful Christian workers.

Shortly after the completion of the railway which shortened the distance between the two points to less than a two hours' trip, the Foreign Mission Board ordered the consolidation of Rajburi and Petchaburi into one single station, the change to become effective from the beginning of 1909. Mr. and Mrs. Cooper remained at Rajburi for four years after this consolidation.

The medical missionaries being needed elsewhere, a national, Moh Tean Koo, was engaged to take charge of the medical work, beginning in 1909 and, although not a fully certified doctor, has continued work successfully until the present time. In 1912, a new agreement was made whereby instead of working on a salary for the mission he be allowed the use of the mission hospital and dispensary building, rent free—besides having the privilege of buying, as much of the drug stock as he wished to use,—and thereafter that the Mission should have no further responsibility for, or share in, the medical finances.

The Siamese government later required the second piece of property which had been loaned to the Mission in Rajburi, using the site with additional adjacent land for building a fine, new market. They gave the Mission a year's notice, which was extended to a three years' period; they also granted the privilege of removing all improvements which had been added at mission expense, and enabled the Mission, through their good offices to purchase a vacant lot for its future work.   Four small buildings were then erected on the new site, one of which affords temporary accommodation for the supervising missionary and the others being for chapel, school and medical work.   The old site was vacated in March 1913.   The Coopers remained in Rajburi a month longer in order to turn over the work to the nationals who, with such supervision and cooperation as could be given from Petchaburi, were to carry things from then on.   In April Mrs. Cooper left on furlough and Mr. Cooper went to Pitsanuloke to fill an emergency vacancy there.   It may be said that there were no funds available to suitably house a resident missionary family on the new site at Rajburi, nor was there any family available to be located there.

Since the time of the consolidation of forces at Petchaburi, Rajburi has continued to be an out-station of the former, without resident missionaries,—and even at the present time the missionary force at Petchaburi is smaller than it should be to handle the work. Similar conditions have surrounded the withdrawal of resident missionaries from Ayuthia and Lampoon, and threaten the existence of of single stations elsewhere.

It is impossible from the meager and fragmentary records available to compile a full and complete story of the faithful labors of those workers who have been placed at Rajburi during the course of its existence.   Most of those from whom we should be able to obtain the most in the way of authentic data are no longer with us, and the entire records of the things accomplished and of the extent of the spreading of the Word will appear only in another world.

———— •◄◆►• ————

CHAPTER XI

THE NARRATIVE OF PRAE STATION

Established in 1893

THE opening of Prae station was preceded by a tour of investigation by Dr. McGilvary in 1892. The next year was the year of the great famine all over this section of the North and Elder Noi of Lampang went to Wieng Tong to proclaim the fact that the missionaries were helping the starving people by giving rice. While in Wieng Tong the Elder preached the gospel and on his return a number of people went with him to Lampang and stayed about a month. The Rev. S. Peoples, M. D., also took a large quantity of rice to Prae by pony caravan and distributed to the people in need. Those who heard the gospel in Lampang showed great interest and about ten persons were baptised, who upon their return to Prae told the gospel story to their neighbors and friends.

In 1894 Dr. Peoples arranged to buy a plot of land for a mission compound along the Me Yome river adjoining the compound of the Bombay-Burmah Trading Corporation, which at that time was a very suitable location. In that year William Briggs, M. D., moved to Prae and was the first resident missionary. Soon afterwards, he was joined by the Rev. and Mrs. William Shields and when Dr. Briggs left Prae, the Rev. J. S. Thomas, M. D., came to take his place. Miss Julia Hatch also joined the Prae missionary force about this time.

The first two elders in the Prae church were Nai Ma of the Iu tribe and Noi Panya. One of the strongest men in the Prae Church was Nan Chai Nuparb, who had come from Chiengmai to work for the Bombay-Burmah Trading Corporation before

the mission station was opened.   Another man who developed into
an aggressive leader in the Prae work was Nai Loom Pantupongse,
who also came from Chiengmai.   He was baptised after coming to
Prae and became an assistant to Mr. Shields.   These two men were
ordained elders and became strong pillars in the Prae church.   During the time of trial and testing when there were no resident missionaries in Prae station they held the church together and were
active in the Lord's work almost up to the time of their deaths in
1924.   These two men had been neighbors and friends for many
years and both died in the same month.   Their lives were living
epistles read by the Prae people and much of the work here is due
of their strong leadership.   The laying of the foundation of the
mission work in Prae was accomplished without any trouble or
persecution, for those in authority greatly respected the missionaries
and have always been very friendly.

In 1902 the Shans of the North rebelled because of the new
taxes levied by the Siamese Government and made a raid on Prae.
There seemed to be great danger and it was quickly arranged to send
the missionary women and children to Lampang and Chiengmai. The
national Christians were greatly alarmed and seeing the women
and children of the mission station preparing to leave, went in a body
to Dr. Thomas, who was the only man in the station at the time,
and begged him not to go.   He assured them that he had no intention
of leaving but they were still much afraid and asked him to put his
promise in writing.   Many of the Christian people and some non-
Christian Siamese took refuge on the mission compound and some
fled across the river.   Dr. Thomas raised the American flag and hired
a number of Sikh watchmen to guard the compound : no one
there was molested but the Shans killed a number of Siamese in the
town, including the Governor.

When the Rev. and Mrs. William Shields and later the Rev. J. S.
Thomas, M. D., and Miss Hatch left Prae, the Rev. Robert Irwin and
Mrs. Mary Irwin, M. D., came, but remained only a short while. After

Rev. J. H. Freeman and Mrs. Freeman

them came C. H. Crooks, M. D., and Mrs. Crooks who also stayed only a short time. Then for a number of years there were no resident missionaries in Prae and aside from a few visits by the Rev. Henry White and others the work of the church was carried on largely by elders Nan Chai and Loom. It is encouraging to note that the church held its own during this time.

The Mission then decided to open Prae station again and the Rev. R. Gillies, D. D., and Mrs. Gillies and the Rev. William Yates were assigned there. Soon afterward, Mr. Yates was compelled to return to America on account of ill health, and Dr. and Mrs. Gillies were joined by E. C. Cort, M. D., and Mrs. Cort and a little later by Mr. Arthur McMullin. Then Dr. and Mrs. Gillies were transferred to Chiengmai and the Rev. and Mrs. Charles Callender came to take their places.

In 1913 the mission station was moved to the east side of the town along the main highway leading to the railway station at Den Jaya. This move was necessary because of the yearly encroachment of the river on the old compound but it was a change for the better. The new compound is more accessible and open to the public and the work has prospered. New hospital and dispensary buildings were built, schools were opened and much teaching which has borne good fruit was done in the country villages. A new church was organized at Ban Pa Pung in 1914. Elder Noi Pawm was the leading elder and evangelist in this section. A day school for the children was also organized in connection with this church. The membership of this church has grown steadily and is scattered over a wide area of country villages.

When Dr. and Mrs. Cort were transferred to Chiengmai, Charles Park, M. D., and Mrs. Park came to take their places. The Rev. and Mrs. R. I. McConnell were also added to the Prae missionary force in 1919, and in the same year Mr. and Mrs. Callender and Dr. and Mrs. Park were transferred to the new work among the Tai people in southern China. They also took with them several families of native workers, so that this new work across the border owes much to Prae station. The Rev. and Mrs. John Freeman were then appointed to Prae and Dr. C. H. Crooks, stationed at Lampang, began to look after the medical work from Lampang. Soon afterward Mr. and Mrs. McConnell were transferred to Chiengmai and Mr. and Mrs. Freeman carried on alone for several years until Mr. Freeman was seriously injured by a fall from his pony while itinerating among the country villages and was compelled to go home where he died.

Dr. Crooks remained in charge of the medical work and the Rev. J. L. Hartzell, who was also stationed in Lampang, took charge of the rest of the Prae work and both made regular visits but there were no resident missionaries in the station for several years. About this time there was a large ingathering of new Christians in the country villages. This was no doubt due to the labors of former missionaries, and Mr. and Mrs. Hartzell moved to Prae in order to devote all of their time to the growing work there. Dr. Crooks then gave up the medical work and it has since been conducted by Mrs. Hartzell who has carried on with the help of national assistants and various physicians from other stations who have come from time to time to do the surgical work of the hospital.

Soon after Mr. and Mrs. Hartzell moved to Prae a new chapel was built at Ban Pa Pung along the main road. This was necessary because of the rapid growth of this country church and about a year later this new chapel had to be enlarged. It was built and the ground paid for almost entirely by native contributions. The membership now numbers over three hundred communicants. About a year later another growing Christian community at Ban Don Moon was organized into a church and a chapel built. Mrs. Freeman gave one hundred ticals toward this chapel as a memorial to her late husband and a school organized there was called the Freeman Memorial School. Kru Kham Tan was put in charge of this school and also acts as lay-pastor for the church.

The church work has also been developing in a number of

small villages along the railway from Me Poak to Ban Dan and small chapels have been built at Ban Dan and Ban Hoi Rai. Elder Tong Yu is in charge of this work and his wife conducts a small school at Ban Hoi Rai. There are about forty Christian households among these villages and steps are now being taken to organize them into a church at Ban Hoi Rai. When this new church is organized there will be four Churches in Prae with a combined membership of over seven hundred. There are also four schools with an enrollment of about one hundred fifty children.

The Christian people are gradually learning to conduct their own churches. The services and preaching of the city church are carried on by a committee of elders and most of the services in the country are conducted by elders. They are also learning to give, and the offerings are increasing. The city church uses the envelope system and pays the salary of one evangelist. The church is self-supporting except that there is no native pastor.

It can be seen from this brief history that Prae station has had more than its share of changes in the missionary force, which is so detrimental to the work. It has been remarked that Prae is the only missionary station in Siam where there are no missionary graves. The answer is easy. It is not that the Prae climate is better nor mosquitoes fewer, but that no missionary has yet stayed long enough to be buried. There have been two periods when no resident missionaries were in the station and for the past five years there has been only one family. It is the poorest equipped station of the mission and there are no fine buildings to be seen, but the work has grown steadily and stands high in the mission list. What might be done in such a fruitful field if properly worked ?

CHAPTER XII

THE NARRATIVE OF NAN STATION

Established in 1894

NAN is the most northeastern province in the outskirts of Siam. It was organized as a station in 1894 by Dr. and Mrs. Peoples. This place was brought to the notice of the Mission first by Dr. McGilvary who, accompanied by his daughter Cornelia, and the Rev. and Mrs. Hugh Taylor, made his first visit to the province in 1890. He then spoke of it as being the most promising outlook for a new mission station of any in the North. "We found the rulers of Nan very friendly and received a cordial reception and found men to take charge of the chapel. There were many to look after our welfare while there and we had the privilege of seeing the last King of Nan Province and had audience with him in the Throne Room. He was very old and very deaf at that time."

The report of this trip by Dr. McGilvary is what induced the Mission to start a station there in 1894, and Dr. and Mrs. Peoples, who had opened the station in Lampang, were given the privilege of opening this station also. They had to man the station there alone for awhile but the Rev. John H. Freeman came out in the fall of 1894 and was sent to their relief. Later Miss Mary Bowman, M. D., accompanied Dr. and Mrs. Peoples on their return from their furlough and was stationed at Nan. (Miss Bowman is now Mrs. Robt. Irwin.)

After Dr. Bowman came to Nan the succession from then on was: the Rev. and Mrs. Henry White, the Rev. and Mrs. A. P. Barrett, and the Rev. and Mrs. David Park. Mr. White nearly died of smallpox while in Nan. Mrs. Barrett suffered from a very severe sunstroke and was compelled to leave the country in 1908. Her leaving was very sudden and at such a time that it left Dr. and Mrs. Peoples alone in the station.

The church of Nan was organized in 1895 with a dozen members mostly transferred by letter from Lampang and Chiengmai. About one third of the charter members are still living and in connection with the church. There has been a steady growth in the church from the first. Three distinct colonies have been transferred to other stations in the mission—Muang Tun, Chieng Khom and Muang Oi. It is a church now of almost six hundred living members. The number of baptisms since the organization of the church has been something over fifteen hundred. These members are distributed over the province : in certain places there are considerable numbers, viz. Wiang Sa, Ban Son, Nan Kiang, See Pome, Muang Poa, Muang Pua, Chieng Khan, and Muang Leh. The city chapel was built in 1907-08 and has been remodelled recently. Two other chapels have been built in the province ; one at Ban Son, which is now used not only as a chapel but for a parochial school as well, conducted by the people ; another chapel at Wieng Sa, which is occupied by the evangelist in charge of the work there, as parsonage and chapel.

An important branch of this church is the new outstation of Luang Prabang Province. This branch consists of about eighty baptised adults and infants. This does not include the Muang Sa group which is under the Lampang church.

The boys' and girls' schools in Nan have produced some very good and efficient workers for this station, and for some other places in the mission, Chiengrai and Prae particularly being beneficiaries of our schools. We have two ordained ministers and graduates of the Theological Seminary in Chiengmai and we have two very promising young men in the seminary at the present time. With the exception of one, all of the members of the present faculties of the two schools are products of the educational work in Nan. The head teacher in the boys' school is a self-educated teacher. As a boy he had one year in the Nan school, and later one year in the Chiengmai school. But after that he was unable to attend school and studied by himself until he was able to pass the teachers' examination and now possesses a teacher's certificate.

Originally Nan province was much larger than it is now. It used to include Muang Khawp, Chieng Hon, Chieng Lom, Muang Ngun, Hong Sa. But these have since been added to the French territory.

The Mission decided to send the Rev. and Mrs. Hugh Taylor to the relief of the station. They arrived early in 1909. Prior to their coming the boys' school had been carried on by Mr. Park but had later been closed. On the arrival of the Taylors, the school was reopened and carried on in a small temple dormitory that was on the compound where they lived. At the same time a number of the girls were gathered together for a little school. This was the beginning of the work of the girls' school at Nan. Two from that company of girls have long been teachers in the girls' school but recently increased family cares have compelled them to give up their teaching.

In 1908 the Parks resigned. Then in 1910 Miss Eula Van Vranken was sent to Nan to take charge of the girls' school but when she had to leave on furlough in 1911 Miss Lucy Starling was transferred from Chiengmai to take her place. In 1912 William Beach, M.D., and Mrs. Beach arrived to take charge of the medical work, relieving Dr. Peoples who then devoted himself to the evangelistic work.

For some time after this, the station was comprised of the Peoples, the Taylors, the Beaches, the Palmers, and Miss Starling. There were no further changes until 1918 when Dr. and Mrs. Beach went home on furlough. At that time Dr. Beach resigned from the mission and joined the U. S. Army. He was reappointed later and sent to Chiengrai. This left Nan without a physician, and Harvey Perkins, M. D., and Mrs. Perkins came in 1920. They stayed in Nan for three years and were then transferred to Chiengmai. Early in 1920 the Rev.

and Mrs. M. B. Palmer were transferred to Bangkok to take charge of the Bangkok Christian College. This left the boys' school of Nan without anyone in charge and Mr. and Mrs. Bronson were assigned to that work. Mrs. Bronson's health failed and they left the field inside of ten months after their arrival.

The present force in Nan comprises the Taylors, the Weisbeckers and the Colliers. The Colliers were assigned to Nan in 1924 and are just completing their first term of service on the field. The Rev. and Mrs. Homer Weisbecker arrived on the field and after a year of language study in Bangkok, arrived at Nan station in October 1926.

The Rev. Robt. Irwin and Mrs. Mary Irwin, M.D., have spent some time in Nan and so have also C. Denman, M. D., and Mrs. Denman.

CHAPTER XIII

THE NARRATIVE OF CHIENGRAI STATION

Established in 1897

THE opening of work in Chiengrai reminds one of the Apostle Paul's early experiences. Scarcely had the Rev. Daniel McGilvary, D.D. established himself in Chiengmai before he started to carry the Gospel message into the far distant parts. It was because of these early trips that groups of Christians were established in several centers in Chiengrai, at Pakuk in Kengtung State and at Muang Sai in French Cambodia. As one meets some of these early Christians who became followers of Jesus during those early trips to the north, we cannot but feel that he was one of the greatest evangelists that the mission has known.

Two other men stand out in the early history of Chiengrai: the Rev. W. Clifton Dodd, D. D., and W. A. Briggs, M. D. Dr. Dodd followed in the footsteps of Dr. McGilvary as one of our great touring evangelists. Beside the work he did in Chiengrai, it was largely because of his faith and efforts that the present work in Yunnan was opened up. Himself a fine linguist, he was able to present the Gospel in a clear and winsome way. Dr. Briggs filled the offices of physician, educator, pastor and builder and did all well. With the exception of one, all of the present buildings of the station were erected under his oversight, and by funds solicited by him. Others have worked with, or have come after, these two men in trying to carry on the work they so nobly began.

At the beginning of the work, because of wars and pestilence Chiengrai was very sparsely populated, but that condition has changed greatly within the past fifty years. In the migration to the north many Christian families have come from Chiengmai and

150

WILLIAM BRIGGS, M.D.

Lampang which have been a great aid in building up Christian communities. There are now eleven organized churches with a total membership of over 1400. The churches are widely separated, three being sixty or more miles distant from the mission station, another being over the border in Kengtung. Though organized into eleven churches, yet their membership is scattered throughout forty villages. Up to the present, most of these churches have been led and served by unpaid Elders, with help from evangelists in the mission center.

Chiengrai is Siam's most northern province covering a district of over seventy-five miles square. The main caravan trail to Kengtung and southern China passes through this province. The government is putting in good macadam roads, one of which goes on to the northern border. Possibly in no part of Siam has means of travel improved more than in Chiengrai. Trips that before took days can now be made in as many hours. Roads which before were teeming with pack ponies and human carriers, now see the familiar motorbus. Districts where rice could not be sold are now open to the markets of the world. Along with improved roads have come improved economic conditions, better educational opportunities, and a more stable form of government.

But we are here interested in the work of Christian missions. In 1896 Chiengrai was opened as a mission station, by the Rev. W. Clifton Dodd, D. D., and C. H. Denman, M. D., and because of the early starting of the work in many places, the work has greatly prospered. Although there are still many problems to be worked out, yet a start has been made which should make Chiengrai one of the strong centers of Christian influence in Siam. There are residences for three missionary families, with money in hand to build a fourth residence. There are also buildings for hospital, schools and church. During the time Chiengrai has been occupied as a mission station thirteen missionary families and three single women have helped with the work. Three Siamese men have been ordained for the ministry with several others in training. Assistants have been trained in the medical and educational departments so that the efforts of the missionaries are multiplied many times by the help received from the nationals.

The beginning of the work is most interesting and in many cases shows marvelous devotion to the cause of Christ. The first Christian was Nan Sawan one of the early converts to Christianity in Chiengmai. He was one of 2,500 people afterward conscripted from Chiengmai and Lampang to repopulate the district to the north of Chiengmai. At first he considered buying himself off, but upon the advice of Dr. McGilvary he decided to go. He soon had a group of believers gathered around him. With Nan Sawan as leader these were organized into the first church in Chiengrai. For several years they remained in Siamese territory, but later because of some trouble with the government they moved over into Kengtung. Their descendants now form the membership of the Pakuk church. This Church has sent three men to the Theological Training School where they took the vernacular course.

Soon after Dr. McGilvary made his first tour to the north, a Christian man, his four sons and their families, like Abraham of old, moved up to the new promised land and settled in Papau. It was not long before these, by their living and teaching, won three more families to join them in the observance of Christianity. Soon strong opposition developed from the local officials. They were forbidden to teach the new religion, and were finally sent in chains to the Prince of Chiengmai. Complaints were forwarded to the Prince stating that these Christians were obstructing the progress of the place by interfering with the laws laid down by the higher powers. The Prince gave them a thorough grilling, but the charges were not found true. Still, just to show his authority, he ordered the leader of the group to be lashed five times with the rattan. Then they were dismissed. Even with this persecution they in no way lessened their efforts for the work of God and their new religion. They bore manfully all difficulties, hardships and privations for the sake of their love for Him and His great love for them. Their numbers increased and now we see the results of their steadfastness in one of the strongest churches in Chiengrai. This church has just completed a small brick chapel at a cost of nearly one thousand dollars. This is the third chapel they have had. The first was made of bamboo, the second of teak and this one of brick. They have outgrown them one by one until even now the seventy-five families nearly fill the new chapel to overflowing. It is interesting to note that the first two men to be ordained to the Christian ministry are grandsons of this early convert to Christianity, and one is now pastor of the church his grandfather helped to establish.

In a village about eight miles from Chiengrai, fifty years ago there lived a teacher in one of the temple schools and very strict in his Buddhistic observances. His son was a trader, at times travelling over into Burma. On one of these trips he came into touch with Christianity. On his return he related to his father the various things he had seen and heard. His father was greatly moved by what his son told and desired to know more. Learning that in Chiengmai there was a man of white skin who had come to tell about the religion of Jesus, he arranged for his son and four others to go to Chiengmai to learn more and to get what literature they could. They remained one month and then returned to tell what they had heard. The result was that the five men and the old Buddhist teacher turned to Christ, and were the beginning of what is now known as the Suan Dawk church. This church has the honor of erecting the first brick chapel outside of the mission station. They were fifteen years in building it, but it now makes a fine center for their worship and social activities.

A native doctor one day received a portion of scripture. He became interested and walked thirty miles to see the missionary located at Chiengrai to find out more about the teachings of Jesus. As a result of his inquiries the missionary and an elder visited his village and the work was begun which has resulted in the organization of the Muang Pan church.

A missionary doctor took a young Christian as a servant. Along with his work he received daily instruction in Christian teachings. Later this missionary and his servant were sent to open a station at Nan. After the work was well started there the servant, who had become the leading elder in the church, was sent with his family out as a home missionary eight days journey from Nan into what is now a part of Chiengrai province. This medical evangelist began a work there, the outcome of which has become the organization of the Chiengkam church.

It would be interesting to search out the history of the beginnings of our other six churches, for no doubt like experiences could be found to show how the Spirit worked on the hearts of different ones to cause the birth of a new church here and there. Many tales might be told of hardships overcome, of persecution endured, and of consecrated service for Him. Here as well as in other lands there are those who according to their light serve the Master faithfully.

Kru Dee, Chiengrai's first ordained minister, is an example of one who has caught the spirit of service and has developed himself so that he has been instrumental in helping many to a better understanding of the Way. Until fifteen years of age he was kept at home without any educational opportunities. Then, after the death of his father, the way opened up for him to study six years in one of our mission schools. After this short course he started a school in his home town to pass on the knowledge he had thus gained. This school he kept going for seven years. When the Theological Training School opened in 1913 he was among the first to enter its doors. Finishing the three years course he was ordained to the Christian ministry. Since that time he has been of great help in carrying on the work of this station. Now others better trained will be able to carry on the work to which he with an unselfish and consecrated spirit has given the best years of his life.

Kru Suk, Chiengrai's second man to be ordained to the ministry has had a somewhat similar experience. Left an orphan at seven, he was taken by Dr. and Mrs. Dodd until he reached the age of fourteen. With them he received much of the training that has given him such a fine spirit in his present ministry. He then attended school until the age of twenty when he was called to serve his time in the army. The next few years he spent in establishing a home of his own. Soon after the opening of the Theological Training School he took the regular course. He is now serving as pastor of the Papau church. This church during the past ten years has prospered greatly under his leadership.

We should not close without a word of tribute to the band of Christian women who have done their share in building up the life of these churches. Two women by their strong outstanding characters did much to win several of the early Christian families to Christ, who later were among the charter members of the Muang Pan church. One woman with her husband settled in a non-Christian village. Soon she had a group of ten families meeting at her house on Sunday morning to join in Christian worship. Another woman moving to a far distant place was constantly seeking opportunity to hand a portion of scripture to an enquirer and to talk to him about the new way of life. These women have stood faithfully by their husbands, and in many cases have taken the lead in the upbuilding of the Kingdom.

As we bring this chapter to a close we cannot but feel that the Spirit of God has been working in no uncertain way, upon the hearts of these people, to lead them out into a better land which we trust is but the beginning of a larger movement towards Him.

CHAPTER XIV

THE NARRATIVE OF PITSANULOKE STATION

Established in 1899

PITSANULOKE: The name stands as a witness of the extent to which the religion of Gautama is dyed with the thought of Hinduism, for the name means, "Vishnu's world." Reverence for Vishnu, the second name in the great Hindu triad, has given his name to an important city on the banks of the Nan river and to a territory of 15,911 square miles in the Kingdom of Siam. It would be interesting to know just why this place was believed to be sacred to Vishnu, "the pervading one", but the writer knows no tradition concerning it. It is of no little interest, however, that Vishnu occupies the place in the Hindu triad corresponding to the place of Jesus in the Christian Trinity, and that the worship and beliefs of the Vaishnavites have many points in common with Christianity.

Within this world of Vishnu are to be found the places around which the beginnings of Siamese history center. Suko Tai, Sawankalok, and Pitsanuloke, are all ancient capitals rich in ruins and traditions. Everywhere are to be found influences that bind the minds of the people to the past and help to keep them loyal to their ancient faith. In the city of Pitsanuloke these influences center largely around the famous image of Buddha known as the Praputachinarat. Like the image of Diana at Ephesus, the idol is known throughout the entire country and receives the homage of kings. Seated in the attitude of meditation it has seen eight or perhaps ten centuries of time pass into oblivion, but the master workmanship of its makers has stood the test of years and it stands today as one of the most perfect examples of bronze idol-casting to be found

Padoongrart School, Pitsanuloke

(Built by Rev. Boon Tuan Boon Itt)

throughout the whole world. When royalty would have taken it to the national capital to adorn a new and beautiful temple there, local pride refused to permit its removal and thus bound Pitsanuloke more closely to its worship.

To the west and south of the Pitsanuloke Circle lies the Circle of Nakon Sawan, the City of Heaven. This Circle, covering an area of 16,278 square miles, is dependent upon the workers of Pitsanuloke station for its Christian culture. From Paknampo as far north as Utradit the field is accessible by railroad, and from Paknampo the Me Ping and Me Yom rivers afford routes to Raheng and Suko Tai, except during the dry season when these rivers are not navigable. If the missionary at Pitsanuloke wishes to visit the eastern part of his field, around Lomsak and Petchaboon, he must hire carriers, don his hiking clothes or mount his horse and make the journey overland in this way. His parish, an area almost as large as the state of Maine, extends from the border of French Indo-China on the east to Burma on the west and has a population of 750,000.

Into this vast, but then unoccupied territory, there came in the year 1897, a new influence. The Rev. B. T. Boon Itt and family, his cousin Kru Tien Pow and family, and Walter B. Toy, M.D., and family had braved the tedious two hundred and fifty mile journey by boat from Bangkok to open a new work in the "far north". After spending some time seeking a favorable place to settle, they finally chose Pitsanuloke as the best center from which to work and began unhesitatingly to establish themselves. They were kindly received by the officials and through their good-will were able to secure a valuable site on the east side of the Nan river. The work was so encouraging from the first that the Mission was requested to open a permanent station and in 1899 Pitsanuloke became a part of the Siam mission. Dr. and Mrs. Toy left on their furlough in 1898 leaving all the work in charge of Kru Boon Itt and his helpers. During their absence, the government reclaimed the site on the east bank of the river and Kru Boon Itt was compelled to seek another location.

On the west side of the Nan river, just south of the Monton barracks, was an old dilapidated temple known as Wat Rang, or Wat Klong Madan. The place was a wilderness and an abode of tigers but the officials were willing to lease it and Kru Boon Itt, nothing daunted by the task of reclamation, rented the property. This lease has been retained but instead of a wilderness there is now a beautiful compound. No one looking at the property to-day would dream that it was once rented because it was considered worthless.

So much has been written about Kru Boon Itt that to give a history of his life at this point would be superfluous. But the story of how he reclaimed the old, overgrown temple ground, to the knowledge of the present writer, has not been told and since it casts more light on the character of the man, it seems worth while to include it here. For this story we are indebted to Nai Jerm, now Mün Wai, the oldest Christian in Pitsanuloke community.

The property that Kru Boon Itt had rented was a typical Siamese jungle. Aside from the dense growth of bamboo and jungle grass, there were five or six large white ant hills, each twelve or fifteen feet high, to be leveled. Superstition prevented the obtaining of local help for this work so Kru Boon Itt and the small group of followers he had gathered about him set to work to do it themselves. Mün Wai was especially impressed with the size of the ants found in these hills. Some, he says, were as large as a good sized beetle, and from these they graduated down to the common size. Kru Boon Itt was impressed also and took pictures of the large ones to send to his friends in America. In addition to the ant hills there was also a large Bo tree which seven or eight people joining hands could scarcely encircle. The work of digging this out devolved upon the same group, for no true Buddhist will help destroy a Bo tree. Led by Kru Boon Itt himself, whose stories "made the work seem like play", Kru Tien Pow, Kru Tien Boon, and the others threw themselves heartily into the task and soon the place was ready for the erection of buildings.

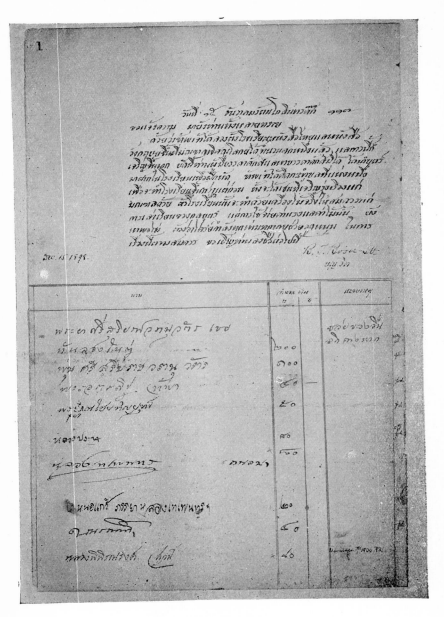

Subscription List
for
Padoongrart School, Pitsanuloke

Expenditures

School Building { *Padoong Rart School* / 7½ × 4 robs. 2 stories high }

Material Cost of Main Building.

	T.	a.
Posts 34 @ 6 =	204	00
Royalty on 16 logs	64	13
Sawing logs at Chek Chongs	77	46
" squaring posts (Gov. Prara)	142	63
Mai Yaong planks Subtotal 39 @ 4 ⁿ	170	40
Teak planks 1ˢᵗ stuff ₱ 12 0 0 @ 24 =	690	00
2ⁿᵈ 12 12 0 0 " 44 =	561	00
3½ 1 4 0 12 " 53	67	07
3 0 5 0 0 " 60 =	11	12
Bamboo	4	00
Grass - Yah kah 2375 @ 4/2 . plus "trunk"	107	32
Nails, screws, locks, hinges + netting	135	00
Cost of labor. Putting up the building	1280	00
" Filling in the first floor with earth	77	48
Ticals -	3599	59

Furnishings.

Book cases 8 @ 7	56	00
Benches 4 @ 4/2	18	00
Chairs 36 @ 2	72	00
Desk 1	12	00
Lamps 4 @ 8/2	34	00
Lamp shades	1	16
Plates	9	00
Spoons and forks	33	00
Glasses 5 dozs @ 1	5	00
Tics	240	16

Cost

of

Padoongrart School, Pitsanuloke

The school established by Kru Boon Itt upon his arrival in Pitsanuloke, enjoyed the confidence of the community from the beginning. In 1898 the records show that it had an attendance of forty boys. When it was moved to the new site on the west side of the river Kru Boon Itt appealed to the community for funds to erect a building and was able to obtain a sum of more than four thousand ticals for this purpose. With this money he built a substantial two-storey teak building which served as dormitory and school room. With the rent allowance granted by the Board he built for himself a bamboo house. A church was built at the same time. The goodwill of the officials toward the work of Kru Boon Itt is shown by the way in which they contributed toward the upkeep of the school. Mün Wai writes that one official gave fifty oxen to be used as food for the boys, and offerings of meat, rice, and vegetables were common. At that time, the only time in its history, the school was entirely self-supporting.

The success and popularity of Kru Boon Itt at Pitsanuloke seem to have been due to two outstanding characteristics. First, a determination to make his work truly indigenous, combined with a willingness to work with his own hands to accomplish his purpose ; second, a genial, sympathetic, Christian disposition and a well-trained body. It is said of him that his boys would stand with open mouths watching him climb trees, or do other feats of physical strength. On Saturdays he visited in the homes of his pupils, or took his boys on hikes. And so he won the hearts of the people as no one else has since been able to do.

Padoongrart, upon Kru Boon Itt's transfer to Bangkok in 1901, was placed under the direction of his cousin Kru Tien Pow who successfully continued the work. In 1903 Kru Tien Pow followed his cousin and the school passed into the hands of the Rev. A. W. Cooper, who with his family had been transferred from Rajburi, and it remained in his charge until his re-transfer to the work in Rajburi in 1906. At that time the Rev. R. C. Jones and family were called from the work at Petchaburi to take charge of the educational and evangelistic work at Pitsanuloke. Mr. Jones retained his position as head of the school until 1913 when the Rev. H. W. Stewart was appointed to the place. For two years the school remained under his care and then passed back into the hands of Mr. Cooper who had been again transferred from Rajburi after the closing of that station. From that time until the coming of the Rev. N. C. Elder in 1927, the work of the school remained for the most part in Mr. Cooper's hands.

Although Padoongrart was perhaps the first institution established in Pitsanuloke, it found itself by the year 1920 outstripped in numbers by the younger Padoong Nari school for girls The latter having outgrown the buildings provided for it, and funds for the erection of new buildings not being available at that time, the old "Boon Itt" building was turned over to the girls' school, and Padoongrart was moved to temporary buildings that had been erected on a newly-leased plot of land near the home of the Lord Lieutenant. This was a deserted temple ground also, and incidentally the one to which the priests from Wat Rang had gone after its destruction. The plan at the time was to erect permanent buildings for the girls' school on this property, but before this could be accomplished the Government reclaimed the site, and as compensation sold to the Mission a small plot of land on the east side of the river, and leased with it sufficient land for the erection of a new plant. The change to the east side made it advisable to transfer Padoongrart rather than Padoong Nari and in 1926 the boys' school took possession of the new property. The growth and success of the Pitsanuloke boys' school is not all due to the efforts of the missionaries who have had it in charge. Without the help of such efficient head teachers as Kru Chuan Chrisnawan, Kru Boon Tam Rongrangsee and Kru Seng Lan Chairatana much less would have been accomplished.

Boon Itt's passion for education was shared by his wife, Nang Kim Hoch, a graduate of the Harriet M. House School and an earnest Christian. While he was building up the school for boys, his wife taught a group of girls, using her own house as a class room. Such were the beginnings of the Padoong Nari school for girls. After the departure of Nang Kim Hoch there is no record that the work was maintained but with the arrival of Mrs. R. C. Jones an effort was made to revive it. This attempt did not meet with very great success for reasons unknown to the present writer, and it was not until Mrs. Carl J. Shellman assumed the principalship of the school in 1913 that the work can be said to have been established· Under the direction of Mrs. Shellman it grew to such proportions that in 1914 a new building was erected for its use in front of the medical house. The station at this time asked for a single lady to take charge of the school, and one year later Miss Helen McClure was assigned by the Mission to this work. During the ten years of her stay in Pitsanuloke the school outgrew its quarters, as we have seen, the roll increasing from twenty-three in 1915 to seventy in 1925. During the most of this time Miss McClure was assisted by able Siamese teachers, of whom Kru Pin Chantrasut and Kru Jaranai Sarakoset deserve special mention for the able way in which they filled the important position of head teacher. When Miss McClure was transferred to Chiengmai in 1925, the Station appointed Mrs. H. W. Stewart to be principal of Padoong Nari. Soon afterwards the husband of Kru Jaranai, an army officer, was transferred to another place and Mrs. Stewart was left with the entire responsibility of the work in her hands. That she has borne it ably is shown, by the fact that the school has held its own in spite of the reduction made in the forces at the Barracks from which a large number of the children come. Late in 1927 Mrs. E. H. Freeman arrived from Lampoon to take over the work at Padoong Nari. Ill health has caused her early resignation, and the school now reverts again into the hands of Mrs. Stewart and her head teacher Kru Som Boon Mahasakon, until the arrival of Miss Winnie Burr who has been appointed by the Board to fill the place.

Conscientious differences of opinion often result in great good. Early in the year 1897 the Mission located Dr. Walter B. Toy and family at Samray, against his wishes, and he consented reluctantly to the arrangement. It was perhaps for this reason that later in the same year he fitted out a large house boat and invited the Rev. B. T. Boon Itt and family to accompany him on a tour to the north. From that tour they did not return but remained to open the work at Pitsanuloke.

The first hospital at Pitsanuloke was Dr. Toy's large boat. Leaving on furlough in 1898 he did not have time to erect a hospital until his return. During his absence Kru Boon Itt carried on the medical work. Mün Wai states that a bamboo hospital had been erected before Dr. Toy's departure but this does not agree with the record of Mr. Cooper, who states that the boat served throughout the time until Dr. Toy's return. Be that as it may, immediately upon his return Dr. Toy set about to erect a place to work and a place to live. He had learned the art of building in his youth and so was fitted for this work. The house had just been completed and some of his goods moved in when it was destroyed by a jungle fire. This misfortune aroused the sympathy of the community and sufficient funds were subscribed, when supplemented by a grant from the Board, to build a comfortable bungalow which served as the medical residence until 1925, when it was replaced by the present substantial dwelling erected by W. T. Lyon, M. D. At the same time Dr. Toy secured sufficient money from the Lord Lieutenant to build a hospital. While not versatile in his use of the language, Dr. Toy had a splendid knowledge of the medical vernacular and the work under his care prospered. He remained in the station until his furlough in 1905. Shortly after reaching his home in Toronto, Canada, he suffered the loss of his wife. Because of this and other circumstances he did not return to Siam under the Presbyterian Board, but in a short time came back in the service of the Government. Afterward he took up independent Christian work at Puket, South Siam.

Carl Shellman, M.D.

During most of his term in Pitsanuloke, Dr. Toy was assisted in the hospital by Nai Soon See, a graduate of the Bangkok Christian High School. This man had a command of three languages and was very capable in his work.

Dr. Toy was succeeded in the station by C. C. Walker, M. D., whose ability attracted attention beyond the mission circles. Unfortunately Mrs. Walker died in a very short time after reaching Pitsanuloke and her husband, overcome by his grief, was not satisfied to stay with the work, so was transferred to Bangkok where he served until 1914.

The place left vacant by Dr. Walker was filled late in 1906 by Carl J. Shellman, M. D., who, until his death 22 March 1919, was the "beloved physician" of the Pitsanuloke community. Kru Soon Tiensiri, who was for many years the assistant of Dr. Shellman, says that he was known and loved by everyone from the common people to those of rank. To save people was the passion of his soul and to do it he gave himself unreservedly to the work. The old hospital was improved and added to, but by 1914 the work had outgrown its capacity and the present building was erected. A dispensary was opened in the city market under the care of Nai Kim Sun Suarun, who was later put in charge of a dispensary at Sawankalok and his place at Pitsanuloke taken by Nai Dee Sawaranaw. Medicines were sold at Pechai, Pechit and Hua Dong, and the receipts of the work amounted to six hundred ticals a month. But at the height of his success the leader was taken. Cholera had broken out in the community and he responded to the challenge of the enemy. While giving himself to the staying of the disease he did not unload his share of other duties on his fellow-workers. His colleague the Rev. A. W. Cooper writes, "Another painfully memorable experience was in March 1919: Dr. Shellman had worked like a beaver all day over arrangements for the closing entertainment of the girls' school, not even telling his wife he was ailing, then slipped home to treat himself for cholera. My wife and I next door had no intimation or suspicion of anything amiss until the next morning when we were called over only to find him in collapse and see him breathe his last ". He saved others, himself he would not save. His remains rest in the Christian cemetery of Pitsanuloke. The hospital he built bears his name in memory of his sacrifice.

For two years following the death of Dr. Shellman, the medical work of the station was under the direction of Miss J. A. Christensen, R. N., whose work among women was especially successful. However, not being a physician, she was limited in the scope of her work. It was with joy that W. T. Lyon, M. D., was welcomed in 1921. During the five years of his residence, the work of the hospital continued to prosper. The present large two-storey dwelling was erected, an up-to-date surgical ward was added to the hospital, and four large concrete tanks, sufficient for the hospital needs, were built. But again the leader was taken. Due to ill health and to other circumstances Dr. Lyon left the work in 1925 and Pitsanuloke was again without medical protection. Early in 1927, J. V. Horst, M. D., and family were appointed to fill this vacancy. Their coming to the hospital in July of the present year has been greeted by an increased interest in the community and promises well for the future.

In the two years intervening between the departure of Dr. Lyon and the arrival of Dr. Horst, the hospital was under the supervision of the Rev. H. W. Stewart and the first hospital assistant, Kru Intoom Sudaharat, did faithful service. While limited by their lack of knowledge, to the treatment of minor cases they were able to keep the hospital on a self-supporting basis. Kru Intoom first began his work under the direction of W. A. Briggs, M. D., of Chiengrai. In 1918 he came to Pitsanuloke as assistant to Dr. Shellman and has continued his connection with the medical work ever since that time. Capable in an unusual degree for a man lacking technical training, he is in truth the " right hand man " of the work. To him and to others before him must go much of the honor for the stability and success of the hospital.

Rev. A. W. Cooper

We have already noted that the first buildings erected in Pitsanuloke were a school and a church. The latter was an open sala in which services were held regularly from the beginning. Mün Wai writes that Kru Boon Itt made tours to Petchaboon and other points, so touring trails were broken early. Dr. Toy took a deep interest in the evangelistic work and in his large boat toured north to the Laos boundary and west as far as Raheng. It was his custom to tour during the rainy season, an idea contrary to that followed by most missionaries. During the years 1901-03 Dr. and Mrs. Toy were alone in the station and the minutes show that several station meetings were held while they were moored to the river bank at some point along the Nan river.

In 1903 the educational and evangelistic work of the station passed into the hands of Mr. Cooper. For three years he served the field, going by boat or by horse to the various points. At that time Pitsanuloke was a very isolated place The railroad had not yet reached so far north, and even bicycles were of no use because there were no roads. Mr. Cooper writes that when they first arrived in Pitsanuloke they found it difficult to obtain suitable food, and that they suffered other inconveniences due to the inaccessibilty. of the place.

The names of Mr. and Mrs. Cooper are so closely bound up with the history of Pitsanuloke station that no phase of the work can be described without including them in it. They had an active part throughout sixteen of the thirty years of the station's life. Although called upon to fill important offices in the mission, Mr. Cooper has given the greater part of his effort to the establishing of this work. He writes, "I put in many years of plodding work there with few, if any, high spots, and waited long for really encouraging results." The marks of his efforts are plainly visible on the foundation stones of the Pitsanuloke work.

Mr. Cooper was re-transferred to Rajburi in 1906, and the Rev. and Mrs. R. C. Jones and family were called from Petchaburi to fill the vacancy in Pitsanuloke.   Mr. Jones was an enthusiastic evangelistic worker and until the end of his service in 1918 gave much of his time to touring.   Every year a tour was made to Petchaboon, a journey of ten days by horse, and in addition, visits were made to other parts.   Under his leadership the Christian community of Pitsanuloke was organized as a church in 1908.   Their place of worship was an open sala, or rest house, but by 1917 the church had grown from sixteen to fifty-three members and the need of a new and larger building led to the erection of the present chapel, for which the money, more than five thousand ticals, was raised throughout the Siamese churches.   At the present time the church numbers sixty-six, and has a constituency of one hundred and seventy.

Late in the year 1911, the Rev. and Mrs. H. W. Stewart were transferred from Rajburi to the Pitsanuloke field.   While not among the pioneers of the work they have had a large share in its growth. Since their coming they have seen service in every department, and with the exception of a short time spent at the Boon Itt Institute at Bangkok, their residence has been continuous.   It is always diffi-cult to evaluate any work until it is completed, and whoever writes the history for the second Centential Celebration will be better able to tell the extent of Mr. and Mrs. Stewart's influence in Pitsanuloke. The present writer can only state definitely that their work will have a permanent niche in the annals of this place.

Unfortunately there are no records of the work done by the evangelistic helpers and by the individual Christians who have done their part in the construction of the Pitsanuloke work. Among these are Kru Boon Mee Boribuna, who for seventeen years has been la-boring in this field ; Kru Seng Saa Chai Ratana and his brother Kru Seng Lan, who have contributed in both the evangelistic and educa-tional fields ; Kru Boon Tam Rongrangsee and Kru Ming Boribuna and Kru Boon Mark Gistarn, all graduates of our boys' school that have come back to preach or to teach.   To these should be added the names of Christian servants who have aided in poling boats or

Mrs. Emma Parker Cooper

carrying goods in order that the field might be cultivated. Nor would it be fair to omit mention of the girls who have gone out from Padoong Nari to the service of their fellow Siamese either as nurses or teachers.

Pitsanuloke: It is still Vishnu's World, but were Vishnu a living god who could sense change, he would realize that the new influence that came to Pitsanuloke thirty-two years ago is slowly changing, not the name of the place, but the hearts of the people into Christnaloks, and "The City of Heaven", into "The City of our God."

———•◄•►•———

CHAPTER XV

THE NARRATIVE OF SRITAMARAT STATION

Established in 1900

THE story of the founding of the Sritamarat mission station really goes back to the early eighties when Nai Kurt and his wife, Nang Make, and a young man left Nakawn Sritamarat by sailing boat, intending to go to Bangkok about 450 miles away, to secure medical aid for Nai Kurt. En route, the boat put into the mouth of the Petchaburi river. Meeting a Christian there and learning that there was a foreign physician and a hospital at Petchaburi, the party decided not to continue the journey to Bangkok, some two days or more distant, but to go to Petchaburi instead. While there the three professed belief in Jesus Christ and were baptised. Nai Kurt was given some special instruction and was supplied with scriptures and other Christian books and then returned to his old home to act as evangelist there.

During the years that followed a number of persons, converted through the influence of Nai Kurt, were baptised at Petchaburi or at the Samray church in Bangkok. No missionary had yet visited the place. Finally the Rev. E. P. Dunlap, D. D., made a trip by sail-boat along the west coast of the Gulf of Siam, hoping to reach Sritamarat. It being late in the season he was turned back by the rough weather. In 1892 the Rev. J. A. Eakin, D. D., and the Rev. C. E. Eckels were appointed by the Mission to visit the west coast and report upon a suitable place for establishing a mission station. They went down in April 1893 by a small coasting-steamer, and were kindly received by the acting-Governor who supplied them quarters during their stay there. They remained about ten days. On

Rev. and Mrs. Charles Eckels

the Sabbaths, services were held in the home of Nai Kurt. Two evening talks were given with the sciopticon showing pictures of the life of Christ and Old Testament stories: large audiences attended. Dr. Eakin was given an opportunity to preach before a gathering at the largest temple: colporteur work was done in the market-place. Dr. Eakin made a trip to the town of Pak-Panang where some Christians were residing. Returning part way by sail-boat, a call was made at the town of Bandon, farther up the coast, to look up a few Christians there, and the party joined the steamer at a point previously agreed upon farther up the coast. In August of that year, Mr. Eckels accompanied by Kru Yuan Tieng-Yok of Bangkok and Kru Boon of Petchaburi, made a second visit to Sritamarat.

Dr. and Mrs. E. P. Dunlap having returned from America early in 1893, they again began visiting Sritamarat as frequently as possible. Dr. Dunlap and others continued to carry on the work during the next few years, using Bangkok as a base. In 1895, the Siamese Government permitted the Mission to lease the piece of ground since known as the "West Compound" on which are now located the first mission residence, the church building and the boys' school building. That same year a church was organized with thirty-one charter members. Some of these had been baptised the year previous at Sritamarat and some were transferred from the Petchaburi and Samray churches.

Soon after the organization of this church, the people built a chapel with board floor and bamboo walls on the lot leased to the Mission by the Government. It should be stated here that Nai Kurt, the first evangelist in the place, had died before this church was organized. During one of Dr. Dunlap's visits to Sritamarat Nai Kurt had received a knife wound on the leg while coming out by night to visit Dr. Dunlap: the wound resulted in the death of this faithful evangelist.

From the time that the lot was secured, Dr. and Mrs. Dunlap spent several months each year in Sritamarat. They first built on the lot, a small shack in which they themselves lived one or more seasons. Later they built a small frame cottage which they occupied for several seasons and then it became the living-place for Dr. Hamilton and Mr. Eckels. Later—after the station was actually opened—Mr. and Mrs. Eckels occupied this house during the first year. It then was made to serve for about four years as a dispensary and temporary hospital. Later it was used for a boys' school building and afterward, with some addition, it served for both boys' and girls' schools until it was finally torn down in 1915.

In the Fall of 1899 the Mission appointed the Rev. Charles E. Eckels and Guy Hamilton, M. D., to open this station. Leaving Mrs. Hamilton in Bangkok and Mrs. Eckels and her children at Rajburi, Dr. Hamilton and Mr. Eckels arrived at Sritamarat on 5 March 1900. A dispensary was opened in a little lean-to room adjoining the chapel. Work was at once begun on a permanent residence. Finding that this would require longer than was at first supposed owing to the difficulty of procuring materials, a second small frame house, was built for the accommodation of Dr. and Mrs. Hamilton. Mrs. Eckels and the children and Mrs. Hamilton were then brought on and the station was fully manned the latter part of June.

In less than three months the condition of Mrs. Hamilton's health made it imperative that they leave the station and a few months later they left Siam permanently. They are now stationed at Shunteh, Shantung mission, China.

During these earlier months of the Sritamarat mission, the lot now occupied by the hospital and physician's residence was turned over to the mission and work was begun on getting it into shape for building, and the foundations of the residence were laid there. The residence on the other compound—the " West Compound "—was occupied by the Eckels family just a year from the day the ground was first broken for it, but the house was still far from completed. The second residence was erected in 1902 and finished early the following year.

William Swart, M. D.

During the latter part of 1901 Dr. and Mrs. Swart were with Mr. and Mrs. Eckels for a few months and Mrs. Swart was taken ill and died there. In the early part of 1902, Dr. and Mrs. Harry Boyd arrived to take up medical work but had only been in Sritamarat four months when her health required a change. At the close of that year Dr. Swart returned to take up the medical work of Sritamarat and was instrumental in raising funds and building the present hospital building which was opened in 1909. In this he was greatly assisted by Dr. E. P. Dunlap.

When the station had been occupied less than two years the Siamese people contributed funds and changed the bamboo walls of the chapel to board. A little later these were painted. Early in 1909 steps were taken towards securing a new church building. A Building Committee, consisting of four Siamese and Dr. Swart, was appointed and funds were contributed regularly for this purpose during a period of two years. The contributions during a third year provided the furnishings. In the Fall of 1912 a neat brick church building was dedicated free from debt. No money had been received from America for either the building or the furnishings. Most of the funds were supplied locally by the people and missionaries of Sritamarat but some additional help was given by most of the other churches of South Siam and a few individuals. A little more than one third of the sum required for the building was supplied by one man in the congregation—Towkaa Soon Nguan. Dr. Swart who had been the moving spirit in the matter of building and who had prepared the plans and had had the oversight of the work of building until the walls were up and ready for the roof-timbers, left on furlough during the Spring before the building was completed and did not return to Siam so never saw the completed church building.

The year following the opening of the station a small school for boys was opened and this was maintained for two years without expense to the Board. It then lapsed for a few years as the teacher was needed in another line of work. Beginning in 1904 a small girls' school was conducted for about three years on the veranda of the " West residence "—also without expense to the Board. It was later closed when the teacher moved away.

Near the close of 1907, the boys' school was re-opened under the Rev. R.W. Post who had come to the station when Mr. and Mrs. Eckels went on furlough in 1906. In 1909 the school came under the care of Miss L. J. Cooper who was transferred to Sritamarat from Bangkok for this special post. With the exception of the time Miss Cooper was on furlough, during which period Miss Beatrice Moeller carried on the boys' school for her, the school was under Miss Cooper's care until her death in November 1918. The boys' school then passed under the care of the Rev. S. E. Kelsey for four years. The brick building which the boys' school now occupies was completed in 1916. It stands on the site of that early Dunlap cottage which housed the boys' school for seven years. When Mr. Kelsey went on furlough in 1923, Mr. Eckels was placed in charge of the school but a year later he and Mrs. Eckels were sent to Nan and a year later to Prae and the Rev. F. L. Snyder took charge of the school from the beginning of 1924, carrying it until he left on furlough in February 1927. Mr. Kelsey did relieve Mr. Snyder for about four months after his return from furlough but, Sritamarat being without a resident physician at the time, it was thought better to transfer Mr. Kelsey to Petchaburi where he could be under the care of a physician as his health was failing. When Mr. Snyder left on furlough, Mr. Eckels, who had by that time returned from North Siam, again took over the work until the time of his leaving for U. S. A. approached. Mr. Snyder, who had meanwhile returned from furlough in May, was again placed in charge of the school in June 1928.

In 1909 the present girls' school was opened under the supervision of Miss Cooper in an annex to the same cottage that housed the boys' school. While the boys' school building was in process of erection, both schools were under the direction of Miss Moeller and were held

Miss Larissa J. Cooper

under the "West house." In 1915 the girls' school was transferred to the "North Compound" where it still continues in rooms in the basement of the mission residence. It has been under the care of Mrs. Eckels, Miss Moeller and Mrs. Snyder. Miss McCague took over the school when Mrs. Snyder went on furlough and it still remains under her care. During the past few years it has greatly increased in numbers, having at the present time an enrollment of about eighty,—of whom more than thirty-five are boarders.

The "North Compound" was leased from the Government in 1909 and a brick residence was erected on it, during that and the following years. It was first occupied by Dr. and Mrs. Wachter who joined the station in 1911.

In 1916 a fourth residence was completed on the same lot. This was converted into a dormitory for the girls' school when Mrs. Snyder had charge of the school.

When Dr. Swart left the station in 1912 the medical work went under the care of Dr. Wachter until the arrival of Dr. and Mrs. P. W. Van Meter near the close of 1913. Dr. Wachter then took up the evangelistic work when Mr. and Mrs. Eckels went on leave in 1914. After their return in 1915 Dr. and Mrs. Wachter gave their attention to evangelistic touring as long as it was possible for Dr. Wachter to do so. Near the close of 1917 Dr. Wachter was transferred to Trang station—then known as Tap Tieng. Mrs. Wachter had gone to the U. S. A. in 1916.

A few weeks before Dr. Wachter moved to Trang, Dr. and Mrs. Van Meter were obliged to leave the station very suddenly because of the condition of Mrs. Van Meter's health—getting off in less than forty-eight hours from the time it was settled that they must go. From that time until the arrival of Dr. McDaniel and family in June 1920 the work at the hospital was under the direction of Mr. Eckels with Kru Chaang as first-assistant.

In 1922 Mr. and Mrs. Snyder, just returned from the U. S. A., joined the station a short time before Mr. and Mrs. Eckels went on furlough.   Dr. and Mrs. McDaniel were obliged to leave in the Fall of 1924 on account of the serious health condition of Mrs. McDaniel. They were detained in U. S. A. because of serious surgical operations which both Dr. and Mrs. McDaniel were forced to undergo and did not return to the field until the close of 1926.

In 1922 Dr. McDaniel began special work in behalf of the lepers of the Sritamarat region.   Injections of chaulmoogra oil were started ; a lot was secured and one building was erected on it, though this building was not completed until after Dr. McDaniel had left for America.   Nothing further was done toward developing the homes for lepers until after Dr. McDaniel's return in 1926, though the regular treatment of the lepers who came for oil-injections was carried out by Dr. T. T. Wen, then hospital first-assistant, who had been trained by the English Presbyterian missionaries at Swatow, China.   After Dr. McDaniel's return however, work was pushed vigorously and has made such strides that the numbers under treatment during one month are out of date by the time another month has rolled by.   Considerable sums of money have been contributed by persons both inside and outside of Siam. His Majesty's Government has given considerable assistance by turning over to the leper work an old building which had been used for a barracks. This building has provided considerable material for the erection of leper homes.   At present there are three buildings for men and two for women.

In closing this sketch of Sritamarat it seems fitting that a word of tribute should be paid to Nang Make, wife of Nai Kurt, and one of the first three persons from Sritamarat to accept Christ. Her name heads the list of charter members of the Bethlehem Church.   When the station was first established, Nang Make volunteered to come and live with Mrs. Eckels and help care for the children.   This she did until finally the family went on leave in 1906.   After the new hospital was opened she served as matron there for about seven years.   Then for about eight more she served as Bible-woman, going on tours with Dr. and Mrs. Wachter and later making some tours with Mr. and Mrs. Eckels, teaching and selling scriptures both in the city and at points outside the city, as long as she was able to go about. For a number of years she lived on the " North Compound" with a grand-niece who was teacher in the girls' school. Lately she has gone to live in the city at a place not far from her former home there. She is now about eighty years of age but still comes to church on Sabbaths whenever she is able. It is a pleasant sight to watch her sing without a book " Phuak sit kong Jesu kow luen me ti phung "—" The people of Jesus, they only have a refuge. "

This in brief, is the story of Sritamarat station. Mistakes there have been. May God forgive them ! And if there has been anything that has helped to bring His Kingdom in this place, to Him be all the glory.

CHAPTER XVI

THE NARRATIVE OF TRANG STATION

Established in 1910

In the year 1910, on November the tenth, when the railroad was being projected south of Petchaburi, and a few miles of track had been laid north from Kantang, then intended as the Penang terminus, Trang station had its birth. At first it bore the name Tap Tieng. The Rev. E. P. Dunlap, D. D., and Mrs. Dunlap sailed from Bangkok, around by Singapore to Penang—up to Kantang in a small Malay pig-cargo boat—on up the river in a decrepit steam launch. L. C. Bulkley, M. D., left Bangkok later, walked the five days overland from Sritamarat and reached the tiny house in an abandoned pepper garden which meant home, an hour or so before Dr. and Mrs. Dunlap arrived. It was late afternoon and no carts to transport food, clothing, and bedding were allowed over the mile and a half of road between the river landing and the house. Kru Thoon,—Chinese evangelist,—Kru Juang,—hospital assistant,—and a Siamese evangelist, with the cook and "boy" made up the party. There was one Christian family to welcome the pioneers. In those days all mail was brought by relays of carriers—six days' walk from Sritamarat to Kantang, and the missionaries must receive and send their mail by messenger to Kantang, two more days' travel, until later the little village of Tap Tieng was dignified with a post office.

For seven months the hospital cottage was the only dwelling: originally just three small rooms intended for a bachelor. It was crowded to the limit when Mrs. Bulkley joined the station force in April. During that hot season Mrs. Dunlap often crawled under the bed to escape the sun pouring in through seams in the outside wall

Rev. E. P. Dunlap, D.D.

of their west room. By the end of May, Dr. and Mrs. Dunlap moved into a small bamboo house (afterwards converted into a stable) on the other compound where they lived nine months watching the building of their home.

On Christmas Eve 1911, Miss J. H. Christensen, R. N., sent to help in the medical work, arrived in Kantang and was handed the undelivered telegram she had sent from Penang to the missionaries at Trang. A group of Englishmen engaged in railway construction were celebrating at the home of Mr. Knight; Miss Christensen was made welcome at the dinner and one of the men gave up his house for the night—there was no hotel in the whole Siam peninsula. She was in time for the Christmas festivities at the station the next day, doubly welcome as baby Katherine was expected in a few days. The house, in the process of being remodelled and enlarged, had not a door or window that could be closed at night. Not many months afterward, four robbers came to the house one night—straight from a goodly haul at a Chinese place, and that same year another kind of visit was made to the other compound: Dr. Dunlap found tiger tracks one morning.

During the first years of the station Dr. Dunlap was very active. Besides his many duties and interests he had been asked by H. E. Phya Ratsada to inspect all the temple schools in the Province. He did a great deal of travelling about and his carriage and pair of Delhi ponies were a familiar sight. Many distinguished visitors came and were charmed with the hospitality of their home; the humblest and poorest received the same loving welcome. On one of his tours while at Panga, Dr. Dunlap received an injury when a rung of the ladder leading up to one of the houses broke under his weight. Two subsequent acccidents while driving in Trang and in America caused much suffering for years. Dr. Dunlap died in Trang on 29 March 1918 surrounded by the people he loved, and who loved him with touching devotion. Interment was in the hillside cemetery,—the gift of his friend H. E. Phya Ratsada. H. R. H. Prince Damrong in a letter to the Rev. J. B. Dunlap, D. D., among other things, said in tribute "He became my personal friend and I consider him to be the true type of missionary" because of "his large-mindedness, lack of prejudice and respect for what is good in the beliefs of others". We who lived in the station with Dr. Dunlap know how he gave unstintingly and unceasingly of his time, strength and money to any and all who sought him, high or low, rich or poor; it is literally true that he would have given the coat off his back to one in need. Mrs. Dunlap continued on in the station for five years, then retired and after two years in America, passed away in December 1925.

H. E. Phya Ratsada, High Commissioner of the six south-western Provinces, had offered to build a hospital if the mission would establish work somewhere in this southern field. Dr. Dunlap on his annual tours in this region had felt the greatest opportunity was here in Tap, Tieng; the wisdom of this choice was confirmed a few years later by the transfer of the seat of Government from Kantang to Tap Tieng: then the town took the name of the province—Trang. In the High Commissioner's scheme of things, Trang was to have an important place. Besides its many natural attractions, His Excellency saw its possibilities in copra, nutmeg, rubber, tin, and cattle for export. He had built a motor road for fifty miles across the peninsula, from the river to the Inland Sea and from Kantang to Sritamarat a hundred miles; he used and kept these roads in perfect condition; and at the entrance to the mountain pass, he maintained a lovely park with guest cottages. His plans included a sanatorium on "Soi Dow," a peak of some five thousand feet near the park. His Excellency and his nephew the Governor, were both brought to an untimely end by revolver shots in February 1913: the mission doctor and trained nurse were in attendance. Not only was the loss to Trang inestimable but organized crime increased alarmingly; gangs of hooded men in black would come to a house, noisily enough, by torch or moonlight, spike all paths, post sentries and then go to work. One such attack resulted in the murder of an Austrian on a rubber estate, when Miss Chris-

Mrs. E. P. Dunlap

tensen was alone at the station, and hers was the painful task of caring for the body and attending to the burial alone.

For some twenty years Trang had been visited by itinerating missionaries. Many have heard of the first Christian who was won by a tract distributed in the market-place by the Rev. John Carrington, D. D. Of his descendants of the third generation, all are Christians,—one is a successful contractor, one is an evangelist and one is second-assistant in the Sritamarat hospital: and the daughter of one is having a year at the Wattana Wittiya Academy preparatory to teaching in the mission girls' school in Trang. Among the early converts were two who had been head-monks in Buddhist temples; both became evangelists. Kru Sook the elder who died in service, had a lovable and magnetic personality above the ordinary. Once when a Tesa (High-Commissioner) called a congress of religions in the market building, Kru Sook presented Christianity before the several hundred assembled in an acceptable and winsome manner. The younger Kru Loop has conducted the church service most of the time since Dr. Wachter's withdrawal from active mission service.

Market-day in Trang is an " event " that " happens " every third day. Hundreds and thousands of country people come into town. Characteristically, Dr. Dunlap saw the opportunity and from the first month of the station's existence, rarely missed a market-day extending a welcome in the corner stall with table, benches, teapot, scriptures and tracts, and picture roll, with the Siamese and Chinese evangelists ready to teach and explain. Without doubt it was a factor in gaining interest in those first years. The church membership numbers many who first heard of God and Jesus Christ in the market-building.

For the first two and a half years, services were held in the hospital chapel room. June 1913 was a notable month: stakes had been set on the new church property purchased in the name of the Christians, and every member was early on the ground to erect the temporary building for worship. There were seventy, including the wives who cooked the picnic dinner, and the entire building of bamboo and thatch with its earth floor and benches of split areca palms was nearly completed in one day. It was use 1 as the church for two years. In November 1915 the brick church building was dedicated; pride and joy mingled with regret that Dr. Dunlap was not present as he had been compelled to go on furlough.

Trang's evangelistic apportionment is about 240,000 people; touring has had its place. The Rev. F. L. Snyder during the six years preceding 1920 did a great deal of itinerating: there are groups of Christians in each of the six provinces, and he spent much time in visiting them and searching out untouched villages. There was an interval of four years when the Rev. Egon Wachter, M. D., was either tied down to both hospital and pastoral duties or unable because of poor health, to go on long trips: Puket and Panga he did visit and often said that he would like to live in Puket after retiring from active missionary work. Dr. Wachter learned to speak Chinese during his last ten years here. Dr. and Mrs. Wachter returned to America in December 1923 but Dr. Wachter's heart was in Siam, so that he lived only a short time in the home land in which he had come to feel a stranger.

The January following, brought the Rev. and Mrs. H. G. Knox and small son down from Bangkok and again the field was toured systematically and enthusiastically, almost every mode of travel being used including bicycle and elephant. For many years regular Sunday services have been held in Chinese at Kantang. Since Mr. Knox's return from furlough a group has been organized at Huey Yot, the mining centre north of Trang, with morning services in Siamese and afternoon services in Chinese. Each year the Christians scattered about the province gather together in Trang for the Christmas festivities.

Not until the fifth year was any one available for educational work in the station. For nine months in 1913, until furlough intervened, a half dozen little girls were gathered together for half a day at the

First House occupied by Rev. E. P. Dunlap, D.D. and Mrs. Dunlap at Trang Station

hospital residence and a Christian girl who had had a year at the Harriet M. House School in Bangkok taught them under daily supervision. Then in 1915 Miss R. O. Eakin, returning to the land of her birth, came to Trang for school work. School there was none, neither equipment nor pupils; and education was as unwanted as in Bangkok fifty years earlier. At first the parochial plan was tried but received insufficient support. For two years the old thatched church building was used, literally creeping as it was with scorpions and centipedes— until it swayed alarmingly and another temporary building was put up to take its place. After six and a half years, when Miss Eakin went on furlough the school was on a substantial basis; the school residence was completed, the lower floor being used for class-rooms.

Mrs. Wachter had been in the station a year and had done her utmost to secure a head-teacher. Failing, the school had to close but reopened in April 1922 with an excellent staff of teachers. During forty years in Siam, serving in several stations, Mrs. Wachter has never been able to resist the call and need for a teacher; here as in the past she put heart and soul into the school, and much of the school's present prestige it owes to Mrs. Wachter; we have known no other woman of the mission more popular and beloved by all of the officials. Miss Eakin returned from furlough in November 1923 with money for the present beautiful building with dormitory, class-rooms and assembly hall. Proof of the Government's good-will and confidence appears in the fact that thirteen girls of their choosing and at government expense, are having a three-years' course at the school, preparatory to teaching in the country districts from which they have come.

Though the hospital was the centre of station activity during the first few years, the medical work had to win its way gradually. Foreign medicine was stranger than the foreigners themselves and surgery more so still. In this part of the peninsula where all officials were accorded a "jungle bonus", "spirit doctors" were numerous and had a very strong hold on the people.

In 1913 Dr. Bulkley was appointed Health Officer by the Ministry of the Interior to help the Government in the fight against cholera. During furlough and transfer Miss Christensen carried the hospital work alone three times, for periods of a year or more each. Dr. Wachter had charge for about five years and trained the present efficient first-assistant, whose wife is hospital matron. Since 1923 Dr. Bulkley has again been in charge of Trang medical work.

Some royal visits to the hospital during those early years have helped immeasurably to establish confidence in foreign medicine. The year 1912 was made memorable by the visit of H. M. Queen Saovabha, H. R. H. Prince Damrong and H. R. H. Princess of Petchaburi;—in 1913, H. R. H. Prince Nagor Svarga and in 1915, H. R. H. Prince Bhanurangsi visited us. When H. M. King Rama VI came to Trang and Dr. Dunlap went to pay his respects, His Majesty came forward to greet him with the word, " My Father's old friend". The present operating room of the hospital was His Majesty's gracious gift at that time.

———◆———

Original Church Building at Trang—New Church in the Foreground

CHAPTER XVII

THE NARRATIVE OF CHIENGRUNG

Established in 1917

Rev. Daniel McGilvary, D. D., is the Nestor of the North Work. The memory of his tours is a constant inspiration to the younger generation. He still lives in the expansion work.

Among Dr. McGilvary's numerous tours was one reaching as far north as Chiengrung (Chinese Kiulungkiang). In 1893 he and the Rev. R. Irwin, following the Mekong river, came into the territory known as the Sipsawng Panna (now Chinese territory). The arrival of Dr. McGilvary in Chiengrung is thus described by one of the Christians who was an eye-witness : " A man with long, white beard, mounted on an elephant. When he dismounted he began teaching out of a book."

In 1897, others made their way into the Sipsawng Panna or Tai Lu country. That year, appointed by the Mission, the Rev. W. Clifton Dodd and Dr. W. A. Briggs made an exploratory tour into this region. By arrangement they met the Rev. Robert Irwin in Kengtung, Burma. He had come up through Burma from Rangoon, en route from America to his mission field in Siam. These three men gave a most enthusiastic report of their tours, at the next mission meeting. Subsequent tours were taken. To quote from Dr. Dodd's book, " The Tai Race " :

" Six tours had been taken into the Lu country from the North Siam Mission before the occupation as a mission station. The first was in 1893 by Dr. McGilvary and Mr. Irwin, as far as the town of

NOTE. The Narrative of Chiengrung is included in this history of Protestant Missions in Siam because this work was started by the Siam Mission which has given five missionary families to the work.—*Ed.*

Chiengrung.   The second was by Dr. McGilvary alone, extending through to Ban Baw He, where the salt wells are and through Muang Pong, and Muang La, returning to Muang Sing.   These are both reported in Dr. McGilvary's Autobiography.   The third was my tour in 1897, only as far as Muang Che ; the fourth the beginning of my journey across Yunnan in 1910; the fifth was with Dr. Lyon in 1915 ; and the sixth the following year was by our Tai evangelists sent out and financed by the Tai church.....In all these tours the Lu people seemed especially eager for our books, and equally eager to hear the preaching and teaching that accompanied them.   Many thousands of people heard the Word of Life."

To quote again from Dr. Dodd's book :

" My greatest surprise, however, was sprung when we went to the big market in Chiengrung town the next morning after our arrival –– another of God's timings......I took over to the market this time four bundles of books, 700.   Before long these were exhausted and I went back and got another armful. Dr. Lyon managed to keep the gramophone going but most of the time he was as busy as the elder and I were in sorting and handing out books.   We worked so fast that our arms ached and still we could not keep up with the impatience of the crowd.   I can see yet those hands stretched out from all directions and can still hear the insistent calls, 'give me two of those sacred books.'   Once more and still once again I went to our stopping place with the Father of the District and ran back to market with an armful of books.   When the market was over we counted and found that no less than two thousand books had been distributed that morning.

" Some results of this book distribution came to our notice at times.   During my visit to Muang Che in 1897 an official who was a Phya received a tract.   He believed its teaching and carried it with him till the day of his death, hoping to hear more.   Some seven or eight years later he was killed in one of the raids on the town.   His wife and son fled for their lives to Muang Yawng.   There they found

REV. WILLIAM CLIFTON DODD, D.D.

the Baptist workers and were baptised.

"In our first tour this year at Muang Yang, a day north from here, a woman came to listen to the reading of a tract, who frequently exclaimed, 'I know that is true.' Her face was drawn with sorrow and weeping. After the crowd had gone I sought her out and heard her story. Her son, a fine young man, had received a tract from me on my tour of 1915. He carried it with him day and night. He believed what it taught and tried to get his friend to believe it too. Last year he was drafted as a soldier and was sent down to Chiengrung. He hoped to see Dr. Mason and learn more about Jesus but before he had an opportunity to call on him, he was taken sick and died suddenly. People said the demons had got him, and his father and mother wept day and night for a month. We told her that if her son did believe on Jesus he had gone to be with Him. At once she seemed to accept this as true of her son. Her sad face lighted up and her burden seemed to roll away. When we saw her again on our way home her face was shining and she said, 'I have not wept since you told me that.'

"Soon after the station was opened here, one Sunday at morning service in Dr. Mason's house, eight men who were strangers attended. When the collection was taken up they were passed by, but each one got up in turn, came forward, dropped in his coin, with the uplifted hands with which they accompany their Buddhist offerings. When told that this was a Christian offering and not to any idol or to make merit, the eldest of the party answered by opening a small parcel and producing several portions of scripture. He said that he had received them from me some two years before when I visited in their village.

"After we arrived we made our first tour to their village, three days away. They seemed almost ready to cut loose from their old moorings and launch out on the promises of God, but they needed a general movement. They were anxious to be delivered from the thralldom of demons but not willing to forsake their sins. Some of the women asked if they learned to sing, would it keep the demons away from their home. One woman said she put our books on a shelf and worshipped them. We lived in their temple, my wife and I, and taught day and night the people who came to us and we visited in their homes but still they were afraid. One man said, 'You have visited us three times in our village. The first time we did not understand clearly. When you come again some of us may be ready to accept.' "

On one of his tours Dr. Dodd was asked by the people if his King had sent him on this embassy. After Dr. Dodd had spoken with great power, telling the people of the great King Jesus, some said to him : " Come and stop in our city as long as you like......We are prepared for the coming of the Messiah."

Thus the soil was well prepared and much seed sown before the station was established at Chiengrung (Kiulungkiang) in 1917 by Dr. C. Mason and the Rev. L. J. Beebe. There is now a good church of over a hundred members at the mission center and work has been started in five other places. The Tai Lu are a very responsive and open-hearted people, and while the work is encouraging, the writer is satisfied that if the people were not forbidden by the ruling class thousands would have accepted Christ all over the Sipsawng Panna.

One of the most interesting features in the development of the work in Chiengrung is the movement among the lepers. Dr. Galt has over seventy segregated in a newly-built village about twenty minutes' ride from the mission compound. They receive treatment of the chaulmoogra oil regularly. Most of them are studying preparatory to being received into the church. Probably there are thousands of lepers in Sipsawng Panna country, the home of the Tai Lu ; the number is increasing rapidly.

Chiengrung station was organized on a basis of five families in order to have a strong center for expansion. God did not wait till five families came before issuing his call to spread northward. The call came in 1921 in the form of a mass meeting in the Red river valley, sixteen days' travel to the northeast.

Mrs. William Dodd

Mass Movement among the Illiterate Tai—
  The Call of the Holy Spirit.

A small woman, Mrs. W. Clifton Dodd, was the leader. She is a woman of strong faith and vision. Before the death of her husband she and Dr. Dodd had toured extensively in Yunnan province. Some six or eight points had been suggested as strategic places to plant stations to reach the Tai in Yunnan and other sections of China and the northern part of French Indo-China. In 1910, when Dr. Dodd passed through the Red river valley on that memorable tour, he prophecied that the Tai in that valley would probably accept Christianity en masse. His prophecy came true.

Mrs. Dodd, accompanied by two Tai evangelists from North Siam and two from the Yangtse valley, left Chiengrung (Kiulungkiang) hoping to found a station in Linganfu.

Arriving at the place in the Red river valley called Yuangkiang, sixteen days' travel from Kiulungkiang, she was told by the Chinese magistrate that she could not proceed any farther on the direct road to Linganfu as robbers infested it. Nothing daunted, Mrs. Dodd asked permission to proceed via Yunnanfu, the capitol, and come down the French railway and thence across from Amichou west to Linganfu. She left some of the Tai workers in Yuankiang and proceeded on the long, round-about route as granted by the official in Yuangkiang.

While she was gone, attempting to reach Linganfu, the mass movement started. Two persons, a woman and a child, were lying in their hovels at the point of death. The Tai evangelists were called to the bedside of the sick. Prayer was offered and a few simple remedies were administered. In a short time the two patients were up and well. From these wonderful cures, word was spread all over the valley. The Tai workers were called to the bedsides of many who were ill. Hundreds gave themselves up to the Gospel message, asking to be taught. Houses were cleansed of demons; the converts promised to cast off all demon worship and to take

Jesus Christ as their Saviour. Spirit shrines by the basket-full were taken down and burned. In an incredibly short time there were between two and three thousand enrolled, including children. Then a terrible persecution broke out. The Chinese official of the Mosha district fined some villagers for becoming Christians; some were driven away at the point of the gun or knife, and threats were made to kill all of the converts—unless they recanted and resumed spirit worship. Most remained faithful.

Letters were written by the Tai workers to the missionaries, telling about the movement and begging us to come and help in that most difficult situation. Mrs. Dodd returned to Yuangkiang and Mosha, where the mass movement started, and not long afterward the Callenders arrived there, and in a few months more the Parks also arrived, the work in Kiulungkiang having been turned over to the nationals till the arrival of Dr. Mason.

For nearly a year services were held under God's blue canopy in the shade of the trees. Until a chapel was built the missionaries lived in native mud-houses. After the chapel was built the missionaries lived in the upper storey and the lower storey was used for services and for school work and other meetings. The converts donated the sun-dried brick;—the missionaries furnished the timbers.

A large group of workers from North Siam, many of them selected by Presbytery, came up and assisted the foreign missionaries. These workers had to travel more than forty days to reach the work—as far in point of time as it is from San Francisco to the same field. This was real missionary work—foreign missionary work—on the part of the Tai workers from Siam.

The fifty churches in Siam, particularly those in the northern part, helped to finance the project. A certain amount of the Central Fund to which the churches give for evangelistic work was devoted to the work in the North. Funds there were from other sources. One of the largest was monies from the Milton Stewart estate. We had no authority to take Board funds appropriated for the current work of Kiulungkiang station and God provided other means.

God opened the door, then shut it upon our enemies (see Rev. 3: 7 ; 8). We were wonderfully kept. His grace was found sufficient. Our boy of ten summers became very ill. Dr. Park had not yet arrived; no physician was there except the Great Physician. It was a complicated case of fever ; the spots seemed to indicate typhus fever. After about twenty days of anxiety and prayer the lad's temperature became normal again—just before the arrival of Dr. Park and family. This happened while we were living in the mud-house of one of the converts—in a room about sixteen feet by twelve. In that room we lived for six months. Many things happened—strange and new : Chinese came,—Tai came,—mountain people came from days away,—bandits and criminals, some seeking our help, some out of curiosity, others to accept Christ. One day a man came into our doorway, his belt full of cartridges, his rifle in hand. He was Chinese ; we could not talk his language. I asked the man of the house after he had left who he was ; the reply came that he did not know. Every box that came into our house was supposed to contain money. Outsiders plotted with the man in whose house we were camping ; he turned traitor. A little dog's barking apprised us of the would-be robbers. The pup had been given to our son by the man of the house. The little dog was faithful ; when a human head appeared in the little opening, watching to find out where our money was kept, he gave a bark and the head vanished. God then led us to set a watch over the room containing our few chattels and go out touring among the many village converts. In a month we came back—the trouble was over. "God is a strong tower ; the righteous runneth into it and is safe."

It was necessary to carry on two schools : one in the Tai language, in order to deliver the Gospel message and to train the catechumens and build up the church ; one in the Chinese language, in order to comply with the Chinese Government's requirements.

Workers from North Siam taught the Tai school,—a Chinese worker from Yunnanfu the Chinese school. This man was sent to us by the C. I. M. at our request. Mr. Chen has proven to be just the right person for this most complicated task. He plays the organ, Chinese flute and cornet; he teaches his pupils these instruments, besides singing. All these, except the flute, he has learned since coming to our mission station. He knew a little English when he came and now he speaks and writes English well. During the present disturbances in China, when all the foreign missionaries have been called out, this man has had charge of all the work in that mass movement.

Local Tai leaders are emerging. There is the fullest of cooperation between the foreign missionaries and the workers—Tai from Siam,—local Tai,—and Chinese. The local workers are mostly supported by offerings on the field. There are over twenty centers where night schools are conducted, mostly by the local helpers. They teach catechumens and prepare them for the sacraments,—teaching them also to read and write.

Six chapels have been built,—the converts supplying the brick and labor,—the mission the timbers. The Tai are poor and possess no timbered land. The year before I left, 225 adults were admitted into the church. I baptised 80 at one time: 60 adults and 20 children. There are now about 400 church members.

Bible study, voluntary service, self-support and self-propagation are stressed. The yearly program of the missionaries is: three months out in the villages, then three weeks with Bible classes at the center, and conference. This is carried on throughout the year. In spite of the disturbed conditions in China, and the absence of the foreign missionaries, a splendid work has been done during the past year. Old work has been strengthened,—new families have been won for Christ. The following is a brief report of the Christmas celebration by the Christians in the main center, no foreign missionaries being present:

" Yuangkiang (Mosha):

Now I have a very happy affair to tell you about, It is in regard to the Christmas holiday. We received the help of God. All things were prepared in advance. $113.30 silver was subscribed altogether. Three beeves were slaughtered costing $70.10 leaving a balance of $42.20. We observed Christmas on two days, December 24th and 25th. The Christians who assembled for the festival numbered about 1100 or 1200. Now I will also report to you the facts occurring on these two days.

I.— December 24th. Exercises, Games and Play, Feast, Evening Entertainment.

II.—December 24th. Christmas Service.

During these two days there were more than a thousand people present each day, what a pity you could not be present. Alas !

(Signed) Ho Jong Chong."

Work Among The Tai Nua In The Muang Baw Region— (Chinese Weiyuan)

Muang Baw (Chinese Weiyuan) is a strategic place. Dr. Dodd, who toured among the Tai Nua (northern Tai) in 1910, estimated their population as 600,000, and Weiyuan at the head of the Mekong river is their rallying point. In all, they occupy twenty-eight districts, all but four of them on the west side of the Mekong.

Mr. Callender made a tour among the Tai Nua in 1921, Dr. Park in 1922, Mr. Beebe in 1925, and Mr. Callender again in 1926. Like the Tai Lu, the Tai Nua received the foreign missionaries with open arms. Great crowds, almost uncontrollable at times, flocked to see the missionaries and to hear their message. Tai men from North Siam, sent and supported by the American Bible Society under their Secretary, the Rev. Robt. Irwin, had worked in this region and we have one Tai Nua communicant at Weiyuan, who is teaching some twenty catechumens—Tai and Chinese. A piece of land has been bought and a building erected which serves as chapel and dispensary. But it is evident that it is too far away from our present stations to be superintended properly from either Kiulungkiang, thirteen days' travel distant, or Yuankiang, twelve days away. There should be be a station organized at Weiyuan at once.

The Yunnan Mission Field—a Summary.

Area and Topography: Yunnan province has an area of 146,718 sq. miles,—almost equal to that of California, and about two thirds the area of Siam. The surface is very mountainous with valleys between the ranges. There are very few large plains or plateaux. Major Davies gives 10,000 sq. miles of plains and 140,000 sq. miles of mountains.

Population: There are no large cities; Yunnanfu, the capital, is the largest with a population of about 100,000. There are a few small cities containing a population ranging from about 10,000 to 30,000 each. The bulk of the population is in villages. Major Davies estimates that there are 400 persons to the square mile in the plains and 40 in the mountains: about two thirds of these are various tribes, one third Chinese. In this estimate the Tai are included as tribes, although, strictly speaking, they are a people by themselves. A fair estimate for the Tai would be 2,000,000, of whom one half are Buddhist and literate. The Tai live in the plains and work in the rice fields. The tribes people live on the hills, many being serfs of the Chinese land-owners who also live on the mountains or on the high plateaux. The total population of Yunnan Province is from nine to twelve millions.

Languages: Yunnan is polyglot; the languages are Chinese and Tai, with numerous dialects spoken by the different tribes. Most of the tribes understand the Chinese language somewhat and may be reached with the Gospel through that medium. Mr. Fullerton's great work among the Lisu tribe is done mostly through the Chinese language. It is recommended that new missionaries study the Chinese language, as well as the Tai; in some places Chinese should be made the major language. On the other hand, Mr. Fraser, of the C.I.M., has done a great work among the Lisu in the extreme west of Yunnan province, and he has learned the Lisu dialect and has translated part of the scripture into their language, employing the Romanized method. Mr. Fraser's work is self-supporting, carried on by voluntary service of the converts—a unique work. The Tai do not know the Chinese language, particularly the Buddhist Tai, and cannot be reached through that medium. Even the non-Buddhist and illiterate Tai who know considerable Chinese and have incorporated into their language many Chinese words and terms, do not readily receive the Gospel message through the Chinese language.

Foreign Missionary Forces: The number of foreign missionaries, including all societies at work in Yunnan province, and some independent workers, is something over forty, which averages one missionary to every 200,000 of its population. In the U. S. A., we are told, there is a church to every 1,000 of its population, and there are many workers in each church. What a contrast! This contrast would not be fair in well-developed fields; but in Yunnan there are very few workers.

Presbyterian Responsibility: The territory falling to the Presbyterians has been pretty well outlined by Providence. There is one station at Kiulungkiang, one at Yuankiang, and work has been carried on in Weiyuan for several years. It is almost equidistant between these three places; a triangle drawn from the three points describes approximately the Presbyterian responsibility in Yunnan. Within a triangle, whose sides are 16, 13 and 12 days' travel apart respectively, the Presbyterian Board is the only society at work. To the north, east and west other societies are at work.

These four societies (the C. I. M., the C. M. S., the P. M. U., and the English Methodist) were appealed to, it being suggested to them that one of them might handle the Presbyterian work in the Red river valley. The result was that a joint statement was sent from the four societies to the Evaluation Conference held at Canton. In that statement they volunteered the information that their societies had more than they could do in their respective fields, and they commended highly the work the Presbyterian missionaries were doing and urged upon the China Council not only to provide adequate forces for Yuankiang, but to recognize what seems to be an evident call to evangelize all peoples within the area mentioned above, and to accept full responsibility for the same.

The Siam mission has ever stood for expansion. She has been fortunate in having men and women of vision. From the Siam mission five families went forth into the expansion work to the northward : the Dodds, Masons, Beebes, Parks and Callenders. Dr. Dodd has gone to his reward and Mrs. Dodd is honorably retired ; the Masons are not now connected with the field. The three other families are still at work. They, with the three newer families, the Galts, Goodenbergers and Campbells, constitute the Yunnan mission. Let us not forget the "heavenly vision" of those who first came into this field,—but complete the task—far and near.

CHAPTER XVIII

MEDICAL MISSIONS IN SIAM

THE first Protestant missionary to Siam was Rev. C. F. A. Gutzlaff, a Doctor of Medicine who arrived in 1828. Ill health and the loss of his wife and children caused his retirement after three years of forceful service. Dan Beach Bradley, M.D., succeeded him, arriving in Siam in 1835, giving nearly forty years of his life to Siam in his ministry of healing.

All folk-medicine and ancient systems of medicine in general, says one writer, have been essentially alike in tendency; in each case an affair of charms and spells, plant lore and psychotherapy, to stave off the effects of supernatural agencies. Dr. Bradley soon found that against all his skill there was arrayed the prestige of ancient superstition, sanctioned by ignorance and custom. He found that he was often sent for as a last resort, and was then expected to perform a miracle.

It is a far call from the little dispensary established by him in 1835 to the five Government hospitals in Bangkok or to the new McCormick Hospital in Chiengmai with its five modern buildings including a Maternity ward, steam laundry, electric light plant, X-ray apparatus or to other institutions less pretentious but also efficient. And we must not forget that of the three institutes in the world where anti-venene serum (for snake bite) is made, Siam possesses one; and that in her Pasteur Institute anti-rabic serum is also made and hundreds of patients every year are saved from a horrible death. There are those of our medical men who have witnessed nearly the whole of this remarkable development and whose work has greatly benefitted thereby. It is, I say, a far call, and yet there is a real connection between them.

Dr. Bradley's was but a beginning, and a small beginning at that. His was however a service in which the best in the art of surgery and medicine was joined to the true spirit of service in the name of the Great Physician, one of whose commands to His disciples was, " Heal the sick ". The practice of the healing art has undergone a vast change since Dr. Bradley's days of service in Bangkok. He had been at work a full year before Dr. Peter Parker, another great missionary doctor, had set foot on Chinese soil to begin his great work. Vaccination against small-pox had not long before been recognized. Chloroform was just coming into use. Ether had not yet been discovered. Pasteur, one of the founders of bacteriology, whose wonderful work has made the whole world his everlasting debtor, was but a boy of twelve, still joyously fishing in the streams of his native France. Profiting, by the discoveries of the immortal Pasteur, Lord Lister made antiseptic surgery possible and thereby conferred a priceless boon on suffering humanity. When Dr. Bradley came to Siam, Lister was but a lad of seven : the wealth of his great contribution to science was still a generation in the future. Dr. Oliver Wendell Holmes had not yet written his celebrated paper on Puerperal Sepsis that was to startle the medical world and to usher in a new era in the practice of midwifery. Only the crudest of clinical thermometers were in use and the hypodermic syringe was as yet unknown. Of course Dr. Bradley and Dr. House had neither the X-ray nor radium,—and yet it was a propitious time to begin the practice of the healing art in a virgin field.

One of the first and greatest benefits Dr. Bradley conferred on the land was his introduction of vaccination in 1840. This event alone is memorable. Probably the first surgical operation under ether anasthesia in Asia—surely in this land—was performed by Dr. House who came out in 1847. Then ether had only been used in surgery for two years. Only two years after his arrival occurred that fearful cholera epidemic which took a toll of fully thirty-five thousand lives in the city of Bangkok alone. Dr. House saved many lives and made a host of friends for himself and the cause for which he was an ambassador.

Lacking many of the efficient weapons that the medical man of today carries with him in his fight against disease, those early doctors rendered an epoch-making service. They paved the way for every advance in medical science that has since then been put to use for the benefit of this land. May we not truly say that since the first patient cared for by Dr. Bradley and the thousands treated by the forty doctors who have followed him in the mission of healing, that they have given *themselves*—they have also appropriated and given freely the most advanced aids that science has approved to help in their mission of mercy. Dr. Bradley did this when he introduced vaccination, as already related, bringing the virus from America on the long nine months' voyage by sailing ship; McGilvary did it when he carried the scabs from vaccinations on the twelve weeks' boat journey to Chiengmai and also introduced life-saving quinine to stay the devastating scourge of malaria. Braddock and McKean, undismayed by a myriad difficulties, successfully made small-pox virus in Bangkok and in the jungles of the far North, making possible the wholesale vaccination of the masses. Their effort conquered the ancient scourge of this people. In 1904 Dr. McKean established a laboratory for the production of vaccine. This was imperatively needed because of the extreme difficulty in securing it from abroad. Throughout a period of ten years, a high grade vaccine was thus produced in large quantities and broad-cast over the northern provinces by the hands of the mission vaccinators who were trained and who numbered as many as 210 at one time. Vaccine was supplied to the other mission hospitals and to the Siamese government. The promulgation of the compulsory vaccination law and the establishment of the Pasteur Institute under Royal patronage made the continuance of this laboratory unnecessary.

In isolated communities where the doctor has no medical colleagues, he himself is often exposed to grave danger. Many of our doctors after having bound up the wounds of this people have finished their work and entered into the Celestial City. Not merely as an entering wedge did they minister to the wounded and the diseased, but by loving service they glorified tasks naturally repulsive and, translating the Gospel of Love into kindly deeds of mercy, they have reached out with yearning hearts for the Master's crown. Thus James B. Thompson, M. D., gave his own life while caring for cholera cases in 1898. On 22 March 1919 Dr. Carl J. Shellman, beloved friend and physician, passed away under similar circumstances. Their memories we hold forever sacred.

In the days before the organization of an efficient Board of Health, His Majesty's Government regularly called on the medical men of our mission to lead in measures for the suppression of great epidemics. H. R. H. Prince Damrong, while Minister of the Interior, called the first conference of mission medical men to consider the health problems of the whole Kingdom. This was in 1903 and annually for several years this conference was held—usually lasting for one day. Many helpful suggestions which resulted in great benefit to the whole country were made in these meetings. This fact is warmly recognized by His Majesty's Government. The very latest tribute to this desire for co-operation was the request of H. R. H. Prince Nagor Svarga that our medical men be represented on the recently organized National Health Council.

The first mission hospital in Siam was built at Petchaburi about 1882. The first Government hospital where modern medicine and surgery were practiced was one of sixty beds for soldiers only, located within the city wall of Bangkok near the Sampeng market gate. A good deal of interest centers around this hospital, in that Dr. Tien Hee (afterwards Phya Saurasin) was placed in charge of it. He had not only been educated in our boys' mission school, but had received his medical education in America, being a graduate of the Medical Department of the University of New York. Modern medicine was on trial in Siam and it won with flying colors.

T. Heyward Hays, M. D., joined the mission in 1886. Up to this time practically all medicines dispensed by the missionaries had been given free. Dr. Hays believed this policy to be wrong and calculated to pauperize the people. He believed that the patient would value the medical service rendered more if encouraged to pay according to his ability. He carried this theory into practice in the American Dispensary which he opened in 1888 and which he ran for a number of years as a mission enterprise. His theory having been proven correct, other mission dispensaries followed in his footsteps and for the first time, instead of being financial burdens to the mission became self-supporting institutions.

But great as has been the value of the help our medical men have rendered during times of epidemics, it has been surpassed by the campaigns carried on by them during ordinary times. From nearly every mission hospital there have issued, from time to time, clear warnings as to improper food and water and strong appeals that all take advantage of vaccination and inoculation as measures of tremendous value in the preservation of life and health. One of our medical men pursuing investigations of his own to account for the anemia and lethargy of such a large proportion of the people in his district, discovered that hook-worm was the cause. Reporting this to the representative of the Rockefeller interests probably caused them to undertake the nation-wide campaign that they have been conducting for several years past with such notable success.

Epidemics have been mentioned as having taken fearful toll of human life at frequent intervals. Nothing has been said, except in the case of hook-worm, of the diseases that afflict a large proportion of the people at all times: they are too well known to all. We are more vitally concerned with the means held efficacious by the people to get rid of them.

A conservative estimate is that seventy-five per cent of the populace still depends on their native doctors in time of illness. The equipment of these medical men for the healing art is the possession of some ancient medical books, which are a strange mixture of plant-lore, astrology and spiritism. The great weight of age-old custom still clings like a millstone around the neck of the sick person consigned to their ignorant care. But a happier day has dawned !

Equipped as never before, encouraged by Royal favor, aided by men and money from the western world, the Government Medical College is now turning out young men well-trained in modern medicine and able to meet a real need and gradually they will replace the doctor who lacks scientific training.

Except for a bountiful supply of pure water in Bangkok, the country in general is without modern sanitary conveniences. The people for the most part being ignorant of the mental rules of health and hygiene, any campaign for preventive medicine is a fight against heavy odds, for even the most skilled medical man.

Notwithstanding nearly a hundred years of work behind us, our medical work is far less efficient than the needs demand. Though we have some hospitals incorporating the latest in architecture and in hospital administration, yet not one of them is equipped as it should be. This is not due to a lack of appreciation of the value of all modern agencies but to the lack of money, together with unfavorable local conditions.

But what value is placed on our medical work by the people of the land ? This is a fair question. Nearly every one of our mission hospitals stands as a strong evidence of the deep appreciation of the people of all classes to the worth of our medical work. The hospital at Petchaburi really became a hospital when the reigning King gladly gave $2,000.00 gold for its enlargement and the women's ward at the same place was built by the bounty of His Queen, for she had seen with her own eyes what was being done for women there. Part of the old hospital at Chiengmai was the gift of two princes in memory of their father, the last Lao King, who was at one time a patient of Dr. McKean's. Trang hospital was

T. Heyward Hays, M.D.

built by the late Phya Ratsada out of gratitude to the late Rev. E. P. Dunlap, D.D., who healed him of a serious malady.   One of the wards at Lampang was built with the help of a man whose heart was full of gratitude for the cure of his wife and son in the hospital. Sritamarat hospital was built largely by the gifts of the Siamese in recognition of the good it had been doing while only indifferently housed,—H. M. King Chulalongkorn himself giving $2,000.00 gold toward the project.   Instances of this kind might be multiplied to include every hospital in our mission.

Medical education has been touched upon.   Our mission has just pride in the part that a son of one of our pioneer missionaries has had in its development.   From the time of his return to Siam after securing his medical education in the United States until his retirement in 1926, Dr. Geo. B. McFarland gave himself to teaching in the Government Medical College,— during that time translating portions of Gray's Anatomy and other standard medical text books into the Siamese language. His faithful work during all these years insured steady growth and made possible the greater things of today and the high hope of a greater tomorrow.

Though the early missionary doctors gave all their services gratuitously yet changing conditions have made it necessary and wise to charge fees commensurate with the patients' ability to pay.   This does not mean, however, that anyone is turned away.   The beggar with only a loin-cloth is as welcome in any of our mission hospitals as the Prince of Royal blood or the wealthy Chinese or Indian merchant.

Not a doctor out here, but has felt the need of intelligent nurses : yet the relatives of our patients often carry out instructions surprisingly well ; any doctor who has been here a long time will testify to their faithfulness as a rule.   He could also bear witness to the contrary, —some instances comic, with no harm to the patient—others alas,— most tragic. This has been a heavy handicap in the endeavor for efficiency.   In the first place he has often had to take in not only one relative of the patient as a nurse, but sometimes the whole family with much of the kitchen paraphernalia. Where a whole room has been available this has been a matter of small moment, though in critical cases it has made for unrest and confusion. One of our hospitals has for twenty-two years furnished the meals for all of its patients but admits the nursing problem to be far from ideal. One of our most efficient hospitals though not provided with graduate nurses has trained a most competent corps of practical nurses and orderlies and the hospital is a model of cleanliness and order. Our mission was a long time in making any provision for the training of nurses. At last however in 1920 a Training School for nurses was established in connection with the new McCormick hospital in Chiengmai—the third in Siam and the first outside of Bangkok. Under the efficient superintendency of a trained nurse of experience, the school has already made good progress and has graduated one class of two nurses, both of which have passed the examination of the Royal Siamese Red Cross Society. The entrance requirement of Matayome VI ensures the possibility of a high grade of training for these nurses. Though still in its youth, the existence of this Nurses' Training School is amply justified. May it soon furnish trained nurses to all of our other hospitals.

It is only fitting that recognition should here be made of the valuable service rendered by men who had received no medical training. As a matter of course, from the very first the healing art has gone hand in hand with the Gospel message—nay has been a very vital part of that message. Had the Master not specifically said,— " Heal the sick ",— yet his disciples must of necessity have taken it as an essential part of their work,— example aways being stronger than precept. There has *never* been a sufficiency of medical men in our mission,– and so McGilvary, McFarland, Dunlap, Eckels and others have stepped into the breach and rendered notable service along medical lines. Nearly all non-medical men have at some time or other given valuable service in directing extensive vaccination

Mrs. T. Heyward Hays

campaigns. Often for periods of several years at a time the Rev. C. E. Eckels did the work of a doctor. Living for a time in a very lawless district where there was no medical man, he was forced by necessity to become a skilful user of the surgical needle.

It is also fitting that we make mention of the medical and maternity work carried on for twenty-five years by our brethren of the Church of Christ at Nakon Pathom. Some of their members having had considerable training along these lines, they have maintained a useful work in a most needy field. At all times they have freely given of their best in their efforts to relieve suffering and to prolong life.

For many years the Government has maintained a Maternity work in connection with the Siriraj Hospital in Bangkok, but it could at best offer service to but a small percent of the cases. In 1922 Mission action provided for the establishment of a Maternity Home in Bangkok. Started in a small way in a populous center, it has served all classes and all races in a most acceptable manner and has maintained a steady growth. Prenatal care of the mother has been an advance step to which many Siamese women have responded. Graduates of the Bangkok Bible Training School are given a subsequent course of training in the Maternity Home if they will take it. Along health lines Siam has no greater need than maternity homes of this high standard. Truly they are a boon to motherhood.

What shall I say of the help given by the wives of the doctors? Those of them who were trained nurses have rendered skillful, valiant service through long periods of years, and this too while their families were growing up around them. Those not so trained have gradually adapted themselves to the needs and have been helpful assistants in the medical work of their stations.

Work done by the Presbyterian mission for the lepers of Siam is one of such importance and significance that it is treated in a separate chapter—but it is most assuredly a part of the medical task.

Though the treating of physical disease is the distinctive mission of the physician, the medical missionary has never forgotten that the Lord taught by example that physical ills and spiritual needs are closely associated and to be " whole every whit " involves a spiritual healing as well as physical. Sometimes the clergyman has helped the medical missionary with the spiritual side of his task. But in each hospital the patients are given instruction which often leads them to the Great Physician who heals their souls. This " by-product " of the medical work is of such magnitude and importance one can not term it secondary but must feel that healing of body and soul are joint aims of the true physician.

We must not forget the faithful and efficient hospital assistants and helpers. Many of them have caught the real spirit of service and have dedicated their lives to the ministry of healing. No time-service theirs but a continual giving of every energy—effort being only measured by the need of the sick. Attaining a high grade of skill, they have combined with it a good degree of administrative ability, that has enabled them to " carry on " during the whole period of a doctor's furlough. Truly much of the credit for the success of our medical work is due such men as these; a credit they would be to any race.

Health conditions from the time of the founding of the mission emphasized the great need of a place for rest and for recuperation after sickness. For more than fifty years the only places our missionaries could go for this rest was Ang Hin or Tachin. Government rest-houses, when not already occupied, were always gladly offered but the journey to either place was attended with great difficulty, a special launch or sail boat having to be provided for the journey. They were at the mercy of wind and tide or other circumstances almost equally beyond human control. Therefore the need for a place of our own, easily accessible and always ready, became increasingly urgent.

Our fellow-workers in the North established such a place

more than thirty years ago when some bungalows were built on the mountain near Chiengmai, where during the hottest season of the year tired bodies and weary minds might find rest for a season. Twenty-five years ago a small double bungalow was built on the beach at Bangtaloo near Petchaburi; this was followed by another by the seaside at Koh Lok; both of these were invaluable. These places being required for Government use, we were given in exchange for Koh Lok the beautiful location at Nong Khae. The first houses there were erected in 1915 and from time to time as our mission grew, others have been added until there are now five. Here sea air and bathing have wrought their miracle for many who have returned renewed in body and mind, ready for the toil of another year. This is also the story of the latest bungalows,— those built at Khun Tal near Lampang in 1922. Here amidst beautiful mountain pine trees, this sequestered spot affords the quiet that so many need and love. Plain almost to crudeness, yet these places of rest have done much to prevent serious breaks in health which would have meant expensive health trips to the Sanataria of nearby countries or journeys to America,— expensive in both time and money.

It has not always been easy to keep mission hospitals open : it has sometimes been a case of " making bricks without straw ". The only dressings the doctors have sometimes had have been worn out sheets or the coarsest of market cloth. Ointment has been dispensed in sea shells and horse hair of their own gathering has furnished skin suture material. But those days are happily gone ; kind hearts have come the rescue. Without doubt one of the greatest helps that has come to our hospitals in recent times has been the whole-hearted co-operation of the good women of our home churches. Out of the help demanded by the fierce carnage of war, has grown an equally loving service for the Prince of Peace. With painstaking care deft fingers make us bandages and dressings of all kinds sufficient to meet our utmost needs, and the need for such is ever recurring—the task of making them knows no end, but love makes it glorified labor. and enrolls them as partners with us, in the healing of the nations.

A hundred years : a few dispensary patients in a floating-house in one city of the kingdom—to ten hospitals, one maternity home, two leper homes and one training school for nurses. These treated in 1926 more than twenty thousand patients! All of these people heard the Gospel story at least once. Many heard it often. Some heard it only to turn away—some to accept and to enter into newness of life with the sure hope of some day dwelling in that blessed land where the inhabitants shall never say, "I am sick". Tribute is surely due those faithful friends at home who have made this expansion of our work possible. Some have built and equipped great hospitals, some an operating room, some a ward, some have provided endowment that the poor might be cared for, some in the winter-time of life have remembered the medical work in their wills. There have been the steady givers and their earnest prayers. Without their help we must have failed. May those who have given out of their poverty, and those who have given out of their abundance, be richly blessed. May they and others realize that all hospitals continually need new equipment to keep abreast of the demands of modern medicine and surgery. We commend to them the needs of all our medical institutions.

When will our task be finished ? Not until all of the lame and the halt and the blind are cared for,—not until the unnecessary dangers of motherhood are banished,—not until the perils to infancy and childhood shall have been infinitely reduced,—not until the demented shall no longer be chained as animals in jungle huts, but shall be in institutions offering a chance for the return to sanity,—not until the nineteen thousand lepers still unreached are safely cared for in Homes or Hospitals and receiving as their birthright the best gifts of modern science,—not until the untainted children of such unfortunates are forever removed from the perils of the leper-life,

—and not until the many victims of the "great white plague" (tuberculosis) are cared for in sanitaria where sunlight, fresh air and an abundance of nourishing food, together with medicine suited to to their needs, open to them a door of hope.

Dedicated to the Mission Doctors who have served
and passed on to their reward.

Where grim Death had stalked in triumph
Through the city streets and lanes;
Where no help had stilled their terror
Where no balm had soothed their pain,—

They did come, the mighty warriors
But without the bugles' blast:
They did come with draughts of comfort,
Yes — they came with help at last.

Though the conflict of their battles
Was unheard by human ears,
Yet the marvels of their healings
Have come down from distant years.

And though still the battle rages
Over mountains and o'er plains,
There's a shout of hope and comfort
At the mention of their names.

Though in heat of battle fallen,
Or in conflict wounded sore,
Theirs the fight that knew no shrinking;
Theirs the victory ever more.

Now that eyes once kind and watchful,
Now that hands once strong and true,
Now are closed and now are folded,
There is work for us to do.

Tasks unfinished left behind them ;
Sacred duty ours to cherish ;
Service full—in spirit, heroes,
Theirs are names that cannot perish.

———·◄♦►·———

CHAPTER XIX

EDUCATION IN SIAM

SEVERAL years ago, after visiting the schools in Siam conducted by missionaries, a former Educational Secretary of the Presbyterian Board of Foreign Missions included in his report the following statement:

"Our schools are not bait to bring pupils near enough to hear the Gospel, but a powerful method of presenting the realities and the practical results of the Gospel in human terms and by normal psychological processes to the consciousness of all their students. The purpose of our mission schools should be recognized as four fold:

1. To provide Christian education for the Christian youth.
2. To win non-Christian boys and girls to Christ through education in a strongly Christian atmosphere and by direct Christian instruction.
3. To permeate Siamese society with Christian ideals and standards, recognizing that there may be many students in our schools who will not be prepared to profess themselves Christian but will carry from their school experience the Christian viewpoint and an understanding and sympathetic attitude toward Christianity.
4. To discover and to train Christian leaders—not only for the churches, but for positions in Government, business and professional life.

"If the Presbyterian missionaries who first came to Siam had not established and fostered schools for the benefit of the youth of the

---

NOTE: Acknowledgment should be made of the debt the author owes to the helpful treatise on *Educational Work in North Siam* by the Rev. W. Harris. That became the foundation of the present chapter.—The Author.

209

land, they would have been untrue to the standards of their denomination which, throughout its history, has been staunch in its support of education. But, more than that, they would have shorn the Gospel they came to preach of part of its meaning if they have not shown that the salvation they were eager for men to accept was for the whole man, and for the whole of his life. The modern movement toward universal education, now world wide, so largely owes its origin to the Christian view of the worth of the individual as to warrant the claim that it is a part of Christ's gift to the world. His belief in the infinite possibilities locked up in every human soul, His behest to love God with all the heart, soul, mind and strength as well as to love one's neighbor as oneself, the dignity and meaning He gave to human life: these call for an emphasis that has been increasingly placed since His time, on the duty of the race to its children. In founding schools, the missionaries were seeking to share the great gifts of the enlightment of mind and enlargement of spirit which elsewhere have been the heritage of Christian people, believing that this service to humanity is included in the command of Christ, 'Go ye and make disciples of all nations, teaching them'."

In 1828 the world had not yet developed a system of universal education. In Siam, formal education was for boys only, and only for such boys as had become novitiates in the temples. Even then learning was limited to reading and writing and to the memorizing of the temple ritual, and by no means was study compulsory. Since there was nothing of Law, Medicine or Science, education was not for *life* but rather for the carrying on of the temple worship.

Moreover since business and official life made such slight demands there was little appreciation of the value of learning. Since the people knew nothing of schools, their worth had not yet been established. Of necessity then, school work began in a very small way. At first the missionaries took a few boys and girls into their own homes to give them a Christian education. It was even difficult to persuade these children to come to them when they promised to feed

A Class of Women which Mrs. House taught to Read, Sew, Wash and Iron

them and charged no fee for board or instruction. Later when schools were formally opened, the first pupils had to be hired to attend classes and to study. But a significant recognition of the value of learning was met with in another quarter when, in 1845, H. R. H. Prince Chao Fah Mongkut invited the Rev. Jesse Caswell to teach him Science. This Royal pupil studied with Mr. Caswell for eighteen months and formed a deep friendship for his tutor. Four months after he had ascended the throne, His Majesty invited three women of the missions to teach the ladies in his Palace. Thus Mrs. Dan Bradley, Mrs. S. Mattoon, and Mrs. John Taylor Jones began in 1851 the first zenana work in the world.

To Mrs. Mattoon belongs the honor of founding the first Presbyterian school—a day-school, gathered together in a Peguan village on 13 September 1852. On the 30th of the same month the Chinese assistant of the mission, Sinsaa Ki-eng Qua-Sean opened a boarding-school on the mission premises beside Wat Cheng, for the sons of Chinese. Dr. House was elected at this time to the office of Superintendent of Mission Schools. By the close of the year this first boarding-school conducted in the Chinese language, could report twenty-seven pupils. These first students complained that it "hurt to study," but they were induced to persevere until by 1857 the work had become large enough to demand larger quarters and the school was moved farther down the river to Samray where the Presbyterian mission had acquired a larger site. Two years later (1859) a girl pupil was admitted to the school,—a noteworthy event —and the following year (1860) the language used in the school was changed from Chinese to Siamese, because the teacher, Sinsaa Ki-eng Qua-Sean, had died and his successor, Kru Keo, was Siamese. The formidable subjects taught, Philosophy, Arithmetic, Geography, Composition and Astronomy may well have put a strain on both the language and the young pupils.

The year 1860 seemed to have marked a turning point in the work of the mission. In February of that year, the Rev. D. McGilvary and Dr. Dan Bradley made a tour to Petchaburi and while there met a Siamese official, Khun Raja Mat, จมื่น ราชามาตย์ who offered to support a missionary in Petchaburi for a time and to assist in securing a site for the mission, if in turn they would teach him English. This offer which had been prompted by the success of the school work of the mission, was accepted and the next year the Rev. and Mrs. S. G. McFarland and the Rev. and Mrs. Daniel McGilvary began work in Petchaburi. An industrial school for girls and women was started by Mrs. McFarland in 1865 and the boys' school was started in 1873 by the Rev. James Van Dyke.

In 1871 Mrs. Carrington, following the example of Mrs. McFarland, started an industrial school for girls in Bangkok, being allowed Tcs. 12.00 per month for her school. This school however followed very different lines and was apparently soon absorbed in what became the Harriet M. House School. In 1872 Miss Anderson, who had come out to Siam with Mrs. House primarily for work in the Wang Lang School for which Mrs. House had been raising money during her health-trip to America, started an "infant school." By this was not meant a Kindergarten but a school in which the pupils were little children. The previous efforts for girls were with girls somewhat older who were attracted by the industrial features of the instruction rather than by the instruction in the "Three R's". In May 1875, these various girl pupils were gathered together and formed the nucleus of the Wang Lang School that then had its birth. The name of the school was changed in 1892 to Harriet M. House School, in honor of Mrs. Samuel R. House, whose faith and effort had provided a home for it. From small beginnings the school grew until it had out-grown its Wang Lang home. In 1921, under the leadership of Miss Edna S. Cole whose hand had then guided the school for thirty-six years, a new location was secured, buildings were erected and the boarding-school was transported in toto. A day-school was continued at the old Wang Lang site until the property was sold in 1925. The boarding-school was renamed

Miss Anderson and her " Infant School "

Wattana Wittiya Academy and started on a new era of service to the womanhood of Siam. The original plot of land was increased by purchase and by a gift in memory of Mrs. Mary Root McFarland who had, throughout her twenty-eight years in Siam, ever been a good friend of the Wang Lang School. On the death of T. Heyward Hays, M. D., the school became beneficiary to the income of a fourth part of his estate, which provides the wherewith for additional improvements year by year. Ample grounds, splendid modern buildings and a wonderful heritage makes the Wattana Wittiya Academy a school of far-reaching power, influence and importance.

During the period 1865-1885, the work at Petchaburi had gone steadily forward until at the end of those decades ten schools were being conducted in the market and Lao village near there. During this time the boys' school at Samray had been growing steadily, the work being greatly strengthened when in 1890, the Rev. John A. Eakin and the Rev. John B. Dunlap joined the teaching staff. The following year the name was changed to Bangkok Christian High School —the name that had been borne by Mr. Eakin's private school which he had brought with him when he joined the mission (in 1890). Mr. Dunlap was soon taken from the educational work and put in charge of the mission press, but Mr. Eakin continued to direct the course of the school for about fifteen years—to its very great benefit.

In view of the fact that the east side of the Menam Chaophya was rapidly developing into the residence section of the new Bangkok, it seemed that a boys' school should be located there to provide Christian education for the boys of that section of the city. It was therefore decided to started a new Bangkok Christian High School on the east side of the river. Land having been secured and buildings erected, in 1901 Dr. Eakin took charge of the new Bangkok Christian High School and began for this school a new period of growth and influence. The name was later changed to Bangkok Christian College. The site which was then in the very out-skirts of the city, is now in the heart of the city, and the grounds that then seemed ample for any possible future development, have come to be utterly inadequate for the school as it has developed during this quarter of a century. A site has now been selected far to the east beyond the outskirts of the present city—and there a new Bangkok Christian College is being built.

The school situation, as it existed when the early missionaries reached Bangkok in 1828, Dr. McGilvary found practically duplicated in North Siam when he went to Chiengmai in 1867. Only two women in the province could read and but few of the men : only those who had entered the priesthood were literate. Here again the need for learning had to be demonstrated. Since the boys could learn to read and write in the temples, the first successful school established was for girls. Mrs. McGilvary gathered a few girls about her and taught them Siamese, sewing, Bible, knitting and household economy. "They were really private pupils, living on our premises and in our family". It is interesting to recall that out of that little band of Lao girls whom Mrs. McGilvary gathered about her and trained with so much care came some of the noblest women of the Lao church. This was about 1875 ; and from this nucleus four years later was organized the Chiengmai girls' school under the superintendence of Miss Cole and Miss Campbell. To-day it occupies a beautiful campus and was first known as Prarachaya School and now as Dara Academy.

Many girls have come to Dara from all of the other mission schools for girls in the North, there gaining a higher education than is possible to give them in their own village schools, and the added vision and breadth that comes from residence in a capitol city—for Chiengmai has a long history of political power as the seat of the strongest of the northern Princes. Many of these girls return to their homes to teach in the schools there. Thus is the influence of Dara Academy wide and invaluable.

The first boys' school in Chiengmai was organized in 1887 by the Rev. D. G. Collins, and under his supervision it grew rapidly.

Eight years later the teaching force was strengthened by the assignment to the school of the Rev. William Harris.   In 1899 the Rev. D. G. Collins was relieved from school work that he might devote himself entirely to the work of the press which was printing in the Lao character and Mr. Harris then became principal.   Under his principalship, during the years that have intervened, the school has steadily progressed, exerting an influence intellectually, morally and socially. In 1906-7 the school was moved from the old buildings and site to a large, attractive site.   H. M. King Rama VI,—then still Crown Prince —while on a visit to the North, laid the corner stone of Butler Recitation Hall and gave a new name to the boys' school—The Prince Royal's College.   The grounds were laid out and plans for an adequate group of buildings were made.   The accomplishment of this task has been materially hastened by the generous gift of the late T. Heyward Hays, M. D., who, by his Will, left to the Prince Royal's College one fourth of the annual income of his estate.   The splendid foot-ball field and the new dining commons have thus been made possible— and more to follow.

By the time that mission stations were opened at Lampang, Prae, Chiengrai and Nan in the North, there was already a Christian community in each place and education was in demand so that schools for boys and girls were opened almost synchronously with the founding of each station.   All of these schools had boarding as well as day departments and to them were brought the Christian children from the out-stations as well as the local pupils.   In the early days it was out of the question to attempt out-station parochial schools, owing to the lack of native teachers and the widely scattered country flocks.   These central schools had the advantage of being under the constant over-sight of the missionary in charge ; on the other hand they were a very expensive means of education, as, to a large extent, both board and tuition were of necessity free.   It was therefore possible by this means to provide for but a very limited number of pupils.

The first out-village parochial schools were organized by the Rev. J. H. Freeman about 1900 in connection with the various churches and Christian communities in Lampoon province under his charge, and it was due largely to his example and precept that this idea was adopted by one station after another, until now it forms a part of the educational policy of the mission throughout North Siam. These parochial schools are usually held in country chapels with most meager equipment.

Industrial education has not kept pace with mental training in our schools. In the matter of manual training the girls' schools have as a rule excelled the boys'. The former have always taught sewing and various lines of domestic economy, with the result that our Christian school-girls have been conspicuous as successful home-makers.

The first extensive attempt at industrial education for the boys was made in Lampang about thirty-five years ago, the aim being to establish an Agricultural School. This was a most laudable object, for Siam is an agricultural country, pure and simple, whereas the methods and implements used are crude and inefficient. The mission procured a tract of about 30 acres of rice land, and a grant of $5,000 from the Board in New York; American farm implements and a pumping engine for irrigation work were purchased. But the foreign machinery proved unsuited to the local needs and the maintainence expenses of the pumping plant prohibitive. So this first attempt proved a failure.

Various other attempts on a small scale have been made by other schools of the mission in carpentry, masonry, gardening etc., the most elaborate of these being the tannery in connection with the boys' school in Lampang. This effort was a success in that a plant was equipped and training given until the project was economically successful and the plant was sold to the national manager who continues to operate it. In spite of the strong desire of educational leaders to the contrary, it must be admitted that the industrial effort

H.M. KING RAMA VI.

of the mission schools has not kept pace with the mental. This is
due to a number of causes, but the desire persists and will, it is
hoped, eventually lead to a re-adjustment of curricula in keeping with
vocational needs.

In the matter of medical education the mission has made the attempt to train a few assistants in connection with the various
hospitals. Some of these have become very efficient as non-profes-
sional assistants. In 1914-15 about $25,000 gold was raised for the
purpose of building and equipping the first laboratory of the proposed
mission medical school; the first class was organized in May 1916.
About that time the Royal Medical College began new plans leading
toward improvement of its staff and training and it seemed unnecessary for the mission to continue its plan for developing a Medical
College.

Theological education has suffered many vicissitudes. The first
effort to establish a theological school was in 1883. Five years later
a more successful attempt was made and the " Theological Training
School" continued its existance for five or six years, doing some excellent work, the fruits of which are still manifest. But this too
came to an untimely end. Finally in 1912 the generous gift of
$15,000 for the specific object of establishing a theological seminary
placed the mission under obligations to erect this new school on solid,
permanent foundations, physical and spiritual. To-day it has a staff
of five instructors and is known as the McGilvary Theological Seminary. Special account of this institution is given in a chapter
dealing with the Training of Christian Leaders.

In connection with the McCormick Hospital in Chiengmai a
school for the training of nurses was founded in 1923. A suitable
laboratory was equipped and instructors provided. Feeling that it
should be possible to attract better educated young women for this
training, the attempt from the first was to make the entrance
requirements as high as possible—quality, not quantity being the
aim. The result has exceeded the hopes of those who have given

so unstintingly of their time and effort to the new enterprise. The first graduating class of two also successfully took the examination of the Royal Red Cross Society and the present year's graduating class came to their nurses' training with Matayome VI or higher educational preparation. The training of these young women has been greatly helped by Miss Civili Sinhanetra who after completing her education at Prarachaya and Wang Lang, was sent by the Rockefeller Foundation to Peking for thorough training as a nurse. Since her return to Siam she has been connected with the McCormick Hospital and has given invaluable assistance to the Nurses' Training School.

In 1921 Miss McCord began a Bible Training School for girls. After the old Wang Lang site was sold, the Bible Training School formally opened its doors in rented quarters near the Maternity Home. This has made co-operation between the two institutions possible and a course in Bible instruction is being followed by a course in midwifery for those who are willing to take it. This institution is still in its infancy but it embodies a definite effort toward the training of women evangelists.

A stupendous task lay before the Siamese Government in creating an adequate Educational Department and developing a system which would lead to universal education. The establishing of schools, training of teachers to man these schools and the changing of public sentiment in favor of universal education for boys and girls was a task requiring decades of effort. The mission has been privileged to have a part in the achieving of this purpose. In the early years especially many of the boys and girls trained in the mission schools were invaluable in the teaching of some of these Government schools. The mission school helped create the desire for education and helped solve some of the problems of curriculum and training. Especially in the Government girls' schools was the influence of the mission girls' schools felt. Between the mission schools and the Educational Department of the Siamese Government happily a most cordial and mutually helpful relationship has existed. In 1878 H. M. King Chulalongkorn appointed the Rev. S. G. McFarland, D. D. as his first Superintendent of Instruction and the Principal of the first new King's College for Princes and sons of Nobles. One of the sons of this missionary, G. B. McFarland, M. D., organized the Government Medical College and remained with it for thirty-five years. Miss Cole was offered the principalship of a Government girls' school though the offer was not accepted. To-day the peculiar need which faced the Government in those days is supplied for it now has well organized schools for both boys and girls and a compulsory education law which is helping to bring about a higher degree of literacy among the people of Siam.

For a number of years the Mission has been working toward a uniform educational policy and a uniform curriculum. The Government curriculum is the basis in all mission schools and the policy of the Mission is to train both boys and girls in each one of the central mission stations as far as High School entrance. The two schools in each Chiengmai and Bangkok provide for the higher education for those who want to continue or who can be sent for further training for mission work.

The Government Educational examinations are taken by the pupils in the various mission schools and this proves gainful to these schools as well as helpful in making the education of Siam uniform. In cities where both Government and mission schools exist they cannot be said to compete. The mission schools largely minister to the needs of the Christian community. In several cases in smaller communities, the Government has waived the right to establish schools in consideration of the fact that the mission schools had already been established and were doing good work. The co-operation and friendly consideration of the Educational Department has been of incalculable value to the educational work of the mission and calls forth the highest possible appreciation from the corps of mission workers.

One other mark of Government courtesy should here receive mention. The mission schools have been also Christian schools. Though Siam is a Buddhist land and Buddhism the State religion, there has never been the least compulsion on the part of the Government in regard to the teaching of that religion in the mission schools. The decree of Religious Toleration issued by H. M. the late King Chulalongkorn in 1878 has found fullest observance by the Educational Department of H. S. M.'s Government.

In the early decades of the century now past Siam had few opportunities to come into contact with outside thinkers, to know and be helped by the intellectual movements of the time. Such was the calibre of the founders of the leading mission schools that they were able to pass on to this country some of the stimulation to the betterment of human life through Christian education which more advanced countries were then experiencing. Their motives were identical with those of the founders of schools and colleges in America during that period, expressed thus in the words of an early president of Wellesley College, "To put all that is truest and finest, sunniest and strongest into their lives,......to give them all that the years have brought to my own soul, God helping me."

It is the property of light to spread, of seeds to take root and grow in neighboring gardens. So in Siam many schools have indirectly benefitted by the Christian idealism prompting the motives and determining the objectives in the mission schools. Men and women, especially those who have been able to give many continuous years to one school, have enjoyed influential contact with the Siamese responsible for the national educational system. Far more important than any external patterning has been the silent contagion of spirit, the desire to serve, concern for character, the spirit of fair play—an influence that touches the most vital need. The largest contribution of the Mission to education in Siam has been in these intangible, but indispensable values.

CHAPTER XX

EVANGELISM IN THE NORTH

EVANGELISM in northern Siam began with a venture about equal to some of the aviation expeditions of the present day, one lone family with two small children making a three months' journey to their new location beyond the mountains. Another family would join them a year hence but they were to wait five years before a physician could reenforce them for a short time and seven years before a medical man would be a permanent part of their force. At that time the Presbyterian mission in Siam had two other stations and Dr. House was their only medical man.

The intensely interesting experiences of Dr. and Mrs. McGilvary and Dr. and Mrs. Wilson and their heroic faith during those early years are related in another chapter of this book.

The first decade was a period of many trials and patient waiting. At the end of this period the church numbered only nine communicants. Yet the annual report says "We must wait quietly, hopefully, prayerfully for the salvation of God in this land." The first chapel, a small bamboo structure, was built during the last year of this period and "some cases of illness in the Viceroy's palace had been treated successfully."

The second decade opens more encouragingly. Ten are added to the church membership during the first year and the report says of them, "Their deportment has been very exemplary. We think the Laos are going to make working Christians. A number of these have been gathered in as the original disciples were. 'He first findeth his own brother Simon......and brought him to Jesus.'"

During this second period reenforcements from America

221

made possible the establishment of a regular hospital and of a boarding school which greatly increased the appeal of the Christian movement to the minds of the people. Reenforcements also made possible a much larger amount of itineration. The period closes with more than four hundred in church membership, a fourth of whom had been added during the last year of this second decade.

The third ten year period opens with the organization of a new church (Chieng San) in the Chieng Rai province and it is recorded that " this hopeful beginning is due in large measure to the blessing of God upon the efforts of one man, formerly an elder in the Chiengmai church. About five years ago he was compelled by government order to remove with his family to Chieng San, which was then resettled after lying waste for many years. His piety was not only substantial enough to withstand a change of scene such as has proved disastrous to the spiritual life of some but through all these years he has been a living power for Christ. The missionaries at each successive visit have had the joy of baptizing at least one or two persons who had been instructed by him or his family in the way of life ".

During the third and fifth decades there were periods of large accessions followed by periods of consolidation and more thorough instruction and organization. The consolidation periods came somewhat automatically, being necessitated by limited resources and the limited force of workers.

From the very beginning a prominent feature of the work has been the relief of suffering and instruction as to the cause and cure of the most common diseases. This has been regarded by both missionaries and Lao evangelists as a very important part of the gospel message. Examples sufficient to fill a whole book could be furnished by the various stations. Here is one that comes to mind:— Word came from Muang Pao, four days' journey distant that many of the Christian people were ill with malarial fever. Their

Sri Chinmoon Church

stock of medicines was exhausted and two deaths had occurred already. It was during the height of the rainy season and the roads were almost impassable. Elder Sao cheerfully undertook the task, for which his work in the mission hospital peculiarly fitted him. Dr. McKean prepared a supply of medicines for him. Elder Sao's report is in part as follows:—

"Upon arriving at Muang Pao, I consulted with Rev. Chi Ma and we began work together. All of the Christian homes were visited, some of them many times. We instructed the sick and encouraged them. We prayed with them and treated the sick. Each evening a meeting was held for study and worship. A school with sixteen children in attendance was organized and a class of fifteen men spent five days in studying the Scriptures". Ninety patients were reported cured.

Relieving distress is one form of evangelism that appeals strongly to the people. When an epidemic occurs, those who are able to work are very willing to contribute liberally to supply the needs of any who are destitute. Relief of suffering often leads to the embracing of Christianity by those who first become acquainted with the gospel message in this form.

Practical sympathy with those in distress through witchcraft accusation, or slavery, or with such diseases as leprosy, smallpox, or malaria, have had an appeal to the hearts of the people as being the very essence of the gospel.

In former years witchcraft accusation and the sympathy and helpfulness shown by the missionary in such cases led many to become Christians. One such household supplied the nucleus of the Bethel church. From this group have come two ordained ministers of large usefulness, the Kev. Pannya Jayavanna and the Rev. Kham Ai Jayavanna; also the wives of two others of our most prominent ministers, the Rev. Semo Wichai and the Rev. Ban Chong Bansiddhi. Several teachers in our mission schools have come from this group.

Thanks to the Government, slavery has been abolished and

persecution on account of witchcraft charges has been forbidden for many years.

One of the characteristics of the Lao people is the tendency to act as households and groups of households rather than to act individually. This is especially true in religious matters. Many examples of this could be given in all our mission stations. One or two will suffice.

Noi Chi and his wife moved to a new district where farming land was cheaper. They were the only Christians in the district but they soon had led four other households to become Christians and had taught them to sing several hymns and to read the scriptures before the first visit of the missionary was made.

Noi Duang Keo and his family decided to accept the gospel message. He immediately became solicitous about his parents and other relatives and ere long eight entire households of them had become Christians.

It has been the custom to make much use of tracts and portions of scripture. This is especially true of the fifth and sixth decades, when the people everywhere have been much more ready to receive and read them. A house to house canvass is made and this is repeated at intervals and is fruitful in conversions. The American Bible Society has cooperated very largely and efficiently in this form of evangelistic effort.

Many years ago a neighbor of Nan Chi of Lampang province loaned him a copy of the Gospel according to St. John. He read in the ninth chapter the story of the healing of the blind man. The sympathy and healing power of Jesus appealed and after putting them to the test in his own household, he and his family accepted Christ as their personal Saviour and have been very zealous and faithful.

Thus the work has grown until now we have in our five northern stations thirty-nine organized churches.

The stress that has always been laid upon evangelism in northern

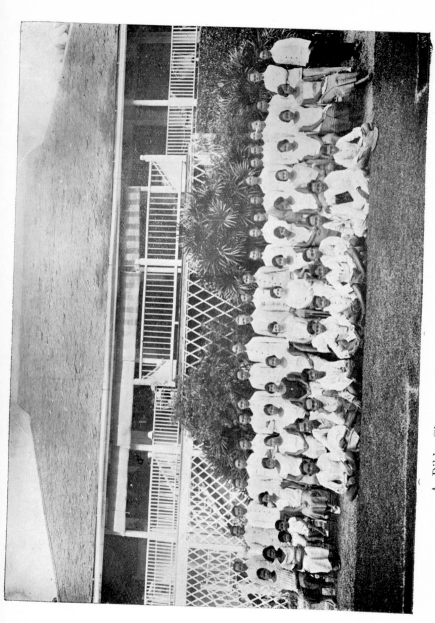

A Bible Class At The Campbell Residence, Chiengmai.

Siam, has developed a Christian church that is strongly self-propagating. Other elements have entered into this development: the early practice of witchcraft; the patriarchial organization of society; the isolation from the thoroughfares of the world; the bondage of fear under which the worship of spirits placed many:— these and many more things have conspired to assist the trend toward self-propagation of Christianity in the North. But one must not overlook the fact that the seed was carefully and prayerfully sowed. By example and precept the founders of the Christian church in North Siam, taught that each one has an unalterable responsibility for telling others what the Lord has done for him. And so the church has grown strong—in strengthening others.

The simpler days of the Nineteenth Century are gone—in North Siam as elsewhere—but the generation gone, or nearly gone, passes on to a more highly trained new generation traditions and a habit of religious life and walk that should mean a greatly enlarged leadership and broader evangelization of North Siam. The missionary "must decrease"—but the work will increase.

CHAPTER XXI

THE TRAINING OF CHRISTIAN LEADERS

In any view of our Lord's earthly ministry the training of the twelve is one of its most essential elements. The latest great missionary conference—the meeting of the International Missionary Council at Jerusalem—has emphasized afresh the vital importance of more through theological training on all mission fields.

In Siam as elsewhere this has been one of the most difficult parts of the missionary program to carry into effect satisfactorily The following pages are concerned mainly with North Siam and simply attempt a brief historical sketch of the various endeavors to secure to the church there an instructed leadership, for it is only in the last three years that a theological seminary for the whole mission has been in actual existence.

From the earliest days of the work in the North, Dr. McGilvary fully realized the necessity for well equipped national leaders. He put a great deal of time and labor into the instruction and training of picked and tested men among the early converts; no more fruitful work has ever been done in the northern field than was accomplished by some of those men. First among them was Nan Inta, the first baptised convert and the pioneer Lao evangelist and companion of Dr. McGilvary on his early tours. In speaking of the arrival of Dr. C. W. Vrooman in January of 1872, Dr. McGilvary says: "He found Nan Inta at the point of death from acute dysentery; and his first trophy, was the saving of that precious life. Had he done nothing else, that alone would have been well worth while." All through those early years man after man was taken under Dr. McGilvary's personal instruction and solidly grounded in Christian faith and knowledge.

In 1885 when the mission had been strengthened by several new

Early National Pastors of North Siam

are as follows :—

wer row, from left to right :—Noi Chai Ma, Chai Ma Nan Panya Pook.
cond row :—Nan Soopa (son of Nan Inta the first convert), Nai Wong,
anta, the first ordained Minister of North Siam, Nai Lin.   Third row :—
ng, Oon, Chailangka.   These three last were not ordained.   The eight
en in the lower row were ordained.   Of these eleven persons only Noi
hai Mai, Chai Ma and Panya are living.

arrivals and a Presbytery had been organized, the task of providing theological training seems to have been uppermost in Dr. McGilvary's mind. He writes: "I was then full of the idea of a theological training-class. My experience of the accumulated power added to the missionary's efforts by having such assistants as Nan Inta, Nan Suwan and Noi Intachak, raised in my mind the question, why not increase the number?" He wanted to organize a class of six or eight men and in a carefully prepared paper laid his views before Presbytery.

The disappointing outcome is best stated in his own words: "Presbytery took hold of the scheme with much ardor, but on far too large a scale and with far too formidable and too foreign apparatus. A regular 'Board of Education' was created with rules and regulations better suited to American conditions than to those among the Lao churches." One of the main difficulties was in regard to provision for the men's support. When this proved unacceptable the candidates declined to commit themselves to a scheme of training which they did not understand. The whole experiment was killed (by too much "red tape" Dr. McGilvary thought) before it had any chance of being tried out.

Dr. McGilvary however continued as was his wont to give all the instruction he could to his helpers individually. One of the most notable of these was Nan Ta who subsequently became the first ordained minister in the North. This man had been a protege and "luk keo" of the old Chiengmai Prince Kavilorot and had been one of those marked out for vengeance because of his Christian faith. Being warned, he fled the country, got across into Burma and wandered about for nine years, carrying with him a Siamese copy of the Gospel of St. Matthew which he had received from Dr. McGilvary in the early days. Not till after the publication of the Edict of Toleration did he venture to return to Chiengmai where he found his wife and infant daughter (then nine years old) still preserved to him. Dr. McGilvary thus describes his appearance upon his return in 1879:

"I saw a handsome man of medium height but of striking figure, larger and more portly than is usual among the Lao, and thirty-three years old, as I learned. It was evident that he had been spared and kept for some wise purpose. And so it proved. As a church member, as a ruling elder, and afterwards as an ordained minister, he was a power in the church till the day he was taken up. Thousands heard the Gospel from his lips, and many were drawn by his words and by his life into the fold of Christ."

The next attempt at the organization of a training school took place in 1888 under the Rev. W. C. Dodd, D. D. Mr. Dodd (as he then was) had collected a class of some twenty students, and when he and Mrs. Dodd were put in charge of the work at Lampoon the training class was moved to the latter place. For some six or seven years the school continued under the care of Mr. Dodd and later under the Rev. Robert Irwin. By 1894 the school had sent out a considerable number of evangelists,—between forty and fifty in all,—and the number of converts largely increased, the year 1893 being one of the banner years in this regard.

But as yet there was only the one ordained minister, Kru Nan Ta. He was then in his prime, doing a work of outstanding value. Ought there not to be more ordained workers like him? This question came up at the meeting of the mission and Presbytery in 1894. There were a number of men who had had two, three or more years of training, and of these nine were presented for examination before Presbytery. Dr. McGilvary tells us that the move at this time was against the advice of Dr. Dodd who was absent on furlough. The first thought was that one or two might be ordained to meet the immediate needs of the work, but eventually six were chosen for ordination and three for licensure.

That, however, was the time when ideas of Dr. Nevius were claiming wide-spread attention and making a strong appeal, and their trial in other fields was being urged by the Board. So the Lao churches were called upon to support the newly ordained minis-

McGilvary Theological Seminary

ters who were expected to be content with what the churches would give to maintain them. The result was that at the end of a single year this whole forward movement practically collapsed, the training school had to be abandoned and its reorganization was postponed for seventeen years.

Some of the principal mistakes which account for this second failure are fairly evident: (1) Missionary ideas were too much in the foreground; the churches and the students were largely passive. (2) The attempt to move forward was too rapid and sweeping, while conditions required a cautious and gradual advance. (3) The men ordained or licensed, with possibly one or two exceptions, were not ready for such a test as was imposed upon them. They expected larger pay than they have received as evangelists and were told to accept what the churches, through a plan of assessment, could raise for their support. (4) Both the churches and the ministers misunderstood what the mission was about, thus making failure inevitable. In Dr. McGilvary's judgement no party involved—the mission, the churches, the ministers and indirectly the Board—was free from blame for the undeniable back set caused by the closing of the training school at that time.

The six men who received ordination were the Reverends Pook, Wong, Oon, Chaima Sr., Chaima Jr. and Pannya. The licentiates were Chailangka, Nan Supa and Noi Lin. Three of the former—the Revs. Pannya and the two Chaimas,—still survive and are in good standing as ministers. Chaima Sr. is the oldest minister in Siam, at least of the Presbyterian mission, estimates of his age ranging from eighty-five to one hundred years. Chaima Jr. has for thirty years lived in Muang Sai in the Kamoo country and doubtless has had much to do with holding the Christian community there together through all its years of isolation, till today the signs of life and progress are unmistakable.

During the interval between 1896 and 1912 training work in the North, apart from instruction given in connection with the

general evangelistic work, was practically confined to an annual
class for elders and evangelists,—generally of about a month's
duration.   There were also the vaccination campaigns conducted by
Dr. McKean, extending over a number of years and achieving results
of the highest practical importance to the north country.   Large
numbers of men were sent out in all directions.   Vaccination was
combined with evangelistic work and at stated intervals the men
were required to attend classes both for instruction in vaccination
and for Bible study.

All along in the Lao churches the office of ruling elder has
been one of the corner stones of church organization.   It harmonized
with the social structure under which the people lived.   Each village had been used to be directed by its head-men ; each family or
group of families had had its guardians without whose sanction no
important decision could be taken.   So in each church the eldership
proved the most fitting instrumentality,—whether for instruction,
discipline or general leadership in the Christian community.   In all
the country churches many pastoral functions including the conduct
of public worship has devolved on the eldership.   Character, intelligence and knowledge of scripture on the part of their elders have
been perhaps of more vital importance to the welfare of these
churches than any other one factor that could be named ; nor in any
future development is it ever likely that the church can prosper
without a well instructed and high grade eldership.   The idea of
the pastorate on the other hand has still to win its way—partly because its place has been taken by the eldership with a missionary
acting as stated supply ; partly because the question of pastors'
salaries is yet an unsolved one in the northern areas.   This is the
question now lying immediately in front, to which the churches and
the mission must co-operate in finding an early solution.

Between 1896 and the reorganization of the Theological
Training School in 1912, only four men were ordained to
the ministry in North Siam namely, the Reverends Semo Wichai, Nan

Ti and Kham Ai Jayavanna in Chiengmai, and the Rev. Wong in Lampang.   Ordination in each case was conferred in view of general ability and knowledge or on the ground of services already rendered to the church.

The mission at its meeting in January 1912 once more undertook to provide for the regular training of leaders. The Rev. Henry White was appointed to take charge of the proposed seminary and it was transferred to Chiengmai station. In the following year the Rev. R. M. Gillies was also assigned to this work. The Reverends Semo Wichai and Kham Ai Jayavanna were appointed as Bible teachers. Mr. White was obliged by ill health to give up the work and return to America in 1920. The rest of the staff have carried on till the present time, with the addition of the Rev. A. W. Cooper who joined the school in the fall of 1927.

In 1913 a gift of money from Mr. Louis S. Severance of Cleveland, Ohio, made possible the present seminary building, which was dedicated in 1915 on the occasion of the visit of Dr. Robert E. Speer and his party, but not actually occupied until the following year. The seminary has now completed fifteen years of teaching, its annual term averaging over six months, and its average attendance between twenty-five and thirty men.   Until quite recently it has ministered exclusively to the better instruction of elders and evangelistic workers, thus seeking to strengthen the churches in their most immediate needs.   Its aim has been to be a center of continuous influence upon the churches. The call from Yunnan provided opportunity for what was practically foreign mission work. First and last over thirty men have gone to that field for periods ranging from one to four or five years.   Gradually a course of training for prospective pastors was undertaken and since 1920 ten men have been ordained : In Chiengrai, the Rev. Dee Ariwong, the Rev. Sook Kunasvasdihi and the Rev. In Kham Pinit; in Nan, the Rev. Tammawong Charoen Pong and the Rev. Pannya Chairangsee; in Lampang, the Rev. Phat Chindawong and the Rev. Dee Intrapan; in Chiengmai the

Rev. Birk Kantaratt, the Rev. Champoo Wongtaree and the Rev. Kham Chan Kantamit. Apart from seminary students, Chiengmai has also ordained the Rev. Ban Chong Bansiddhi, for many years head teacher at Prince Royal's College, and now in charge of the City Church at Chiengmai. Some of these men have proved unequal to their high calling but most of them are giving useful service and a few have taken honorable places of leadership. Seven or eight more have completed a course of training which might lead in the future to their appointment as country pastors.

Recent years have brought about two marked changes in the development of the seminary—the average age of students has gone steadily down, the majority now being young men; and the number drawn from our mission schools has steadily increased. Of course the two things go together. Formerly the early training of most of our workers was received in the temples, now we must depend practically altogether on pupils from the mission schools.

The latest advance step in our theological training work, and in some ways the biggest, was taken in January 1925, on the occasion of the visit of Dr. and Mrs. Cleland B. MacAfee. By this step the seminary at Chiengmai has become in fact as well as in name a mission institution, its students at the present time representing seven of our ten mission stations. The inauguration of the theological course of four years with English text books, confined to students of the 8th Matayome standing, has radically changed the character of the seminary and has created problems which the church and the mission have yet to solve. The curriculum, the teaching staff and the financial support of the institution are all in a process of evolution. The Centennial finds us with seven students in the advanced grade; five in their third year and two in their first year; also with a tentative constitution and Board of Directors charged with the task of working out a future policy.

With the help of various members of the mission as lecturers and with the valuable aid of the Rev. S. J. R. Ensign since June of last year, it has been possible to get this new venture fairly under way, but only thorough co-operation between the church and the mission can we secure its future. The way must be found to make it as rapidly as possible a Siamese and not an English institution, and a sound basis must be found for its financial support. The failure of earlier attempts, owing mainly to money difficulties, is a standing warning that the present undertaking is also doomed to disappointment unless a permanent solution can be found to this problem of support.

At the end of one hundred years since the Gospel first reached Siam, what confronts us with regard to theological training is not an achievement but rather a complicated problem. Our task is to turn that problem into an achievement. How shall it be done? There is only one way—that we find and follow the mind of Christ.

CHAPTER XXII

LEPROSY IN SIAM

" In all the long procession of the ages there is no more truly tragic figure than that of the leper. His cup is full to the brim with bitterness, and includes in it every ingredient of sorrow. He is an out-cast and life for him holds no hope. Indeed, the very word has become the synonym for all that is foul and repulsive."

Leprosy is a world disease. It is to be found in all lands, but it thrives best and does its horrid work most extensively in tropical and sub-tropical lands, although it is known in cold countries,—even in Iceland.

Neither history nor legend give any information as to the time or manner in which leprosy came into Siam. It would seem probable that the disease came with the Tai people as they moved downward from China during several centuries.

The actual extent of the malady and the total number of lepers in the Kingdom is not known with any degree of accuracy. A census of the leper population taken some ten years ago, showed about seven thousand recorded cases. But like all attempts at making a leper census this one must have given very inaccurate results and the figure named evidently is much below the actual number of leper people.

The two chief reasons for inaccuracy in making a leper census are the census-taker's lack of knowledge regarding the disease and also and particularly the unwillingness of the leper and his friends to have him registered as a leper. Their passive resistance is usually very effective.

It is probable that in a population of less than ten millions, Siam has approximately twenty thousand people infected with lep-

His Majesty the King addressing a company of leper men.

rosy, many of these being incipient and unrecognized cases.

Desultory and ineffective aid was given to leper people locally in Chiengmai beginning in 1892 but it was not until 1908 that organized work was begun, this being the first organized effort for lepers in the Kingdom.

In that year a gift to the mission by His Siamese Majesty's Government of a plot of land for an asylum made possible an attempt to establish a work for these needy folk. This plot, comprising more than one hundred acres, consists of the lower half of an island in the Maping river five miles below the city of Chiengmai. It is admirably located and in every way well adapted to the purposes of the Asylum.

In October 1928 the Asylum completed its twentieth year. The growth has been slow and gradual, but continuous. There are now three hundred and fifty patients in the institution. During these twenty years ten hundred and ninety-five patients have been received.

The hearty encouragement and the generous financial support of the Mission to Lepers, British, during many years made expansion along conservative lines possible. During later years the chief support has come as ample allowances from the American Mission to Lepers. The people of Siam have given generous aid in support of the work both in money gifts and in the erection of buildings, no less than twelve of which have been supplied, chiefly by the Royalty and Nobility.

In addition to gifts from individual Siamese, generous grants in aid were received from His Siamese Majesty's Government during a period of several years.

In 1924 through the kind offices of His Royal Highness the Prince of Nagor Svarga, Vice-President of the Siamese Red Cross Society, the Chiengmai Leper Asylum was placed upon the Government Budget for ten thousand ticals per year,—the equivalent of four thousand five hundred dollars, U. S. gold. This amount is approximately one third of the annual outlay for maintenance and is a most highly appreciated favor.

On a visit to Chiengmai in January 1927, His Majesty the King accompanied by the Queen evinced his interest in His Leper subjects by visiting the Asylum. At this time His Majesty graciously gave command for the metalling of the road leading from Chiengmai to the Asylum. The work now having been completed the Asylum is very greatly the gainer by this Royal donation.

In 1924, Dr. T. Heyward Hays of Bangkok by his will left to the Asylum one fourth of his estate, the interest from which is to be used annually for the benefit of the Asylum.

In the inception of the work His Royal Highness Prince Damrong, at that time Minister of the Interior, gave his personal and official aid in securing a grant of the land and gave his moral support to the project.

An endeavor has been made to render community life as nearly ideal as is possible in a community where marriage and real family life are not allowed.

To this end the Siamese form of local self-government with officials elected by themselves is in use and gives much satisfaction. A hospital and dispensary, a church, schools for men and women, a Siamese physician, a sanitary squad, uniformed home guards, a welfare committee, a community store and grocery market, blacksmith and carpenter shops, tailor shops for the men and for the women, etc. give to this community the semblance of a well regulated village, rather than that of a hospital or " an abode of living death," as a leper asylum at times has been designated.

Indeed instead of an atmosphere of gruesomeness there is rather one of good cheer and contentment. In as much as nearly all of the patients in the Asylum have become believers in Christ, there is no doubt that the assurances of the Gospel contribute in a very large degree to their peace of mind.

Garden plots are given to those who are able to work. All such persons are encouraged to raise vegetables and fruit for their own use. Experience has shown that the active, busy leper patient is

Ministers' Village. Five of these cottages were built by the Royalty and nobility of Siam : one by an uncle of the King, two by brothers of the King and two by noblemen of high rank.

more contented and makes much more rapid progress toward cure than the indolent, inactive patient; hence all our people are encouraged to work either in their own gardens or in the care of the village streets, of the cocoanut palms and the village door-yards. Flowers are grown in profusion and a degree of village pride is evident.

In 1923 the Siamese Red Cross Society began a work for the lepers of Southern Siam and in 1924 the Red Cross Leper Asylum was dedicated at Prapadaeng in Bangkok. His Majesty King Rama VI and Her Majesty the Queen Mother made liberal contributions to the original building fund while the Royalty and Nobility also contributed generously. His Majesty's Government makes good grants in aid for yearly maintenance.

This asylum is well operated and is doing a valuable work with nearly two hundred patients in its wards. The call for enlargement is insistent for there still are many leper people in and near this great city who are in urgent need of care.

The Department of Public Health operates an out-door leper clinic in Bangkok where several hundred patients receive treatment free of all cost. Out-door clinics form a useful and inexpensive method of treating leprosy, but this method has distinct limitations inasmuch as the chief value of out-door clinic treatment lies in securing the early cases in whom there is good hope of improvement, whereas experience shows that the patients who come to such clinics, for the most part, are advanced cases in whom hope of improvement is more problematical.

The work for lepers in Sritamarat was begun by Dr. E. B. McDaniel as a small out-door clinic in 1922. The attendance has increased slowly but steadily, some four hundred patients having received treatment. Inasmuch as many patients come from a distance, it has been found necessary to provide shelter, residence and support for these and this has resulted in the formation of the Nakon Leper Home with some seventy in-patients.

There are now ten buildings with a good area of land. Generous contributions have been received from many individuals and business firms, with a fine spirit of co-operation on the part of many people. His Siamese Majesty's Government has donated an additional area of twenty-five acres of land that is suitable for growing fruit and vegetables. Members of the Royal and official class have manifested an interest in the work. With a probable leper population of two to three thousand lepers in this area, the need for expansion and for adequate support is apparent and there is good prospect of growth into an institution of great value to the community.

In Petchaburi and in Trang Dr. Bulkley has made a beginning of work for lepers.

For some years past Tai speaking leper patients from Yunnan Province, China, have come to the Chiengmai Asylum in considerable numbers. They have come with great difficulty on foot over mountain trails,—a journey of from twenty to twenty-eight days.

Dr. Galt of the Presbyterian mission in Chiengrung (Kiulungkiang), Yunnan, has begun a work for lepers of that region and now has seventy people in his Asylum. Although this region is beyond the political boundaries of Siam yet the people are Tai and this interesting development of leper work in a very needy field should be mentioned in this connection.

In the four asylums mentioned the accepted treatment is by the use of Siam-grown oil of Hydnocarpus anthelmintica (Chaulmoogra Oil). Some five or six species of Hydnocarpus trees grow abundantly in the forests of Siam, the fruit of which probably would produce oil sufficient for the treatment of the two or three million lepers of the world.

While treatment with Chaulmoogra oil and its derivatives gives the best results of any remedy hitherto used, yet it is very far from being a specific for the cure of the disease. While we may well rejoice in the effectiveness of this remedy, undue optimism as to the ready curability of leprosy should be avoided.

Hay's Memorial Injecting Clinic with open air dressing station in the rear, Thaw Chapel.

Leprosy is not only a world disease, it is a world problem. No solution is at hand as yet. There is great encouragement however in the fact that governments are becoming more and more aware of the need of caring for the leper and of preventing the spread of this disease.

Siam has made a beginning. There is a growing consciousness in the public mind that persons infected with leprosy should live apart from family and friends.

His Majesty the King is interested in all efforts to rid His Kingdom of this malady. Princes and nobles, the Department of Public Health and the Siamese Red Cross Society are giving attention to the leper problem and there is every reason to hope that the interest will grow in strength and effectiveness until means and measures are found to eradicate leprosy from Siam.

CHAPTER XXIII

WORK AMONG THE CHINESE IN SIAM

IN an age when men are crying for bigger and better things in life, business and religion, we in the missionary cause of Christ must often find our comfort in the age old words of wisdom, "Despise not the day of small things." Certainly this is true of the work among the Chinese in Siam. In looking back over the past century to that day when the Rev. Jacob Tomlin and the Rev. Carl Gutzlaff arrived in Siam, where within two months time they had exhausted their meager supply of scriptures among the Chinese of Bangkok, and looking upon the many thousands of Chinese who have come to Siam since that time, we are forced to admit that in the missionary efforts among this people, the "day of small things" is still with us, but by no means is it a day to be despised.

"Strangers working with strangers in a strange land" might well be given as a title to the missionaries working among the Chinese in this land of the "Yellow Robe." But, in comparing the number of workers with the statistics on Chinese immigration to Siam, it is readily seen that the increase in our missionary force has not corresponded proportionately with the increase of the Chinese strangers, who have flowed into this friendly land during the past one hundred years. To-day, they form a large part of the population in all of the larger cities and towns throughout the kingdom. Most of these are being neglected today through the lack of workers and the necessary funds to carry on the work. Two or three years ago, the Harbor Department's statistics showed an annual increase of 30,000 adult Chinese over a period of ten years, over and above the number that returned to China and those who were born and died in the land. In a recent report on "Chinese Migration to Siam" for the period April to August 1928, inclusive, there were 50,564 Chinese men and women who arrived from China, and 29,032 who returned, leaving a net increase of 21,532 for that five months period. On the other hand, our missionary force now working with these many thousands of strangers, consists of two families and one single woman in the capitol city of Bangkok, one family in the Petchaburi field, and three other workers who from their work among the Siamese devote a portion of their time to reach the Chinese in their fields of labor. " A day of small things !—yes, from the number of workers on the field,—BUT A DAY WHICH IS NOT TO BE DESPISED. The mustard seed has not yet developed into the greatest of all herbs, but the signs of life and self-expression on the part of the nationals, lead us to hope for an unusual growth within the next few years.

From the time that the American Baptist Board withdrew their missionary force from Siam until the present date, the Baptist Chinese Christians have continued to carry on a regular chapel for their Christians who come to this land from China. For a number of years one of the missionary staff of the Baptist mission at Swatow, made an annual visit to Bangkok to look after their mission interests and to advise and encourage the Christian Chinese here. Since the death of the Rev. John Foster, D. D., of the Baptist mission at Swatow, there have been but two visits made, one by the Rev. Mr. Grovesbeck in 1923 and one by the Rev. A. H. Page in 1928.

The Presbyterian Chinese church in Bangkok (known as the Third Church of Bangkok) was founded in the year 1896, sixty-eight years from the date of the arrival of the first Protestant missionaries on these shores. Its growth has been slow, and many have been the difficulties which have retarded its growth throughout the years. Oftentimes an occasional wind of opposition has been able to do more damage in a few weeks than all the united efforts of the church for good in as many years. One of the greatest handicaps in the early days of the Chinese church, was the necessity of conducting and supervising the work through the medium of the Siamese language.

First the message was given in Siamese, then interpreted into Chinese. But for the past few years the services have been entirely in the Chinese language, the missionaries themselves speaking it.

The first missionary supervisor of the Chinese work in Bangkok was the Rev. F. L. Snyder, assisted by a Chinese named Kru Choi. The first meeting place was a small rented building on the Raja-wongse Road, where the light from the Chinese Presbyterian church began to shine dimly into the vast darkness. In consulting one of the older Chinese Christians, it was learned that at that time there were only seven members, five having come from China and two who had been received into the church in Siam. In the year 1897 a Chinese named Ang Kia Eng and one Nai Tham were baptised, and two years later the wife of Ang Kia Eng was also baptised. In 1899 the church moved to Samyek and that same year there came two other Chinese from China, Ang Tong E and Lim Seuy Kee, and these became the first elders of the Chinese Presbyterian church in Bangkok. From the year 1903 to 1907 the Chinese pastor was Chung Kia, the missionary supervisor at that time being the Rev. J. B. Dunlap, D. D. In 1910 the church was moved to the Plang Nam Road, the present meeting place of the Tie Chieu congregation, and from that time until the year 1915 the church was under the supervision of Dr. Dunlap and Mr. E. M. Spilman.

The Siam mission had long realized that to do the most efficient work among the Chinese in Siam, they must have a missionary who could devote his time to the study of the Chinese language and so be able to direct this work in their own native tongue. For seventy-five years this request had repeatedly been made but until 1915 it was not possible for the Presbyterian Board of Foreign Missions of New York, to accomplish its desire along this line. Then it sent out the Rev. and Mrs. Graham Fuller for Chinese work in Bangkok. Shortly after their arrival, Mr. Fuller was granted permission to make a visit to China to study some of their methods of working with the Chinese there and also to obtain some help for his own language study. As the

Early Leaders in 3rd Presbyterian Church, Bangkok

Left to right:—Nai Chek Muk Saa Pei, Kru Choy, Rev. W. G. McClure, D.D.,........,
Nai Tong E (a Professor of Chinese Literature).

overwhelming majority of Chinese in Siam now speak the Tie Chieu dialect, Mr. Fuller naturally went to Swatow for this help and later he and Mrs. Fuller began their study of that dialect. With the coming of the Fullers, the Chinese work began to prosper, so that within a short time the Siam mission felt the need of another family for the Chinese work. In 1919, the Rev. and Mrs. A. G. Seigle were also appointed for Chinese work in Bangkok and upon their arrival were assigned to the study of the Cantonese dialect. Later Mr. Seigle began the organization of the Cantonese branch of the Chinese church. In 1920, the need of a single woman to have charge of the Cantonese girls' school was felt and in response to this call, the Board sent out Miss Alice Schaefer who en route spent a year in the Language School at Canton and arrived in Bangkok in 1924 to take up this school work.

While the progress of the Chinese church during these years has not been record-breaking, yet there has been a slow, steady growth which inspires hope for bigger and better things in the next few years. The church record for the year 1913, shows a membership in the Chinese church of forty adults, most of these being of the Tie Chieu dialect. The church record, giving the membership of the two main bodies of the Chinese church for the year 1928, shows a membership of 169 in the Tie Chieu group, 107 in the Cantonese group. This number does not include the hundreds who crowd the doors of these meeting places during the Sunday morning services. There were fourteen adults and twenty-five children baptised during the past year, together with a number who were received by letter from China. With the increase in membership, there has also come the increase in financial support, so that to-day, with the exception of the rent for the two chapel buildings, both of these larger bodies of the church are entirely self-supporting. The money raised during the year for benevolences, congregational and other expenses, amounted to Tcs. 1,945.74 by the Tie Chieu group, and Tcs. 1,716.51 by the Cantonese group, making a total of Tcs. 3,662.25 for the Chinese church during the past fiscal year.

In 1917, Mr. Fuller engaged the first Cantonese preacher, a man by the name of Yee Khee Meng.   But owing to his ill-health, he was compelled to give up this work after a very short time. In 1919, when Mr. and Mrs. Seigle arrived in Siam, there were about ten Cantonese Christians meeting with the Tie Chieu group for their Sunday worship.   But, as this was an entirely different dialect from their own, they were unable to get very much spiritual food.   Immediately Mr. Seigle began a service for the Cantonese Christians, using the English language and his language teacher, Mr. Choi Tsun Sun, interpreting the message into the Cantonese.   At that time Mr. Choi was not a Christian but later he was baptised and was received into the church.   After his conversion, Mr. Choi was able, with a little help, to conduct the preaching services by himself, which he did for more than a year.

At this time the Cantonese were meeting in the same building in Plang Nam Road with the Tie Chieu group, but at a different hour. Later, at the invitation from the Resident-Secretary of the Boon Itt Memorial Institute they moved to the lower floor of the Boon Itt Memorial building. Once every two months the Tie Chieu group joined them in the Communion service in this place.   In December of 1926, the Cantonese decided to have a small place of worship all their own, so after subscribing more than ticals five hundred, for the alteration and furnishings of a chapel near Sam Yek, they moved in and the first service was the Christmas service of that year.   The Chinese church plans for the near future, include an Institutional Church building, in which these present divided congregations may be united into one large church and united in a effort to reach the thousands of their fellowcountrymen in Siam.   At present each separate group has its own pastor, elders and deacons for their individual group work, but all unite together in one large meeting to face the problems that concern the church at large.

One of the most encouraging features of the Chinese church work at the present time, aside from the fact that the church is almost entirely self-governing, is the present plan of distributing the scriptures, and the opening of Bible classes in the different sections of the city.   For a number of years Mr. Fuller and Mr. Seigle have assisted the Rev. Robert Irwin, of the American Bible Society, in the distribution and sale of the scriptures, the Bible Society supplying the scriptures and providing for the wages for the colporteurs, the missionaries supervising the men, receiving their reports, and paying the salaries.   This past year the responsibility for the distribution of the scriptures was laid upon the church, and it was a joy to see the spirit with which the church went at this new task.   For weeks the missionary, Chinese pastor and Bible women, went from house to house distributing on an average of one hundred and seventy-five portions of scripture daily, and with each portion went a personal message to the receiver. The church members were each given a number of scriptures to distribute in his own community, and many of them came back for a further supply of books. Another way in which the church is finding its way into the different communities, is through the Bible classes which are held in the homes of Christians or of friends of the church.   At some of these meetings there are as many as sixty persons, many who hear the Gospel story for the first time. From these Bible classes we have been able to get some of the children to attend Sunday School at the church on Sunday morning. Here the Ford car, a gift from the Westminster Church of Bloomfield, New Jersey, plays very important part.   Sunday after Sunday the prospect of a ride in the Ford is a drawing card in getting some of the children to Sunday School.

During these years, while the church has gone forward, many things have happened which have brought joy to our hearts ; still there have been apparent defeats which have brought much sorrow. In the fall of 1918, some Chinese friends came to Mr. and Mrs. Fuller asking that a mission school be opened for Chinese boys, promising to help in whatever way they could. The Presbyterian mission consented and the Chinese raised Tcs. 40,000 which purchased a piece of property adjoining the Bangkok Christian College, with the understanding that this school was to be a Chinese Department of the Bangkok Christian College. A Chinese Board of Directors was formed, and contracts drawn up between them and the mission. The school very shortly had more than one hundred pupils. Feeling encouraged, in the spring of 1919 the Chinese Board of Directors opened a school for girls, the Loyal School, the mission granting the use of the ground floor of the Rev. Graham Fuller residence for this purpose. About this time, the Siamese Government began enforcing the law, that all teachers of schools in Siam must know Siamese :those not knowing any Siamese were given one year for opportunity to study and at the end of that time were to take an examination. Then if anyone failed to pass, he was not permitted to teach. All but one of the teachers in the boys' school, being unwilling to comply with the law of Siam in this particular, left and entered other lines of work. New teachers were secured from China at a great expense. Their salaries were very high and the running expenses of the school were heavy. From this time, the school was not self-supporting, so in 1924, because of the lack of funds, the school was closed. During the life of the school, twenty boys were brought to know Christ as their Saviour and were baptised and were received into the church. Others were influenced, but because of the home opposition, did not join the church. In June 1929, one of these Chinese boys who was converted while in this school, will graduate from the Union Theological Seminary at Canton, China, and will return to Siam to teach and preach Jesus Christ to the Chinese of Bangkok. The Loyal School for girls continued to grow and to prosper until October of 1926, when the spirit of patriotism ran high in the hearts of the Chinese people. Unfortunately, that year the Chinese Republic day fell on Sunday. The children requested that they be allowed to have a big tea party and celebration at the school on that day. The principal told them they might return to the school, sing their National anthem and salute the flag, but she could not grant permission to have the tea party and celebration on Sunday, but that they might have it on the following day. This refusal caused much commotion among the students who went on a strike, eighty per cent leaving the school. As the school was on a self-supporting basis, with a monthly expense of over five hundred ticals, it was impossible to carry on. Since the closing of the school, many requests have come from the Chinese that we re-open it. It is our hope that in the very near future we shall be able to open these schools, where we believe the seed of God's Word has been sown, and from which we are still expecting big results.

Mention should be made of the Chinese work which is being done by those in Siamese work in some of the other stations of our mission. The Rev. R. W. Post, though using the Siamese language as a medium, has a growing work among the Chinese in the North Petchaburi field. At present there are two ordained Chinese preachers working in this field. Along the Rajburi river, among the Hakka Chinese, there are three Christian Chinese groups.

The Rev. Loren S. Hanna has a growing work among the Chinese in Lampang. Last year the Chinese completed their small brick chapel in the market, and the interest in the church has increased greatly. The pastor is a very earnest and zealous Christian worker, laboring to win those of his people in this place far removed from their native land. The Chinese meet for their morning worship with the Lao Christians in the Lao church, and at their own church in the afternoon.

Trang has very large Chinese population of various dialects. One-third of the members of the Trang church are Chinese. The Rev. Gaylord Knox is in charge of the evangelistic work in the Trang church field, and he reports an ever increasing interest among the Chinese in the Gospel story. At Huey Yot, about 18 miles from Trang, there is a group of ten Chinese Christians who are paying two-thirds of the chapel rent. At Kantang there is another group of twenty who own their own place of worship. More than thirty years ago the Plymouth Brethren, an English mission, opened up a work at Tongkah, the island of Puket, with a resident medical missionary and a Chinese evangelist. This group was in a flourishing condition for some twenty years. For more than ten years this place had no resident missionary, but the Chinese Christians carried on their regular services. A few years ago, the Christians of Puket asked our mission to send a man to take up the work there, guaranteeing his support and assistance in the school and church work, but owing to the lack of workers we were compelled to refuse.

In looking over the Chinese situation throughout the kingdom of Siam, the words of our Master are brought to our minds with renewed emphasis, namely, "The harvest truly is great, but the laborers are few: pray ye therefore the Lord of the harvest that He send forth laborers into His Harvest." "Say not ye, there are yet four months, and then cometh the harvest? Behold I say unto you, Lift up your eyes and look on the fields; for they are white already to harvest......I send you to reap that whereon ye bestowed no labour; other men labored, and ye are entered into their labors."

CHAPTER XXIV

THE AMERICAN BIBLE SOCIETY

THE Bible Society is built on what, at first, was an assumption, viz. that the Bible is God's book and also man's, because "it has the same living power to change men of every race which it has shown among those of our own race."

The organization of the English and Foreign Bible Society in 1804 "for Wales" and "the World," "had the effect of an electric shock that quickened men's faculties" in America and "within six years time more than a hundred Bible Societies had been organized in the United States with the simple purpose of providing Bibles for the poor who had not means of supplying themselves" and to extend its benefits, when possible, to foreign lands. To better meet this need of the fast-growing frontier settlements the national American Bible Society was formed in 1816.

The record is not at hand which definitely states when the American Bible Society began to take a part in the providing of scriptures in Siam, but in the Centennial History of the Society printed in 1916, there is definite reference to the work of Bible translation and revision carried on by the Rev. Chas. Robinson, who joined the A. B. C. F. M. mission in Siam in 1834. Quoting from this history:—"Another early mission of the American Board (A. B. C. F. M.) was in Siam, having been commenced by David Abeel in 1831 and continued until about 1850 when the missionaries were withdrawn. During the time of their stay in Bangkok the missionaries set up a printing office, manufactured Siamese type, and with the money granted by the Society, issued in Siamese the New Testament and some books of the Old Testament." Apparently this grant of money by the American Bible Society was continued not only as long as the A. B. C. F. M. mission in Siam continued its existence, but was also made to the American Presbyterian mission after it took up work in Siam. The early Presbyterian Board letters to its Siam mission contain repeated requests for more definite and fuller reports as to how the funds of the American Bible Society were expended. Since the earliest efforts of the Baptist mission in translation of scripture portions stressed their own baptismal beliefs, the other missionaries felt the necessity of also translating the scriptures. The result was doubtless a gain, for it brought a broader and greater effort to this task, and laid the foundations for the later united effort along this line and the final evolving of the one common Siamese translation of the scriptures which is today undergoing revision—as has been the case ever since the first beginnings at translation by Gutzlaff.

A very interesting fact connected with this translation of the scriptures lies in the fact that the printing and distributing of these scripture portions and other religious literature, really made the printing press of today. The need felt by the missionaries, led to their experiments with printing presses, type casting and the forming of a Siamese printed character. The earliest type bore the characteristic slant of script; the perpendicular printed letter was a much later development.

Another evidence of the part the early printing of the scriptures had on printing in Siam is brought out in the following quotation from the Rev. Chas. Robinson, taken from the same Centennial History of the American Bible Society:—"This mission has introduced in your books the division of words in printing, as is done in other languages. The Siamese generally acknowledge that this makes the book much easier to read than those printed in the Siamese method which runs the words together." It might be added that this modification has also extended to the written language: most modern Siamese printing and writing follows this division into words.

เรื่องข่าวดีประเสิฐ แห่งพระเยซูเจ้า,ที่ศิศชื่อไยฮันได้เขียนไว้.

หนัาต้นบท ๑.

๑ ในที่แรกเดิมนั้นองค์คำก็ยงอยู่,แลองค์คำนั้นอยู่กับด้วย
พระเจ้า,แลองค์คำนั้นก็เปนพระเจ้า.

๒ พระองค์นั้นตั้งอยู่แต่แรกเดิมกับด้วยพระเจ้า.

๓ พระองค์ได้ทรงสร้างสาระพัดทุกสิ่งสิ้น,จะหาสิ่งอันใดๆ
นอกจากที่พระองค์ไม่ได้สร้างนั้นไม่มีเลย.

๔ ในพระองค์นั้นมีชีวิตรตั้งอยู่, แลชีวิตรนั้นเปนที่สว่างแก่
มนุษทั้งปวง..

๕ รัศมีนั้นส่องสว่างไปถึงที่มืด,แต่มืดนั้นมิได้ยอมให้สว่าง
นั้นเข้าไป.

๖ ครั้นอยู่มามีบุรุษผู้หนึ่งชื่อไยฮัน.

๗ บุรุษนั้นพระเจ้าได้ใช้ให้มาเปนพญาณสำหรับที่จะได้อธิ
บายความสว่างนั้น, เพื่อจะให้คนทั้งปวงเชื่อถือด้วยเหตุท่าน.

๘ อันไยฮันมิไช่สว่างนั้น,เปนแต่พญาณว่าถึงสว่าง.

๙ สว่างนั้นแลเปนสว่างเที่ยงแท้,ซึ่งได้สว่างทั่วไปแก่มนุษ
ทั้งปวงที่บังเกิดมาในโลกย์นั้น.

๑๐ พระองค์ได้อยู่ในโลกย์นี้, แลพระองค์ได้สร้างโลกย์นี้,
แต่มนุษในโลกย์นี้มิได้รู้จักพระองค์.

Much of the effort of the early missionaries centered around the tract house where scripture portions as well as tracts were distributed. The early Chinese and Siamese assistants of the missions spent most of their time in going about among the people talking to them and giving out these books and explaining them. Just what portion of this work was dependent upon the funds given by the American Bible Society cannot be ascertained by the records at hand, but certainly the missions and the Bible Society worked together in this matter.

One of the Presbyterian missionaries most interested in this phase of the work was the Rev. John Carrington, D. D. Ill-health necessitated the resignation of Mr. and Mrs. Carrington in 1875. But in 1889 he was returned to Siam by the American Bible Society as its first Foreign Secretary to Siam. Dr. Carrington toured extensively distributing scripture portions wherever he went. The climate of Siam seemed unsuited to his wife and finally she was again forced to return to America, but Dr. Carrington remained alone in Siam until his death in 1912, carrying on patiently and bravely the work so dear to his heart. During his later years, a very familiar sight was this old, white-haired man trudging through the streets, with his out-stretched left hand filled with scripture portions, the curved handle of his umbrella, perchance, hooked on the out-stretched arm while with the right he offered the books to all who would take them. Means of transportation was still primitive and so most of the time he went on foot, until his swollen feet, encased in ill-fitting shoes became almost unbearably painful. But still he persevered, never speaking one word in anger or complaint, but sweetly and kindly trying to bring to others the Word of Life which had brought peace and comfort to his own soul. The actual cause of his death was cerebral congestion, probably induced by over exposure to the sun—for he was seventy-two years of age when he died —and to the time of his last illness he never ceased his work. During the lucid moments after he was taken sick, over and over again he would say, "I am so tired; but oh, if I only had the strength to go out and take them these precious books!" Dr. Carrington passed on to his reward but many today testify to the matchless devotion of this godly man to the cause of making Christ known. His work had been largely confined to South Siam,—translating, printing and other forms of endeavor being subordinate to the actual distribution of scriptures.

Rev. W. H. Cameron and Mrs. Cameron were appointed assistants to Dr. Carrington in 1909 and they carried on for a short time after his death. In 1911 the Rev. and Dr. Robert Irwin were appointed to the vacant post and the work has been under their supervision ever since. Coming to the work from a long experience in North Siam, they brought to the new task that was theirs a background which has given a new direction to the work of the American Bible Society. The Agency, while not lessening the work in South Siam, began then to reach out to the other branches of the Tai race and to provide the scriptures in the various Tai dialects and in the languages of the hill tribes. Wherever possible it has been our aim to work through the missionaries, furnishing them scriptures and money, they securing and superintending the helpers. The work has been difficult and slow but something has been accomplished. Many hundreds of thousands of scripture portions have been distributed in all parts of Siam. It is not an exaggeration to say that in a general way the American Bible Society has extended its work all over Siam. In the southern Shan States of the Salween river, circumstances have made it necessary to send men from Siam at great expense a few months only each year and these men have distributed many thousands of scriptures, but not more than half the country has been covered by these tours. The British and Foreign Bible Agency of Burma is responsible for carrying the scriptures to the Tai west of the Salween. South China has probably as many Tai as Siam, less than half of whom are literate, but we have only touched them in half a dozen spots in Yunnan. We have a Tai-speaking Chinese, with his Tai wife from

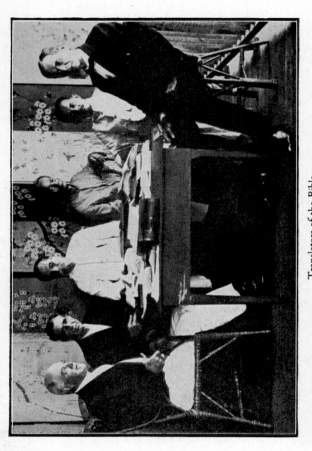

Translators of the Bible

Left to Right:—Rev. J. A. Eakin, D.D., Rev. R. Irwin, Rev. A. W. Cooper, Rev. Yuan Tien Yok, Rev. Kim Heng Mangkonphan, Rev. W. G. McClure, D.D.

Chiengmai, in training at the Alliance mission school of Wuchow preparing to go to the Tai of Kwang-Si next fall if the way opens. China Inland missionaries of Kwei-chow have made a beginning with the Tai there.

It is only two years since the French authorities began to allow mission work in Luang Prabang province. We at once united with the American Presbyterian mission to put two Siamese families into Luang Prabang city for colporteur and evangelistic work. The Rev. and Mrs. Fullerton of the Pentecostal Missionary Union, driven from their Lisu and Tai field near the Black river, spent several months across the French border and distributed several hundreds of Gospels to the Tai of Muang Hou. There are still, at least a third of the Tai without the scriptures or Christian instruction.

Our men have done more or less regular work among four of the hill tribes,—the Kamu of French Laos, the Yao, Miao and Musso of Siam, and they have made occasional visits, to the Karen and L'wa along the Burmese border. The Gospel according to St. Mark has been translated into Musso and the First Epistle of St. Peter into one dialect of the Kamu.

As early as 1830, Dr. Gutzlaff had translated the whole Bible into Siamese though it was not printed. This translation formed the basis of most of the subsequent translations. Portions of the Bible began to be printed in Siamese as early as 1829-30 but the first entire Bible printed in Siamese was completed in 1893 and that in Tai Yuen only last year, 1927. Owing to the extreme bulkiness of the Siamese and Tai Yuen New Testaments, in 1915 both were reduced in size at Yokohama by the photo-zinc process. In 1923 the earthquake destroyed all of our plates, valued at over eleven thousand ticals. The Siamese New Testament is now in the hands of the Revision Committee and plates are being made in Bangkok as rapidly as the books are ready. Next year should see the whole revised Book in the hands of readers.

The Tai Lu New Testament is also in process of preparation,

plates being made from hand-written copy.   This dialect seems to be the favorite for nearly all of the Tai of China as well as a part of the Shan States and French Laos.   The appearance of the page is very pretty.   In 1923 a small edition of the Gospel according to St. Matthew was printed in Tai Ya but it will probably not be reprinted. Scriptures for the Tai Lao, or Laotians, of Luang Prabang are purchased from the Swiss Mission of Song Khone and scriptures for the Tai Ngiu (Shan) are purchased from Rangoon.

In 1915, a system of embossed braille writing for the blind was prepared, parts of the Gospels written and two blind Tai Yuen persons taught to read and write in that dialect.   No further interest was shown by anyone until last when year three blind Siamese at Patriew asked to be taught and a teacher was sent them for five months.   His support was made possible by gifts from friends in and around Bangkok. Funds were exhausted in February and the teacher had to stop at the end of March.   The system is adapted to all dialects of the Tai language.   A much larger use should be made of it to bring hope and cheer into the now dreary lives of the multitude of blind in this and surrounding Tai countries.

The churches of Siam are slowly becoming interested in Bible Sunday.   More than half now observe the day and most of those make us an annual offering.   As yet, only one church in our Agency has put us on their budget, Chiengrung,—for six Yunnan dollars a month.   A hundred copies of the Bible Society Record, received from the Home Office, have been distributed gratis to friends each month.

For the last seven years our expenditure has averaged Tcs. 50,000 and our receipts from all sources outside of America, Tcs. 2,780.

Our unfinished task for the Tai people stretches away into the unknown regions of China, Tibet, Tonkin, and Hainan. We must follow the Tai to the farthest limits of their abodes, and provide for their spiritual needs or see that someone else does it. We must do the same for all of the mountain tribes within this territory, —except China ; the British and Foreign Bible Society has assumed that responsibility.

Translators of the Tai Yuen Bible

CHAPTER XXV

INDEPENDENT MISSIONARY WORK IN PUKET

Established in 1890

PUKET, an island located off the south western coast of Siam has long been known outside of Siam because of its rich tin mines. Colonists from India worked these mines as much as 2,000 years ago and possibly were the founders of the town there. About the 15th century A. D. Chinese merchants began to take interest in these mines and as a result a large Chinese population poured in to work the mines. To-day there is a population of approximately 30,000, most of which are Chinese. For years the revenue from these tin mines has flowed into the Government Treasury and has made Puket one of the valuable parts of Siamese territory. Of late, however, the drop in the price of tin has reduced this revenue.

Missionary work was begun in Tongkah Puket about 1883, by Brethren working in Penang, Singapore and the Federated Malay States, when some of the Chinese Christians from Penang went up to Tongkah to earn their living. On arriving they found a Mr. Jansen in the employ of the Siamese Government, who gathered them into his house and taught them by speaking in the Malay language which in turn was interpreted into Chinese by one of their number. Mr. Macdonald and Mr. Hocquard, missionaries in Penang, visited them occasionally and in 1885 had the joy of baptising the first convert. These visits were continued until 1890 when Mr. Ashdown and Dr. Amner went up to reside permanently, and later, having married were joined by their wives.

After living there a few years during which time there was a growing assembly, Mr. Ashdown and wife went to Singapore to relieve a missionary going home on furlough and later went to Penang where he now resides and labors.   Dr. Amner continued to live in Puket and cared for the work until about 1920 when he left for good. During the following years there was no resident foreign missionary until Dr. and Mrs. W. B. Toy returned to Siam and took over the work in 1926.

CHAPTER XXVI

THE WORK OF THE S. P. G. MISSION IN BANGKOK

Established in 1903

"S. P. G." are the initials of the Society for the Propagation of the Gospel in Foreign Parts, which is a handmaid of the Church of England, for the purpose of carrying on missionary work under the direction of the Bishops in charge of the various missionary dioceses. The mission at Bangkok is under the jurisdiction of the Bishop of Singapore.

Work was started here in 1903, by the late Canon William Greenstock, when he was already a very old man.

Canon Greenstock's history is interesting. He had taken his degree in England, and was preparing for Ordination to the Sacred Ministry when he had a very serious illness, and the doctors said it was not wise for him to stay in England. The climate of South Africa was suggested. He went there and was rewarded in time by complete recovery to health. He was ordained in the diocese of Grahamstown where he served for thirty-five years doing pioneer work in two different posts, acquiring fluency in the Kaffir dialects. Afterwards he returned to England and spent five or six years doing "deputation" work there.

In 1894 he came to Bangkok as Chaplain of Christ Church. As a boy he had wanted to come to Siam, and his wish was fulfilled in old age. Canon Greenstock was always a missionary at heart: and in 1903 he resigned the Chaplaincy to become an S. P. G. missionary.

His health was beginning to fail, but he had a most courageous spirit and managed to hold services in a little chapel in the city, at Wat Lieb and make pastoral visits, chiefly amongst the people of half European or Ceylonese descent. Early in 1910, the Canon's daughter, Mrs. Grey, came to stay with her father because of his increasing weakness, and helped him very considerably during the last two years of his life. She began a little school on the Rong Muang Road chiefly for the children of Ceylonese fathers holding positions on the railway.

Canon Greenstock died in Bangkok in March 1912, and his body lies in the Protestant cemetery. Very soon afterwards, Mrs. Grey returned to England. Two laymen kept services going at the mission chapel for some time, until Dr. Hillyard, then the Chaplain of Christ Church, took charge.

In August 1913, after a good deal of consideration, it was decided to move the mission to a more central position, and to make an effort to organize a school for Eurasian and Siamese children, in addition to maintaining the Sunday morning service.

Many difficulties confronted those in charge of the newly organized school. In January 1914, the Rev. C. R. Simmons offered himself to the S. P. G. for service overseas, and was told of the urgent need that existed in Bangkok. He was able to meet Mrs. Grey in England, and was told some details of the place and the work, and finally decided to come. In that year the Great War broke out placing serious difficulties in the way of Mr. and Mrs. Simmons' setting out for Bangkok. They sailed, however, on November 7th, and landed in Bangkok on 17 December 1914. Before arriving here, they had broken their journey at Singapore, staying for a few days with Bishop Ferguson Davie, who urged Mrs. Simmons to take charge of the mission school and build it up. The Bishop hoped that other help for the school would soon be forthcoming, but disappointment after disappointment had to be endured. The lady who was to come and take charge of the school to relieve Mrs. Simmons, was prevented from doing so by the death of her brother in the war. The Society in London, also throughout the war, were unable to send any financial help beyond Mrs. Simmons' salary.

Canon Greenstock

However, the work was taken in hand at a house in the New Road, near the present General Post Office, and was slowly built up in spite of set-backs. Pastoral and evangelical work went on, in and through and beside the educational work, and the little chapel continued to be a center of congregational life.

Early in 1915 it was decided to move the mission to larger premises, at Wat Takien, where the school, of about seventy boarders and one hundred day scholars, remained for nearly seven years. On these premises in adjoining compounds were separate schools,—one for girls and one for boys.

The necessity of making another move had to be faced in 1922 on account of disturbing changes in the neighborhood of the school. Premises were rented in the Rajadamri Road, which are now well-known as the girls' school of the mission, S. Mary's, S.P.G. The good work of Miss Siggins, Miss Parkinson and Miss Brandle is connected with the days in Rajadamri Road. The boys' school had very reluctantly to be closed, but was re-opened in new premises at Keo Fah House, in the New Road, when Mr. and Mrs. Simmons returned from leave in 1923.

From there, the boys' school was moved to more suitable premises, in the Siphya Road, in May 1926, and is carried on under the name of S. Peter's, S.P.G.

Miss F. Pope, an experienced missionary who had served in several parts of the world, gave her services at S. Peter's, for about a year, and carried on gallantly until her departure in March 1927, when Rev. C. W. Norwood and Mrs. Norwood arrived from England, and took up their abode at S. Peter's. A little later still the staff was further strengthened by the arrival of a Principal and Assistant for S. Mary's—Miss A. Lattimer, B. A., and Miss G. M. Hewerdine.

The mission has now room for at least two more workers, and an even more urgent need for funds. The work exists to give a good and definite Christian upbringing to all children who come under the influence of the schools. School life centers round the two chapels, where besides the daily prayers, the boarders and some of the day scholars take part in the regular Sunday services, which the members of the mission congregation also attend. Daily Scripture lessons are given, in Siamese and English.

The new Bishop of Singapore (the Right Reverend Basil Coleby Roberts) visited the mission in the early part of 1928 and will, we hope, visit Bangkok at least once a year.

Rev. C. R. Simmons and Mrs. Simmons

St. Mary's School, S. P. G.

CHAPTER XXVII

THE WORK OF THE CHURCHES OF CHRIST MISSION, NAKON PATHOM

Established in 1903

THIS is one of the missions supported by the Churches of Christ in Great Britain. Originally it was an extension of their mission to the Mons (Talaings) of Burma. The effort in Siam was started in January 1903 by Mr. Alfred Hudson of the Yeh mission, who crossed the mountains and travelled down the Menam Qua Noi to Kanburi in a small dugout and so down the Meklong river to the group of Mon villages served by the railway station of Nakon Choom. At that time the railway had been constructed only to Rajburi and the first trains were made up of ballast trucks with corrugated iron roofs and very solid wooden benches. Mr. Hudson had a small cottage of bamboo and thatch erected on a plot of rented ground and was at once able to converse with the people whose language is practically the same as that spoken by their fellows in Burma.

A few months later he was joined by Mr. Percy Clark who had recently arrived at the Yeh mission station and who travelled to Bangkok by steamer. The two erected a more substantial house and worked together until Mr. Hudson's return to England in 1905. By that time a small group of converts had been gathered and an attempt at school work had been made, while medical aid had been rendered free of charge to the many needy folk who came to seek it from far and near. The first church was established at Nakon Choom in 1903 and consisted of two Christian Karens from Burma,

a Burmese from the Tavoy church, the Mon patriarch, Ok Puh and a
Siamo-Chinese young man,—the last two being the first fruits of the
mission and possibly the first ever baptised in the waters of the
Meklong river. That church has grown to number over three
hundred souls at the present time though many of this number
reside at a distance from Nakon Pathom and can seldom get to the
meetings there. Altogether 371 persons of ripe years have been
immersed into the name of the " Living God."

A Mon Patriarch who sought his Creator.

He was a tall thin man of over sixty-four with a keen, intelligent face and he had heard somewhat of the Gospel message from
a fellow Mon who some years previously, had come over from Burma
on a mission to his people here, and who had returned to Burma
again. Ok Puh had been struck by the thought of a Creator God
and when he had pondered over that first sublime chapter of Gene-
sis, he decided to make a visit to Bangkok and try to find someone
who could tell him more. Just about that time the missionaries
from Yeh arrived so he was able to hear and ask about the Gospel
of the "Living God" to his heart's content. He was also baptised in
the running waters of the Meklong and remained a most faithful
follower of Christ for the remaining twenty years of his life. His
funeral was the occasion of a most remarkable witness to the consis-
tent life of this patriarch, given by a large company of his people.

Removal of the Mission Headquarters to Nakon Pathom.

The first lady of the mission, Mrs. Clark, arrived in Siam in
January 1906, and in June the headquarters of the mission were transferred to the town of the great pagoda, then called Pra-pathom,
as being more suitable for general mission work, more accessible to
all the Mon centres in Siam, and yet near enough to the rustic
first home of the mission at Nakon Choom to allow of frequent
visits there. Hired premises were secured in the middle of the town
and schools for boys and girls were at once opened, being the
first organized schools in the district. These schools have con-

Church of Christian Mission, Nakon Pathom

tinued to operate ever since and, together with a mission school for Chinese recently added, have a total of about three hundred scholars. Large numbers of former scholars have now grown up to be useful and honored citizens in many places.   The boys school is now under the charge of Mr. Hugh Jenkins and the girls' school is under the care of Miss Halliday who has been connected with the educational work of the mission for about thirteen years.   Until 1920, except for the two furloughs taken in that time, the whole of the school work was under the direction of Mr. and Mrs. Clark.

Medical and Maternity work.

From the very first the urgent calls for medical help were responded to and it was fortunate that both Mr. and Mrs. Clark had received a considerable amount of special training which they could use and add to as need demanded.

Superstitions frequently prevented the help which would otherwise have been given, but gradually the confidence of the people was won and many lives saved whilst other patients were persuaded to go to Bangkok and receive more skilled treatment there.   In those days outbreaks of smallpox were common and the missionaries often found whole families down with this awful disease and no one to help them with the sick folk.   Great praise is due to the policy of widespread, free vaccination which has freed the country from that scourge but before the Government vaccinators were organised for the great task, the missionaries had the privilege of vaccinating thousands of people free of any charge.   Cholera used to be far more rampant than it is now and there, alas, it was little that could be done to stay the terrible ravages but still the gospel of "boil your water" was sounded wherever the missionaries went and many a household is today remembering that advice to its salvation.   At Nakon Pathom a modest hospital dispensary was put up when as yet nothing else had been done for the relief of suffering and the missionaries were able to give help in great numbers of cases as well as to train their people in caring for wounds and sores, giving out quinine until the folk knew its value and were willing to pay for it, and otherwise making the way of later-comers in public welfare easier. Work amongst the women has prospered greatly and the ladies of the mission carry on an extensive midwifery practice by means of which a great number of lives have been saved. Mrs. Clark was privileged to act as lecturer on obstetrics to the nurses at Siriraj Hospital, Bangkok, for about two years and she also trained women to act as her own assistants. She was able to get many people to trust her in their time of need and to make more and more general the giving up of foolish and most harmful practices connected with childbirth. Other ladies with special training have followed to the great benefit of the people. But now-a-days the advent of motor vehicles and roads which permit of much easier and quicker access to the people in need, have also reduced the toil and risk of long journeys on foot or by pony across the flooded or burning plains, by day and night, and also make more possible the bringing in of patients to be treated at the hospital, —to their great benefit and to the saving of the welfare worker.

Evangelistic Effort.

The work started amongst the Mon people was facilitated by the coming of Mr. and Mrs. Halliday from Burma in 1910. They stayed until 1922 when they returned to Maulmein to continue work amongst the same people there. Mrs. Halliday was able to give maternity help to the women and Mr. Halliday's Mon scholarship is too well known to need comment here. His book on the Talaings is now the standard work and so is his Dictionary of their language. By means of the motorboat "Dayspring," he and Mr. Clark toured amongst the villages of the waterside of the three rivers, taking with them preachers who could speak in the Mon, Siamese, and Chinese languages. Mr. Halliday had long been given responsibility by the American Baptist mission for the Mon translation of the scriptures. These they carried with them.

Of later years an effort at consolidating and intensifying the

Boys' School, Nakon Pathom

Girls' School, Nakon Pathom

work in the villages near Nakon Pathom has been the policy, with only occasional long distance tours but it is hoped that before long the national staff may be strengthened and full touring work may be added to the present efforts, for it is realised that the parish is at least as wide as the Monthon of Nakon Chaisri. Nakon Choom is still visited and many patients are treated in their homes or brought to Nakon Pathom ; the spiritual needs of the people are recognized to demand concentrated effort for our Saviour's first words to the cripple were " Son, be of good cheer, thy sins are forgiven ", and truly any one who considers the cause of most of the suffering that comes for our help must realize that much of it is due to lack of spiritual life and moral restraint.

Amongst the people of Siam who have labored with us in the gospel, we may mention the name of Meh Weo who was Mrs. Clark's first helper and the first teacher of the first girls' school in Nakon Pathom. She is still rendering earnest help in the teaching of the women and village folk. Also the name of Chun Kwang, who laboured with us in those early days, both amongst the Siamese and Chinese for he was bi-lingual and very much in earnest, must be mentioned. He laboured with us about six years and now one of his sons is in the Theological Seminary at Chiengmai and a daughter is in the Bible Training School in Bangkok. The work he started amongst the Chinese has grown and a number of his converts are still holding fast to the Faith.

Amongst present day workers, we must mention Meh Luan, a Bible woman and nurse, educated partly at Nakon Pathom and partly at the old Wang Lang School under Miss Cole to whom both she and this mission owe much for the workers she helped to train. Meh Luan is gifted with the ability to tell Bible and other stories to children and grown-ups in a most effective manner.

Kru Yosart is our most efficient Siamese preacher and he is much appreciated especially by the simple country people who form his chief audiences. He was brought up in our school and served as teacher before entering on his army service, which left him not less but more decided in his Christian convictions,—a thing uncommon enough to merit notice.

Meh Chu, who has for many years rendered most valuable service as a nurse, must be mentioned; her face has been a most welcome one in a great many homes in this district.

There are others, simple folk, untrained but capable of gracious influence, such as old Pah Kam who says that when she first believed in Jesus it was as though a load of cocoanuts had been taken off her chest,—homely words depicting a real experience. She has no greater joy than to bring folk to hear the gospel or to tell them of her own knowledge of what Christ can do for them.

The church at Nakon Pathom now meets in the beautiful chapel built four years ago. Siamese, Chinese and Mons find their common bond of union in the great Founder of their Faith. Christianity is a unifying religion and one which by its high standard of conduct and aim makes for the highest kind of earthly citizenship as well as that of the Kingdom of Heaven. The development of a sensitive conscience and self denial for the good of others makes the religion of Jesus the greatest force for righteousness and service that the world has ever seen.

Hospital, Nakon Pathom

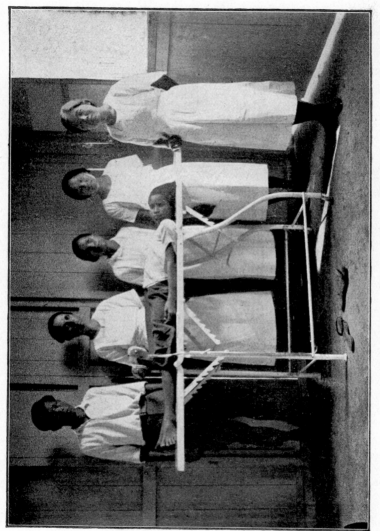

Operating Room, Hospital, Nakon Pathom
Mrs. Clark and her Assistants

CHAPTER XXVIII

THE SEVENTH-DAY ADVENTIST MISSION

THE Seventh-Day Adventist denomination was founded in the U. S. A. in the year 1844. For the first thirty years of its history no foreign mission work was undertaken, but in the year 1874 the first missionary was sent outside of North America.

Early realizing the evangelizing influence of the printed page, Seventh-Day Adventists have long carried on a strong publishing program.

Beginnings in Siam

It was the publishing work that first definitely drew attention of our Mission Board to Siam. A colporteur came to Siam from Singapore selling Chinese literature, and upon his return he reported a company of people keeping the Sabbath. This hastened the sending of missionaries to open a mission in Siam. In December 1918, the Rev. and Mrs. E. L. Longway arrived in Bangkok and early the following year the Rev. and Mrs. F. A. Pratt joined them and together the two families began a definite work for the Chinese. Colporteur work was undertaken with pleasing results, many thousands of ticals' worth of Siamese and Chinese literature having been sold. Also tens of thousands of pages of small literature have been given away by the workers and the lay-members. Colporteurs have travelled over nearly the whole of Siam and thousands of religious and medical books have been sold.

In May 1922, Mr. and Mrs. Longway were transferred to Central China, thus leaving the Siamese mission with but one foreign family. However in January 1923, the Rev. and Mrs. R. P. Abel arrived in Bangkok to take up work definitely for the Siamese people.

The growth of the Seventh-Day Adventist mission has been slow but steady. At present we are operating four chapels,—two in Bangkok and one each in Ban Pong and Korat. The standard has been held high and no one is admitted into the church by baptism who has not given up smoking, drinking, and betel-nut chewing. There have been some remarkable cases in which the Lord has given victory over these particular habits.

At one time, when holding a Bible-reading with a Chinese young man, a weaver by trade we tried to study in the shop where many men were working but the noise was too great. We finally went to a room in the rear that was used for dyeing cloth. This was the lower part of a dwelling house. We sat there in quietness studying God's Word. After a few minutes we noticed that there seemed to be a disturbance outside, for the people were talking in a very loud voice. Upon enquiry we found that the owner of the house was afraid that if we studied the Bible in that place we would drive their gods away. The only thing we could do was to go to another place to finish our Bible-reading. Thus the seed is sown "by all waters"; sometimes we are welcomed heartily; at other times the door of opportunity seems closed and we pass on to another place.

In the year 1927, we published 10,000 copies of the Chu Chart Temperance Magazine and within three weeks, they were all sold. We printed another edition of 10,000 copies and they were sold also. Through the help of some of the leading firms of Bangkok we were able to supply the pupils of the majority of schools in Bangkok with a free copy each. Words of appreciation have not been lacking and we feel that this magazine had had a decided influence for good in Siam.

We have also published a medical book which has sold well. Time will not permit to tell of some of the interesting experiences enjoyed in circulating this book. It may be sufficient to say that in one place the judge of a Provincial Court adjourned proceedings so that he and others present might have an opportunity to buy copies

Group of Seventh-Adventist Chinese Members

Mrs. Pratt's Sewing Class

of this medical book.   Our experience has shown us that the Siamese people are fond of reading and that they will buy religious literature if it is prepared in an attractive manner.

Extensive tours have been made by the mission workers, over the greater part of Siam, with a view to the extension of the work in the future.   We take this opportunity of expressing our appreciation of the work of our loyal Asiatic laborers who through their faithfulness, perseverance and industry have made possible any degree of success which has been attained.

CHAPTER XXIX

UNOCCUPIED FIELDS IN SIAM

IT is quite interesting to find out for ones self what an *occupied* field is. Don't ask any body to tell you; don't look in a Foreign Mission Glossary; just take the maps and statistics and figure it out for yourself. That is what we did.

All over the great fields of India and China we found that as a rule very few mission stations are so isolated as not to have two or more neighbor stations within fifty miles of each other. Make that condition a minimum rule and apply it to Siam. There are only two places where one can stand and reach two other mission stations in that radius. Nagor Pathom as a center would include Petchaburi and Bangkok, and Lampang would include Chiengmai and Prae. The former circle has 46 missionaries in it, and the latter has 38. 20,000 square miles can just barely squeeze in under this rule as occupied. How about the other 175,000 square miles of Siam? Unoccupied! But we are reminded that with the area rule we have not taken into consideration density of population, although it should be noted that it takes more time and labor per capita to reach a scattered population than a concentrated one. China is four and three fourths times as densely populated as Siam. Its average mission station has a little over 400,000 population in its 2,000 square miles. The average mission station of Siam has 735,000 people in its 17,700 square miles.

Let us turn to Burma, a neighbor where conditions very much like those in Siam prevail. It is a country a little larger with a population somewhat more scattered. Burma's 7,000,000 people are ministered to by a mission force of 350 in 50 stations. Siam, with 8,150,000 people and 102 missionaries, is outclassed four to one.

The monotony of the find is broken when we look eastward to French Indo-China where people and conditions are much like those in Siam. In this country, which is one and a third times as large as Siam and has twice the population there are 13 stations with 33 missionaries! One for every 515,000. We could loan the Christian Missionary Alliance and the Christian Missions in Many Lands 57 missionaries to help occupy their field in French Indo-China and still have as many left in Siam, in proportion to the population, as they would have after the addition borrowed from here. According to one standard Siam is not occupied according to the other Siam is fully occupied.

We are not satisfied with either of the above conclusions. Not finding the answer to our quest in comparing ourselves with others let us try comparing ourselves with ourselves. If they were fully manned the five mission stations in the North would be sufficient for the territory they cover. If we were to add fourteen missionaries to the present force, thereby bringing the average per population up to what it has been in China, we would then feel that the North was well stationed well manned: occupied.

Turn now to the rest of Siam. The first thing we note is one great section 250 miles wide and 450 miles long that has only one station, Pitsanuloke, in it. One can keep fifty miles away from that one station and block out one section two hundred miles square and another one hundred and twenty-five miles square that are absolutely unoccupied. Here we could locate six new stations each having 10,000 square miles for territory as its field. They might be established at the following centers, viz. Korat, Ubol, Roi Ed, Lopburi, Raheng and Nong Kai. Start the work in each with evangelistic and medical families and then as soon as they are going well add another evangelistic family; then bring in the educational workers as soon as there are Christian children to educate. Two other mission stations at Chantaboon and Patani would be necessary to fill up the smaller unoccupied sections to the southeast of Bangkok and in the extreme south of the peninsula.   Eight new mission stations and eighty additional workers! This in addition to the necessary reenforcements to the stations already existing! Does it startle one? It is not a vision as bold as the one which the first missionaries to Siam saw.

A section of this chapter should consider the Lao and Kamoo population of Luang Prabang.   Eastern or French Laos lies along the eastern border of Siam as far south as Cambodia.   The people are closely related to the Yuan Laos of North Siam.   In Savanaket the Swiss mission have work among them.   Vieng Chan is occupied by the Roman Catholics.   The Gospel has been preached, in a way, in the Northern section or Luang Prabang, for a good many years by the North Siam mission. Dr. McGilvary was the pioneer in this work and was followed by Dr. Dodd, Dr. Peoples, Dr. Campbell and Mr. MacKay.   A growing Christian community has been established among the Kamoos to the north of Luang Prabang and the Rev. Chaima was left in charge.   Then occurred a hiatus of some twenty years. After the long silence it was learned that this company of converts still held together, true to their faith.   Lampang station sent another family to assist in the work of grace that was reviving among them and now there is steady growth reported in this section.   The Presbyterian Mission and American Bible Society arranged for an evangelistic tour to Luang Prabang which confirmed the impressions reported by the early pioneers in this region.   This tour was followed up by a number of tours by national workers from Nan station. In the fall of 1925 a second tour was authorized by the mission which led to the definite allocation of this field to the charge of Siamese nationals.   This scheme for occupation of the new field was recommended to the National Church.   The Presbytery of North Siam adopted it and a beginning of that work was made in December 1926 by the settlement of two evangelistic families from Nan station, for a three years stay in the city of Luang Prabang.   The work is developing far beyond original expectation and bids fair to call for reenforcements soon. The hope is that the church will go at it with vigor. It is a foreign field within their reach, a field that responds in such a way as to fire the zeal of those who take a hand in the work. It is a field worthy of the utmost effort of those who seek to take the Gospel of Christ to it.

When we view these unoccupied fields we are forcibly reminded to pray as our Lord enjoined : " Pray ye therefore the Lord of the harvest that He send forth laborers into His harvest." May the Church of Siam lift up its eyes and, seeing the unoccupied fields, thrust out into them. Millions on millions at our very doors are destitute of the Bread of Life. And may the Church in America which has begun a good work not draw back from its responsibilities but perform until the day of Jesus Christ.

NATIONAL LEADERSHIP

CHAPTER XXX

OUTSTANDING MEN AND WOMEN OF SIAM

THE Christian Church is made up of individuals who have accepted Jesus Christ as their Saviour and leader and whose lives reflect something of the image of their perfect model. Jesus Christ demonstrated his belief in the individual man when He said, "It is finished." Humanly speaking, *it was ended* : the leader was smitten; His followers, weak and afraid, were scattered. But with divine insight and unlimited faith in those whom He had been molding during the years of His ministry, He could look down through the years and in great assurance say, "It is finished." He had made salvation possible ; to His disciples he was giving the task of making this salvation known. The task He imposed upon the church is not yet ended and much remains to be done before the "kingdoms of this world become the Kingdom of our Lord and of, His Christ," but His disciples in many lands have put their shoulders under the burden, and, looking upon them as our Lord looked upon His little group of disciples of old, we too can look down the years and see the fulfilment of His plan—when "all shall know Him from the least unto the greatest," and it shall truly be *finished*.

The life stories of some of those who have taken upon themselves the name of Christ in this land are here briefly written down, most of them of the generation which has passed on to their reward. They are the "goodly heritage" of the present generation and because they have reflected some of the divine glory, many who today are bearing the "burden and heat of the day," find a larger and richer service. So as we read over these brief stories of transformed lives, may we not also catch a glimpse of the *finished* task, and take courage.

Sinsaa Puan

Sinsaa Puan was a member of the Chinese Baptist church of Bangkok, associated with this church and with the Baptist missionaries from youth till death. At the age of 18 he joined Dr. Dean and two years later began going about preaching. He was largely instrumental in starting the churches at Patrieu, Chonburi and Panat, and served those churches for many years. At one time he worked with the Chinese church at Wat Koh in Bangkok but later returned to Panat and remained there until his death. His whole life was devoted to preaching and he never entered into any kind of business. The money that came to him was simply enough for the daily living expenses and when he died he left his children only the inheritance of a faithful Christian life, lived wholly in the service of his Lord.

Luang Petch Songkram

Nai Boon-Nart Chi-Sawn, later given the title Luang Petch Songkram, was born in Thai-Pawn, in the Trang province. His wife was Nang Nu. Luang Petch Songkram was a very well educated man with versatile accomplishments. He wrote both poetry and prose: he had an extensive knowledge of the occult art and could foretell future events. He was an ardent Buddhist and thought much on religious subjects. One especial article of his belief was that TRUTH is the greatest thing in the world. His quest for truth led him constantly to seek for a fuller revelation of it.

He came to believe that surely there must be a Creator-god since the universe is so infinitely more wonderful that the simple mechanisms which we are constantly making and which can not come into being without our effort and creative genius. Thus his mind was ready for the reception of the Christian teaching of the divine creator. Luang Petch Songkram was thirty years old when he received a book from the Rev. John Carrington, D. D. There was no

Sin Saa Puan

missionary there but he read and believed what he found in that book and accepted the Christian God as the one whom he had long sought. There was no opportunity for him to receive baptism until the Rev. E. P. Dunlap, D. D., went to Trang when this man gladly went to him and received baptism. He then erected a red flag in front of his house, saying that that sign was for a testimony that here lived a Christian.

He called together his relatives and friends and about thirty others were also baptised. His children became earnest Christians and now the fourth generation of Christians,—descendents of this man, form a part of the membership of the Trang church.

Finally Luang Petch Songkram felt that the end was near and told his family that before the day ended he would be gone. At about 10.00 a. m. he bathed, lit a candle, inhaled its fumes and watched it burn. As the candle flickered out, he drew his last breath and his soul went to seek its Maker. He was seventy-two years of age when he died.

Three Generations of Bible Women

Nang Boa Lai was a Bible-woman for many years in the Lampang city church. She was not very well educated but she was wise and made a little learning go a long way. For years she went from house to house teaching the new converts among the women to read and to pray. The latter she insisted on because as she would often say, "How can one be a Christian if she cannot pray ?" She was a woman of real dignity and commanded the respect and won the love of her pupils. She was a women of deep spiritual life and some excellent leaders have come from her pupils, including two Bible women and one deacon of the church. After many years of zealous and successful work, the Lord called her to the heavenly home : then her mantle fell on her daughter Nang Boa Koa. She is a worthy daughter of her mother and is now in charge of the work. Whenever she is ill or unable to serve, her daughter Nang Thom Kao takes up the work and carries it on successfully.   On asking a member of the class how Nang Thom Kao conducted her classes she replied, "Just like her mother and grandmother before her".   So these Bible women of three generations are doing their part to hold the Christian women of their church true to Christ and are training them as witnesses for their Master.

Tau Kaa Lung Ruen

For many years Tau Kaa Lung Ruen served as a nurse in the Lampang hospital.   He came into the hospital first as a patient in a helpless and apparently hopeless condition.   God surely sent him to us.   He was cured. After he became a Christian his whole life and thought seemed given to the service of God.   In his work as nurse he was faithful to every duty, kind and thoughtful in his care of the poor and suffering who came to the hospital.   Few men in our work have done more to comfort and relieve the distresses of his people.   Although burdened by many duties he constantly taught by word of mouth the truth his life so beautifully exemplified. Nothing could exceed the joy he had over the conversion of his patients.   He served in the Lampang medical work for over two decades and then was called home to his reward.

Tau Kaa Lung Kao

Not many years after the first resident missionaries came to Lampang there came into their employ a man by the name of Kao.   He proved himself reliable and dependable.   As years went by he was faithful to every duty, kind and unselfish in his work for others.   His wife whose name was also Kao was a woman of very unusual intelligence and of great personal charm. In due time this man was made an elder and then was called Tau Kaa Lung Kao.   He had the boarding department of the boys' school for years and he and Meh Tau Kao cared for these boys as they would have cared for their own children.   For years he was a father and a shepherd to the Christians; many a disagreement has he

Sitting, left to right :—
Rev. Semo Wichai, Rev. Pannya Jayavanna
Standing :—Rev. Kham Ai Jayavanna

settled and sent all away happy. He served long and faithfully and after he was retired still went about preaching the Word of which he is so good a witness. Now he is too old to carry on active work but he still attends the Sunday morning service and is a blessing in our midst. Of him it can truly be said, " to live is Christ ". Three of his sons are elders—two in the city church and one in the Muang Nyon church.

Rev. Pannya Jayavanna

The Rev. Pannya Jayavanna was born at Bethel, Lampoon, in 1861. He served in the Buddhist priesthood for seven years and was baptised and united with the Christian church in 1886. Two years later he married Nang Kao Wonna. For a number of years Kru Pannya toured with Dr. McGilvary, being under instruction as an evangelist. He also studied under the Rev. Robert Irwin, and was finally ordained elder of the Chiengmai church. In 1896 he was ordained to the Christian ministry and became pastor of the Chiengmai church. He has three children,—Nai Muang Chai (Khun Ni-worn Rokapadh), Nai Boon Lert and Nang Kao Kanlaya.

Rev. Semo Wichai

The Rev. Semo Wichai was born in Chiengmai the very year that his father first met one of the missionaries—1868. The second time he met a missionary was in 1875 when he met Dr. M. A. Cheek. In the meantime he had been many years in the Buddhist priest-hood. In 1877 he was baptised, together with his wife, Nang Wondee and in 1880 he became an elder in the Chiengmai church. That same year his son Nai Semo was baptised. The father died in 1894.

Nai Semo worked in the forests near Chiengmai for many years. In 1893 he married Nang Kam Baw Jayavanna and they have had nine children. One of these is the wife of the Rev. Ban Chong Bansiddhi, pastor of the Chiengmai church at the

present time and another is Kru Charoen Wichai, one of the city
evangelists in Bangkok.

Nai Semo Wichai was ordained elder in the Chiengmai church
and in 1911 was ordained to the Christian ministry and became
pastor of the Chiengmai church. At the present time he is one of
the staff of the McGilvary Theological Seminary.

Rev. Kham Ai Jayavanna

The Rev. Kham Ai Jayavanna, son of Nai Sao Jayavanna and
Nang Chan Fong was born at Ban Bann, Lampoon on the 15th of
February, 1880. He was educated at Prince Royal's College and
after graduating there assisted Dr. McKean for eight years at the
hospital in Chiengmai. He then joined the Internal Revenue
Department of the Government. After a brief service there he
studied Local Government and being qualified for the position of
Nai Umpher served in that capacity at Madka, Chiengmai for three
years. He again joined Dr. McKean and assisted in the making of
vaccine in the mission laboratory. For a time he then took up law
but shortly joined Dr. Campbell and took up Bible study. For
three years he served in the Post Office and Telegraph Office at
Lampang, returning to Chiengmai to take a position as teacher in
the McGilvary Theological Seminary in 1914. In 1919 he was
ordained to the Christian ministry and still continues teaching in the
Seminary.

His wife is Nang Bua Keo and he has nine children.

Nang Same

Nang Same and her husband Nai Yoo were two of the early
Christians at Petchaburi. Humble folk they were with no remarkable places of leadership in the Christian community. Nai Yoo was
a mission washman and they lived in a little cottage on the mission
compound. Week by week their home and the home of Kru Klai,
on the same compound, alternated as the meeting-place for the

Nang Same

Christians for their weekly service of prayer. Nang Same is now the oldest Christian in Petchaburi.

Rev. Yuen Tieng-Yok

Rev. Yuen Tieng-Yok, or Kru Yuen as he was known by all of the present generation, was born at Supanburi in 1850. His mother Nang Muang died during his infancy and he was cared for by her relatives until he was about six years old. Then his father who was a cloth merchant brought his little son with him on a trip to Bangkok. Their boat was moored near Wat Cheng and there the boy soon made the acquaintance of the little lads who were attending the new Presbyterian mission boys' school nearby. Nai Yuen's father being Chinese soon made the acquaintance of the Chinese teacher of the mission school, Sinsaa Ki-eng Qua-Sean. The result was that Nai Yuen was placed under the care of Dr. Mattoon and entered this mission school where he was educated and cared for. When he was twelve years of age, his father died and the last outside tie was broken. When the school was transferred to Samray, Nai Yuen went along. Later he entered the home of the Rev. S. G. McFarland, D. D., at Petchaburi and paid for his schooling and board by doing domestic work commonly done in Siam by a " boy ". Some of his friends finally left school and he asked permission to leave too, but for a long time he was unable to get the consent of Dr. McFarland. Finally the consent was reluctantly given and Nai Yuen left the missionary home and became an apprentice to a tailor, getting only board for his services. Finally this tailor and the Rev. S. J. Smith had some difficulty which resulted in the imprisonment of the tailor. Then Nai Yuen regularly carried food to the jail to his master. The Rev. N. A. McDonald. D. D., seeing the difficult situation into which the lad had fallen persuaded him to return to school again.

At eighteen years of age Nai Yuen was baptised, for the religious teaching of the schools had found a ready response in his heart.   Dr. House urged him to become a preacher but Nai Yuen replied that he was not a ready speaker and so was unfitted for that task.   But Dr. House knew his boy ; he felt that Nai Yuen had certain traits which would make him unusually successful in the ministry.   He was finally licensed to preach and went about teaching, distributing and selling Bibles and other religious literature. Twice he made trips to Ayuthia, the first time being with Dr. Carrington and Kru Keo.

Finally a teacher was needed in the Petchaburi school and Kru Yuen was asked to take the position, which he did temporarily. After two months he left there and returned to Bangkok.   Since the work in Ayuthia had not prospered as much as anticipated, he was not returned there but began selling Bibles with Kru Keo near Wat Samcheen.   Two years later the situation at Wang Lang demanded a resident Siamese family and the mission asked Kru Yuen and his wife to go to Miss Cole's assistance there.   For more than ten years he faithfully served at Wang Lang.

Upon the return of the Rev. B. T. Boon Itt to Siam, he felt that there should be a resident pastor for the Samray church and that it should no longer be served by a missionary acting as stated supply. Kru Yuen was called to this church and accepting, was ordained. Later when the Fourth Presbyterian Church of Bangkok was organized in connection with the Bangkok Christian High School which was built on the east side of the river, the Rev. Yuen Tieng-Yok served both the new church and his own charge—the First Church. It was planned that he should be relieved from the First Church and give his whole attention to the Fourth Church, and Kru Kim Heng Mangkarabundhu, then Principal of the Samray boys' school, was suggested as the successor for the Samray church.   This plan was never carried out and the Rev. Yuen Tieng-Yok remained Pastor of the First Church until his death, while other provision was finally made for the Fourth Church.

One cannot estimate the value of such a life as that of Kru

Rev. Yuan Tieng Yok, Wife, Son and Grand-children

Yuen. Gentle and kindly, patient and sympathetic, earnest and consecrated—such men are the " salt of the earth." Those of us whose memories go back some twenty years or more to the days when he was in the full vigor of his manhood, take delight in remembering how fully he entered into every phase of the life of the Christian community. No party was complete without him and his quaint humour; no theatrical was really funny unless Kru Yuen played a leading part; no undertaking succeeded so well without his whole-hearted assistance; no hour of sorrow or suffering but needed his tender sympathy. For years he carried on—brave and true. The first church in Bangkok to attain self-support was his church. Money was not always forthcoming and the salary paid him was never large, but Kru Yuen's is a name we all love and honor and his memory is a priceless inheritance of the Christian community of Bangkok.

He died in his 79th year on 27 September 1927, as the result of influenza and complications, and was buried in the old Christian cemetery at Samray where so many before him had been laid to rest. The Rev. Yuen Tieng-Yok was thrice married and his widow, Nang Serm, survives him. He had one son by the second marriage and two sons and one daughter by the third. His grandson is today one of the ruling elders in his grandfather's church and one who carries much of the responsibility for leadership there.

Rev. Part Chindawong

The present pastor of the city church of Lampang was one of three brothers who became Christians. One brother served as an evangelist for some years when a wasting disease, from which he had suffered some time, ended what appeared to be a very promising and valuable career in evangelistic work. The youngest brother also died,—but after a much longer period of service and while always faithful, he did not have the strong personality of either of the other two brothers. In the beginning the Rev. Part

Chindawong served as an evangelist acceptably. In the last years of Dr. Wilson's life when at times he was almost helpless, this man was his most devoted caretaker. With loving zeal he gave his life at that time to the friend he loved so dearly. After Dr. Wilson's death he returned to his former evangelistic work. He had taken the regular training in the Theological Seminary and for several years previous to his ordination and installation as Pastor he acted as Pastor's Assistant. He is a man of pleasing personality, gentle and courteous· He appears to have won the confidence of the congregation he serves and is proving a good shepherd of the people. As the church is now self-supporting no missionary sits in his meetings of the Session ,—so he and his eight elders must bear the sole responsibility for their church, both spiritual and financial.

Kru Tien Pow Viradhien

Nai Tien Pow Viradhien was the son of Nai Boi and Nang Hong, born at Bang-Ba, on 23 Jan. 1873. When but ten years old his mother died and his father put him under the care of the Lord Abbot of the Wat at the mouth of the Bang-Ba canal. He studied Siamese there until the death of his father when he entered the priesthood as a novice or nane. He was so diligent in his study and made such progress in learning about Buddhism that he was sent to preach instead of the priests and won quite a reputation as a Buddhist preacher. Before reaching his majority, he left the priesthood and wanting to study English, went to Samray and lived with his aunt while studying in the Samray school. She was nurse to Mrs. E. P. Dunlap's children and her husband was the Dunlap cook. About three months after Nai Tien Pow went to live with his aunt, the Dunlaps were transferred to Petchaburi and Nai Tien Pow returned to his old home at Rajburi. Kru Tien Su, a relative and a teacher in the Samray school, realizing that Nai Tien Pow was so eager to study brought him back from Rajburi and had him live

Kru Tien Pow Viradhien

Family of Kru Tien Pow Viradhien

with him at Samray.   But when Kru Tien Su went back to Rajburi himself shortly, Nai Tien Pow once more returned to his old home. In 1889, some one brought Nai Tien Pow to Dr. Eakin with the arrangement that he was to remain in the Samray school four years and graduate.   At the end of three years, however, Nai Tien Pow was graduated from the Samray school where he was a great favorite with teachers and pupils for his eagerness in study and his proficiency—especially in Arithmetic,—a subject in which he had no equal.

After Nai Tien Pow's graduation in 1892, he returned to Rajburi where he helped Dr. Wachter both as teacher and in the Dispensary.   In 1893, he was baptised and in 1895 he married N. S. Kim Hong.

In 1897, he went with the Rev. Boon Itt and Dr. and Mrs. Toy to help start the new station at Pitsanuloke.   He was teacher there for six years, helping to build the Padoongrart school for boys, the hospital and the church.   The pupils in his school showed such proficiency in their studies that their teacher won much renown therefrom.

In 1903, he followed the Rev. Boon Itt to Bangkok and entered Government service in the Government Dispensary.   But he was there a very short time when Dr. Eakin asked him to go to the Bangkok Christian High School as teacher.   This position he held until three years later when his health failed and he made a vain attempt to stay the disease which had fastened itself on him.   On 9 Nov. 1906 he died of tuberculosis, when but 35 years of age.

He was one of the most promising of the young men who were just entering upon their life work as Christian men and leaders. His death was a great loss to the Christian community.   He was a member of the Board of Directors of the B. I. M., a member of the Government Teachers' Association, and a teacher in the Samray S. S. at the time of his death.   Kind-hearted and brilliant, he was much loved and passed on to his five children a rare heritage.   The children are Nai Sadap (now Luang Prakat), Nang Sangat Sakulkan, Nang Karoon Taiyong, N. S. Prayat and Nai Salak.

Nang Kim Hawk Suddikam

Kru Kim Hawk was born on the 22nd of April 1878 at Bang-Pa, Rajburi. She was the daughter of Nai Hong Yee, of Chinese descent, and Nang Ngawk, a Cambodian. An older brother is Nai Chur, and a younger brother Nai Kim Saa is a Customs Official, now bearing the title Luang Pah. When a child, Meh Kim Hawk studied with relatives. Then she was entered in the Wang Lang School where she remained until she graduated in 1896. She began teaching there but left shortly afterward to marry her cousin, the Rev. Boon Tuan Boon Itt. She and her husband went to Pitsanuloke and there she proved a right loyal helper, entering very fully into his work and proving just the one to fill the wife's place in that missionary home. She started the girls' school in Pitsanuloke, teaching it until they left there six years later for the new work in connection with the Fourth Church of Bangkok. Three children were born to them, the youngest but an infant when Kru Boon Itt died. The son, Dr. Samuel Bentoon Boon Itt, after graduating at the Bangkok Christian College went to the P. I. for further study and since his return has entered Government service at Siriraj Hospital.

In 1907-8 Nang Kim Hawk married Kru Pluang Suddikam, then teacher in the B. C. C., since then ordained and now Pastor of the Fourth Church of Bangkok.

When her children were little Nang Kim Hawk decided to start a little school in her own home for them. Neighbors began asking to be allowed to send their children to the school and little by little it grew. New buildings had to be built; other teachers were employed. Today there are between two and three hundred pupils in this school. After their graduation at the Wang Lang School the two daughters returned to help their mother in her school, teaching

Mrs. Kim Hock Boon-Itt

until they were married—and afterward. This school, the Padoong Darunee—is one of the strong Christian schools of Bangkok, exerting a tremendous influence.

Rev. Kim Heng Mangkarabundhu

Nai Kim Heng was born in 1875 at Bang-Pa, Rajburi. His father was a Chinese named, Nai Tai. His mother was a Siamese named Nang Soon. His father died when Nai Kim Heng was an infant and his mother supported him until he was fifteen years old. She then married again. Her husband was Nai Churn, the cook of the Rev. E. P. Dunlap. This brought the boy into the Dunlap home at Samray. His mother became the nurse for the Dunlap children and her own boy was put into the Samray school. When Dr. and Mrs. Dunlap were transferred to Petchaburi, the cook, nurse and Nai Kim Heng went along. There he studied for a time under Miss Cort later returning and finishing his education in the Samray school. In 1892 he was baptised and became a member of the Samray church where he also taught a S. S. class. He had an open, kindly disposition and was very popular. He began teaching in the Samray school and finally became Principal of the school, a position he held until he was called to the pastorate of the Second Church of Bangkok in 1915. He then resigned and was ordained, serving that church until some time after the transfer to Wattana from Wang Lang had forced the organization of the Fifth Church. For a time he served both churches but the Second Church called to its leadership another Bangkok teacher and the Rev. Kim Heng Mangkarabundhu was free to devote himself entirely to the Fifth Church.

Later, in an emergency after the resignation of the Rev. Yuen Tieng-Yok from the First Church at Samray, the Rev. Kim Heng Mangkarabundhu again extended his ministry to cover two churches. This arrangement lasted for a year and a half.

Kru Kim Heng was the first Siamese President of the Conference of Christian Workers—an office he has held several

times.   He is one of the Board of Directors of the Boon Itt Memorial
Institute ; one of the Bible Revision Committee—and still the actual
pastor of the First Church, near which his home is, for he belongs to
the whole Christian community and his heart is big enough to
make him the one to whom everyone turns in both joy and sorrow.

Sinsa Kai-eng Qua-Sean

Sinesa Ki-eng Qua-Sean was a Chinese from Amoy who come to
Siam to seek a living. He had been educated as a doctor and was well
versed in the occult art as was customary with all such physicians. He
went to Rajaburi where he settled, marrying Nang Hay. They had
five children,—three sons and two daughters. Their names should
be mentioned because they and their descendents have played an
important part in the Christian church of Bangkok. Nai Pen, Nang
Tuan, Nang Koon, Nai Hong Yee and Nai Tien Soo. Sinsaa Ki-eng
frequently came to Bangkok and finally met the missionaries. He
became the Chinese teacher of the Rev. S. Johnson and in 1844 was
baptised by him.

About five years later, the work of the A. B. C. F. M. mission in
Bangkok ended and Sinsaa Ki-eng was encouraged to transfer his
membership to the Presbyterian church which had just been organized seven days before. He thus became the first non-missionary
member of that church.

At first Sinsaa Ki-eng taught religion for the missionaries but
finally in 1852, with mission sanction, he gathered together a little
boys' school for sons of Chinese parents and began to teach them in
their own language. He went with the school when it was transferred
to Samray and taught there until his death in 1859. He placed his
children in school and taught them and his wife the new religion that
he had found. His wife never was baptised but one by one his children
did all accept Christ. Meh Tuan perhaps more than any of the rest
bore the impress of her father and gave herself fully to the Christian faith.

Nang Tuan

Finally Sinsaa Ki-eng began to realiz that the end was near and one day gave a great feast for all of his family. The day passed in great pleasure. The following day the old man told his family that the end was approaching. Since he had not been ill and even then seemed quite all right, the family did not realize that the end was so near. But it was so and before the day ended, he had let his mantle fall on other shoulders.

Nang Tuan

The second of Sinsaa Ki-eng Qua-Sean's children, Meh Tuan, was born at Bang-Pa the very year that her father accepted Christ as his Saviour. Upon her a double portion of her father's spirit seems to have fallen. Educated in the mission school at Samray, she became very proficient and could do many things well. At the age of 21 she married Nai Ban Sooie, a man of Chinese extraction, a seller of posts. They made their home at Bang-Pa but Nai Ban Sooie was frequently away selling loads of posts. On one such trip to Bangkok he fell sick with cholera and died. A servant came back to tell the news but when a search was made it was impossible to find the body. He had never become a Christian though apparently he did not oppose his wife in her religious life.

After his death, Nang Tuan decided to bring her little family of two sons and one daughter to Bangkok. Two hopes induced this move,—(1) She wanted her children to come under Christian instruction, and (2) she wanted to be near a church herself. She went to Samray in 1873 and shortly afterward was sought by Mrs. House to take the important position at the new Wang Lang School which she held so efficiently for more than ten years. The baby daughter had died and the two little boys were placed in the Samray boys' school.

Realizing that education was a very great gain to her country, she persuaded many of her relatives and friends to come from Bang-Pa to Bangkok to study. One in particular of this group should be mentioned for she was especially beloved of Nang Tuan, Meh Kim Hong, who later became the wife of Kru Tien Pow Viradhien.

Nang Tuan later resigned from the Wang Lang School and took up the study of nursing. At one time she taught sewing and embroidery in one of the Palaces. She was of the same generation as Meh Esther and like her clever, diligent and ambitious. Nearly the whole of her life she supported herself.

The crowning joy of Nang Tuan's life was the return of her eldest child, the Rev. Boon Tuan Boon Itt from America, ready to enter upon his missionary work in Siam. Her dreams were coming true; her son was to make the Master she had so long served known in the land of his birth. But the younger son too had fulfilled all of her hopes for him. He had moved to Chiengmai where his home has been ever since. In that community he has ever been known for his godly life and good works.

Rev. Boon Tuan Boon Itt

Nai Boon Tuan Boon Itt was born on July 15th, 1865 in the little village of Bang-Pa on the Meklong river just below Rajburi.

"When Boon Itt was eight years old, the little family left Bang-Pa and went to live at Samray," where the church was located of which Sinsaa Ki-eng Qua-Sean was so long a member. The father had died and some change was imperative. There Boon Itt and the younger brother Boon Yee were placed in the boys' school and began their education. When Boon Itt was eleven Dr. and Mrs. House decided to take him with them to America to educate him. Another lad of about the same age also went with them, Nai Kawn.

"In 1881, when the boys were sixteen, Dr. House sent them to Williston Seminary, Easthampton, Mass., to prepare them for college. Here Boon Itt soon became a great favorite. As he began to grasp the knowledge of the Western world he showed an eagerness and a

---

Note,—This narrative of the life of the Rev. B. T. Boon Itt is almost wholly excerpts from an article by Belle Brain appearing in the May 1912 issue of the Missionary Review of the World. The quotation marks indicate the part of narrative thus culled from that longer one.—Ed.

Rev. BOON TUAN BOON ITT

joy in acquiring it that made him a delight to his teachers.   With the students he was equally popular.   As in Siam, he became a leader in athletics.   ' In the gymnasium and on the athletic field, at baseball or football, his lithe and muscular body had few equals,' says one who knew him.   ' His swimming feats and records were never equalled. In the classroom his work was always well done.   In the literary society he was one of the merriest and most faithful.   Everywhere his good humor and hearty laugh were contagious, and his unselfishness was a byword'.

"At Williams, where he took his four years' classical course it was the same as at Williston.   He was an apt and conscientious student, dearly beloved by every one with whom he came in contact. In 1889, when he completed the course, no member of the class had a better general record.

"It was at Williams that Boon Itt found Christ and took Him for a personal Saviour.   He had been faithful in church attendance and had read and studied his Bible, but this was largely the result of habit and from a desire to please his mother and Dr. and Mrs. House. His ideas on religion were indefinite and hazy, and it seemed hard for him to grasp the idea of a personal God.

"When at length the awakening came, it wrought a great change in him.   Making a full surrender to God, he resolved to study for the ministry and return again to Siam as a missionary.   Meanwhile, working through the channel of the Young Men's Christian Association, he became a strong factor in the religious life of the college.

"In the autumn of 1889, Boon-Itt entered Auburn Theological Seminary.

"Early in the summer of 1893, Boon Itt returned to Siam to take up his life work.   For 16 years America had been his home, and those who knew him best felt that going away was a real cross to him—as much of a sacrifice as that made by many an American-born missionary.   Yet he found great joy in the thought of winning souls in Siam.

" Boon Itt's first work was to perfect himself in the language. His English was faultless, and he could read Greek and Hebrew at sight , but his knowledge of his mother-tongue , tho he could still use it, was only that of a boy of eleven.   His mother was ambitious to see him a great Siamese scholar , and the older missionaries urged him on , in the hope that he would be able to make a revision of the imperfect translation of the Bible.

" During his months of preparation he lived at Samray, assisting the work in every way possible.   Everyone soon learned to love and respect him, and his influence in the church and Christian Boys' High School became very great.   ' In his quiet way he tried to show the students the manliest man who ever lived on this earth was Jesus of Nazareth,' says Dr. Eakin.   ' It is noticeable that the young men who came into the church during this period were marked by a stalwart strength of character '.

" Not a little inspiration for his future work was gained by accompanying the Rev. Eugene P. Dunlap on evangelistic tours through the country.   By means of a stereopticon, great interest was aroused among the villagers in the life of Christ and Boon Itt was very happy.   ' It is great joy,' he wrote to America, ' to tell the story of Jesus to the multitudes who have never heard it before.'

" On September 23rd, 1897, an important step occurred in Boon Itt's career—his marriage to his cousin, Maa Kim Hock, a recent graduate of the Harriet House School at Wang Lang.   Boon Itt's bride was heartily in sympathy with his life work, and made him a very good wife. Shortly after their betrothal he received an offer from a commercial house in Siam, at a salary supposed to have been between five and ten thousand dollars.   On submitting it to his fiancee, she heroically answered :   ' I think we will be far happier at the Lord's work on a little money than to leave it for this large sum.'

" Soon after their marriage, Boon Itt and his bride left Samray and went with Dr. and Mrs. Toy to open a new station at Pitsanuloke, a month's journey up the Menam from Bangkok.

Nai Boonyee Bansiddhi and wife

" The special work assigned to Boon Itt being a boarding school for boys, he threw his whole heart into the task. The beginning was small, but it soon attracted the attention of the Government authorities, who set the seal of their approval on it by sending their own sons. As it grew in numbers and popularity a larger building became a necessity, and this was erected at the cost of 4,000 ticals, every tical being secured by Boon Itt from the Siamese at Fitsanuloke.

" His influence over the boys was unbounded. On Saturdays it was his custom to take them on long tramps into the jungle for the study of nature, and the keen personal interest he took in them all won him their deep and abiding affection. But there was a larger work to which God was about to call him. In 1902, when Dr. Arthur J. Brown, of the Presbyterian Board, arrived in Siam on a tour of inspection, he found that the most imperative need was a new church in Bangkok. Young men educated in the mission schools were flocking to the city in ever increasing numbers, and in order to attend church, they must cross the river and go long distances to the suburbs. A great opportunity was being lost and the missionaries were much troubled. In his report to the Board, Dr. Brown wrote as follows :

" 'For this great work a man and a church are needed at once. No other need in Siam is more urgent. The man should be able to speak high Siamese like a native. He should be conversant with Siamese customs and etiquette, and so understand the native mind that he can enter into sympathy with it and for God. There is one man in Siam who meets all these conditions. The man is the Rev. Boon Boon-Itt, one of the most remarkable men I have met in Asia.'

" At first Boon Itt was loath to leave his work at Pitsanuloke, but presently he accepted the call and removed with his family to Samray. There were three children now, a boy and two little daughters.

" As the work progressed, he found it necessary to rent a small house near the site of the new church in the city proper, where new buildings for the Christian Boys' High School were also being erected. While busily engaged on the church, Boon Itt felt that some work ought to be inaugurated for young men during the week as well as on Sunday. For years he had cherished the plan of establishing an institution in Bangkok, with library, reading-rooms, and gymnasium, somewhat on the order of a Young Men's Christian Association, and the time now seemed ripe for it. Friends both in Siam and America showed such interest in the project that success seemed assured.

"But alas! in the midst of it all, Boon Itt was stricken with cholera, and died on May 8th, 1903, after an illness of ten days. For about two months before this no rain had fallen, and there had been much suffering by reason of the heat and the drought. At midnight, when Boon Itt passed away, the wind was rising and dark clouds were gathering. Shortly afterward, the monsoon broke and there were torrents of rain. Of what took place in that house of mourning during the storm, Dr. Eakin gives a vivid picture as follows :—

"'The house shook under the fierce attacks of the raging tempest. Knowing the common superstition of the Siamese, we realized how terrible it might seem to our people that a naked soul should go forth exposed to such a wild war of the elements. But the bereaved wife and mother calmly gathered the friends together in the little sitting-room, passed the hymn-books around and asked them all to sing. Through the long hours of that terrible storm they sang the hymns of Christian faith and hope and comfort.

"'In the intervals they talked of the future. One exprest concern about the new church building. It would be hard to find a contractor to take up work that had fallen from a dead hand, owing to a superstition that the building would be haunted. Then Kru Thien Pow, his devoted assistant, broke down for the first time and wept aloud: "I am not thinking of the new church", he said; "some

The three children of Rev. and Mrs. Boon-Itt

one will be found to finish that.   I am thinking of the Kingdom of Christ in Siam.   Who will take the vacant place in this service ? ' "

"The loss to Siam did, indeed, seem irreparable.   From the field and the Board, from his fellow missionaries and his fellow students, and from the many friends who had known and loved him as a boy in America, a flood of letters came, expressing not only the keenest sorrow, but a strong desire to perpetuate his memory by the erection of a building such as he had in his heart when he died.

" Committees were at once appointed both in Siam and in America.   In a short time the necessary funds were ready, and a beautiful building, known as the 'Boon Itt Memorial', was erected in Bangkok.   All classes in Siam, including members of the royal family and many princes and nobles, gave to the fund and took great interest in the project.   When H. R. H. Prince Damrong, Minister of the Interior, was asked to contribute, he said with deep feeling :—

" 'I am glad to help in the memorial to that splendid man. Boon Itt was a true Christian.   You may not know that I offered him a position which would have led to high titles of nobility from the King of Siam, to the governorship of a large province, and to a large increase in his income.   Yet he declined these high honors and financial benefits that he might continue in the service of Jesus Christ.'

" The ten short years Boon Itt worked in Siam were years of most fruitful endeavor.   His death occurred before he was forty, yet he had already become the acknowledged leader of the Christian Church in Siam.   Christians and non-Christians loved and respected him, and his influence in behalf of God was unbounded."

CHAPTER XXXI

PRESENT SIAMESE LEADERSHIP

"IDEALS are like stars men steer by.   Ultimately they determine the course."   The goal which has been shaping the course of Protestant Missions in Siam for a hundred years has been the establishment of a self-governing, self-supporting, self-propagating church.   From the beginning the missionaries recognized that the problem of establishing such a church was the problem of training leaders.   Today, the extent to which Siamese leadership has developed measures the advance that has been made toward the achievement of the threefold goal.

The fact that advance falls far short of that attained in newer missions in other countries should not blind our eyes to the decided gains that have been made.   If we contrast the meager past with the more abundant present we are prepared to believe in the words of a missionary of long experience, that "the crying need of our time is to urge and speed up the development of national initiative and leadership, to give all needed training for it, and put all needed pressure on the nationals to take a larger share."   The purpose of here tracing the development of Christian leadership in Siam is to encourage those who believe the time is ripe for an Independent National Church.

Who can measure the contribution of the early, seemingly barren decades to the building up of the Siamese church of today ? Much can be traced to the influence of the member received during the first twenty years of the Presbyterian activity, who came by certificate from the disbanding Congregational mission.   For fifteen years, until his death, Sinsaa Ki-eng Qua-Sean was active in promoting the work of the Kingdom of Christ, in talking with his fellow countrymen, in teaching the first school established. He was a strong leader, and looked well to the ways of his own household, for his five children became Christians and they in turn influenced others. Today the names of his descendants with their allied families fill a large space on the church rolls. Many of them hold positions of leadership and add greatly to the strength of the church.

Sinsaa Ki-eng Qua-Sean had been converted as an adult, but long searching for others resulted in so few additions that the training for leadership was directed more and more into the more impressionable years of youth. The man who first held the office of elder, Kru Naa, was given as a child to Dr. House and brought up in that missionary's home. Nang Esther Pradipasena likewise entered at an early age upon the training in the home of Mrs. Mattoon that prepared her for her long service as a Christian witness. When she united with the church in 1861 it was as the first Siamese woman to vow allegiance to Christ. Her faithfulness throughout already nearly seventy years of subsequent life has had an influence, which, while it will never be fully revealed in this world, has to its credit substantial gains to the church which can be reckoned.

The year that saw the first elder ordained, 1867, was the year in which the first Siamese preacher was licensed, and, as if to provide for a time which still lay hidden in the future, a young convert, Nai Keo, was also in that year won to Christ, to later become one of the distributors of the Bible under Dr. Carrington, and a faithful preacher until his death.

The fact that Meh Tuan, a daughter of Sinsaa Ki-eng Qua-Sean, was ready in 1875 to undertake the office of teacher and matron made it possible to begin the Wang Lang School for girls. " Capable, efficient, able to speak English, and devoted to the cause of Christ, she filled the position for many years with abundant success," says her biographer. " But for her faithful and continued service the school could not have grown", is Miss Cole's comment.

In 1877 Meh Tuans' son, Nai Boon Tuan Boon Itt, went to

America with Dr. House to be educated. One may feel sure that the underlying purpose in his being sent abroad was the hope that he would render more efficient service to the church on his return. Sixteen years later those hopes were realized.

Meanwhile, leaders were developing in Siam. Kru Yuen Tieng-Yok had been taken into the mission school near Wat Cheng as a child, befriended by Sinsaa Ki-eng Qua-Sean who had persuaded the father of the boy to entrust him to the missionaries. When he died in 1927 at the age of 78, he left a record of more than sixty years of distinguished service as an evangelist, pastor, teacher and translator. At the time when Miss Cole first came to Wang Lang, that compound was regarded as a complete station, needing a resident evangelist. Kru Yuen was the one selected by the mission for that post; for ten years he rendered invaluable service there. Miss Cole profited much by his advice, and he in turn was strengthened for his later work. In 1895 he was ordained as a pastor, and for over thirty years, until death, fostered the church at Samray, a part of that time in charge also of the Fourth Church, at the Bangkok Christian High School, always taking, besides, a share in all the Christian activities of Bangkok.

Miss Cole encouraged other strong personalities to grow into leaders of ability, both within and without the school. One of these, Phya Vichit, who was for many years head of a government school for boys, made his home at Samray and with his wife, Nang Phun, was influential in all good works. He was a notably good teacher of Siamese to foreigners, and some of his translations are still in use as text books.

In the summer of 1893, Boon Itt returned. He had been educated in an American preparatory school, college, and theological seminary, and was fully qualified to face the problems of mission work on an equality with his American brethren in the Presbytery, as those who knew him testify. He strove to fit into the work with as little friction as possible, but the task of making the Christian church truly indigenous was near his heart. It was a great step in that direction when, in 1897, he and his wife, Nang Kim Hock, together with a cousin, Kru Tien Pow Viradhien, were sent to open a new station at Pitsanuloke, with only Dr. Toy from the foreign group. In 1898 Dr. Toy was absent on furlough, and Boon Itt carried on splendidly. Compelled by the government to choose a new site for their work, he carved it out of the jungle and met every emergency. While his wife started a school for girls he threw his energies into a boarding school for boys. From residents of Pitsanuloke, he secured money for a building and made the school self-supporting,—a powerful influence for good.

In 1920 he was called to work in Bangkok in connection with the Kritsamptawongse Church for which Phya Saurasin, then Phya Montri, had offered to provide a building, above what the Siamese Christians could give. The story of this gift dates back to 1867 when the donor, then a boy and called Nai Tien Hee, accepted Christ and was baptised. Later, his father provided the means for study in America, but after his return he drifted away from the church. The death of his oldest son and the parable that was told him then, in tender reminder, of the sheep that would not follow until the shepherd lifted its lamb in his arms and carried it with him, so touched his heart that he decided to build a church in Bangkok in memory of his son. He hoped that it might be the means of winning many young men. Being a friend and admirer of Boon Itt, it was his wish that he might take charge of it.

In the midst of the task of overseeing the erection of the building, Reverend Boon Itt was stricken with cholera and died on the 8th of May, 1903. Dr. Eakin tells how Kru Tien Pow, Boon Itt's devoted assistant, broke down and wept. "I am not thinking of the new church," he said, "some one will be found to finish that. I am thinking of the Kingdom of Christ in Siam. Who will take the vacant place in the service of Christ?"

His death was indeed a serious set back to what had come to

seem an imminent advance in national leadership and self-determination. On the occasion of a welcome to Rev. Arthur J. Brown, D. D. the year before, Mr. Boon Itt in a public address had said : "It will be readily understood that our people would like to have the management of their own affairs, in religion as well as in other matters, free from foreign domination; but...we do not propose to grasp the reins of control."

Others besides Boon Itt who were being counted on for active leadership were also lost to the cause. Kru Tien Pow, after ten years in the schools of Rajburi and Pitsanuloke, became a teacher in the Bangkok Christian High School. Three years later his health failed, and he died of tuberculosis in 1906, at the age of thirty-five. One of the most promising of the young Christian leaders, his death seemed most untimely but in the lives of his five children, all of whom are taking an active part in the church, his devotion to the cause has had a manifold expression.

One young man had left Siam for study abroad, an aggressive Christian, engaged to be married to one of the outstanding Christian young women. He succumbed to the temptations of worldly preferment. Before his boat reached Siam on the home-journey he sent a letter asking that his name be taken from the church roll. Though he did not wish to have the other obligation rescinded in like manner, his fiancee broke the engagement rather than sever Christian ties.

Samuel, son of Esther, was another whom death removed as he was coming to the front as a leader. Nai Boon Yee, brother of Reverend Boon Itt, and his wife, Nang Soy, who had become an efficient teacher at the Wang Lang School, left Bangkok for the North, where they cast in their lot with the Lao Christians. Kru Tim and Kru Tow, after teaching for over ten years in the Wang Lang School, both entered government service, where they did good work in the newly organized girls' schools but were drawn away from the part they might also have taken in the things of the Kingdom of God.

King's Daughters Circle at Samray

One of the delegates to the Tokyo convention of the World's Students Christian Federation was a promising young nobleman of marked ability as a leader. He bought the land on which the Jane Hays Memorial School now stands with the plan in mind to build there a Christian community, with school, dispensary, and church. He had already made the place a religious and educational center when he met with the disgrace of imprisonment for a political offense and for many years was lost to the church for which he had been enthusiastically working. His fate tended to discourage aggressive leadership, though his downfall was in no way connected with his championship of the Christian faith.

Out of all the group of younger men and women who had seemed at the turn of the century ready to lead the Siamese church to a new position of service and power, there still remained several who were faithful and efficient. They were for the most part women used to looking to the men who were now gone for the public leadership, and they were unable to organize the groups of followers and so use the newly opened opportunities to the full. The movement toward a national church seemed to come to a stand still. It is only as we look back from the vantage point of a quarter of a century later that the quiet years that followed are seen to have been a time, not of stagnation, but of growth.

One of the women whose work counted for much during these years was Kru Soowan......(Nang Vibhajna Vidyasiddhi) who for twenty years was head Siamese teacher at Wang Lang. In Miss Cole's history of the school a fitting tribute is paid to her worth. The church is still benefitting by her service. She is the first Siamese to hold the office of National President of the King's Daughters and as editor of the Daybreak she finds an avenue for another form of service for the women of Siam.

During this time there were schools founded on the initiative of Christian women that have continued to grow and provide centers of Christian influence. One of these is the Padoong Darunee school opened by Kru Kim Hock, first for her own children, and then for the neighbors who besought her to teach their children too, until now the school numbers over 200. Another, the Anugoon Darunee, was founded by Kru Pleek at Samray. She says of the founding of the school:—

"Until 1902 I had never thought of starting a school—I had thought of teaching as something utterly unsuited to my desires. But in that year the loss of my two small children brought me to ask God what it was that He wished me to do with my life. I realized that if I were to die I would have no gift to offer Him, for hitherto I had done nothing for Him. Thinking this over, and praying over it, the verse came to me, 'Take my yoke upon you and learn of me...and ye shall have rest to your souls', and I realized that God was seeking to teach me much that I needed to know before I could work for Him. It was then that Miss Cole comforted me by the thought that my two children had been taken by the Saviour to study in a better school than they would have known here in this world, and from that time my purpose was formed to start a school for the children in my neighborhood that they might know God's love."

From the time that the Bangkok Christian High School moved away from Samray in 1900, the self-supporting school and church there have been carried on without missionary assistance. In 1910 the Samray Christians accomplished on their own initiative the rebuilding of their church. Among the leaders of that period should be mentioned Nang Kim Joi, Khun Krasin and his wife Nang Chang, Phra Pysan, Nai Teang Kim, Luang Krasarp, and Nai Kim Sye Unyawong who has helped his wife, Kru Pleek, in planning for her school. A report of more recent date notes, in regard to a worker who helped to forward the work through these years: "Great credit is due to Miss Lucy Dunlap for the work of the Samray Sunday School and Christian Endeavor. Miss Dunlap is a native Christian who was taken to American many years ago to

First Presbyterian Church of Samray, Bangkok

(Erected in 1910 on site of original Church building and following the old design)

complete her education. For many years she has not ceased to testify for Jesus Christ, even within the walls of hospital or palace."

Younger men were growing up preparing to take the vacant places of leadership. Kru Soon Ho was a teacher at the Bangkok Christian College for many years, for some years head teacher. As an elder in the church, a forceful speaker of magnetic personality, he was long an influential leader. Kru Serm was another teacher whose leadership extended outside the walls of the school room. Kru Kim Heng Mangkarabundhu, a graduate of the Christian High School, was for twenty-two years in charge of the boys' school at Samray. He was a delegate to the Tokyo convention in 1907. His ordination to the Christian ministry in 1915 was the first ordination for twenty years and established a precedent in the matter of the salary due the pastor of a church. Hitherto evangelistic workers and preachers had been paid very meagerly. To call as pastor one who had won recognition as a teacher meant that from thenceforth ministers should be paid as teachers—a worthy step in advance, and one that paved the way for a better educated ministry. Kru Kim Heng was pastor of the Second Church at Wang Lang until after the establishment of the Fifth Church at the new school when the remnant remaining of the Second Church was reorganized under a separate pastorate. By his walk and conversation, by deeds of unfailing kindness and sympathy, he has endeared himself to everyone. His earnest preaching and faithful pastoral care have made him one of the indispensable builders of the church in Siam.

When the Kritsampantawongse church was organized in 1904, it was thought that Kru Kim Heng would take the place of Kru Yuen at Samray and that Kru Yuen would be pastor of the new church. Kru Yuen was in charge of both churches until 1909. Then circumstances made it necessary for him to resume charge of Samray alone, and for seveval years the Fourth Church was in charge of the principal of the Bangkok Christian College. Not until 1918 did the college church call a pastor. Then a former pupil of Kru

Kim Heng, Kru Pluang Suddikam was installed.

Kru Pluang was graduated from the Bangkok Christian High School in 1910 ; taught at Rajburi for one year; in 1906 married Nang Kim Hock Boon Itt, and for fourteen years taught in the B. C. C. There, as Master of Boy Scouts and a valued leader in the work and responsibility of the school, his influence had grown. Twice a month for several years he had preached at the Kritsampantawongse Church, hence the transition to the full time pastorate was a very natural one. In a letter to him from Doctor Mc Clure occurs the following :

"We have felt sure that God has called you to do a great work for Him in Siam. We think of Reverend Boon Itt and yourself as being like Elijah and Elisha ; and we trusted that a double portion of Reverend Boon Itt's spirit had fallen upon you. Siam's great need today is for strong preachers of the gospel of Jesus Christ. We are all expecting much from you and Kru Kim Heng as witnesses for God in Siam."

Today, not only as pastor of the college church, but as the backbone of the Boon Itt Memorial Institute, as leader of the Old Boys Association of the B. C. C., in the work of the Conference Committee, on the Committee for Home Missions, the Centennial Committee and many other avenues of service his power as a leader is felt.

One way in which the influence of the Reverend Boon Itt has been conserved and his memory perpetuated is by the work for young men centering in the Boon Itt Memorial Institute. In an account of the history of its founding written by Dr. Bentoon Boon Itt, the son, the following significant items occur :—

"The evening of April 6th, 1904 marked the beginning of the present Boon Itt Memorial Institute. It was on this date when eleven friends of the late Reverend Boon Itt met for the first time at the home of Dr. E. P. Dunlap to discuss means for raising money for the Memorial building in Bangkok. (The original group included

Rev. Yuan, Luang Vikanedh, Nai Sung, Nai Boon Serm, Kru Thien Pow, Kru Kim Heng, Kru Awn, Nai Chim and three Americans). A few months later the name of Nai Boon Yee, the only brother of Rev. Boon Itt, was added. This committee worked in conjunction with another committee in the United States and raised funds for the Boon Itt Memorial Institute. In 1905 the present site was purchased from Phya Chaiya for Tcs. 19,385. All of this amount was raised in Siam, thanks to the kindness and to the generosity of the friends of Rev. Boon Itt. Part of the list of those who contributed toward this fund is to be found in an Appendix of this volume. It will suffice to mention here His Majesty, King Rama VI, then the Crown Prince, kindly contributed one thousand ticals. H. R. H. Prince Boribat gave five hundred ticals and several other Princes and Government officials, business men and other friends had a share in this Memorial. Nai Boon Yee gave a thousand ticals. The building was completed in 1907 from funds raised among Rev. Boon Itt's friends in the United States.

"The Board of Directors had its birth in December, 1907. The Constitution and By Laws of the Institute were drafted and put into use by this Board of Directors, of which Dr. E. P. Dunlap was president. Dr. G. B. Mc Farland was first Vice President, Kru Soon Ho the second Vice president, Nai Serm the recording secretary. Luang Vikanedh, Nai Kim Sye and Kru Huad were among the members of the Board.

" The Boon Itt Memorial Institute was among the first few clubs in Bangkok. And a member could enjoy himself with games without being dragged into gambling, and could meet his friends and chat with them without being offered a drink, and could sit down peacefully watching the game without being allured and bothered by common women.

" As the work of the Institute flourished and the membership became larger, the work likewise grew heavier, so much so that Kru Thai Pong (Khun Bambat Kadee), then a teacher at the B. C. C.

was engaged as an assistant secretary . . . With the frequent changes in the General Secretary the institute suffered, so that the Mission was at one time seriously considering closing it. A group of Christian leaders, members of the Boon Itt Memorial Institute however, stepped in and requested that they be given full authority to continue the work and the Mission granted them its permission. Thus since December 1923 the Boon Itt Memorial Institute has been under the control of the Board of Directors until this present date."

The Boon Itt has prospered under the control of the Board of Directors and the reports for each of the subsequent years have indicated steady progress. The Directors are all busy men, yet are giving of their time and thought generously to the care and development of the institution, ready and willing to sacrifice for the work which they feel is well worth promoting. The president of the Board this year is Dr. B. Boon Itt, who has both energy and ability adequate to the task.

Two years before the Boon Itt Memorial Institute building was ready for occupancy, there began an organization in Bangkok which was destined to grow also to a strong maturity and to serve the church as a special preparation field for Christian leaders. This was the Conference for Christian workers, modeled after the conferences sucessfully inaugurated at Petchaburi some years before. At first it was a work done *for* the Siamese rather than *by* them. Even as late as 1912 the annual report speaks of Dr. McFarland at the head and early programs attest the small share the Siamese took in the programs. But in 1914 Kru Kim Heng Mangkarabundha became president and from that time on the proportion of foreign and Siamese activity in the work of the Conference has been gradually reversed, until the report for 1927 reads, " In the three conferences of the year interest has been stimulated and aroused for greater church activity. The work of these conferences is entirely in the hands of the Siamese Christian people and is doing much towards their self realization."

Every month four representatives from each of the four
Bangkok churches meet as an executive committee to direct the work
of the organization.   The present chairman is Kru Tart Pradipasena,
the first woman to hold the office.

The initiative and energy that belong to successful leadership
have also been displayed in the work of the Temperance Society.
Temperance work has gone on for a long time in Siam.   By 1923
there were three societies all working for the temperance cause
but somewhat at cross purposes.   A union of the three was effected.
" Twelve officers with the necessary committees were elected, and to
obtain better results, the committees asked older friends to become
advisors.   At present all the officers and committee members are
teachers, pastors, doctors, and other busy people, all with much daily
work to do.   At any rate, they are happy that the work is advanc-
ing," writes Kru Leck Taiyong, who has done much to make the
work of the society an enthusiastic success.   A meeting of their
executive committee is like a roll call of the most active young
people in the various churches.

In still other ways the share of the Siamese is enlarging.   Bible
translation that was formerly largely done by the foreign missionary is now in the hands of a committee, only one member of which is
an American, and he was born in Siam.   They have been making substantial progress in Bible revision over a period of several years with
a gratifying independence of judgment on the part of the Siamese
members. The Daybreak, a Siamese monthly magazine established by
the Mission in 1891, now published under the auspices of the Wattana
Wittiya Academy, has grown from a distinctly foreign type of
magazine to one which reflects the viewpoint of the Siamese and tries
to stimulate its readers to a thoughtful solution of their own problems
for themselves.   Kru Tart Pradipasena, who was assistant editor for
many years laid the foundations for a magazine of a truly indigenous
design, and when she resigned in 1926 to teach the Missionary Language School, Nang Vibhajna has wisely followed the same pattern.

The special Siamese editions of the Siam Outlook have been a forum for the discussion of a variety of subjects, and, even under the handicap of using the English language as a medium, many of the articles have conveyed a thoughtful message. From time to time have appeared translations of Christian books which represent the initiative as well as the labor of Siamese, at times given as a free will offering. A library of all such translations, from Ben Hur to the Prince of the House of David, would more than fill a five foot shelf, proof of the value of this contribution.

That the schools have been indispensable to the church is evident even from this fact alone—from them have come, without exception, all the leaders. In recent years an advance has been made in systematic training for specialized service. The Theological Seminary at Chiengmai began a four years course for the graduates of the Eight Matayome (secondary school), in 1926. Six students enrolled the first year five of them graduates of the B. C. C. "All are interested and earnest in their studies," says the report for the year. "They have the evangelistic spirit. They realize the need of the Siamese church to possess well trained and consecrated leaders."

In 1925, with the help of the Rev. Charoen Sakulgan and his wife, Nang Sangat, a Bible Training School for Women was established in Bangkok which has at present six Bible students doing full work and three special students. The work of this school is very intimately connected with the Second Church, to which the Rev. Charoen Sakulgan was called as pastor in 1922. The report for that year mentions him as a "teacher of long experience at the B.C.C....gifted with the art of leadership. On the Sunday when an executive commission of the Presbytery ordained and installed him in the new church, the Spirit of God was in the service in such a way that every one was moved." He has continued to develop in mind and spirit and evangelistic zeal. In 1928 he was a delegate at the International Missonary Council at Jerusalem, and had also the privilege of a short time in England for special instruction in evangelism. As a result he has become even more serviceable to the church to which he ministers, and to other groups of Christians who call on him for evangelistic work. The Bible Training School provides a home for many of the conferences Kru Charoen conducts. The students teach in the Sunday School, assist in the street chapel work and outside gospel services, and lead the midweek prayer-meetings. Much of the growth of the Second Church the pastor attributes to the influence of the school. During the absence of the missionary on furlough the school was in charge of Kru Charoen and Kru Sangat, who proved fully equal to the responsibility.

Two other institutions have opened the way for young women to prepare for a worthy profession under Christian auspices, The McCormick Hospital School of Nursing at Chiengmai, and the Bangkok Maternity Home with Training Course in Midwifery. In the report for 1927 of the former, credit is given to two Siamese young women for work of a high character: " Fresh from four years at the Peking Union Medical Hospital, Kru Civili Sinhametra has displayed exceptional tact and executive ability as acting superintendent of nurses. Boon Phan Sinhanetra, of our own class of 1926, has acted as head nurse and has been valuable in keeping the ward work up to standard. She also passed the examination of the Red Cross Association, the only standard for nurses this country has at present." In the Maternity Home, Dr. Boon Itt has kindly given time to instructing the student nurses. These students have also had training in the Women's Bible School, since the plan is to train them as Deaconess nurses.

Training for teaching is receiving new emphasis, in preparation for the increased demand for qualified leaders. Some of the secondary schools of the mission have furnished teachers to smaller schools as well as provided recruits for their own faculties for many years, but stressing special preparation for the work will further improve the quality. One school reports in 1928 : " The school has never been so well manned with Siamese teachers, everyone of the twelve being an active Christian, and everyone having the good of the school at heart. Since 1922 one or two of our best graduates have in succession attended the Manila Normal School preparing for work here, and at present the school has four of these on the faculty. The Siamese teachers take responsibility for the printing department, the publishing of the College News, the Sunday School, the Christian Endeavor, the Temperance organization, the College Band, the book room, the Boy Scouts, athletics, and such special activities as occasion may call forth. " This is indeed not only training for leadership but leadership itself.

Note the aspects of present day Siamese leadership which indicate an advance toward the three-fold goal. That the government of the church is ready to pass without upheaval or disturbance into the hands of the people of the land is the outcome of years of enlarging responsibility borne by the elders of the session and by the men who have been ordained as pastors. The churches which have pastors of their own have made a success of self-government. In the three Presbyteries which have oversight of the churches, half of the members are Siamese or Chinese. The moderator is seldom an American. From the present degree of independence to the establishment of an indigenous church, separate in organization entirely from the church in America, is but a moderately difficult step.

The goal, in the second instance, is one of *self-support*. What is the relation of adequate Siamese leadership to the achievement of this end ? Each time that a Siamese pastor has been installed, there has followed a remarkable increase in the contributions of the congregation because of its more definite objective and greater incentive for sacrificial giving. Tithing and stewardship take on a new significance when a regular salary must be provided. Of the annual amount of about 14,000 ticals given for church and congregational expenses, by the more than fifty organized churches, over 8000 is contributed by the six churches supporting their own pastors. That not all their gifts go into the one channel of pastoral salary is shown by the fact that one-third of the total for benevolences comes from the same source. Nor do these churches have either a large membership or exceptionally wealthy members to account for the larger proportion of their giving.

The ideal for our schools and hospitals has long been self-support. The effort to provide trained teachers and hospital assistants has been repaid not only in the primary gain of better service rendered, but in the secondary benefit as well, of being the means of attracting a larger clientele. When the Siamese have a larger part in the management—a step contemplated in the proposed Boards of Directors for our higher schools—a natural channel well be provided for increased gifts from Siamese in recognition of the philanthropic work of these institutions.

Most important of all is that the church be *self-propagating*. Since 1924 a Home Mission Committee, composed of Siamese pastors, laymen and women has been at work collecting funds, experimenting with short campaigns, studying the situation, awakening the Siamese church to a sense of responsibility for the unevangelised. In Bangkok, all of the outreaching evangelistic preaching in the small street chapels is done by Siamese. The mission has oversight of several of the chapels, but for many years the Siamese, through the Conference of Christian workers, have assumed all the effort and expense connected with the work of one chapel, in which over 3000 people by actual count were reported in 1925 as coming that year to hear the preaching of the Word. "In regular order and sequence the work is planned for the year and the appointments are faithfully met by volunteer workers", reads the report.

From the Theological Seminary have gone forth workers into widely separated parts of the field—to the province of Yunnan, China, and down to the Malay peninsula, and to the borders of Burma on the west and into French territory several day's journey beyond the Cambodian river on the east. Those who volunteered to undertake work among the Tai beyond the borders of Siam, and who went with their families for a definite term of years to Yunnan, have on their return brought back to the churches which sent them forth some of the same stimulation to missionary evangelism that that has stirred Christians since the time of Paul and Silas.

Whether this evidence of the growing ability of the leaders of the Siamese church warrants an optimistic faith or prompts a more cautious conservatism to expect a slower development, there is nevertheless much cause for gratitude that one hundred years of labor have yielded a return intrinsically potential of greater harvests to come.   The years may be long before the kingdom of Siam becomes a Christian nation, but what Christian doubts that in the Providence of God His plan for Siam will some day be consummated ?   Toward that consummation points the present day development of Siamese leadership.

APPENDICES

APPENDICES

BIBLIOGRAPHY

ABEEL, DAVID—*Abeel's Residence in China and the Neighboring Countries 1830-1833* (Revised and reprinted from the American Edition—1835 James Nisbet & Co., Berners St., London)

ANONYMOUS—*Guide Book to Bangkok and Siam* (Bangkok, 1904)

BANGKOK CHRISTIAN COLLEGE—*College News* (1921)

BANGKOK TIMES—*Calendar* (Manuscript—1822-1900)

BRADLEY, REV. DAN B., M. D.—*Bangkok Calendar* (1859-1873)

BRADT PARTY, THE—*Around the World Series of Missions* (Chapters VII-IX) (Missionary Press Co. 1912)

BRAIN, BELLE M.—*Boon Itt, A Christian Leader of Asia* (See Missionary Review, Vol. XXV, No. 5, May 1908)

BROWN, REV. A. J., D. D.—*The Expectation of Siam* (N. Y. 1925) and *Nearer and Farther East* (Chapter V-—1908)

CADDY, MRS. FLORENCE—*To Siam and Malaya* (London-1889)

CANDEE,—*New Journeys in Old Asia* (Chapter XI, XII) (F. A Stokes Co. 1927)

CARTER, A. CECIL—*The Kingdom of Siam* (Putnam Sons, N.Y. 1904)

"COMMITTEE, THE".—*Siam from Ancient to Present Times* (Bangkok 1928)

CORT, MARY LOVINA—*Siam, The Heart of Farther India* (Randolph Co. 1886)

CURTIS, MRS. LILLIAN—*The Laos of North Siam* (Phila. 1903)

DODD, REV. C., D. D.—*The Tai Race* (Iowa, U. S. A. 1923)

DUNLAP, REV. E. P., D. D.—*Report of Petchaburi Church* (Manuscript-1883)

DWIGHT, HENRY OTIS—*The Centennial History of the American Bible Society* (N. Y. 1916)

FELTUS, REV. GEO., A. M., B. D.—*Samuel Reynolds House* (N.Y. 1924)

FREEMAN, REV. JOHN H.—*An Oriental Land of the Free* (Phila. 1910)

FRENCH, MRS. H. S. G.—*Scenes in India* (Boston-1847)

314

GRAHAM, W. A., M. R. A. S., F. R. G. S.—*Siam* (2 Vols. London-1924)

GUTZLAFF, REV. C. F. A.—*Journal of Three Voyages, 1831, 1832, 1833* (London—3rd. Edition)

HARRIS, REV. W.—*Educational Work in North Siam* (Manuscript 1915)

LE MAY, REGINALD—*An Asian Arcady* (Cambridge-1926)

LEONOWENS, MRS. ANNA HARRIETTE—*The Romance of the Harem* (1872) *An English Governess at the Court of Siam*

MALCOM, HOWARD—*Travels in South-eastern Asia* (2 Vols. Boston —1839)

MC CLURE, REV. W. G., D. D.—*Brief Survey of the Siam Mission* (1915)

MC DONALD, REV. N. A.—*Siam: its government, manners, customs etc.* (Phila. 1871)

MC FARLAND, REV. S. G.—*Letters* (Manuscript—Letter Press, 1876-1885)

MC GILVARY, REV. DANIEL, D. D.—*A Half Century Among the Siamese and Laos* (N. Y. 1912).

Minutes of The Various Presbyterian Mission Stations (Manuscript)

NEALE, F. A.—*Narrative of a Residence in Siam* (London-1852)

PRESBYTERIAN BOARD OF FOREIGN MISSIONS—

    Siam and Laos (Phila. 1884)

    Report of Deputation of Presbyterian Board of Foreign Missions to Siam, Philippines, Japan, Chosen, and China, —April-November 1915 (N. Y. 1916)

    The Foreign Missionary (Vols. IX, XII, XIII, XIV, XVII, XXVIII-XXXII, XXXIV, XXXVII, XXXIX-XLII)

    Mission Letters—(1847-1884 Original manuscript)

    The Home and Foreign Missionary (Vols. XIII-XV, XVII, XIX, XX-XXVII, XXIX, XXXII, XXXIV, XXXV)

Record of Actions of Siam Mission (Bangkok-1926)

Records of the First Presbyterian Church of Bangkok—(Manuscript 1849-1899)

ROBINSON, REV. CHAS.—*Sketch of the Origin of Protestant Missions In Siam (See Bangkok Calendar 1866)*

ROYCE, NANCY—*A Sketch of the Life and Character of Mrs. Emelie Royce Bradley* (N. Y)

SIAM MISSION—*Siam Outlook* (1921-1924, 1927, 1928)
Notes from South Siam (1921)
Annual Reports (1912-1921)

SMITH, REV. S. F.—*Missionary Sketches: A Concise History of the Work of the American Baptist Missionary Union* (Boston-1887)

SMITH, REV. S. J.—*Reminiscences* (In manuscript)
Brief Sketches of Siam from 1833 to 1909 (Bangkolem Press —1909)
Siam Repository (1869, 1870, 1871, 1872, 1873, 1874)

SMYTH, H. WARRINGTON—*Five Years in Siam—1891-1896* (John Murray—London)

SNYDER, REV. F. L.—*Resume of Educational Work in South Siam* (Manuscript)

SOMMERVILLE, MAXWELL—*Siam on the Meinam from the Gulf to Ayuthia* (Phila. 1897)

SPEER, ROBERT E.—*Presbyterian Foreign Missions* (Phila. 1902)

STRONG, WILLIAM E.—*The Story of the American Board* (Pilgrim Press, 1910)

TAYLOR, BAYARD—*Siam* (Compiled and arranged by Geo. B. Bacon (N. Y. 1893)

THOMPSON, P. A.—*Lotus Land* (Lippincott Co. 1906)

THOMSON, J., F. R. G. S. *The Straits of Malacca, Indo-China, and China; or Ten Years' Travels Adventures, and Residence Abroad* (N. Y. 1875)

TURPIN,— *Histoire de Siam* (Translation by B. O. Cartwright 1908)

VINCENT, FRANK—*The Land of the White Elephant* (N. Y. 1874)

WOMAN'S FOREIGN MISSIONARY SOCIETY OF THE PRESBYTERIAN CHURCH—*Historical Sketch of Missions in Siam* (7th Edition— Revised by Rev. A. W. Cooper, 1915)

WORLD MISSIONARY ATLAS—(1925)
YOUNG, E.—*The Kingdom of the Yellow Robe*
หม่อมเจ้า นพมาศ — นิราศ ลอนดอน, ตั้ง เจ้าพระยา (พ.ศ. ๒๔๖๑)
หมอ ดี. บี. บรัดเล — ประชุม พงศาวดาร ภาค ที่ ๓๑ จดหมายเหตุ เรื่อง
มิชชันนารี อเมริกัน เข้ามา ประเทศ สยาม (พ.ศ. ๒๔๖๙)
หลวงจินดาสหกิจ (ละม้าย ธนะสิริ) — ประวัติ ของ แม่เต๋อ (พ.ศ. ๒๔๗๑)
พระราชนิพนธ์ ใน พระบาทสมเด็จพระจุลจอมเกล้าเจ้าอยู่หัว —
ประชุมพงศาวดาร ภาค ที่ ๓๓
บุรพภาค พระธรรม เทศนา
เฉลิม พระเกียรติ พระบาทสมเด็จฯ พระนั่งเกล้า เจ้าอยู่หัว (พ.ศ. ๒๔๖๙)

Roster of Missionaries According to their Missionary Societies, Given in Chronological Order.

† Honorably retired.
* Died in Siam.
‡ Transferred to China.
** Contract Teachers.
— Still in active service

NETHERLANDS MISSIONARY SOCIETY.

    1828-1831 Rev. Carl Friedrich Augustus Gutzlaff.
* 1830-1831 Mrs. C. F. A. Gutzlaff.

LONDON MISSIONARY SOCIETY.

    1828-1832 Rev. Jacob Tomlin.

THE AMERICAN BOARD OF COMMISSIONERS FOR FOREIGN MISSIONS.

   1831-1832 Rev. David Abeel.
   1834-1845 Rev. Charles Robinson.
   1834-1845 Mrs. C. Robinson.
‡ 1834-1846 Rev. Stephen Johnson.
* 1834-1841 Mrs. S. Johnson.
   1835-1848 Rev. Dan Beach Bradley, M. D. (Later joined A.M.A.)
* 1835-1845 Mrs. D. B. Bradley.
   1838-1839 Rev. Stephen Tracy, M. D.
   1838-1839 Mrs. S. Tracy.
   1838-1839 Rev. Mr. Robbins (or Robins).
   1838-1839 Mrs. Robbins (or Robins).
* 1840-1840 Rev. N. S. Benham.
   1840-1841 Mrs. N. S. Benham.
* 1840-1842 Rev. H. S. G. French.
   1840-1843 Mrs. H. S. G. French.
‡ 1840-1846 Rev. L. B. Peet.
‡ 1840-1846 Mrs. L. B. Peet.
* 1840-1844 Miss M. E. Pierce.
* 1840-1848 Rev. Jesse Caswell.
   1840-1849 Mrs. J. Caswell.
   1840-1849 Rev. Asa Hemenway.
   1840-1849 Mrs. A. Hemenway.

THE AMERICAN MISSIONARY ASSOCIATION.

    * 1850-1873 Rev. Dan Beach Bradley, M. D.
    * 1850-1893 Mrs. D. B. Bradley.
      1850-1855 Rev. L. B. Lane, M. D.
      1850-1855 Mrs. L. B. Lane.
      1850-1855 Rev. Josiah Silsby.
      1850-1855 Mrs. J. Silsby.
      1866-1873 George G. Graham.
      1866-1873 Mrs. G. G. Graham.
      1871-1874 Rev. Cornelius B. Bradley.
      1871-1874 Mrs. C. B. Bradley.

THE AMERICAN BAPTIST BOARD.

    * 1833-1851 Rev. John Taylor Jones, D D.
    * 1833-1838 Mrs. Eliza Grew Jones.
      1835-1884 Rev. William Dean, D. D. (1842-1864 served in China).
      1835-1835 Mrs. W. Dean (Died en route).
      1836-1845 Rev. Robert Davenport.
      1836-1845 Mrs. R. Davenport.
    * 1836-1837 Rev. Alanson Reed.
      1836- ? Mrs. A. Reed.
   ‡ 1836-1837 Rev. J. L. Shuck.
      1838-1842 Mrs. William Dean (Miss Theodosia Barker).
    * 1839-1841 Rev. Cowdon H. Slafter.
      1839-1881 Mrs. C. Slafter (Later became Mrs. W. Dean).
   ‡ 1839-1848 Rev. Josiah Goddard.
   ‡ 1839-1848 Mrs. J. Goddard.
    * 1841- ? Mrs. Judith Leavitt Jones.
      1843-1868 J. H. Chandler.
      1843-1868 Mrs. J. H. Chandler.
      1846-1847 Rev. Erastus N. Jencks.
      1846-1847 Mrs. E. N. Jencks (Died on passage home).
    * 1848-1889 Mrs. Sarah Sleeper Jones (Later became Mrs. S. J Smith).
      1848-1855 Miss Harriet Morse.
    * 1849-1868 Rev. Samuel Jones Smith, LITT. D.
   ‡ 1851-1858 Rev. William Ashmore, Sr., D. D.
   ‡ 1851-1858 Mrs. Martha Ashmore.
   ‡ 1854-1863 Rev. Robert Telford.
   ‡ 1854-1863 Mrs. R. Telford.

1864-1870 Miss Augusta Fanny Dean (Married Rev. J.
Goddard).
* 1864-1865 Rev. Cyrus H. Chilcott.
‡ 1866-1871 Miss Adelle M. Fielde.
1868-1868 Rev. William M. Lisle.
1868-1868 Mrs. W. M, Lisle.
‡ 1869-1873 Rev. S. B. Partridge.
‡ 1869-1873 Mrs. S. B. Partridge.
1882-1893 Rev. L. A. Eaton.
* ? -1891 Mrs. L. A. Eaton.

THE PRESBYTERIAN BOARD.

1840-1844 Rev. William P. Buell.
1840-1844 Mrs. W. P. Buell.
1847-1865 Rev. Stephen Mattoon, D. D.
1847-1864 Mrs. S. Mattoon.
1847-1876 Rev. Samuel R. House, M. D.
1849-1852 Rev. Stephen Bush.
* 1849-1851 Mrs. S. Bush.
1856-1876 Mrs. S. R. House.
1856-1857 Rev. Andrew B. Morse.
1856-1857 Mrs. A. B. Morse.
* 1858-1911 Rev. Jonathan Wilson, D. D.
* 1858-1860 Mrs. Maria Wilson.
* 1858-1911 Rev. Daniel McGilvary, D. D.
* 1860-1923 Mrs. Daniel McCilvary.
1860-1878 Rev. S. G. McFarland, D. D.
1860-1878 Mrs. S. G. McFarland.
1860-1886 Rev. Noah A. McDonald, D. D.
1860-1884 Mrs. N. A. McDonald.
1862-1873 Rev. S. C. George, D. D.
1862-1873 Mrs. S. C. George.
1863-1864 Mr. J. F. Odell.
1866-1868 Rev. Patrick L. Carden.
1866-1868 Mrs. P. L. Carden.
1866-1885 Mrs. Kate Wilson.
1869-1875 Rev. John Carrington, D. D. (Later joined Am.
Bible Soc.)
1869-1875 Mrs. J. Carrington.
1869-1886 Rev. James W. Van Dyke.
1869-1880 Mrs. J. Van Dyke.
1871-1881 Rev. John N. Culbertson.

1870-1873 Chas. W. Vrooman, M. D.
1871-1873 Rev. R. Arthur.
1871-1873 Mrs. R. Arthur.
1871-1873 Miss E. S. Dickey.
1872-1876 Miss Arabella Anderson (Married Rev. Henry
Noyes, D. D.)
1874-1877 Miss Susie Grimstead.
1874-1882 Sarah M. Coffman.
1874-1891 Miss Mary Lovina Cort.
* 1875-1918 Rev. Eugene P. Dunlap, D. D.
1875-1925 Mrs. E. P. Dunlap.
* 1874-1886 Marion A. Cheek, M. D.
1874-1883 Mrs. M. A. Cheek.
1878-1880 Rev. J. M. McCauley.
1878-1880 Miss Jennie Korsen (Married Rev. J. M. McCauley).
1878-1881 Miss Belle Caldwell (Married Rev. J. N. Culbertson).
1879-1884 Miss Mary E. Hartwell.
1879-1882 Miss Hattie H. McDonald.
* 1878-1881 Miss Mary M. Campbell.
† 1878-1924 Miss Edna S. Cole.
1880-1882 Rev. Charles S. McClelland.
1880-1882 Mrs. C. S. McClelland.
1880-1896 Miss Laura Olmstead (Married Rev. J. A. Eakin).
1880-1885 Ernest A. Sturge, M. D.
* 1880-1920 Rev. Samuel C. Peoples, M. D.
1881-1885 Mrs. E. A. Sturge (nee Mrs. Turner).
1881-1886 Miss Mary H. McDonald.
* 1882-1883 Rev. Charles D. McLaren.
† 1882-1924 Mrs. C. D. McLaren (Married Rev. Egon Wachter.
M. D.)
1882-1885 Miss Linnelle (Married Mr. S. Cross).
1882-1883 Miss Florence Wishard (Married Rev. Albert
Fulton).
1882-1885 Miss Antoinette Warner.
† 1882-1922 Miss Sarah Wirt (Married Rev. S. C. Peoples, M. D.).
1882-1883 Rev. John P. Hearst (Transferred to Japan).
1882-1883 Mrs. J. P. Hearst (Transferred to Japan).
1882-1903 Miss Isabella Griffin.
1884-1895 Miss E. Westervelt (Married Rev. S. Phraner).
1884-1886 Rev. Chalmers Martin.
1884-1886 Mrs. C. Martin.
1884-1922 Rev. Egon Wachter, M. D.

* 1884-1891 Miss Jennie Neilson (Married T. Heyward Hays,
M. D.)

* 1886-1891 T. Heyward Hays, M. D.

* 1886-1927 Rev. W. G. McClure, D. D.

1886 — Miss Mary J. Henderson (Married Rev. W. G.
McClure, D. D.).

* 1886-1891 Miss Jennie Small.

* 1886-1898 James Thompson, M. D.

1886-1893 Mrs. James Thompson.

1886 — Rev. A. Willard Cooper.

1886-1887 Mrs. A. W. Cooper.

1886-1919 Rev. William C. Dodd, D. D.

1886-1917 Rev. David G. Collins.

1886-1924 Mrs. David G. Collins.

1886-1888 A. M. Cary, M. D.

* 1886-1886 Mrs. A. M. Cary.

1887-1890 Miss Van Emmon (Married Rev. Christian Berger).

1888-1890 Rev. Christian Berger.

† 1888-1928 Rev. J. B. Dunlap, D. D.

† 1888-1928 Miss Mary Stokes (Married Rev. J. B. Dunlap, D. D.)

† 1888-1927 Rev. John A. Eakin, D. D.

† 1888-1928 Rev. Charles E. Eckels.

1888-1890 Benjamin Paddock, M. D.

1888 — Rev. Hugh Taylor, D. D.

1888-1925 Mrs. H. Taylor.

† 1887-1925 Miss Belle Eakin (Married Rev. W. C. Dodd, D. D.)

* 1888-1905 Miss Kate Fleeson.

1889 — James W. McKean, M. D.

1889 — Mrs. J. W. McKean.

1889 — Miss Cornelia H. McGilvary (Married Rev. W
Harris).

1890-1918 William A. Briggs, M. D.

* 1890-1891 Mrs. W. A. Briggs.

1890-1895 Rev. Stanley K. Phraner.

* 1890-1891 Mrs. S. K. Phraner.

1890-1906 Rev. Robert Irwin.

* 1890-1927 Miss S. Emma Parker (Married Rev. A. W. Cooper)

1890 — Rev. Frank L. Snyder.

1890 — Mrs. F. L. Snyder.

1890-1891 William Lee, M. D.

1890-1891 Mrs. W. Lee, R. N.

* 1890-1918 Miss Larissa J. Cooper.

1891-1894 Rev. Evander B. McGilvary.
1891-1894 Mrs. E. B. McGilvary.
1891 — Miss Margaret A. McGilvary (Married Rev. R. M.
Gillies, D. D.).
1891-1905 Walter B. Toy, M.D. (Later entered independent work)
1891-1905 Mrs. W. B. Toy.
1891-1898 Miss Elsie Bates (Married Mr. Vernon Kellett).
1891-1901 Miss Elizabeth Eakin.
† 1891-1928 Miss Margaret Galt (Married Rev. C. E. Eckels).
1891 — Miss Annabel Galt.
1892 — Miss Emma Hitchcock (Married Rev. J. H.
Freeman).
1892-1918 Mrs. W. A. Briggs.
1893-1895 Miss Annie Ricketts (Married Mr. Charles Barley).
* 1893-1903 Rev. Boon Tuan Boon Itt.
1894 — Rev. Howard Campbell, D. D.
* 1894-1920 Mrs. H. Campbell.
1894-1922 Rev. John H. Freeman.
1894-1903 Rev. William Shields.
1894-1900 Mrs. W. Shields.
1893 — Miss Julia Hatch (Resigned 1903-1916 ; Married
Rev. H. Taylor, D. D.).
1894-1903 Rev. J. S. Thomas, M. D.
1894-1903 Mrs. J. S. Thomas.
1894-1907 Rev. C. H. Denman, M. D.
1894-1907 Mrs. C. H. Denman.
1895-1906 Miss Mary Bowman, M. D. (Married Rev. Robert
Irwin).
1895-1907 Miss Margaret Wilson.
1895-1908 Carl C. Hansen, M. D.
1895-1907 Mrs. C. C. Hansen.
1895-1899 Miss Hattie Ghormley.
1895-1899 Rev. L. H. Curtis.
1885-1899 Mrs. Lillian Curtis.
1895 — Rev. William Harris.
† 1896-1923 Rev. Charles Callender.
† 1896-1923 Mrs. C. Callender.
* 1896-1897 Rev. F. L. Lyman.
† 1896-1926 Mrs. F. L. Lyman (Married Rev. J. A. Eakin, D. D.).
1897-1903 Mrs. Kim Hock Boon Itt.
1898-1913 William Swart, M. D.
* 1898-1901 Mrs. W. Swart.

† 1899-1902 Rev. James Waite.
† 1899-1902 Mrs. J. Waite.
† 1899-1902 Rev. Alexander Waite.
  1899-1923 Rev. David Park.
  1899-1923 Mrs. D. Park.
  1899-1906 Miss Edna Bissell.
  1899-1921 Rev. Robert C. Jones.
  1899-1921 Mrs. Jessie Magill Jones.
  1899-1901 Rev. Archie McKee.
  1899-1901 Mrs. A. McKee.
† 1899-1901 Guy Hamilton, M. D.
† 1899-1901 Mrs. G. Hamilton.
  1901-1902 Rev. Harry Armstrong.
  1901-1902 Mrs. H. Armstrong.
† 1901-1902 Harry Boyd, M. D.
† 1901-1902 Mrs. H. Boyd.
  1902   — Rev. Richard W. Post.
  1902   — Mrs. R. W. Post.
  1902-1921 Rev. Henry White, D. D.
  1902-1921 Mrs. H. White.
  1902   — Rev. Roderick M. Gillies, D. D.
  1902-1904 Rev. C. A. MacKay.
* 1902-1903 Mrs. C. A. MacKay.
† 1903-1920 Rev. Howell S. Vincent, D. D.
† 1903-1920 Mrs. H. S. Vincent.
  1903-1921 Miss Edith M. Buck.
  1903-1904 Howard Cornell, M. D.
  1903-1904 Mrs. H. Cornell.
  1903   — Edwin B. McDaniel, M. D.
  1903   — Mrs. E. B. McDaniel, R. N.
** 1903-1921 Rev. R. O. Franklin (Contract teacher 1903-1908 ;
             Regular missionary 1913-1921).
** 1903-1921 Mrs. R. O. Franklin (Contract teacher 1903-1908 ;
             Regular missionary 1913-1921).
  1903   — Miss Ednah Bruner (Married L. C. Bulkley, M. D.).
  1904-1913 Charles C. Walker, M. D.
* 1904-1906 Mrs. C. C. Walker.
  1904   — Charles H. Crooks, M. D.
  1904   — Mrs. C. H. Crooks.
  1904   — Miss Mabel Gilson (Married E. C. Cort, M. D.).
  1904-1907 Rev. A. P. Barrett.
  1904-1907 Mrs. A. P. Barrett.

1904-1910 Miss Elizabeth Carothers.
1905 — Lucius C. Bulkley, M. D.
1905 — Miss Margaret C.McCord.
1905-1907 Rev. Hugh Moody.
1905-1907 Mrs. H. Moody.
1905-1913 Mrs. W. Swart.
* 1906-1919 Carl Shellman, M. D.
1906 — Mrs. Carl Shellman (Married Rev. H. Campbell,
D. D.).
1906-1922 Miss Eula Van Vranken.
1906 — Rev. Marion B. Palmer.
1906 — Mrs. M. B. Palmer.
‡ 1906-1923 Claude W. Mason, M. D.
‡ 1906-1923 Mrs. C. W. Mason.
1908-1925 Miss Bertha Blount (Resigned 1916-1918; Married
G. B. McFarland, M. D., Affiliated missionary 1925—)
‡ 1908-1923 Rev. Lyle J. Beebe.
1908 — Edwin C. Cort, M. D.
1909 — Miss Lucy Starling.
1909-1914 Rev. William O. Yates.
1909-1981 Mr. Samuel Conybeare.
1909-1911 Mrs. S. Conybeare.
1909-1912 Mr. Albert Caldwell.
1909-1912 Mrs. A. Caldwell.
1909-1917 Mr. Edward M. Spilman.
1910 — Rev. Herbert W. Stewart.
1910 — Mrs. H. W. Stewart.
‡ 1910-1923 Miss Marie Collins (Married Chas. Park, M. D.).
1910-1911 Rev. Donald C. MacCluer.
1910-1911 Mrs. D. C. MacCluer.
* 1910-1915 Miss Daisy P. Campbell (Married Rev. Ray
Bachtell.)
1911 — Rev. Ray Bachtell.
1911-1920 Mr. Henry P. Reid.
* 1911-1913 Miss Ruth Shewbridge (Married Rev. L. J. Beebe).
1911-1921 Clarence A. Steele.
1911-1921 Mrs. C. A. Steele.
1911-1913 Mrs. Charles C. Walker.
1911 — Miss Johanna Christensen, R. N.
1911 — Miss Alice J. Ellinwood.
1912-1917 Mrs. E. M. Spilman.
1912-1920 Miss Beatrice Moeller.

1912 — Miss Bertha M. Mercer.
1912-1915 Mr. Arthur McClure.
1912 — William Beach, M. D.
1912 — Mrs. W. Beach.
1912-1920 Miss Addie Burr (Married Mr. Henry P. Reid).
1912 — Rev. Jacob L. Hartzell.
1912 — Mrs. J. L. Hartzell.
1912-1915 Miss Kate P. McKean.
1912- ? Mr. Arthur McMullin.
1912-1926 William Lyon, M. D.
1912-1926 Mrs. W. Lyon.
1912 — Miss Hazel Brunner (Married Rev. L. Hanna),
‡ 1912-1923 Charles Park, M. D,
1913-1918 Miss Harriet Worthington.
1913-1918 Paul Van Metre, M. D.
1913-1918 Mrs. Paul Van Metre.
1913 — Rev. Paul A. Eakin.
1914 —- Miss Helen McClure.
1914 — Miss Ruth Eakin.
1914-1925 Mr. Newell T. Preston.
1914-1925 Mrs. N. T. Preston.
1914 — Miss Maud C. Maxwell (Married Rev. Ray Bachtell).
1915-1916 Miss Alta Irwin.
‡ 1915-1918 Miss M. Niederhauser (Married Rev. L. J. Beebe).
1915 — Rev. Graham Fuller.
1915 — Mrs. G. Fuller.
1915-1919 Rev. Royal G. Hall.
1915-1919 Mrs. R. G. Hall.
1916 — Miss Gertrude Shearer (Married Rev. P. A. Eakin).
1916 — Rev. Spafford E. Kelsey.
** 1917-1918 Mr. Paul Hinkhouse.
1917 — Rev. Allan Bassett.
1917 — Mrs. A. Bassett.
‡ 1917-1923 Miss Martha Taylor (Married E. Perry; Transferred to China; Returned 1921-1923; Transferred
to Chiengrung)
1917-1921 Mr. C. L. Maylott.
1917-1921 Mrs. C. L. Maylott.
1919-1925 Miss Sarah Strong.
1919 — Rev. Lorin Hanna.
1919-1926 Rev. Ralph I. McConnell.
1919-1926 Mrs. R. I. McConnell.

1919-1924 Paul A. Reichel.
1919-1924 Mrs. P. A. Reichel.
1919 — Rev. Albert G. Seigle.
1919 — Mrs. A. G. Seigle.
1919-1924 W. Harvey Perkins, M. D.
1919-1924 Mrs. W. H. Perkins.
1920-1926 Miss Irene Taylor
1920 — Miss Lucy Niblock.
1920 — Miss Faye Kilpatrick.
1920 — Rev. H. Gaylord Knox.
1920 — Mrs. H. G. Knox.
‡ 1921-1923 Rev. E. Perry.
1921 — Miss Agnes Barland, R. N.
** 1921 — Mr. R. W. Moore (Contract teacher 1921-1924;
Regular missionary 1926—)
1922 — Mr. J. Hugh McKean.
1922 — Miss Mabel L. Jordan.
1922-1924 Mr. Robert Cummins.
1922-1924 Mrs. R. Cummins.
1922 — Niels Nedergaard, M. D.
1922 — Mrs. N. Nedergaard, R. N.
1922 — Mr. G. O. Robinson.
1922 — Mrs. G. O. Robinson.
1922 — Mr. C. A. Allen.
1922 — Mrs. C. A. Allen.
1923-1927 Miss Sara Ann Watterson (Married J. E. Davies)
1923 — Miss Alice Schaefer.
1923 — Rev. Paul H. Fuller.
1923 — Mrs. P. H. Fuller.
** 1923-1924 Mrs. M. C. Rand.
1924 — Miss Ruth Bibler (Married Asher B. Case)
** 1924 — Mr. Asher B. Case (Contract teacher 1924-1925;
Regular missionary 1925 —)
1924 — Douglas R. Collier, M. D.
1924 — Mrs. Mary Collier, M. D.
1925 — George Bradley McFarland, M. D. (Affiliated missionary)
1925 — Miss Helen G. McCague.
1925 — Miss Margaret A. Neuber.
** 1925 — Miss Esther Twelker.
1925 — Rev. Homer G. Weisbecker.
1925 — Mrs. H. G. Weisbecker.

** 1925-1926 Mr. Clarke Brockman.
** 1925-1928 Mr. A. R. Hammond.
    1926 — Henry Rust O'Brien, M. D.
    1926 — Mrs. H. R. O'Brien.
    1926 — Rev. John Lyman Eakin.
    1926 — Mrs. J. L. Eakin, R. N.
    1926 — Mrs. R. W. Moore.
    1926 — Miss Sadie Lemmon, R. N.
** 1926-1928 Miss Jeanne Sloan.
    1926 — Rev. N. C. Elder.
    1926 — Mrs. N. C. Elder.
    1927 — Rev. Kenneth P. Landon.
    1927 — Mrs. K. P. Landon.
    1927 — Rev. K. E. Wells.
    1927 — Mrs. K. E. Wells.
    1927 — John V. Horst, M. D.
    1927 — Mrs. J. V. Horst.
    1028 — Thomas M. Proctor, M. D.
    1928 — Mrs. T. M. Proctor.
    1928 — Miss Winnie Burr.
    1928 — Rev. John S. Holladay.
    1928 — Mrs. J. S. Holladay.
    1928 — Miss Mary Eakin.

AMERICAN BIBLE SOCIETY.
    *1889-1912 Rev. John Carrington, D. D.
    1989-1912 Mrs. J. Carrington.
    1909-1911 Rev. W. M. Cameron.
    1909-1911 Mrs. W. M. Cameron.
    1912 — Rev. Robert Irwin.
    1912 — Mrs. Mary Irwin, M. D.

SEVENTH DAY ADVENTISTS.
    1918-1922 Mr. E. L. Longway.
    1918-1922 Mrs. E. L. Longway.
    1919 — Rev. F. A. Pratt.
    1919 — Mrs. F. A. Pratt.
    1923 — Mr. R. P. Abel.
    1923 — Mrs. R. P. Abel.

SOCIETY FOR THE PROPAGATION OF THE GOSPEL.
    *1902-1912 Canon William Greenstock.

1914 — Rev. Cecil R. Simmons.
1914 — Mrs. C. R. Simmons.
1920-1925 Miss L. M. Siggins.
1921-1922 Miss A. E. Brandle.
1924-1926 Miss D. S. Parkinson.
1926-1927 Miss F. Pope.
1927 — Rev. C. W. Norwood.
1927 — Mrs. C. W. Norwood.
1927 — Miss A. Lattimer.
1927 — Miss G. M. Hewardine.

CHURCHES OF CHRIST.

1903-1905 Mr. Alfred Hudson.
1903 — Mr. Percy Clark.
1906 — Mrs. P. Clark.
1910-1922 Mr. R. Halliday (Transferred to Moulmein).
1910-1922 Mrs. R. Halliday (Transferred to Moulmein).
1910 — Miss Esther Halliday (Absent five years during the War).

1923-1924 Mr. Brown (Now in Indian mission).
1923-1924 Mrs. Brown (Now in Indian mission).
1923-1928 Mr. Bratton.
1923-1928 Mrs. Bratton.
1925 — Mr. H. Jenkins.
1925 — Mrs. H. Jenkins.

INDEPENDENT WORK.

1890- ? Mr. W. D. Ashdown.
1890-1920 Dr. Amner.
? ? Mrs. Ashdown.
? -1920 Mrs. Amner.
1926 — W. B. Toy, M. D.
1926 — Mrs. W. B. Toy.

List showing where Physicians have been located, when Medical Work was started (Hospitals were not always established until later dates), and periods of service.

Bangkok,—1835—	Rev. D. B. Bradley, M. D.	1835-1873
	Rev. Stephen Tracy, M. D.	1838-1839
	Rev. Samuel R. House, M. D.	1847-1876
	Rev. L. B. Lane, M. D.	1851-1855
	T. Heyward Hays, M. D.	1886-1891
	C. C. Walker, M. D.	1906-1913
Petchaburi, —1861—	E. A. Sturge, M. D.	1880-1885
	J. B. Thompson, M. D.	1886-1898
	Benj. Paddock, M. D.	1889-1889
	W. R. Lee, M. D.	1890-1891
	W. B. Toy, M. D.	1892-1896
	W. J. Swart, M. D.	1899-1902
	E. B. McDaniel, M. D.	1903-1915
	L. C. Bulkley, M. D.	1915-1921
	Neils Nedergaard, M. D.	1922-1927
Chiengmai, —1867—	C. W. Vrooman, M. D.	1872-1873
	M. A. Cheek, M. D.	1874-1886
	S. C. Peoples, M. D.	1886- ?
	M. A. Cary, M. D.	1886-1888
	J. W. McKean, M. D.	1889 —
	Rev. C. H. Denman, M. D.	1894-1905
	C. W. Mason, M. D.	1906-1918
	E. C. Cort, M. D.	1908 —
	Mrs. Mary Irwin, M. D.	1921-1922
	W. H. Perkins, M. D.	1922-1923
	Douglas Collier, M. D.	1925-1925
	H. R. O'Brien, M. D.	1926 —
Lampang, —1885—	S. C. Peoples, M. D.	1885-1890
	W. A. Briggs, M. D.	1890-1894
	Miss Mary Bowman, M. D.	
	Rev. J. S. Thomas, M. D.	1894-1897
	C. C. Hansen, M. D.	1899-1908
	C. W. Mason, M. D.	

		E. C. Cort, M. D.	
		C. H. Crooks, M. D.	1908 —
Prae,	—1893—	W. A. Briggs, M. D.	1894-1900
		Rev. J. S. Thomas, M. D.	
		C. H. Crooks, M. D.	
		Chas. Park, M. D.	1915-1919
		E. C. Cort, M. D.	1912-1915
Nan,	—1896—	Rev. S. C. Peoples, M. D.	
		Chas. Park, M. D.	
		W. H. Beach, M. D.	— 1918
		W. H. Perkins, M. D.	1920-1922
		Douglas Collier, M. D.	1925 —
		Mrs. Mary Collier, M. D.	1925 —
Chiengrai,	—1897—	Rev. C. H. Denman, M. D.	1897-1906
		W. A. Briggs, M. D.	1900-1918
		C. H. Crooks, M. D.	1906-1908
		W. M. T. Lyon, M. D.	1912-1920
		W. H. Beach, M. D.	1920 —
Pitsanuloke,	—1899—	W. B. Toy, M. D.	1899-1905
		C. C. Walker, M. D.	1906-1907
		C. J. Shellman, M. D.	1906-1919
		W. M. T. Lyon, M. D.	1920-1926
		John V. Horst, M. D.	1928 —
Sritamarat,	—1900—	Guy Hamilton, M. D.	1900 (6 mos.)
		Harry Boyd, M. D.	1902 (4 mos.)
		W. J. Swart, M. D.	1902-1912
		Rev. Egon Wachter, M. D.	1912-1913
		Paul Van Meter, M. D.	1913-1917
		E. B. McDaniel, M. D.	1920 —
Trang,	—1910—	L. C. Bulkley, M. D.	1910-1915, 1922 —
		Rev. Egon Wachter, M. D.	1917-1922
Puket,	—1890—	Dr. Amner.	1890-1920
		W. B. Toy, M. D.	1926 —

Roster of Missionaries Who have died in Siam,

Giving date of death and place of burial.

INDEPENDENT, *Bangkok.*

1831 — Mrs. C. F. A. Gutzlaff.

AMERICAN BOARD OF COMMISSIONERS FOR FOREIGN MISSIONS AND
AMERICAN MISSIONARY ASSOCIATION, *Bangkok.*

1840 — Rev. N. S. Benham.
1841 — Mrs. S. Johnson.
1842 — Rev. H. S. G. French.
1844 — Miss M. E. Pierce.
1845 — Mrs. D. B. Bradley.
1848 — Rev. Jesse Caswell.
1873 — Rev. Dan Beach Bradley, M. D.
1893 — Mrs. Sarah Blachly Bradley.

AMERICAN BAPTIST BOARD, *Bangkok.*

1837 — Rev. Alanson Reed.
1838 — Mrs. Eliza Grew Jones.
1841 — Rev. Cowden H. Slafter.
   ? — Mrs. Judith Leavitt Jones.
1851 — Rev. John Taylor Jones D. D.
1864 — Rev. Cyrus H. Chilcott.
1889 — Mrs. Sarah Sleeper Smith.
1891 — Mrs. L. A. Eaton.
1909 — Rev. S. J. Smith.

SOCIETY FOR THE PROPAGATION OF THE GOSPEL, *Bangkok.*

1912 — Canon William Greenstock.

AMERICAN BIBLE SOCIETY, *Bangkok.*

1912 — Rev. John Carrington, D. D.

THE PRESBYTERIAN BOARD OF FOREIGN MISSIONS.
Bangkok.

1851 — Mrs. S. Bush.
1860 — Mrs. J. Wilson.
1881 — Miss Mary M. Campbell.

1883 — Rev. C. D. McLaren.
1895 — M. A. Cheek, M. D.
1897 — Rev. F. L. Lyman.
1903 — Rev. Boon Itt.
1921 — Mrs. T. Heyward Hays.
1924 — T. Heyward Hays, M. D.
1927 — Rev. W. G. McClure, D. D.

Chiengmai.

1891 — Mrs. S. K. Phraner.
1911 — Rev. D. McGilvary, D. D.
1920 — Mrs. H. Campbell.
1923 — Mrs. D. McGilvary.
1927 — Mrs. A. W. Cooper.

Near Raheng.

1887 — Mrs. A. M. Cary.

Petchaburi.

1891 — Miss J. Small.
1898 — J. Thompson, M.D.
1905 — Miss K. Fleeson.
1906 — Mrs. C. C. Walker.

Lampang.

1891 — Mrs. W. A. Briggs.
1903 — Mrs. C. A. MacKay.
1911 — Rev. J. Wilson, D.D.

Nan.

1920 — Rev. S. C. Peoples, M.D.

Chiengrai.

1913 — Mrs. L. J. Beebe.
1915 — Mrs. R. Bachtell.

Pitsanuloke

1919 — C. Shellman, M.D.

Sritamarat.

1901 — Mrs. W. Swart.
1918 — Miss L. J. Cooper.

Trang.

1918 — Rev. E. P. Dunlap, D.D.

APPENDIX V

Kings of the Chakkri Dynasty

King Rama   I — Pra-Putta-Yot-Fa-Chulalok................1782-1809 — 27 yrs.

King Rama   II — Pra-Putta-Loet-La-Nopalai................1809-1824 — 15 yrs.

King Rama   III — Pra- Nang Klao................1824-1851 — 27 yrs.

King Rama   IV — { 1st King Mongkut Pra Chom Klao................1851-1868 — 17½ yrs.
                   (2nd King Pra Pin Klao)

King Rama   V — King Chulalongkorn Pra Chula Chom Klao.....1868-1910 — 42 yrs.

King Rama   VI — King Maha Vajiravudh Pra Mongkut Klao .....1910-1925 — 15 yrs.

King Rama   VII — King Prajadhipok Pra Pok Klao................1925 —

(A sketch of the origin of the first Protestant Mission in Siam, with an account of the first Missionaries, their reception by the Siamese, labors &c. By the late Rev. C. Robinson,—Missionary of the A. B. C. F. M. Written A. D. 1841.)
(Copied from The Bangkok Calendar of 1866.)

PROTESTANT MISSIONS IN SIAM.

To the Rev. W. H. Medburst it is believed belongs the honor of first projecting a Protestant mission to Siam. As early as 1827, he proposed to visit Siam, Cambodia and Cochin China, for the purpose of distributing books among the Chinese inhabiting the countries; but was for some reason prevented. In 1828, he left Batavia for Singapore in order to join Rev. Messers Tomlin and Gutzlaff, and proceed with them to Siam. But on his arrival at Singapore he was disappointed to find that they had sailed for Siam two days before his arrival at Singapore. Not willing to give up the enterprise, and not finding any vessel that was to sail direct to Siam he went on board of a small native prow, which was to sail up the gulf as far as Singora (Sungkla) hoping to find a passage from thence to Siam. Having visited Singora, and some other places in the vicinity, he returned to Singapore, not being able to get a passage either to Siam, Cochin China, or Cambodia.

On the 4th of August, 1828, The Rev. Jacob Tomlin and the Rev. Charles Gutzlaff, embarked for Siam on a Chinese junk, and reached Bangkok on the 23rd of the same month.

At their first interview with the chief authorities, they obtained leave to reside in Bangkok and prosecute their labors among the Chinese. The Portuguese Consul Segnior Carlos de Silveira, treated them with great kindness, and furnished them a house on his premises, and even took their part when they were threatened with expulsion from the country by the influence of the Roman Catholics. The house they occupied stood on the bank of the river about three rods above the tamarind tree which now stands by the landing place at the Portuguese Consulate. This house was afterwards removed to the spot where Mr. Jones and Davenport's house now stands, and was rented by Mr. Abeel when he arrived.

Messrs. Tomlin and Gutzlaff, for the first fortnight, were daily out conversing with the Chinese and giving them books. This, as might be expected, roused the enemy. Surmises and malicious charges were thrown out against them, representing them as coming to the country as spies, and endeavoring to excite the Chinese to rebellion &c. The king himself caught the alarm, and fancying the books were the great source of the evil, ordered specimens of them to be translated, but finding nothing in them objectionable, the missionaries were permitted to remain. It is said, however, that a royal edict was issued forbidding any one from receiving their books under a severe penalty. Minions of the government seized the tracts when found in the hands of the people, and M. Carlos was censured for having taken the missionaries into his house, and was even ordered to turn them out on peril of incurring displeasure but he continued to befriend them to the end. Mr. Hunter, an English merchant then residing in Bangkok, was requested by the P'rak'lang to take them out of the country in a ship which was going to Singapore.

They immediately appealed to the P'rak'lang, Minister of Foreign Affairs, wishing to know the cause of this persecution, and why they were to be driven out of the country without a hearing or anything proved against them. They appealed to the Treaty then recently made with England, and claimed an equal right to remain with the Romish priests, and also claimed, in case they were not permitted to remain, that the Siamese authorities should put into their hands a written document stating the causes of their expulsion, which might be satisfactory to the English Government. This remonstrance produced the desired effect, and the P'rak'lang gave them permission to remain, only requesting them to be more sparing in the distribution of their books, and imitate the " quiet Padres."

The storm having passed, they returned to their work, cautiously distributing books, and dispensing medicines as they found opportunity. The people soon acquired confidence in them, and came in multitudes for books and medicines. In a little more than two months they " scattered among the people " twenty-five boxes of Chinese books, leaving only two boxes in their possession.

In the mean time, feeling the want of Siamese books, they commenced the study of the Siamese language, and also a translation of the Bible from the Chinese into the Siamese, employing a Chinaman by the name of King (who had Siamese but imperfectly) and Hon, a Burmese (who also knew Siamese) the latter writing down in Siamese from the mouth of the former who read from the Chinese version. Having distributed all the books and medicines and the health of Mr. Tomlin having failed, it was determined that he should return to Singapore to recruit his health and get a fresh supply of books and medicines. He embarked on the 14th of May 1829, leaving Mr. Gutzlaff alone to pursue the work in Siam. During the first six months after their arrival, Messrs. Gutzlaff and

Tomlin had completed the translation of the four gospels, and the epistle to the Romans in the Siamese, and had proceeded with an English and Siamese Dictionary as far as the letter R.

Just before Mr. Tomlin left, he drew up a brief account of the Mission for six months, at the request of Captain Coffin, an American gentleman, to be forwarded to the American churches. After the departure of Mr. Tomlin, Mr. Gutzlaff continued to pursue his work alone in Siam for several months. Having at length prepared a tract in Siamese containing a brief "View of the Christian Religion", and also a translation of a part of the New Testament, Mr. Gutzlaff left Siam for a short time, and proceeded to Singapore in order to get them printed. While on this visit he was married at Malacca to Miss Maria Newell, a pious young lady, who formerly resided in the family of the Rev. Andrew Reed, D. D. of London. She was connected with the London Missionary Society. In February 1830 Mr. Gutzlaff with his wife returned to Siam in an American ship, commanded by Captain Davidson, who was also the bearer of another letter to the American Board inviting them to send missionaries to Siam. Mr. Gutzlaff and his devoted companion zealously pursued the work of translating, hardly allowing themselves time for rest or sleep—daily employing a number of copyists.

During his residence in Siam, he, together with Mr. Tomlin, translated the whole Bible into Siamese, a considerable portion of it into the Laosian and Cambodian languages, and prepared a dictionary and grammar of the Siamese and Cambodian. These translations, from the manner in which they were made, necessarily were very imperfect. On this account only two gospels were ever printed viz;—Luke and John. All these translations were afterwards delivered by Mr. Gutzlaff into the hands of Mr. Robinson, as donation to the A. B. C. F. M. together with a number of native books in the Siamese, Laosian and Cambodian languages. The English and Siamese Dictionary was previously taken by Mr. Jones when he left Singapore, and constituted the basis of the dictionary since prepared by Mrs. Jones. The native Siamese books presented by Mr. Gutzlaff are still in the Mission, the Manuscript translations, being on Siamese paper, were used as covers to other books.

Mr. Gutzlaff and his zealous companion continued their labors with their accustomed ardor, and perhaps to the injury of Mrs. Gutzlaff who on Feb. 16, 1831, gave birth to two infant daughters. In consequence of uterine hemorrhage she died in a few hours. One infant died at its birth, the other survived till near the middle of June, when its spirit returned to Him who gave it.

Thus Mr. Gutzlaff was bereaved of his worthy companion a little more than a year after their marriage. Being now alone, and his own health requiring a change, he determined to leave Siam on an exploring voyage to China, a project which he had long contemplated.

On the 3rd of June 1831, Mr. Gutzlaff went on board of a junk bound to Tientsin in China, leaving his infant daughter with a native nurse, and having made arrangements to place her in the care of Mrs. Thomson at Singapore by the first opportunity. While detained on the bar Mr. Gutzlaff was informed of the death of his child. some days after the event. The junk finally got under way on the 18th June, only a few days before the arrival of the Rev. Messrs, Abeel and Tomlin. Mr. Tomlin hoped to reach Bangkok before Mr. Gutzlaff left, and if possible to detain him for a half year or a year to revise the translation of the Sacred Scriptures in Siamese.

MISSION OF THE A. B. C. F. M. IN SIAM

When Rev. Messrs. Tomlin and Gutzlaff first visited Siam they came for the purpose of exploring the field, without any special direction from the Societies with which they were connected. In other words they came on their own responsibility. Finding things favorable in Siam, Mr. Tomlin first wrote to the Directors of the London Missionary Society urging them to send missionaries to Siam. But the Directors not only discouraged their hopes of assistance for the mission in Siam but also at Singapore dismissed Mr. Thompson, Mr. Tomlin's only associate. Messrs. Tomlin and Gutzlaff also wrote to Rev. J. Judson of Burmah requesting books, and missionaries from that field, on account of the many Burmese and Peguans in Siam. But the Burmese Mission had no men to spare.

They then wrote to the Prudential Commitee of the A. B. C. F. M. by Captain Coffin, as before mentioned, in 1829. This letter, written by Mr. Gutzlaff, first called the attention of the Prudential Commitee to Siam as a missionary field. Soon after the receipt of his letter the Board directed the Rev. David Abeel, who went to Canton in 1829, as Chaplain of the American Seamen's Friends Society, and who afterwards entered the service of the Board, to proceed on a tour of observation to Java and other islands to ascertain the state of the Dutch churches on those Islands, and also to proceed to the Capital of Siam on a mission of investigation. This visit was to be preparatory to the establishment of a mission in Siam which the Board had some time contemplated. Accordingly Mr. Abeel left on the 28th December, 1839, and proceeded to Batavia, and thence to Singapore, where he providentially met with Mr. Tomlin just on the eve of sailing for Siam the second time.

On the 17th of June, 1831, Messrs. Abeel and Tomlin left Singapore and sailed for Siam, in the Sophia an Arab ship having an English commander. They reached Bangkok on Saturday evening July 2nd, and were kindly received by the Portuguese Consul, Segnior Carlos de Silveira, Mr. Tomlin's old friend. When they arrived they were much disappointed to find that Mr. Gutzlaff had left for China only twelve days before they reached the Bar.

They brought with them a stock of medicines, half a dozen boxes of Chinese books, and 300 copies of the Siamese tract before mentioned. Gutzlaff had left seven boxes of Chinese tracts. They took up their residence at the house previously occupied by Messrs. Gutzlaff and Tomlin.

They found the people as eager as ever for books, and their house was frequently thronged with patients, and applicants for tracts. They soon found their scanty supply of Siamese tracts exhausted. They were much encouraged in their work, and mentioned the cases of a number of interesting inquirers frequently visiting them. They particularly mentioned a priest who copied a considerable portion of the New Testament. Soon after their arrival they established public worship at their house on the Sabbath, in Chinese. A number of Chinamen who attended their Sabbath exercises appeared not far from the kingdom of God. Among these Mr. Tomlin thus speaks of their two servants boys—"None have interested us more or given better evidence of a change of heart than our two Chinese servant boys." One of them referred to Chai Hoo (see Tomlin's journal page 64) afterwards went to Singapore with Mr. Tomlin, and lived with Mr. Abeel till he left for America. He was baptised by the Rev. Ira Tracy, and is still a member in good standing in the Church at Singapore.

Mr. Tomlin also mentions three other Chinamen who appeared more than usually interested in the truth viz:—his cook Chong Po, Tay, and Go the Chinese teacher of Mr. Abeel's.

Respecting the importance of this field, Mr. Abeel in his communication to the Board under date of August 25th 1831, says "One thing I feel anxious to urge, and that is the importance of immediate assistance. A host of missionaries with the spirit that can hazard their lives for their Lord and Master would have little difficulty in finding stations and employment. As Bangkok is a new station, and one which should by all means be retained, it appears highly important that at least two or three should be sent to this place as soon as possible." He adds in the same communication, "the claims of Siam are perhaps of more immediate urgency than any other place in these regions. Besides, my fellow laborer (Mr. Tomlin) is not likely to continue long in Siam. He has left Singapore now without a Chinese missionary, and his family are still there."

It appears evident that Mr. Abeel considered himself as finally located in Siam, and nothing but ill health could have induced him to leave, even for a time. Owing to the remarkable overflowing of the river, which covered the whole country for two months, and the want of suitable exercise, Mr. Abeel, brought down by a low lingering fever, reluctantly concluded to visit Singapore with Mr. Tomlin, who on account of the illness of his wife, and his own health, was obliged to leave Siam.

After a residence of little more than six months in Siam, Messrs. Abeel and Tomlin left on the 7th January 1832 for Singapore where they arrived on the morning of the 13th. Having visited Singapore and Malacca, Mr. Abeel with partially restored health, embarked alone for Siam in a junk on the 18th of April, anxious to reach Bangkok before the sailing of the junks for China, that he might furnish them with Christian books. On the 19th of May, after a tedious passage, he reached Bangkok, and was cordially welcomed by his former friend Mr. De Silveira. He found the Siamese much more reserved than formerly. Soon after his arrival a second Edict was issued, prohibiting the people from receiving his books. It was however conceded that he might give books on board the junks for China of which there was about 50 (out of 80) still lying at anchor in the river.

Daily, while dispensing medicines to the sick, he had opportunities to dispense the word of life to multitudes. He was much encouraged by the numbers and good attention of those who attended the Sabbath exercises.

This meeting was continued during Mr. Abeel's absence in Singapore. "The most hopeful circumstance", says he, "connected with the mission is the number of attendants upon the Sabbath exercises. For the greater part of the time between twelve and twenty Chinese have been present. Our auditory has been gradually increasing by a species of management, which had I remained, would probably have swelled to a large congregation. In conversing with the numerous applicants for medicine, I told such as I thought could well attend, of our church service, and appointed that day and hour for them to come for a fresh supply of medicine. Many who commenced their attendance, through these means, became too much interested in their new pursuit to discontinue it. Besides this, about half a dozen have enjoyed the benefit of daily worship and catechetical instruction. The effect has been, that the majority have had their ideas on the doctrines of Christianity greatly enlarged, and a few have manifested such an effect of the truth upon their hearts, as I sincerely hope may prove to them the door of an eternal day. These have rejected their idols, and established the worship of the true God. I have ventured to baptize none, and consequently denominate none of them converts. The most hopeful have lived too far distant to bring them under such a course of instruction as seemed important where the mind is just emerging from gross darkness.

"The one who was baptized by my predecessor Gutzlaff, appears to know the truth in the love of it."

The person here referred to, Bunty, returned from a visit to China and Cochin China, July 6th and was very useful to Mr. Abeel in assisting in the Sabbath exercises. Before Abeel left Siam the second time, he formally appointed Bunty to conduct these exercises in the presence of all present, and made arrangements with Mr. Silveira for the house, which he had occupied, for them to meet in on the Sabbath after his departure. His last interview with "his little flock" was very interesting.

Under date of October 14, Mr. Abeel says—"Since the commencement of our Sabbath service, I have never seen such fixed and thoughtful attention as was apparent towards the close of this morning's exhortation. The spirit of the living Saviour was doubtless in our midst, and the hearts of many, I sincerely believe, felt his sacred presence. Again the sadness of separation came over my spirit, and again I commended this little band to the Shepherd and Bishop of souls."

Among the other wants which occurred which he thought would tend to promote the objects of the mission, he mentions the construction of a brick walk between the mission premises and the Chinese settlement. Also his agreement with Prince Chow-Fah which afforded advantages for acquiring the Siamese language and opened a door for instructing him in the Christian religion. Mr. Abeel became acquainted with Prince Chow Fah at his first entering Siam, who ever treated him, and Messrs Gutzlaff and Tomlin with marked kindness. He also mentions Koon Sit (Prahnai wai) as one from whom the missionaries might expect much. Continued ill health obliged Mr. Abeel to leave Siam the second time, after a residence of about six months.

Nov. 5th he left Bangkok for Singapore in a schooner chartered by Robert Hunter, Esq., the English merchant mentioned by Mr. Gutzlaff as a gentleman to whom he and his associate were under peculiar obligations. Through his influence and the kindness of Capt. Norris, Mr. Abeel was laid under new obligations for his passage to Singapore free of expense.

Soon after his arrival at Singapore, the truly excellent and pious chaplain Rev. Robert Burn died. Mr. Abeel who had ministered to him in his illness, and attended him in his departing hour, finding his own health improved, and being invested by the people to minister to them in the Gospel, he consented to defer his visit to America, hoping it might not be necessary to leave on account of his health, and thus diminish still more the small number of missionaries in the field. While engaged in the duties of the chaplaincy he continued the study of the native languages and attempted to supply every Chinese family in the place with Christian books.

While thus engaged his health again yielded to the influence of the climate and he was reluctantly obliged to leave the field, and in accordance with an invitation of the Board, to revisit his native country.

May 25th, 1833, he embarked for England in an English ship. After having spent sometime in England, Holland, Germany, France and Switzerland, he returned to the United States.

It appears that Mr. Abeel intended soon after he came, to make Siam the principal field of his missionary labor, and that nothing but ill health caused him to leave; or in other words had his health been good he would have continued to be a missionary to Siam. The Board it seems, considered him as such, and in their Reports have denominated him a missionary to Siam.

Early in the year 1832 it was publicly announced by our Board that they intended to send missionaries to Siam.

In Aug. 1832, Rev. Messrs. Stephen Johnson and Charles Robinson were accepted by the Board, and the field of their labor designated to be Siam. Rev. Ira Tracy was at that time expected to be associated with them, but he was afterwards designated to China.

Sept. 25th, 1832, while Mr. Abeel was yet in Siam, Rev. John Taylor Jones was appointed by the Baptist missionaries at Burmah as a missionary to Siam, and left Maulmain for Singapore.

While Mr. Jones was detained at Singapore, Mr. Abeel arrived from Siam. Previous to his embarkation for America, Mr. Abeel mentioned to Mr. Jones the "little company of worshippers" he had left in Bangkok, and requested him to encourage them to meet as they had done till other missionaries should arrive.

(Here ends what Mr. Robinson wrote of the origin and progress of the Protestant missions. What follows is supplied by the Editor of the Calendar.)

Rev. John Taylor Jones, missionary of the American Baptist Board arrived in Bangkok from the Burman Mission, March 25th 1833, being accompanied by his family, of which Samuel Jones Smith (now Rev. S. J. Smith,) was a member. Mr. Jones being designated to the Siamese, devoted himself mainly to them, but in the mean time took a general supervision of the Chinese inquirers left by Mr. Abeel. By the aid of interpreters, and with the blessing of God, he was enabled to keep the little flock together, meeting on the Lord's day, to pray and read the Scriptures, and exhort one another. In the course of the same year there were three Chinese among them who appeared especially awakened. Their names were Chek Peng, Chek Chia, and Lai Seng. These Mr. Jones baptised on the 8th. of Dec. They all are reported to have died within two years of their baptism.

Rev. Messrs. Stephen Johnson and Charles Robinson with their wives sailed from Boston June 10th, 1833, in company with Rev. Messrs. Samuel Munson and Henry Lyman in the ship Duncan, Captain Randal, bound to Batavia, were they arrived Sept. 30th. From thence they proceeded to Singapore, where they remained about nine months for the want of an opportunity to sail for Siam. Mr. Johnson and wife embarked Nov. 14th. in a ship bound to Siam; but calm, head winds, and strong opposing currents compelled them to return to Singapore and spend their time as best they could seven more months preparatory to their future work. The two families left Singapore July 9th, 1834, and reached Bangkok on the 25th. They also took with them a stock of medicines and Chinese books, and labored much as their predecessors had done. They had prepared themselves at home with some knowledge of the medical art, and felt almost compelled to practice it after their arrival, such was the urgency and frequency of applications for medical treatment. The great prominence thus given by them and their predecessors to the treatment of the indigent sick, led the people of Siam to call them all Doctors of medicine, which epithet has ever since been given by them to all Protestant missionaries whether they dispense medicine or not.

The reception which the P'rak'lang gave Messrs. Johnson and Robinson was to them quite encouraging. When told the object of their coming he replied, "this is very remarkable," and appeared to be quite at a loss to know why missionaries should come so far, one or two at a time, for such an object.

The little company of Chinese, who had so long met on Sabbath days to pray and read the Scriptures, they reported as being still constant in their meetings seeking the Saviour of sinners under the general supervision of Rev. J. T. Jones of the Baptist mission.

Not long after their arrival they succeeded in renting of a petty magistrate called Nai Klin a lot just at the upper side of the landing of Wat Koh, and erected two rough dwelling houses of teak boards, and moved into them early in the year 1835. Up to that time they had lived in the neighborhood of the Baptist mission.

APPENDIX VII.

Extract from "Missionary Sketches" by S. F. Smith D. D.
Fifth Edition 1887.*

MISSION IN SIAM.

The First Missionary in Siam.—Geography of Bangkok.—
The First Baptism.—The Chinese Work in Bangkok.—Dr. Dean
and other Re-enforcements.—The First Church Organized.—Death of
Mr. Slafter.—Progress and Mystery.—The New Testament in
Siamese.—Arrival of Mr. Ashmore.—Death of Dr. Jones.—Tokens
of Growth.—Another early Summons.—A Year of Refreshing.—
The Siamese Work Suspended.—Changes in the Mission.—Remark-
able Ingathering.—Latest Intelligence.—Review.

The first mission in Asia undertaken by the American Baptists,
after the mission in Burmah, was the mission in Siam. The first
missionary of the Baptist General Convention to Siam was Rev.
John Taylor Jones. He was originally designated to Burmah, and
arrived in Maulmain in February, 1831 ; and had already made such
attainments in the language of Burmah, that he was able to preach
to the people in their own tongue. But he was set apart by the
choice of his brethren to commence a mission in Siam ; and, taking
passage for that country by way of Penang and Singapore, he
arrived in Bangkok March 25, 1833.

Bangkok is the capital of Siam, but only a small portion of the
population is composed of Siamese people. The principal races in
the city, besides the Siamese, are the Chinese and Burmans. The
city is twenty-five miles from the sea, on the river Meinam, "mother
of waters." The river is two miles wide at its mouth, but less than
half a mile wide at Bangkok, which covers an island in the river,
and extends along both shores, several miles, above and below. The
population of the city is variously estimated. Dr. Malcom set it
down at about 100,000 ; Gutzlaff at 410,000 ; Tomlin estimated the
Siamese population at 8,000 ; Abeel thought the priests alone
numbered 10,000. Of the entire population of the city, Gutzlaff
estimated the Chinese at 350,000.

The religion of Siam is Buddhism. In this respect, the
different races are on the same footing. They all have the same
idolatry, and are alike ignorant of the true God. The previous

---

* This record came to hand after the chapter covering the work of the American
Baptist Board was already in print.—Ed.

residence of Mr. and Mrs. Jones in Burmah prepared them to be useful at once to the Burmese people in the city; and they embraced every opportunity to tell them of the way of salvation. During the period after they left Maulmain, and before they reached Bangkok, they had become somewhat acquainted with the Siamese language, having studied it, with the aid of such teachers as they could find, much of the time for a period of six months.

Mr. Jones sat down to his solitary work of perfecting his knowledge of the language of the Siamese, at the same time making known the gospel message to other races also, as he had opportunity, and to the Chinese through the Siamese. He did not labor long without seeing some fruit. The Lord's Supper was administered for the first time in Bangkok, Dec. 1, 1833; Mr. Jones and his wife being the only communicants. A week later, Dec. 8, the first baptism was administered. The candidates were three in number, all Chinese, and all men.

At so early a period in the work, considerable progress had been already made in the preparation of a Siamese dictionary, as a help to future missionaries. In this work Mrs. Jones was an important helper, devoting much time for a whole year in arranging and copying the materials. The Chinese work seemed to be thrust upon the mission from the beginning. But Mr. Jones steadily devoted himself to laboring for the Siamese. Notwithstanding, a little assembly of a dozen Chinese was accustomed to meet at his house for worship, led by Bunti, one of the Chinese converts baptized. They had the Bible in Chinese, and several tracts, which were freely distributed. Mr. Jones had completed in September, 1833, a catechism on geography and astronomy in Siamese, besides translating into that language a small Burman tract containing a summary of Christian doctrines.

In 1834 Rev. William Dean and wife joined the mission. This was the commencement of the Chinese department; and Mr. Dean was the first foreigner who ever studied the Tie Chiu dialect, which is the dialect chiefly spoken by the Chinese of Bangkok. He first preached in that language in August, 1835, to an audience of thirty-four. In two months the congregation increased to fifty. Three more Chinese converts were baptized in December, 1835; and one of those baptized at the first time of the administration of the ordinance died in Christian triumph in March, 1836,—the first-fruits

---

Note.—His appointment was made in 1834, but his arrival in Bangkok was in 1835. Mrs. Dean died en route at Singapore.—Ed.

of the Chinese in Bangkok to Christ. In the mean time, Messrs. Alanson Reed and J. L. Shuck had been appointed missionaries to the Chinese of Siam, and sailed from Boston in September 1835, reaching Bangkok July 1, 1836. Mr. Reed in March, 1837, took a floating house on the river, and established a new centre for Christian worship two miles above Bangkok, from which many excursions were made, and many tracts distributed. But his labors were of brief duration. On the 29th of August, only five months after the commencement of this enterprise, he was called to put off the harness and to wear the celestial crown. He died at Bangkok at the early age of thirty years. The same month Mr. Shuck was transferred to the empire of China, and commenced a mission in Macao, which, in March, 1842, was transferred to Hong Kong.

Mr. Davenport, a preacher and printer, arrived in Bangkok in July, 1836, to join the mission, bringing with him presses and types in both Siamese and Chinese. He labored in Siam about nine years, and then returned to this country on account of impaired health; and died of disease contracted during his mission life, Nov. 24, 1848, aged thirty-nine years.

By March, 1837, Mr. Jones had made some progress in translating the New Testament into Siamese, portions of which were printed and in circulation. A sheet tract containing the Ten Commandments was printed, to be pasted on the walls of the houses of the people, after the national custom. On the 1st of July, 1837, during the visit of Rev. Mr. Malcom, the first church was formed in Bangkok. The occasion was one of rare interest. The actors, the circumstances, the surroundings, the memories and associations of the past, the hopes and promises and at the same time the uncertainty of the future, made the scene one never to be forgotten.

In the year 1839 Rev. Josiah Goddard was added to the Chinese department of the mission, and Rev. C. H. Slafter to the Siamese. A chapel was built, and three Chinese were added to the church by baptism. The attendance on Chinese worship was about twenty, and on the Siamese, from thirty to fifty. Mr. Slafter carried with him to Siam a second printing press. Up to this date more than forty thousand copies of different works had been printed embracing nearly a million pages. An English and Siamese school was taught by Mrs. Davenport; and a small Chinese school by Mrs. Dean, Mrs. Reed and others.

Note,—This first sheet tract was printed on the first press brought to Bangkok by Dr. Bradley for the A. B. C. F. M. mission. Mr. Davenport of the Baptist mission helped do the work. — Ed.

Mr. Slafter's missionary life was soon ended. He reached Bangkok Aug. 22, 1839; and died April 7, 1840, aged twenty-nine. His widow, after an intervening marriage, became the wife of Dr. Dean, and still lives, a loving and efficient worker in the cause of missions. The brief service which Mr. Slafter was permitted to render to the missionary enterprise is one of the mysteries of Divine Providence, concerning which we are compelled to say, " We know not now, but we shall know hereafter."

In October, 1839, three more Chinese converts were baptized, making the native members nine, and the whole church, including missionaries, seventeen. The New Testament in Siamese was completed, except Hebrews and Revelation, in December of this year; and in 1840 fifty-eight thousand copies were distributed.

In 1841 another step was taken in advance. Besides the baptism of six Chinese and one Siamese, a class in theology was formed by Dr. Dean; and thus a beginning was made of training native Chinese preachers to aid in the work of preaching the gospel to their countrymen. But in February, 1842,—so precarious are the plans of men under the mysterious operations of Divine Providence, —on account of impaired health Dr. Dean removed to Hong Kong; and, except for a brief visit in aid of Dr. Jones in 1850, he returned no more as a Christian laborer to Bangkok till 1864.

Near the close of 1843, Mr. J. H. Chandler, a printer and machinist, joined the missionary force, after a short residence in Maulmain, and served the Union thirteen years. He was a deacon of the Chinese church, and a man of great mechanical genius. Though not a preacher, his influence in Siam was very important. Siam at that time had a king and princes of intelligence and culture, who understood the advantages of modern improvements, and desired their introduction into the kingdom. One of the princes was in constant intercourse with Mr. Chandler; and the latter both instructed him, and aided him in carrying out his projected improvements. A printing-office on his premises and a steam-boat in the river Meinam were among the fruits of this enlightened spirit in the palace. Mr. Chandler was able by his mechanical skill to give a stimulus to the nation in a new direction, which in the end will undoubtedly help the cause of Christianity.

In 1844 the missionaries travelled several miles into the interior to distribute tracts. They made arrangements to commence an out-station some miles away from Bangkok. About this time a house and land were purchased in Bangkok for aged, poor, and sick members of the church. Thus religion bore its legitimate fruit.

The same year the New Testament in Siamese, by Dr. Jones, was finished and published. But the next year mission-work in the Siamese department was suspended, on account of the absence of Dr. Jones, who found it necessary to re-visit his native land. Mr. and Mrs. Davenport, also in impaired health, were obliged to relinquish the mission. Mr. and Mrs. Jencks joined the mission Dec. 14, 1846, but made only a brief stay on account of the feebleness of Mrs. Jencks, who died a year afterwards on the passage home. Some attention was given to compiling a Tie Chiu dictionary for the benefit of present and future missionaries. Calls for religious tracts became more numerous, an unusual number of which went into the families of princes and nobles. About seventy copies found their way into the family of one of the highest princes, who sent his servant every Sabbath for a long time to obtain them. The Chinese hearers at the chapel now numbered from thirty to forty-five.

In March, 1848, Mr. Goddard removed to Ningpo, in China, and commenced a mission there, which still lives,—the son now having in efficient charge the work which his father efficiently began. Mr. Goddard was a missionary in Bangkok eight years, and in Ningpo six,—a man of good report, and still spoken of in China with honor.

Miss Harriet H. Morse, who had been previously connected with an Indian mission near Lake Superior, joined the mission Feb. 18, 1848, specially to labor in the Siamese department. She did excellent service till January, 1855, when failing health compelled her to return to America.

Mr. and Mrs. Ashmore joined the mission in April, 1851, and remained in connection with it nearly seven years. Mr. Ashmore has since been a most efficient and trusted missionary at Swatow, in China. The native church now began to understand and practise the grace of liberality. In 1848-49 they supported the principal native assistant entirely for the year, besides sustaining two schools, in part, more than six months. In 1850 the assistant died, and Dr. Dean returned for a few months from Hong Kong to Bangkok. The church numbered thirty-five members, of whom thirty were native believers.

A great calamity now befell the mission. Jan. 4, 1851, the buildings and property of the mission were entirely destroyed by fire, involving a loss of from ten to fifteen thousand dollars. And still another disaster : in September of this year Dr. Jones died, the father of the mission. He was an excellent and highly honored missionary, and won the respect and esteem of the Siamese court. His knowledge of the language is said to have been wonderfully extensive and accurate, and the testimony of some of the best-educated of the people was that in this respect few natives could equal him.

This year a decree was issued, tolerating Christian worship and missionary itineracy. By invitation of the king, the female members of the mission visited the palace daily, to instruct the ladies of the court in English. The contributions of the church were equal to one dollar per member.

In 1853 eight Siamese converts were baptized. In 1854 Mr. Chandler, who had been temporarily in America, returned to the mission, and Rev. Robert Telford was added to the laborers. He did faithful service for ten years, and returned to the United States in 1864, on account of the failure of Mrs. Telford's health. After the death of Dr. Jones, Rev. S. J. Smith, born in Hindostan, and who had been associated with Dr. Jones for several years, having been appointed a missionary in 1848, married the widow of Dr. Jones, and has ever since been helpful in the Siamese work. Mrs. Smith, being familiar with the language, taught a boarding-school of forty-two pupils in 1857 at private charges. The next year her pupils numbered sixty-six; the Bible and religious works were the principal text-books. Mr. Smith, as interpreter for the Siamese government, and owning an extensive printing-establishment, bears his own expenses, and labors as he has opportunity in the gospel, without being any longer dependent on the funds of the Union.

A second place of public worship was opened in 1859, and in 1860 there was a period of special religious interest. The native members formed a "Society for the Diffusion of the Religion of Jesus," which supported one colporter.

In 1861 a new chapel was erected, and more than two thousand dollars were subscribed towards the building by the first and second kings, nobles, princes, &c. In 1863 the Chinese church, by the departure of Mr. Telford, was left without a missionary. The Chinese church then numbered thirteen, and the Siamese twenty-eight. Since that time, no missionary has been sent from this country to labor in the Siamese department.

In August, 1864, Rev. Cyrus A. Chilcott sailed from New York to join the Chinese mission in Bangkok. High hopes were centred in his coming. Young, ardent, gifted, it was easy to anticipate for him many years of usefulness. But God seeth not as man seeth. In just one year and five days his labors on earth were ended, and he was called to higher service. Miss Fielde, his betrothed, left this country to join him, eleven days before his death. No telegram could reach her in mid-ocean, and she learned her loss only on her arrival in China. But she remained a faithful and devoted missionary for several years in Bangkok, and since that time in connection with the mission at Swatow, in China. Dr. Dean returned, after several years' absence, to Bangkok, and Miss Fielde labored under his direction.

In the report of 1867 is a mingled wail of sadness and song of hope. The work, though feeble, was, in the judgment of Dr. Dean, worthy to be cherished and carried forward. Since the church was organized, in 1837, fifty-one Chinese had been baptized. Much preparatory work had been done, and there was sufficient ground to labor on in hope. God "himself knew what he would do"—as the sequel will prove.

Rev. William M. Lisle and wife joined the mission, full of hope, in January, 1868; but he was almost immediately prostrated by disease, and compelled to flee for his life to his native land. The next year, 1869, the mission was re-enforced by Rev. S. B. and Mrs. Partridge. Mr. Partridge had been a signal-officer of great bravery during the war of the Rebellion, and was fitted to do valiant service for Christ. He came at the right time. The year preceding had been a year of precious ingathering, such as the mission had never seen, and forty-five Chinese converts were baptized,—a number equal to all that had been baptized during the preceding thirty years of the mission. Many of these converts resided at the out-stations, and they were the garnered fruit of the labors of many missionaries now departed or fallen asleep. The year 1868 was also a year of rich blessing. Two chapels were dedicated, and two churches organized at the out-stations.

In 1869 the work for the specific benefit of the Siamese was suspended, for the reasons that no very satisfactory results of labor had been reported for several years, the work for the Chinese in Bangkok was far more encouraging, and other fields of more promise claimed all the funds that were at the command of the Committee. Notwithstanding, through the present Mrs. Dean and Mr. and Mrs. S. J. Smith, all of whom understand the Siamese language, seed has continued to be sown among the people of that race, in the hope that it may be watched over by the Divine Spirit, and by and by bring forth fruit unto eternal life.

In 1871 Miss Fielde was transferred to the station at Swatow. In 1872 the question was suggested by the Executive Committee, whether it was expedient to maintain a mission for the Chinese at

Bangkok, instead of concentrating the efforts of the brethren on some spot in the great empire of China itself. Dr. Dean, with his knowledge and wide and long experience, favored the continuance of the work in Bangkok. Mr. Partridge, however, was transferred to Swatow four years from the time he began his work; and Dr. Dean was left alone, with his family, in Bangkok, in charge of the Chinese department. Mrs. Dean, who learned the Siamese language in the earlier period of her residence in Siam, continued to teach the women and children of that race; and in 1872 two of the former were baptized. The number of members on the roll of the three churches was seventy-eight; but the lamp burned somewhat dimly. However in the year 1873, thirty were baptized, and three or four young men were instructed in a theology class, with reference to future usefulness as preachers of the gospel.

The year 1874 was the most remarkable in the entire history of the mission. All the out-stations received large additions by baptism, as well as Bangkok; two new churches were constituted, two chapels were finished, and a pastor ordained. The spirit of inquiry was awakened among the Siamese: the women, and even Buddhist priests, came to Mrs. Dean for instruction. Many others abandoned idolatry, and asked for baptism, professing their purpose to lead Christian lives. When we hear of eleven baptized at one station, seventeen at another, twenty-five at a third, and eighty-four at a fourth, we cannot forbear to exclaim, "What hath God wrought!" The additions by baptism to all the churches were one hundred and forty. The pastor's heart was made glad, like Simeon's in the temple. The work continued into the next year, and ninety more were baptized, making the whole number three hundred and seventeen. The following is a summary of Dr. Dean's labors up to the year 1876. In his forty years of service, Dr. Dean has gathered six Chinese churches, superintended the building of four Chinese chapels, ordained three Chinese pastors, besides training two who were ordained by others, and baptized three hundred and thirty-nine Chinese disciples, of whom twelve became preachers of the gospel.

The year 1876 indicated a natural re-action after so great a blessing. This year also Dr. Dean made another brief visit to his native land; and his absence was evidently felt by the people, who notwithstanding the presence of their native pastors, were as sheep without a shepherd.

In 1877 we find a report of six churches, 418 members, and 61 baptized during the year. At one of the out-stations 24 were baptized, and 80 sat down together at the Lord's Supper. Every one of the newly baptized gave his contribution towards a new chapel about to be built. At another out-station, seven were baptized, and another chapel in the place of one that had been burned was projected. The pastor was a Chinese convert, the first baptized at that point. A very effective force of native preachers is being raised up; one of the native preachers is supported by the church, another by Dr. Dean. There are seven chapels, two ordained and six unordained native preachers, six churches, and five out-stations. The Chinese work in Bangkok is apparently crystallizing into permanent form, and with an increase of laborers it would be even more fruitful.

Singularly enough the Government of Siam has arrayed itself in favor of the religion of Christ. A proclamation was issued in October, 1878, of which the following is an extract:—

"Whoever is of the opinion that any particular religion is correct, let him hold to it as he pleases : the right or wrong will be to the person who holds to it. In the treaties and in the customs of the kingdom of Siam, there is no prohibition against persons who shall hold to any particular religion. If any one is of the opinion that the religion of the Lord Jesus is good, let him hold to it freely.

"Whenever there is government work, persons who hold to the religion of the Lord Jesus must perform it. No religion is henceforth allowed to interfere in government work. Whoever shall hold to any system of religion, let him do so freely. Let no Phraya Lao, Taosaan, or common person, being a relative or a master of a person holding to the religion of the Lord Jesus, interfere in any affair which that religion does not permit or allow to be done, as worshipping spirits, feasting spirits, and various employments on Sunday. Let there be no compulsion or constraint to practise or to do any thing of the kind : it is absolutely forbidden. Only war and business of absolute importance are excepted. At such times they must serve on Sunday, but let there be no impositions."

The mission to the people of Bangkok has been full of vicissitudes; and the residence of the missionaries there has been, generally, of brief duration. Dr. Jones, the first resident at the station, was there eighteen years; Dr. Dean has labored there twenty-two years; Mr. Davenport and Mr. Telford, nine years each; Mr. Goddard, seven and a half; Dr. Ashmore and Miss Morse, seven years each; Miss Fielde, six years; Mr. Partridge, four years; Mr. Chilcott, one year; Mr. Slafter, less than eight months; Mr. Reed, five months; and Mr. Lisle was forced to return home immediately after his arrival. Dr. Jones, Messrs. Davenport, Goddard, Chilcott, Slafter, and Reed, are dead; Dr. Ashmore, Mr. Partridge and wife, and Miss Fielde, were transferred to China.

The history of this mission illustrates the nature of the pilgrim-life of missionaries, moving hither and thither like shepherds' tents; the long and discouraging labors which often seem of little avail; and the manner in which, at his "set time," God interposes, and the seed, long buried, springs to life, and brings forth fruit.

Dr. Dean wrote, some time since, in this strain: "The cause is the Lord's, and his work is soon to prevail, however much may be the trial to our faith and patience. The everlasting God, Jehovah, fainteth not, neither is weary: therefore we need not faint."

In January, 1879, the king of Siam published a proclamation of religious freedom to all persons in his kingdom. Within the last few years, also, he has instituted many other measures of reform, and is considered the most civilized and progressive native ruler in Asia, with the exception of the emperor of Japan. Mrs. Dean was obliged to return to America in 1881 on account of failing health, and died in Boston, Mass., Jan. 16, 1883. Dr. Dean still remains on the field, and in 1882 Rev. L. A. Eaton went out to assist him in his work. The Chinese, among whom they are laboring, are rapidly increasing in numbers and in commercial and political strength in Siam. In this respect they offer an encouraging field for missionary work; but they have formed protective societies among themselves, which are very powerful, having even the power of life and death over the members. These societies are hostile to Christianity and to the government, so that the mission is laboring under considerable disadvantage at present. The churches number five; and the members are given at five hundred, which is probably far too high an estimate.

[The first letter of the Presbyterian Board of Foreign Mission
to its out-going missionaries in 1846.]

Mission House,

New York, 10th July 1846.

Rev. S. Mattoon

Dr. S. R. House, M. D.

Dear Brethren,

In going out to resume the Mission to Siam, it is proper that you take with you the instructions of the Executive Committee in reference to that field of Missionary labor.

1. When you are permitted to enter upon your work, we shall be glad to hear from you once a month, or as near these periods as you have an opportunity of sending. Letters by way of Canton will come with those of the brethren to China. Thin paper must be used for one letter a month via Canton overland. Other letters with your Journals, annual reports etc., sent by way of Canton will reach us by ships from China.

2. As you go to a people about whom the church knows very little, it will be important for you to communicate in a form suitable for publication, any information that will illustrate their manners and customs, their moral condition, their forms of idolatory and superstition, and in short anything that will make your friends here, and the church at large better acquainted with this benighted land.

3. Your first and great duty will be to prosecute the study of the Siamese language, that you may be able to make known to them, in their own tongue, the wonders of Redeeming Love. Every year's experience has more and more convinced the committee of the importance of Missionaries' becoming acquainted with the native language. In ordinary circumstances, without this knowledge, they can be of little benefit to the natives. Indeed so important do the Committee deem this subject, that they will consider it to be their imperative duty to withdraw from the fields of labor any Missionary who cannot, or who does not in a reasonable time, make himself so far master of the proper native language, as to be understood by those who hear him. Think not then dear brethren that the time is lost, when you are acquiring an element of usefulness, without which all your other acquirements will be to a great extent useless.

4. The Foreign Missionary work is comprised in three directions, each important and none of them interfering with each other.

There are—the direct preaching of the Gospel,—the translating, printing, and distributing the Bible and religious publications, and such an oversight of the course of education as is necessary for training up, with the blessing of God, a native ministry.—So soon as you are able to speak the language of these people, it will be your duty and your privilege to preach to them the Gospel, both publicly and from house to house, as the providence of God may open.—In translating the Bible and suitable publications into the language of Siam, some progress has been made by the Missionaries of sister churches who have preceeded you. But yet much remains to be done, and when your knowledge of the language will permit, this branch of Missionary labor will claim your attention. As printing presses are now in operation in Siam under the care of other Missionaries, it will not be necessary till more laborers are sent out to join you, to have a press connected with our Mission. The course of education will also claim your attention. But for the first year at least, your time and strength will be so taken up in learning the native language that even if the way be found open to engage at and in this branch of Missionary labor, you could not take charge of it. Nor do the Committee at present possess such definite information as to enable them to decide what will be the measures most proper to be adopted a year hence. Until we hear from you, nothing will be decided in regard to this subject. In the mean time you will keep this branch of labor in view, and communicate to us the facilities and prospects in relation to it, and an estimate of the expense of supporting such a system, as in view of all the circumstances you may judge to be the best for that field of labor.

5. It is a consideration of much interest that one of your number possesses a knowledge of the healing art. This like all other acquirements of the Foreign Missionary, must be used as auxiliary in making known the Gospel to the benighted heathen. The knowledge and practice of medicine by many other Missionaries in Siam, have already done much for the course of Missions among these people; and in time to come a continuance of these works of mercy will do much to give you friendly access to them. Thus while imitating the example of our blessed Lord in healing the diseases of the body, you will be aided in making known to them the only remedy for the diseases of the soul. We leave it to yourselves, dear brethren, to decide on the best course to be pursued in the medical labors of the Mission. A little experience when you reach your field of labor, will enable you to decide on what is proper to be done.

6.   Cultivate dear brethren a spirit of confidence and of peace with each other.   Missionaries being so much associated with one another together, and having but little intercourse with others, are more tempted to jealousies and rivalries among themselves than are their brethren in the ministry at home : and hence the frequent exhortations in the word of God to —" love one another"— to " be kindly affectioned "—" to keep the unity of the spirit in the bonds of peace "—apply with peculiar force to them.   It becomes us all to bear in mind that we are imperfect creatures, that we all have our faults, and all have need to forbear much with each other.

Cultivate also a spirit of kindness and friendship, and good offices with the missionaries from other churches, for they too are engaged in the Lord's work.   Altho they see not in all things with us, yet to all who love the Lord Jesus, we most cordially bid God's speed.

7.   Altho the way is opened to preach the Gospel in all parts of Siam, yet the residence of the Missionary, it is understood, has been restricted to Bangkok.   In this city therefore you will take up your abode ; but in your journeys for preaching and distributing tracts you will take notice of the most eligible places for Mission stations, to be occupied when the way is opened.   You will at first rent such houses as you may need.   But you will ascertain whether ground for building can be secured by purchase or on lease, and at what price, with an estimate of the cost of suitable buildings.

8.   The salary of Mr. Buell when in Siam, was fixed at his own request at six hundred dollars per annum for himself and his wife and fifty dollars for each child.   In the usual proportion that of a single missinary would be four hundred fifty dollars per annum. These sums for your salaries may be taken for the present, but if you find on experience that they are too low or too high they can be altered to what is found to be the proper amount.   House rent, teachers' wages, purchase of books for study of the language, public postage, and expense of itinerating will be charged to the Board.   Your salary will commence when you reach Siam.   Your expenses in Macao and passage from thence to Siam will be charged to the Board.

9.   We send you herewith fifteen hundred dollars in silver. From this you will pay your expense in Macao and in Singapore, if you have to touch there, and your passage from China to Siam. The balance, which will probably be $ 1,000 or $ 1,100, you will take with you for the support of the Mission in Siam·   For the first year we have made the following estimate—

sistants for the Office, being not less that $ 1,200, to say nothing of other expenses, to be taken out of the same) is hoarded for future use.

The subscriber regrets much that his Office is unavoidably two miles up town, so far away from the centre of the Foreign community, as to render it difficult of access against strong tides. He would do all in his power to remove this inconvenience to his customers, and hereby pledges himself to take the greater part of the trouble of communication between them and the Office upon himself, by dispatching promptly to them all proof sheets, with direction to his express, to wait, if requested, for their revision, and bring them back for correction—and thus to go and come with the proofs until the matter is pronounced ready for the press, and the finished work is put into their hands. He also promises, that their work shall be executed with all possible dispatch, especially when such is expressly desired.

January, 1st 1864.

D. B. BRADLEY.

APPENDIX XI

Welcome

A hymn written by Rev. Jonathan Wilson, D. D.

Oh ye messengers of Jesus who have come to tell His love
Yours be peace which never ceases,
Precious gift from God above.
Welcome friends, we give you cheer.

Leaving kindred brought you sadness,
Look above! You have a friend
Who can fill lone hearts with gladness,
He'll be with you to the end,
Though 'mongst strangers you'll find cheer.

God's own Son left Heaven's glory,
Stooped to drink man's cup of woe,
Jesus died! Oh tell the story,
Jesus' love let sinners know
Speed the message! Give them cheer.

Satan's hosts are sure to meet you,
Armed for conflict, strike them down!
Warfare ended, Christ will greet you
With " Well done"! receive the crown."
Soldiers brave, we bid you cheer.

Tribes in darkness wait your pity,
Carry them Heaven's wondrous grace.
Then within the Golden City
You shall see Him face to face.
Shout ye saints! Christ gives us cheer.

But the teacher was not only kind and patient but competent and ever ready to help, while the pupils were so glad of interesting work for all those uneventful days so that it was not long before the tangle of tones began to unravel and progress became apparent. By the time the end of the journey was reached the Tones (the Key to the Language) had been mastered. And these new Missionaries strangers in a strange land and among a strange people were so thankful to find that when out among the natives they could get on fairly well with their little stock of words and phrases.

Captain Paul did not "double Cape Horn" as was expected, but went in search of more favorable winds, away far to the south—so that the little Maury found herself among the sleet and snows of a stormy southern winter and oh, how cold and uncomfortable it was. There was no fire on board the ship except what was in the cook room and that was sacred to the cook himself. Sometimes when the passengers were almost perished with the cold, they would beg the the cook to get a piece of a board and heat it in his oven and bring it to the cabin—then all would gather around it to warm their hands and feet. Those southern storms were often terrific and sometimes they were the innocent cause of real fun. One day when the dinner table had been cleared off but the table cloth had not yet been removed an unexpected wave came dashing over the deck and down the passage into dining saloon and state rooms. As the ship rolled from side to side these barrels and barrels of sea water carried every movable thing back and forth with them—books and pencils, hats and coats and wraps were being washed from side to side of the saloon, while the owner of the deluged articles—on chairs and tables were vainly trying to fish them out, to the great amusement of the more fortunate ones of the party. While in the midst of this excitement in the saloon, Capt. Paul came rushing down and snatching the table cloth from the table, calling to the steward to bring buckets, he began to mop up the deluge of sea water. Of course there were shouts of merriment over the novelty of the occasion. But matters looked more serious when ways and means of drying the injured property had to be discussed.

Once a terrible storm came up in the night. The great waves came thundering against the sides of the ship and made her "reel and stagger like a drunken-man". At times it did seem as if every plank in her sides would be shivered to splinters. The wind was simply awful and above the roar and clash of wind and hail and waves the passengers could hear the officers yelling and screaming their orders to the poor sailors in such terribly profane language that man's curses seemed more dreadful than the rage of the elements. Suddenly there was a crash that brought every one to their feet. For a moment the ship stood still—surely she is broken to pieces and is settling down into the raging ocean. For hours of that fearful night the storm raged on—at last the morning came but it was still almost as dark as night. Neither sea nor sky was to be seen, but air and water were a boiling seething undistinguishable mass. Then the cause of the crash in the night was reported—the storm had broken the top from one of the great tough masts and hurled it into the sea. Later on the Captain quietly remarked, we lost a man last night. He was ordered aloft to take in a sail that had been torn by the wind and was never seen afterwards, " Poor, poor fellow was it you that the Captain cursed so unmercifully in the night and did you go to the bottom of the sea with those dreadful curses ringing in your ears !" And now he only says "We lost a man."

Expenses for Building the Klong Kachang Church, Petchaburi.

1868=1872

	Ticals
Place purchased	380.00
Filling up with earth	76.00
Fence	89.62
Brick bought	54.00
Bringing brick to the place	57.00
Cutting and splitting palm trees	7.62
Timber purchased	340.00
Sawing	200.25
Place purchased to make brick	104.00
Bamboo	16.75
Making brick for chapel	270.00
Digging foundation	11.62
Hinges, locks, nails, iron screws	61.75
Shell lime	214.50
White stone lime	31.25
Chalk for temporary roof	7.25
Molasses for masonry	26.25
Work on chapel	30.75
Masons	513.00
Carpenters	412.50
Watchman's house	10.00
Night watchman for the materials	26.00
Putting on the roof	13.39
Entire expenditure in Petchaburi	2,953.50

APPENDIX XIV

(Report of the Petchaburi Church, by Rev. E. P. Dunlap, D.D.)

The Presbyterian Church, Petchaburi.

A COMMITTEE appointed by the Presbytery of Siam consisting of Revs. S. Mattoon, D. McGilvary and S. G. McFarland met at Petchaburi May 9th 1863 and organized the Presbyterian Church of Petchaburi with five members: three natives and two Americans. The church was placed under the care of Revs. McGilvary and McFarland, and continued under their care for three years. Since that time, 1867, this church has been served by the following Stated Supplies:—

Rev. S. G. McFarland	...	nine years
Rev. Jas. W. Van Dyke	...	three years
Rev. J. M. McCauley	...	One year
Rev. C. S. McClelland	...	One year
Rev. Eugene P. Dunlap—present S. S.—six years.		

Since its organization this church has chosen seven Ruling Elders. Three have died, one removed to another church and three are still serving this church.

This church has also furnished six candidates for the ministry. Three of this member have been licensed to preach. One of the three after faithfully preaching the Gospel for several years died in 1881. The remaining two are still preaching in this field. Of three remaining students one died died during his course of study two are still pursuing their studies.

As to the contributions of this church, we are unable to make a full statement. It appears from the church record that the first collection was taken six years after the organization. The contributions for the years 1881-1887 are $942. + The contribution for '87, $240—total $1182.

The growth of this church may be traced as follow:—

Original Membership	...	...	5
Accessions during the First Decade	...	...	23
„ „ „ Second „	...	...	87
„ „ the past five years	...	...	143
Whole number from the beginning	...	...	253
Died	... ...	30	
Dismissed by certificate	... ...	64	
Excommunicated ...	... ...	12	106
Present membership	... ...		147
Whole number of baptized children	... ...		70

The following churches have been organized from this church :—
(1st)   The Presbyterian church of Bangkaboon organized June 1st
        1878 with nine members.

Whole number received from beginning ...		52
Died	7	
Dismissed by certificate	1	8

Present membership   44

(2nd)   The Presbyterian church of Pak Talay organized Jan 5th
        1884 with sixteen members.

Whole number received from the beginning ...		31
Died	2	
Excommunicated	3	5

Present membership   26

(3rd)   The Presbyterian church Ta Rua Ban Pai organized July
        26th with eleven members.

Whole number from the beginning   ...   23
Present membership   23

(4th)   The Presbyterian church Ban Laam organized Feby 27th
        1887 with twelve members.

Whole number from the beginning   ...   15
Present membership...   ...   15.

E. P. DUNLAP.

APPENDIX XV.

Partial subscription list for B. I. M.

H. R. H. The Crown Prince (H. M. King Rama VI)	Tcs. 1,000.00
H. R. H. Prince Paribatra	500.00
H. R. H. Prince Jumbor	100.00
H. R. H. Prince Devawongs	100.00
H. R. H. Prince Divakorn	100.00
H. R. H. Prince Naresr	100.00
H. R. H. Prince Naris	100.00
H. R. H. Khechara	100.00
Teachers and pupils of Bangkok Christian High School	319.00
Teachers and pupils of Wang Lang School	260.00
Siamese members of Boon Itt Committee	760.00
Hon. Hamilton King and Family	500.00
Phya Wailayoot	1,785.00
Family of Phya Wailayoot	200.00
Dr. and Mrs. G. B. McFarland	300.00
Luang Sophone	500.00
Nai Boonyee Bansiddhi	1,000.00
Phra Montri	500 00
Mr. and Mrs. Kellett	500.00
J. W. McEven	300.00
Dr. T. Heyward Hays	500.00
H. Hooker	250.00
Dr. and Mrs. E. P. Dunlap	250.00
L. Lot	200.00
Major O. Busch	250.00
I. H. Moore	100.00
Edwin H. Strobel	300.00
I. Mackay	100.00
Edward M. Ambrose	100.00
V. Guldberg	100.00
Mr. and Mrs. Inagaki	100.00
A. M. Bruce	100.00
Luang Apai Winit	100.00
F. Sampson	100.00
Montgomry Scheyler	100.00
A. Westenholz	100.00
A. W. Cooper and family	100.00
W. A. G. Tilleke	100.00

Dr. and Mrs. J. B. Dunlap	...	...	...	100.00
A Friend ...	...	...	...	100.00
Disciples of Chiengmai	...	...	...	100.00
Luang Anupan	...	...	...	100.00
Miss Edna Brunner	...	...	...	100.00
W. I. White ...	...	...	...	100.00
L. Th. Unverzagt	...	...	...	100.00
F. L. Snyder ...	...	...	...	100.00
Rev. and Mrs. Post	...	...	...	100.00
Miss A. Galt ...	...	...	...	100.00
Dr. W. J. Swart	...	...	...	100.00
Ch. Brockmann	...	...	...	100.00
J. K. Black ...	...	...	...	100.00
Henry Linn ...	...	...	...	100.00
Dr. E. Reytter	...	...	...	100.00

APPENDIX XVI

TABLE I

STATISTICS OF SIAM	Date of first work in this field	Total	Ordained men	Unordained men	Wives	Unmarried women and widows	Short-term workers, included in foregoing	Residence stations
	1	2	3	4	5	6	7	8
American Societies								
American Bible Society ..	1890	2	1	0	1	0	0	1
Presbyterian Board of Foreign Missions, U.S.A. ..	1840	91	24	12	34	21	1	10
Seventh-Day Adventist General Conference ..	1919	4	0	2	2	0	0	1
TOTAL		97	25	14	37	21	1	12
British Societies								
Churches of Christ in Great Britain, For Miss. Comm. ..	1903	3	0	1	1	1	0	1
Society for the Propagation of the Gospel (S.P.G.) ..	1903	2	0	0	0	2	0	1
TOTAL		5	0	1	1	3	0	2
Grand total of all five societies		102	25	15	38	24	1	14

(Taken from World Missionary Atlas for 1925—Table 1,—Foreign Staff,—Page 84.)

1. Owing to inevitable duplication of stations by the various societies, the totals in column 8 are in excess of the total number of cities occupied.

Table II.

MEDICAL WORK IN SIAM. (Including Laos)	Physicians-Men	Physicians-Women	Trained Assistants-Men	Trained Assistants-Women	Hospitals	Beds in Foregoing	In-Patients	Dispensaries	Treatment in Dispensaries	Total Individual Patients	Total Treatments	Medical Fees Received U.S. Gold
	1	2	3	4	5	6	7	8	9	10	11	12
Presbyterian Church in U. S. A. Board of Foreign Missions	8	0	10	10	9	246	2,042	14	27,823	17,653	28,723	36,145
Churches of Christ in Great Britain, For. Miss. Comm.	0	0	0	0	1	—	—	1	—	—	—	568
Grand Totals, 2 Societies	8	0	10	10	10	246	2,042	15	27,823	17,653	28,723	36,713

(Taken from World Missionary Atlas for 1925—Table VI,—Medical,—Page 154).
1. Estimate by the Society or from one of its publications.

Table III

SCHOOLS IN SIAM (including Laos)	Total under Instruction in all schools	Kinder-garten		Elementary schools				High and middle schools				Indus-trial schools		Teacher training schools		Educational fees for all schools, U. S. Gold.
		Kindergartens	Pupils	Schools	Total pupils	Boys	Girls	Schools	Total pupils	Boys	Girls	Institutions	Total Students	Institutions	Total Students	
	1	2	3	4	5	6	7	8	9	10	11	12	13	14	15	16
Presbyterian Board of Foreign Missions, U. S. A.	2,848	2	27	48	2,655	1,559	1,096	4	109	72	37	0	0	0	0	54,204
Churches of Christ in Great Britain, For. Miss. Comm.	283	0	0	4	283	76	107	0	0	0	0	0	0	0	0	
Church of England, S. P. G.	86	0	0	1	86	0	86	0	0	0	0	0	0	0	0	
Grand Total	3,217	2	27	53	3,024	1,635	1,289	4	109	72	37	0	0	0	0	54,204

(Taken from the World Missionary Atlas for 1925.—Table III,—General Educational,—page 126)

Table IV

GENERAL STATISTICS OF THE NATIONAL CHURCH IN SIAM (Including Laos)	Total	Native Staff			The Church											
		Ordained Men	Unordained Men	Women	Organized Churches	Self-Supporting Churches-Inc. Col. 5	Other Places Having Regular Services	Communicants Added During the Year	Christian Community Totals Cols. 10,11,13	Communicants	Non-Communicants Baptised	Total Baptised Total Cols. 10, & 11	Others Under Christian Influence	Sunday School	Sunday-Schools Teachers and Pupils	Contributions for Church Work, U. S. Gold
	1	2	3	4	5	6	7	8	9	10	11	12	13	14	15	16
American Societies																
American Bible Societies	45	1	42	2	0	0	0	0	0	0	0	0	0	0	0	0
Presbyterian Church in U.S.A. Board of Foreign Missions	396	11	195	190	49	33	188	557	14,724	8,222	6,046	14,268	456	107	7,687	28,270
Seventh-Day Adventist Denom. General Conference	6	0	2	4	2	—	—	30	122	122	0	122	—	3	110	1,000
Totals, 3 Societies	447	12	239	196	51	33	188	557	14,846	8,344	6,046	14,390	456	110	7,797	29,270
British Societies																
Churches of Christ in Great Britain, Foreign Mission Comm.	13	2	10	1	2	0	4	28	—	—	0	—	—	2	—	139
S. P. G. Diocese of Singapore	4	0	1	3	1	0	—	—	—	—	—	—	—	—	—	—
Totals, 2 British Societies	17	2	11	4	3	0	4	28	0	0	0	0	0	2	0	139
Grand Totals, 5 Societies	464	14	250	200	54	33	192	615	14,846	8,344	6,046	14,390	456	112	7,797	29,409

(Taken from World Missionary Atlas for 1925—Table II-The Church in the Field,—page 101).

APPENDIX XVII

Partial list of Gifts to the Missions by the Kings and Queens of this Dynasty.

H. M. Phra Nang Klao

1839	Reward to Dr. Bradley for inoculations,	...		2 catties

H. M. King Mongkut

1851	Land for the Presbyterian Mission behind Wat Cheng.				
1852	Land for the A. M. A. Mission.				
1853	Protestant Cemetery Grounds.				
	Gift to Mrs. Caswell,	...	...	... $	1,000.00
	Gift to Mrs. Caswell,	...	...	...	500.00
	Tombstone for Rev. Jesse Caswell.				
1861	Land for the Protestant Chapel.				

H. M. King Chulalongkorn

1877	Petchaburi Girls' School,	...	... $	1,000.00
1887	Petchaburi hospital and medical work,	... Tcs.	2,400.00
	Land for Christ Church.			
	Sritamarat Hospital,	...	... $	2,000.00
	Lampang Hospital,	...	... Rs.	2,000.00
	Land for the Lampang Hospital.			
	Subscription toward purchase of B. C. C. land,	20	catties

H. M. Queen Sawang Vadhana

1887	Petchaburi hospital—Womans' ward,	... Tcs.	1,600.00
1920	Wattana Wittiya Academy,	...	... ,,	1,000.00

H. M. Queen Sowapa Pongsi

Wang Lang School,	...	... 20	catties
Wang Lang School,	...	... Tcs.	2,000.00

H. M. King Rama VI

	Operating room for Trang hospital,	... Tcs.	1,000.00
	B. I. M. land,	...	... ,,	1,000.00
1914-22	Grant to the leper work in Chiengmai,	... ,,	27,545.00
1923-25	Grant to the leper work in Chiengmai,	... ,,	30,000.00
1918	Woman's Ward, Hospital, Petchaburi,	... ,,	800.00

H. M. King Prajadhipok

1927	Gift to Lampang Girls' School,	... Tcs.	300.00
1927	Road metalled to Leper home, Chiengmai,	„	22,000.00
1926-28	Annual grant to Leper Home, Chiengmai,	„	30,000.00
	Prince Royal's College, ...	... „	350.00
1927	Gifts to Mission work, North Siam, viz.	... „	5,000.00

Dara Wittiya Academy,	... Tcs.	700.00
Lampoon School, well,	... „	200.00
Theological Seminary Library, ...	„	900.00
Chiengrai, Sanitary system-2 schools,	... „	1,400.00
Lampang Girls' School,	... „	700.00
Nan, equipment, both schools, ...	„	600.00
Prae, surgical equipment,	... „	500.00

	Ticals	5,000.00

H. M. Queen Rambaibarni

1927	Gift to Pitsanuloke Girls' School,	... Tcs.	200.00
	„ „ Dara Wittiya Academy	... „	300.00

APPENDIX XVIII

Brief list of important dates 1828=1928

1828—Arrival of Rev. Carl Gutzlaff & Rev. Jacob Tomlin.

1831—Beginning of A. B. C. F. M. work by Rev. David Abeel.

1833—Beginning of American Baptist work by Rev. J. T. Jones, D. D.

1833—First Treaty between Siam & U. S. A. drawn up.

1835—Arrival of Dan Beach Bradley, M. D.

1835—First printing press brought into Siam.

1836—Baptist printing press arrived.

1837—First surgical operation performed by Dr. Bradley.

1837—First Protestant Church in Siam organized—Baptist.

1839—First Government Proclamation printed.

1840—Vaccination first successful, by Dr. Bradley.

1840—Presbyterian Mission started.

1844—First steamer ever seen in Siamese waters arrived.

1845—H. R. H. Prince Chao Fah Mongkut began to study with Rev.
Jesse Caswell.

1846—A. B. C. F. M. transferred all Chinese work to China.

1849—Severe epidemic of spasmodic cholera.

1849—A. B. C. F. M. mission ended.

1849—First Presbyterian Church organized.

1850—A. M. A. work started.

1851—Destructive fire on Baptist compound.

1851—H. M. King Mongkut granted site to Presbyterian mission.

1851—Rev. John Taylor Jones, D. D. died.

1851—Missionary ladies began to teach in the Palace.

1852—H. M. King Mongkut granted site to A. M. A. mission.

1853—Royal Grant of land for Protestant Cemetery.

1856—U. S. A. Consulate established.

1856—British Consulate established.

1857—Presbyterian mission moved to Samray.

1859—Baptist chapel near the British Consulate dedicated.

1861—Royal grant of land for the Protestant chapel.

1861—Petchaburi mission station started.

1861—New Road started.

1864—Protestant Chapel opened.

1866—First Meeting of the Ladies' Bazaar Association.

1866—Permission granted for the starting of Chiengmai station.

1868—Baptist mission ceased Siamese work.

1870—Wang Lang property bought.

1870—Proclamation of religious liberty by the Regent.

1875—Wang Lang School opened.

1878—Royal Proclamation of Religious Toleration by
H. M. King Chulalongkorn.

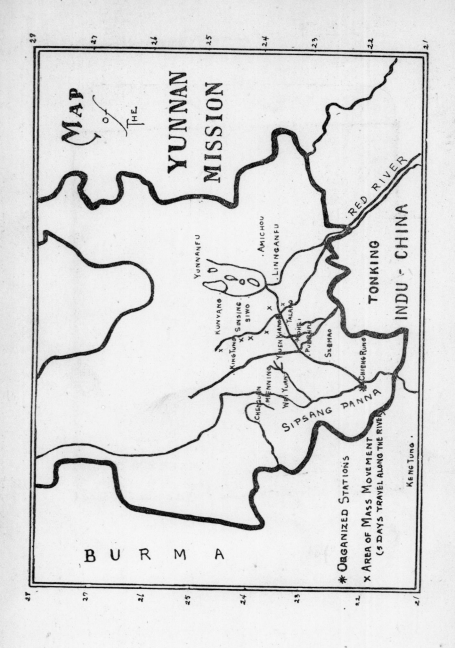

MAP of THE

YUNNAN MISSION

BURMA

· YUNNANFU

· AMICHOU

· LINNGANFU

× KUNYANG
× SINSING
KINGTUNG × × SIWO

× × TALANG
YUEN YANG ×
× × P·OSHE·
P·U·ERH·

SZEMAO

× CHENG RUNG

CHEOGUAN
× MENNING
WENYUNG

SIPSANG PANNA

TONKING

RED RIVER

INDU - CHINA

✱ ORGANIZED STATIONS
× AREA OF MASS MOVEMENT
(5 DAYS TRAVEL ALONG THE RIVER)

· KENGTUNG ·